The
United Nations

The
United Nations

Policy and Practice

edited by
Jean E. Krasno

LYNNE
RIENNER
PUBLISHERS

BOULDER
LONDON

Published in the United States of America in 2023 by
Lynne Rienner Publishers, Inc.
1800 30th Street, Suite 314, Boulder, Colorado 80301
www.rienner.com

and in the United Kingdom by
Lynne Rienner Publishers, Inc.
Gray's Inn House, 127 Clerkenwell Road, London EC1 5DB
www.eurospanbookstore.com/rienner

Library of Congress Cataloging-in-Publication Data
Names: Krasno, Jean E., 1943– editor, author.
Title: The United Nations : policy and practice / [edited by] Jean Krasno.
Other titles: United Nations (Lynne Rienner Publishers, Inc.)
Description: Boulder, Colorado : Lynne Rienner Publishers, Inc., 2023. |
    Includes bibliographical references and index. | Summary: "Clearly
    explains the UN's history, functions, and day-to-day operations"—
    Provided by publisher.
Identifiers: LCCN 2022045451 (print) | LCCN 2022045452 (ebook) | ISBN
    9781955055840 (hardcover) | ISBN 9781955055901 (paperback) | ISBN
    9781685852825 (ebook)
Subjects: LCSH: United Nations.
Classification: LCC JZ4984.5 .U5416 2023 (print) | LCC JZ4984.5 (ebook) |
    DDC 341.23/1—dc23/eng/20221020
LC record available at https://lccn.loc.gov/2022045451
LC ebook record available at https://lccn.loc.gov/2022045452

British Cataloguing in Publication Data
A Cataloguing in Publication record for this book
is available from the British Library.

Printed and bound in the United States of America

5 4 3 2 1

Contents

1   The United Nations in an Uncertain Global Context   1
Jean E. Krasno

2   The UN Landscape   5
Jean E. Krasno

3   Founding the United Nations   29
Jean E. Krasno

4   Promoting Human Development   57
Jacques Fomerand

5   Supporting Human Rights   85
Bertrand Ramcharan

6   The Evolution of Peacekeeping Operations   105
Jean E. Krasno

7   Democratization and Electoral Assistance   139
Massimo Tommasoli and Therese Pearce Laanela

8   Addressing Human Security   159
Kimberly Gamble-Payne and Jean E. Krasno

9   Disarmament and Arms Control   179
Randy Rydell

10   Financing the United Nations   197
Wannes Lint

11   Confronting the Authority of the Security Council   231
         Jean E. Krasno

12   Achievements and Challenges   261
         Jean E. Krasno

List of Acronyms   275
Bibliography   279
The Contributors   287
Index   289
About the Book   303

1

The United Nations in an Uncertain Global Context

Jean E. Krasno

The United Nations, created in 1945 following the end of World War II, plays a pivotal role in the global environment—a role that is compounded if you include the many UN agencies, funds, and programs. Yet this worldwide UN system remains largely unnoticed in the media and, unfortunately, in the curricula of many colleges and universities, even though Model UN clubs are very popular on campuses. The goal of this edited volume is to address this void and offer a useful overview of the key functions, policies, and practices of the United Nations.

In these chapters, the authors examine how the organization has evolved over time beyond its original intended focus on international peace and security. The United Nations as a body has undertaken a gradual shift toward an emphasis on human security, human rights, humanitarian assistance, the creation of global norms, protection of the environment, ways to address climate change, and support of democratization, to name a few of its program areas. Peacekeeping, which was never envisioned in the writing of the UN Charter, has now become one of the most important activities of the United Nations. Troop-contributing countries send hundreds of thousands of soldiers around the world to work toward providing peace and stability to countries emerging from conflict or, at times, caught in the midst of upheaval. These peace operations have become more and more complex and multidimensional as the UN endeavors to address the root causes of these conflicts. The UN Peacebuilding Commission and Fund is an example of member states coming together to assist fragile nations in finding ongoing, long-term stability.

The UN provides a mirror onto the world around us. If what is seen through that looking glass is fractured, the UN will reflect those fissures in its ability to function. At the end of the Cold War, hopes were high that the members of the Security Council would be able to work together to solve threats to the peace, but the Council can be dysfunctional at times, particularly when the interests of the major powers are at stake. The Council represents only one aspect of the UN's work. More needs to be understood about the other vast enterprises that the United Nations undertakes in seeking political and peaceful solutions to disputes through the daily work of the UN system as a whole as it, for example, provides emergency food aid through the World Food Programme (WFP), assists children in need through the UN Children's Fund (UNICEF), and copes with global health concerns through the World Health Organization (WHO). It is hoped that this book will provide a window into the work of the UN—its policies and practices—by delving into both its productive and its less productive sides. The United Nations is the single universal organization that can take up any issue and bring nations together to solve global problems such as climate change and the growing inequality between rich and poor, thus setting values for our worldwide community.

An edited volume like this one has the advantage of being able to capture the experiences of those who have worked within the UN system while also drawing on the expertise of UN scholars. That advantage is well reflected in the chapters that follow. In Chapters 2 and 3, Jean E. Krasno focuses on how the UN has adapted to the shifting global environment. Chapter 2, "The UN Landscape," presents an overview of the bodies, functions, and practices of the organization and how they have grown and changed. Chapter 3, "Founding the United Nations," discusses the origins of the UN and how and why certain concepts were built into the Charter. For example, many people question why the five permanent members of the UN—China, France, Russia, the UK, and the United States—were given the power to veto any Security Council resolution. How that came about is captured in Chapter 3.

Chapters 4 and 5 examine the more human face of the organization. In Chapter 4, "Promoting Human Development," Jacques Fomerand explains the evolving role of the United Nations in human development, including the creation of the UN Development Programme (UNDP) in 1965, the launch of the *Human Development Report* in the early 1990s, and the establishment of the Millennium Development Goals in 2000 and then the Sustainable Development Goals in 2015. In Chapter 5, "Supporting Human Rights," Bertrand Ramcharan delves into the progressive attention that the United Nations has given to human rights since the writing of the Charter. This chapter includes a careful analysis of the growth in the number of human rights agreements, as well as the breadth of the issues they address.

Chapters 6, 7, 8, and 9 examine the UN's changing role in areas related to peace, security, and democratization. In Chapter 6, "The Evolution of Peacekeeping Operations," Krasno addresses the evolution of peace operations from simply creating buffer zones between two warring parties to conducting complex peace operations that must deal with intrastate conflicts where there is no dividing line among competing groups. Peacekeeping has become one of the most important activities of the United Nations, and over the years it has taken on a more expansive multidimensional character. There are at present twelve peacekeeping operations around the world, along with twenty-eight political missions that seek to find peaceful solutions to disputes.

In Chapter 7, "Democratization and Electoral Assistance," Massimo Tommasoli and Therese Pearce Laanela address the fundamentals of democratization through the electoral process, which could only have been placed on the UN's agenda after the end of the Cold War. The UN has been overwhelmed by requests from states for electoral assistance, helping to establish national electoral commissions, supporting voter registration, observing the balloting process, and offering legitimacy by declaring an election free and fair.

In Chapter 8, "Addressing Human Security," Kimberly Gamble-Payne joins Krasno in examining nontraditional concepts of security in the areas of global health, climate change, and migration. While these three issues at first may seem to be disconnected concerns, they are, in fact, intrinsically intermingled. More than 281 million people have been displaced and are on the move, escaping conflict and the effects of climate change, intense weather events, floods, and drought.[1] The devastating Covid-19 pandemic has exacerbated the plight of migrants, who often find themselves in crowded conditions with no protection from the spread of the virus and discriminated against over fears that they may be sources of infection. These factors all contribute to the loss of human security.

In Chapter 9, "Disarmament and Arms Control," Randy Rydell traces the history of UN efforts to eliminate weapons of mass destruction and regulate conventional arms. This chapter underscores the fact that "the UN's work on disarmament has produced far more than words alone and that it continues to confirm not just the UN's relevance but also its indispensability in fulfilling its core mandate to maintain international peace and security."

Chapters 10 and 11 examine UN politics, processes, and practice, offering insight into the work that the organization carries out as it balances the requests and demands of the member states while simultaneously negotiating within an atmosphere of internal political competition. In Chapter 10, "Financing the United Nations," Wannes Lint lays out the complexities of how mandates are translated into plans and budgets. How a mandate is implemented, what member states collectively budget for these projects, and ultimately the amount each member state will end up paying are a result of complex political negotiation processes. In Chapter 11, "Confronting the Authority of the Security Council," Krasno discusses ways to maneuver around the Security Council when it is unable to act. The "Uniting for Peace" resolution, written by the UN General Assembly in 1950 to deal with the outbreak of the Korean War, sets the stage for a process that has enabled the General Assembly to take up an issue when the Security Council has failed to do so or is presumed unwilling to be proactive. This maneuvering process is not well known but has often been used by the General Assembly to circumvent a Security Council that has been thwarted by the veto of a permanent member, as was the case in 2022 regarding the Russian aggression in Ukraine.

In Chapter 12, "Achievements and Challenges," Krasno describes UN accomplishments, but also looks at the perils and pitfalls that lie ahead. The task facing the United Nations is to remain relevant during a time when major powers may refuse to cooperate for the greater good. Important to remember, the UN is constituted by its member states and reflects the aspirations and willingness of its members to act. As we see in this volume, the Secretariat operationalizes the mandates handed to it but also adds its own normative perspective and implements the practice on the ground, thus becoming an actor within the process. In this book, we offer an inside perspective into the workings of the organization and the UN's intense engagement in contributing to the peaceful solution of conflict in an increasingly complex international environment.

Note

1. International Organization of Migration, *World Migration Report 2022*, https://worldmigrationreport.iom.int/wmr-2022-interactive.

2

The UN Landscape

Jean E. Krasno

The purpose of this chapter is to paint a broad landscape of the United Nations (UN) and its work. The organization, with its 193 members in 2022, can be viewed from several perspectives: as a focal point for global security issues, a world forum for debate, a network for developing universal norms and standards, and a vehicle for humanitarian assistance around the world, to name a few. The six principal bodies of the United Nations make up the core of the organization, but its outreach goes far beyond the core to include a myriad of loosely affiliated funds, programs, agencies, and other related bodies. Since its inception in 1945, the UN has continued to grow and adapt to the challenges of a complex and changing world environment. Some activities that in 1945 appeared to be focal points of the organization's landscape have now retreated from the foreground and in some cases have completely disappeared over the horizon, replaced by more relevant endeavors. Still, the central purpose of the UN continues to be to maintain international peace and security. The Security Council, which holds the primary responsibility for the maintenance of international peace and security, therefore remains the most publicly visible body. At the same time, the Secretary-General is the single most important individual and symbolic representative of the United Nations to the peoples of the world.

One of the most important recent evolutions in the UN has been the changing focus of the organization from a primary concern for national security to the inclusion of human security within the state. The notion of state sovereignty as a centerpiece of the intergovernmental body is still key. Yet this is beginning to include the *responsibility* of the state to protect its citizens, however controversial, and not to simply accept the sovereign immunity of the state from interference when the state is unable or unwilling to protect its people, or when it may be the perpetrator of violence. Involvement within the state does not necessarily mean intervention through the use of force but also includes development assistance and peacebuilding. The Millennium Declaration, which was adopted by the member states in 2000, calls for the eradication of poverty, access to clean water and sanitation, and access to sustainable sources of energy. The Declaration's new emphasis on human security and the human condition evolved into the Millennium Development Goals (MDGs) under the leadership of Kofi Annan, UN Secretary-General at the time, who explained that he wanted to return the UN to the "peoples" as it is written in the UN Charter. The MDGs were to expire in 2015, but because of their relative success, the member states collaborated to reinvigorate the concept by creating the Sustainable Development Goals, a set of seventeen goals to be achieved by 2030.

With two devastating world wars fresh in their memories, the founders of the United Nations wanted to create an organization that would prevent the outbreak of a third global conflict. Also, uppermost in their minds was the Great Depression and the economic disequilibrium that had preceded World War II, which many believed had contributed to the outbreak of the war. Therefore, the founders envisioned conflict prevention to incorporate several different approaches, including military might but not limited to it. The countries that gathered in San Francisco to finalize the United Nations Charter hoped that the nations that had united to fight and defeat the Axis powers would remain united to prevent future aggression and preserve peace—hence the name "United Nations." The concept was that the five major powers that had the largest militaries and had fought together during the war— the United States, the UK, the Soviet Union, China, and France—would lend their military might to the UN to fight any would-be aggressors. These five members were given permanent seats on the UN's fifteen-member Security Council. In addition to the use of military force, coercion was to also include pressure through the imposition of economic sanctions and diplomatic isolation.

The use of coercion or the threat of force or sanctions, as spelled out in Chapter VII of the Charter, is only part of the picture, however. The UN was also established to be a forum for dialogue and an environment in which negotiations and diplomatic solutions might replace war to settle disputes. Chapter VI of the Charter, titled "Pacific Settlement of Disputes," also calls for conciliation, mediation, negotiation, and arbitration in the peaceful pursuit of settlement of disputes. Economic and social inequities that might contribute to conflict are also addressed, as well as the means to prepare non-self-governing territories and colonies for independence, in the hope of avoiding wars of independence or conflict over these territories. All these tools for the prevention of conflict, however encompassing, depend on the cooperation of the collectivity of the member nations, something that is not always forthcoming. In addition, because the UN does not have its own military or its own economic resources, the organization is dependent on voluntary and assessed contributions by member states to implement its decisions.

Allocation of Tasks and the Six Principal UN Bodies

Each of the aforementioned functions is allocated to one of the six principal bodies of the United Nations: the Security Council, the General Assembly, the Secretariat (headed by the Secretary-General), the Economic and Social Council, the Trusteeship Council, and the International Court of Justice.

The Security Council

The maintenance of international peace and security is primarily the responsibility of the fifteen-member Security Council. The Security Council, with its authority to create resolutions that are binding on all member states and with the influence of the permanent five members (the P-5), is the center of power within the UN system. The P-5 include: China, France, Russia, the UK, and the United States. The ten nonpermanent members, also referred to as the elected ten, are chosen by two-thirds of the General Assembly for a two-year term and then have to go off the Council for at least one year before being reelected. Five of these ten members are elected each year, so not all ten go off the Council at the same time. The nonpermanent member seats are allocated by region to maintain a more global balance on the body. Three seats are allocated to Africa, two for Latin America and the Caribbean, two for the Asia-Pacific Group, one for Eastern Europe, and two for Western Europe and other. Two nonpermanent members, Brazil and Japan, have held seats on the Council more often than other states: Brazil has served eleven times, and Japan by 2023 will have served twelve times. Some fifty states have never been elected to the Council.[1]

To pass a resolution, there must be nine votes in favor. However, the permanent five (P-5) not only have the privilege of continually holding a seat on the Council while the other ten countries are elected for two-year terms, but they also have the veto power, which means any one of the five can vote "no" on a resolution and prevent its passage. Therefore, in order to pass a resolution, there must be nine votes in favor and no negative vote from any of the P-5. As of July 8, 2022, 246 vetoes have been cast, primarily by the Soviet Union/Russia followed by the United States, but every member of the P-5 has exercised the veto at some point.[2] Some are challenging the rights of these five to continue to hold these positions of power. The distribution of military and economic strength since 1945 has changed significantly, and the economies of Germany and Japan are now much greater than those of the other P-5 members, with the exception of the United States and now China. However, the combined military capacity of the five is still significant, and the constitutions of both Germany and Japan still place limitations on their abilities to send troops abroad, thus constraining their capacity to contribute to collective security. Efforts to reform the Security Council since its last enlargement in the 1960s from the original eleven members to fifteen have failed in recent years. The Charter states that any amendments must have the concurrence of the permanent five members, and no permanent member is likely to vote itself off the Council. Efforts to enlarge the Council to include the bigger economies, such as Japan, Germany, Brazil, India, and perhaps South Africa, have also been met with resistance by competitors and lack of agreement. The members of the UN seem to be resigned to accepting the Council in its present form at least for the time being. Nevertheless, the Council must be seen as effective and living up to its responsibility to uphold peace and security, or countries may decide to turn to other bodies to take on this role.

The General Assembly

The General Assembly, which comprises all the member states (originally 51 countries in 1945 and now 193 in 2022), fulfills the function of a central forum for global dialogue wherein pressing issues of concern from population growth, development, the environment, and climate change to humanitarian issues can be discussed. Each fall, the General Assembly opens with a general debate, during which foreign ministers and heads of state/government take the podium to express their governments' positions on the challenges of the day. General Assembly resolutions are not binding in the same way as Security Council resolutions but are considered recommendations and offer a "sense" of the member-ship, meaning a reflection of support and agreement among the member states. Voting is by majority rule, and there is no veto. Yet the General Assembly has the authority to determine the budget of the United Nations, or "power of the purse," which can shape policy on what receives funding or not. Because of its nearly universal membership, its pronouncements can offer a kind of moral authority or a collective con-science, as they did for many years in condemning the practice of apartheid in South Africa, and more recently condemning Russian aggression in Ukraine. That is not to say that all the work of the General Assembly and the interests of its members have moral overtones. As with all large bodies, much of the work is tedious and repetitive and the interests of some may be in direct opposition to others. Nevertheless, the UN is the only place where all member states have permanent rep-resentatives as ambassadors throughout the year, so that when a crisis or issue arises, formal and informal conversations can take place conve-niently in a timely manner.

The General Assembly has six main committees, which deal sepa-rately with issues ranging from disarmament to international law. Each committee includes all the member states.

First Committee: political and security issues, including disar-mament and other national security concerns, conflict, and peacekeeping.

Second Committee: economic and financial issues affecting the global community, including the Sustainable Development Goals.

Third Committee: social, humanitarian, and cultural issues that are related to humanitarian crises.

Fourth Committee: decolonization-related issues and special political missions. Because there are no longer any colonies, this committee does not meet frequently.

Fifth Committee: administrative and budgetary issues, which include determining the budget for the organization.

Sixth Committee: legal issues, creation of new treaties, and over-seeing the work of the International Law Commission (ILC).

These committees can also create subsidiary bodies. For example, the Sixth Committee created the ILC, a body of legal experts, to advise the committee and prepare draft documents, such as developing language for treaties. It has continued to function throughout the decades and, for example, formulated drafts for the eventual statute that established the International Criminal Court, which went into effect in July 2002.

A very important role of the General Assembly over the years has been to oversee the decolonization of some eighty countries that were not under the trusteeship system but are now sovereign independent members of the UN. Chapter XI of the Charter, titled "Declaration Regarding Non-Self-Governing Territories," pronounced that it was the responsibility of the colonial powers "to develop self-government" in the territories under their control, "to take due account of the political aspirations of the peoples, and to assist them in the progressive development of their free political institutions."[3] In 1946, eight member states produced a list of their combined non-self-governing "colonial" territories, which came to a total of seventy-two. By 1959, eight of them had become independent. Because of the slow pace of decolonization, in December 1960 the General Assembly passed resolution 1514 (XV), titled the "Declaration on the Granting of Independence to Colonial Countries and Peoples," also known as the "Declaration on Decolonization."

The declaration called for immediate steps to be taken to end colonial practices, and the UN gradually oversaw elections in many of these countries as they transitioned to independence. East Timor, which joined the UN in 2002, is one of the latest to become independent, along with South Sudan, which in 2011 became the most recent state to become a member of the UN.[4] Other territories that are self-governing, like Kosovo and Taiwan, plus others that are striving to become independent, such as Palestine, are still not UN member states due to the veto of one or another member of the P-5 blocking their membership. In 2012, with support of the members of the General Assembly, Palestine was given the title of "Non-Member Observer State." This status gives Palestine the right to observe meetings of General Assembly bodies, but without a vote. The title "observer state" offers Palestine the recognition of being a state. Other entities with observer status, but without the term "observer state," include the International Committee of the Red Cross, the Holy See, and the European Union, to name a few. With observer status, these organizations can sit in on meetings of the member states but cannot vote.

The Secretariat and the Secretary-General

The Secretariat is the organ that administers and coordinates the activities of the United Nations. The functions of the Secretariat, a complex bureaucracy, include supporting the work of the Security Council, the

General Assembly, the Economic and Social Council, and other main bodies of the UN by servicing meetings, preparing reports, and implementing decisions. For example, if the Security Council authorizes the deployment of peacekeeping troops, the Secretariat must contact troop-contributing countries and make arrangements for sending soldiers under UN auspices into the field. While the Security Council is tasked with addressing issues of peace and security and the General Assembly offers the opportunity for open debate and consensus building, the Secretariat has become the focal point for diplomacy in crisis situations, wherein the "good offices" of the Secretary-General and his (or her) representatives are put into play. The term "good offices" refers to mediation capabilities offered by the Office of the Secretary-General and its envoys to find a peaceful solution, using the high-level and impartiality of the office. As head of the Secretariat, the Secretary-General can create new staff positions. Under Secretary-General Kofi Annan, the UN created the position of Deputy Secretary-General. Over the last few years, the Deputy has performed different roles. Today, the Deputy Secretary-General Amina Mohammed has been the coordinator for the Sustainable Development Goals.

The Executive Office of the Secretary-General directs the Secretariat, which is divided into fifteen departments and offices. These departments and offices include the Department of Political and Peacebuilding Affairs (DPPA), the Department of Peace Operations (DPO), Department of Operational Support (DOS), Department of Global Communications (DGC), the Office of Legal Affairs (OLA), the Office for Disarmament Affairs (UNODA), the Department of Economic and Social Affairs (DESA), the Department of Management Strategy, Policy and Compliance (DMSPC), the Office for the Coordination of Humanitarian Affairs (OCHA), to name a few. There are other specialized offices that focus on specific issues, such as the Office of the Special Representative of the Secretary-General for Children and Armed Conflict, the Office of the Special Representative of the Secretary-General on Sexual Violence in Conflict, and the Office of the Special Representative of the Secretary-General on Violence Against Children.

The Secretary-General is elected by the General Assembly upon the nomination of the Security Council, and so far, the Security Council has never nominated more than one candidate. So, in the end, the General Assembly has rubber-stamped the person chosen by the Council. Since 1991, UN member states put pressure on the Security Council to select a Secretary-General from rotating geographic regions in order to represent the broader world. However, this recommendation is only informal and can be ignored if the Council prefers a specific candidate, as it did in 2016 in electing António Guterres, the fourth Secretary-General from Europe. The Secretary-General is elected for a five-year term and can be reelected. António Guterres began his second term in 2022. The founders of the UN originally conceived of the Secretary-General as primarily an administrator. However, Article 99 of the Charter gives the Secretary-General the authority to bring an issue before the Security Council, thereby leaving open a door for the Secretary-General to also play a political role in leading the administration of the UN. While the position has become considerably more dynamic over the years, it must be remembered that the Secretary-General serves the member states and has no assets, military, or budget of his or her own to implement policy decisions. While there are some discretionary funds available to the Secretary-General for specific projects, like democracy building or crisis assistance, these funds are limited. While it often appears to the public that the Secretary-General is the face of the UN and the political leader of the organization, similar to a president, this is a false impression.

The position can be used as a bully pulpit to promote multilateralism and place issues like climate change, human rights, poverty eradication and HIV/AIDS on the world's agenda, providing a kind of moral compass for the organization. But the Secretary-General must walk a very fine line to maintain the legitimacy and impartiality of the office and of the UN while not offending any of the major powers. The personality of the Secretary-General can determine the role of the office. Javier Pérez de Cuéllar preferred to keep a low profile and delegate mediation between disputing parties to talented staff members. Dag Hammarskjöld often inserted himself directly into negotiations and in so doing suffered the wrath of member states like the Soviet Union, which called for his resignation. Boutros Boutros-Ghali lost the confidence of the United States and was not granted a second five-year term. Kofi Annan used his office to promote human rights and lead the United Nations in addressing global challenges, particularly those that affected the most vulnerable in society. In attempting to maintain a balance between the principles of the UN in support of peace and the interests of the major powers, he was able to gain the support of the P-5 members and was elected to a second five-year term. However, during his second term, the United States lost confidence in him over his position that the 2003 war in Iraq, which failed to gain Security Council authorization, was illegal under international law. Ban Ki-moon used his position at the helm of the organization to keep climate change high on the agenda of member states. And António Guterres has worked to achieve gender equality at the highest levels of the Secretariat and to reform the UN to be better fit for purpose.

The following is a list of the Secretaries-General who have served the UN over the years, so far all men:

- Trygve Lie (Norway), 1946–1952
- Dag Hammarskjöld (Sweden), 1953–1961
- U Thant (Burma/Myanmar), 1961–1971
- Kurt Waldheim (Austria), 1972–1981
- Javier Pérez de Cuéllar (Peru), 1982–1991
- Boutros Boutros-Ghali (Egypt), 1992–1996
- Kofi Annan (Ghana), 1997–2006
- Ban Ki-moon (Republic of Korea/South Korea), 2007–2016
- António Guterres (Portugal), 2017–present (reelected in 2021 to a second term)

In the lead-up to the election of António Guterres in 2015 and 2016, there was a campaign to elect a woman Secretary-General at the same time that the members of the General Assembly demanded a more open process. Instead of the secret manner in which the Council met to discuss possible candidates in the past, member states could now openly nominate candidates. Each candidate made a presentation to the full membership of the General Assembly to which members of civil society were invited. This was a first attempt to make the process more open and more democratic. Of the thirteen candidates who were nominated, seven were women. The General Assembly even held an open debate among the candidates that was televised. In the end, however, the Council once again nominated one candidate, which the General Assembly then confirmed.

The Economic and Social Council

The Economic and Social Council (ECOSOC) was established in the Charter to serve as the central body for discussing international social and economic concerns, to initiate studies and reports, and to promote humanitarian issues. ECOSOC also has the authority, along with the General Assembly, to call international conferences and to consult with nongovernmental organizations (NGOs). The global conferences on human rights, the environment, population, and women's rights, to just name a few, have been some of the most important contributions made by ECOSOC. These global conferences provide an important forum for including the voices of civil society in the workings of the UN. For example, NGOs affiliated with ECOSOC and the DGC sometimes participate directly in the conferences or in parallel NGO forums in a way not possible in other UN bodies. There are more than 6,000 NGOs in consultative status with ECOSOC, with additional NGOs affiliated with DGC and some 400 accredited to the Commission on Sustainable Development. Holding this status means that these NGOs are able to send observers to meetings of ECOSOC and its subsidiary bodies. NGOs are increasingly viewed as important partners, not only in representing civil society in the formulation of policies but also in implementing policies and norm promotion in countries around the world.

ECOSOC, a fifty-four-member body, convenes one five-week session each year, held alternately in New York and Geneva, Switzerland. The member governments are elected by the General Assembly for three-year terms. Seats are selected based on geographical representation: fourteen allocated to Africa, eleven to Asia, six to Eastern Europe, ten to Latin American and the Caribbean, and thirteen to the group of Western European and Other states.[5] Its year-round work is carried out by its subsidiary commissions and committees. Some of these bodies include the Commission on Human Rights; the Commission on the Status of Women; and the Regional Commissions for Africa, Europe, Latin America and the Caribbean, Western Asia, and Asia and the Pacific. ECOSOC originally had eighteen members, but with a growing number of countries joining the UN from the developing world, the body was expanded in 1965 by a Charter amendment to include twenty-seven members and was enlarged again to its current membership of fifty-four in 1973. Although ECOSOC is given the status of one of the six main organs of the UN, it actually functions under the General Assembly and is often criticized for duplicating the work of the Assembly's six main committees. Some critics have called for ECOSOC's elimination, but the majority of its membership, which represents developing countries, is unlikely to listen to these demands.

The Trusteeship Council

Having fulfilled its function, the work of the Trusteeship Council is one of the activities of the UN that has disappeared over the horizon. Considered one of the six principal bodies of the UN in the Charter, the Trusteeship Council was established to administer the eleven original trust territories and prepare them for independence or self-government. That work has been accomplished, but the Council still exists in theory, and the UN continues to maintain the elegant Trusteeship Council chamber at UN headquarters next to the ECOSOC chamber. The trusteeship territories are not to be confused with colonial holdings. Entities under trusteeship were (1) territories held by the League of Nations as mandates and inherited by the UN, (2) territories detached from enemy states after World War II, and (3) territories voluntarily placed under the system.

Membership on the Trusteeship Council had its own peculiar system. It included member states that had been given administrative authority over a trust territory, plus all of the permanent five countries, and a number of members not administering a territory but elected by the General Assembly to serve three-year terms. The total number of these elected member states had to equal the number of countries who were administering a territory. The concept was that the administering state had to prepare the territory for independence while the additional member states were on the Council to review this progress and hold them accountable. The role of the Council was to supervise the governance of the territories by the administering state and to receive petitions and grievances by the inhabitants seeking redress. The Council would make an annual report to the General Assembly on its work, thereby delegating accountability to the administering state. In this way, it was to the advantage of the administering state to rid itself of this responsibility, and the Council eventually put itself out of business by its success. In 1994, the last of the territories, Palau, a Pacific Islands territory, gained its independence and became a member of the UN. Formally, the Trusteeship Council still exists, but with only the P-5 as members. There have been suggestions that the Trusteeship Council could oversee failed states and prepare them for good governance and capacity building. But so far, the member states have not taken up this concept.

The International Court of Justice

The International Court of Justice (ICJ), also known as the World Court, is one of the six principal organs of the United Nations and replaced the Permanent Court of International Justice, which had functioned during the incarnation of the League of Nations. All members of the United Nations are automatically members of the ICJ, and the Court's statute is part of the UN Charter. The Court, which is located in The Hague, Netherlands, settles legal disputes between states. Individuals cannot bring cases to the Court, and no individual can be tried under the Court's auspices. The ICJ can also offer advisory opinions on legal matters, but only designated UN bodies such as the General Assembly or the Security Council, not states, can request an advisory opinion.

The fifteen judges sitting on the Court are elected by the General Assembly upon the nomination of the Security Council members, who receive a list of qualified candidates from the Secretary-General. A judge on the Court serves a nine-year term and can be reelected, and no country can have more than one judge on the ICJ at a time. The permanent five countries of the Security Council always hold five of the fifteen seats. Every three years, five members are elected, so that not all fifteen leave at the same time. Thus, the replacement of judges is staggered so the institutional memory of cases before the Court is sustained. The full fifteen judges can hear a case, or they can create a smaller body comprised of a few judges (called a *chamber*) if the parties bringing a dispute to the Court so request. For example, in 1993, the Court established a seven-member chamber to deal with environmental cases falling within its jurisdiction. In addition, if a party to a dispute asks for an additional judge, perhaps from its own country, that request can be granted if none of the current fifteen are of the party's home state.

Many cases deal with boundary or territorial disputes, and most are brought voluntarily by the parties to the Court. Some examples of cases brought before the Court include the dispute between the United States and Canada regarding the Gulf of Maine; the border dispute between Nigeria and Cameroon; the territorial dispute between Namibia and Botswana; a dispute on sovereignty over islands between Indonesia and Malaysia; and the dispute between Finland and Denmark regarding passage through the Great Belt.[6] More recently, other types of cases have emerged—for example, on genocide and humanitarian rights. Bosnia and Herzegovina brought Serbia before the ICJ on grounds that Serbia had been responsible for perpetrating genocide in Bosnia and Herzegovina during the war in the Balkans in the 1990s. In 2019, the Gambia brought a case to the ICJ against Myanmar, accusing the country of carrying out genocide and ethnic cleansing against the Muslim Rohingya people of Myanmar's Rakhine province.

During the Cold War, the number of cases brought to the ICJ were rather few, but this changed dramatically after the Cold War ended in 1991. According to Roselyn Higgins, a judge on the Court from the UK who also served as president of the ICJ:

> It is no coincidence that by 1992 the Court had over twelve cases waiting for disposal. This is exactly because states from all over the world

are coming to the Court, not reluctantly dragged there by reference to instruments they now wished they had never signed, but voluntarily. This undoubtedly reflects an increasing confidence in the Court, not only as an institution of great competence and impartiality but one perceived as capable of ensuring that its interpretation of international law is at once predictable and responsive to diverse legitimate needs.[7]

Higgins's prediction that the Court would begin to hear more and more cases has proven correct. Even by 2004, the ICJ had twenty-two cases on its docket. By the end of 2021, the ICJ had delivered 179 judgments since its first case in 1947.[8]

In addition to cases brought by states, over the years the Court has issued twenty-seven advisory opinions (such as the responsibility of member states to pay the expenses of the United Nations). Under Article 19 of the UN Charter, member states are required to pay their annual dues to the organization or lose their vote in the General Assembly. Some countries had been refusing to pay their peacekeeping dues, and the UN requested a legal opinion from the Court as to whether peacekeeping dues would be considered part of a country's financial responsibility to the UN. The decision of the Court was affirmative. Another request for an advisory opinion was on the legality of the security wall that Israel had built along the dividing line between the State of Israel and the Occupied Territory, land captured by Israel in the 1967 war. The judgment claimed that the part of the wall built within the Occupied Territory was not legal but left open the question as to whether the whole wall was legal. In 2010, the ICJ issued an opinion on the case of Kosovo and its legal right to unilaterally declare itself independent. Serbia did not recognize the breakaway province as a new independent state, and the General Assembly held a special session to request an advisory opinion of the ICJ. The decision of the Court was that Kosovo had the right to unilaterally declare independence, but to be really independent a state had to be politically recognized by other countries. As of this writing, 117 countries have formally recognized Kosovo, with the exceptions of Serbia, Russia, and others.[9]

Voting Procedures Within the UN System

The United Nations utilizes an amalgamation of voting mechanisms borrowed from both domestic and international practices and grafted onto the decisionmaking procedures in the different UN bodies. Voting is a paramount activity in the UN and subject to extensive lobbying and vote trading. To illustrate, decisions are taken by vote in the Security Council, the General Assembly, ECOSOC, special committees of the Council and Assembly, UN-sponsored global conferences, treaty conferences, and the governing bodies of the UN funds, programs, and agencies that make up the UN system. At least four voting mechanisms function simultaneously, with variations among different bodies:

- the egalitarian practice of one country, one vote, borrowed from international law and treaty conference practices;
- the elitist great power privilege tradition, which evolved in Europe (the P-5 veto privilege);
- majoritarian decisionmaking, borrowed from democratic theory and practice; and
- consensus, or unanimity, based on European conference procedures and practices.

Consensus, or unanimity, as had been required by the League of Nations, was seen as a stumbling block and had to be replaced when the UN was created. Unanimity meant that one country, no matter what its intentions might be, could block any action emanating from the League. Although consensus recognizes the rights of each sovereign state, its use can enable inaction. That practice was to be avoided, and the United Nations abandoned consensus in favor of majority voting in standing bodies. However, consensus has been retained in some instances for multilateral treaty agreements and the formulation of precise language for UN declarations, to demonstrate solidarity. Conferences and other declarations that intend to represent global norms generally strive for consensus but may resort to majority rule if outliers continue to hold positions that would undermine the intent of the document. For example, in finalizing the Statute for the International Criminal Court (ICC), member states chose majority voting to avoid watering down the agreement in order to satisfy those countries who wanted to weaken the ICC.

The Security Council has the most complex system of voting among the UN bodies because its operating procedures include a mixture of the four elements.

- Egalitarian practice of one country, one vote: each of the fifteen members of the Council has one vote.
- Great power elite privilege: the five powers—China, France, Russia, the UK, and the United States—while having one vote each, also have permanent, unelected seats on the Council; the remain-

ing ten serve two-year terms, are elected by the General Assembly and cannot serve consecutive terms.
- Majoritarianism: an affirmative vote of the Council must have a supermajority of nine votes in favor to pass; eight would be a simple majority.
- Unanimity: affirmative consensus of the five permanent members must be achieved for a resolution to pass; even one P-5 negative vote, or veto, blocks passage; an abstention is not considered a veto and does not block a resolution from passing if there are nine votes in favor; the veto cannot be used on procedural matters, such as placing an item on the agenda of the Council.

To further complicate matters, under Article 27, paragraph 3, of the Charter, regarding decisions under Chapter VI (peaceful settlements of disputes), if a permanent member is a party to a conflict and the Council takes up the issue, that member must abstain from voting. By adding this provision, the founders wanted to be sure that even the P-5 would need to heed calls for peaceful solutions, such as mediation, negotiation, arbitration, judicial settlements, and so forth. In practice, however, this provision in the Charter has never been imposed on a member of the Council. On the other hand, that permanent member's vote is restored if the resolution falls under Chapter VII, which deals with enforcement measures. In writing the Charter, the founders understood that the major powers would need to agree on the authorization of the use of force; fighting among the major powers was to be avoided. In addition, these powers would not have joined the UN if force could be used without their consent. Yet, it was hoped that under Chapter VI all nations would accept peaceful means for resolving disputes.

On a few occasions, the Security Council, under manipulation primarily by the United States, has been able to circumvent the major power veto. Under the General Assembly "Uniting for Peace" resolution created in 1950, if the Security Council is unable to act, the issue can be moved to the General Assembly by a procedural vote in the Council or by a majority vote in the General Assembly itself. The "Uniting for Peace" resolution was enacted to avoid vetoes by the Soviet Union during the crisis on the Korean Peninsula in the early 1950s. The Soviet Union was supporting the Communist North, and the Western powers were militarily engaged in support of South Korea and wanted the legitimacy that UN authorization would provide. However, the Western powers on the Council played a trick on the Soviet Union regarding Korea. They voted to remove the Korean issue from the agenda of the

Security Council, to which the Soviet Union wholeheartedly agreed. However, if the Council is no longer engaged in a matter, the General Assembly, according to the Charter, can take it up. And so, a few days later, the General Assembly took up the Korea issue, and any further resolutions on the matter were exercised by the General Assembly.

In fact, the first time the "Uniting for Peace" resolution was enacted was during the 1956 Suez crisis, ironically to avoid vetoes by France and the United Kingdom, who had colluded with Israel to attempt to take back the Suez Canal after Egypt's president Gamal Abdel Nasser had nationalized this key waterway. This resulted in the General Assembly authorizing the first deployment of armed UN troops and the creation of the term "UN peacekeeping." Over the years, through "Uniting for Peace" or other methods, issues have been taken up by the General Assembly a number of times.[10] One recent example was on February 16, 2012, in regard to the conflict in Syria when the Council had been unable to agree on how to proceed. Under the principle that the Security Council was unable to act, a majority of the General Assembly membership took up the Syria issue, passed a resolution proposing a plan of action, and called upon Secretary-General Ban to name a special envoy to mediate the crisis.[11]

In 2022, the Security Council once again made use of this tool, "Uniting for Peace," regarding Russian aggression in Ukraine. In this case, the Council members had confidence in the members of the General Assembly to cooperate in condemning Russia's actions in a democratic European state. The United States may have lost its dominant influence in the General Assembly since the mid-1960s when many new developing countries began to join the United Nations; nevertheless, Russia's aggression was perceived as a threat to world peace and even possibly leading to the outbreak of a third world war. This is not to say that now the Council is willing at all times to circumvent a veto. It will depend on the critical nature of the events. However, the General Assembly may opt to take over an issue if the members decide the Security Council is not living up to its responsibilities.

Voting in the General Assembly is dramatically simpler than in the Security Council. All decisions are taken by majority vote, no consensus is required, and there are no vetoes. Each member has one vote. Decisions on important issues are made by a two-thirds majority of those present and voting, which may not comprise the entire membership. These important issues include final approval of the budget, peace and security, election of members to the Security Council and ECOSOC, the admission of new members to the United Nations, the expulsion of members, and other such questions the Assembly decides are important. All other resolutions require a simple majority of those present and voting. Because resolutions emanating from the Assembly are not binding, it was not considered essential to have 100 percent agreement, and members not agreeing with the outcome are not required to comply. Plus, the principle of consensus in the League of Nations had crippled the League from being totally effective. On the other hand, budgetary assessments on member states established by the General Assembly, as written in the Charter and confirmed in the ICJ, are obligatory.

The election of the Secretary-General is an interesting case in which both the Security Council and the General Assembly are involved. The Charter states in Article 97, "the Secretary-General shall be appointed by the General Assembly upon the recommendation of the Security Council." In practice, this has meant that the Security Council, after deliberation and a voting procedure that includes the veto, has selected its choice of a single candidate and the Assembly has always approved that choice. However, in the election in 1991 to replace Pérez de Cuéllar, whose term ended in December 1991, the General Assembly took the initiative to declare that it would only approve a candidate whose nationality was African. Until that point, Secretaries-General had come from Europe, Asia, and Latin America but not from the African continent. The Africa Group in the Assembly essentially had enough members to block any candidate not emanating from Africa, and therefore the Security Council had to take the threat seriously. Boutros-Ghali of Egypt was elected and took office January 1, 1992, right at the end of the Cold War. When Boutros-Ghali only served one term and not the expected two, the Assembly reaffirmed its demand that another African had to succeed Boutros-Ghali in order to give Africa its fair representation. The Council then nominated Kofi Annan of Ghana, who then served two five-year terms. For the time being, it was expected that the Secretary-General should rotate among the continents, and in 2007, Ban of the Republic of Korea was selected to begin the rotation back to Asia. As Ban's two terms were coming to an end in 2016, the Central and Eastern Europe Group claimed it was their turn. However, as stated above, the Security Council reneged on the concept of geographic rotation and chose Guterres of Portugal, constituting the fourth from the continent of Europe.

Voting in the remaining principal bodies of the UN is by simple majority, including decisions by the ICJ, for which the president of the Court, also one of the fifteen judges, can break a tie if one should occur. Voting by the governing boards of the UN's programs, funds, and agencies is determined by each organization's own procedures, as is voting by treaty bodies.

UN Programs, Funds, and Specialized Agencies

There are a myriad of organizations within the UN system that focus on specific issues. Some examples of UN programs, funds and agencies are the UN Development Programme (UNDP), the UN Children's Fund (UNICEF), and the International Atomic Energy Agency (IAEA). Although it is beyond the purview of this chapter to elaborate on all of these programs, funds, and agencies, some degree of discussion offers an appreciation for the enormous scale of activities undertaken by the UN. At times the relevance of the UN is questioned, but this attitude reveals a general ignorance of the tremendous work the UN carries out on a daily basis around the world on issues of humanitarian assistance and economic technical development, as well as educational issues ranging from the environment to population, human rights, and the role of women. A handful of bodies in the UN system are discussed below.

The World Bank—which includes the International Bank for Reconstruction and Development (IBRD) and the International Development Association (IDA)—and the International Monetary Fund (IMF) were created in 1944, prior to the UN's inception, as part of what is known as the Bretton Woods Institutions, named after the location in New Hampshire where the first organizational meeting took place. They are considered a part of the UN system as "specialized agencies," but the UN has no decisionmaking authority over the Bank or the Fund, which are governed by representatives of their member states. The World Bank, headquartered in Washington, DC, has 189 member countries, which are responsible for how the institution is financed and how the money is spent. The IBRD raises almost all its money (US$30.523 billion in 2021) in the world's financial markets.[12] It issues bonds to raise funds and passes on the interest rates to its borrowers. The Bank makes loans for development and reconstruction. Originally, those loans were to rebuild Europe and Asia after World War II, but now the Bank issues loans around the world. At Bretton Woods, the IMF, also headquartered in Washington, DC, was established to make short-term loans to help countries resolve balance-of-payment problems in order to stabilize their monetary systems so that international trade and business could grow and thrive. In addition, the IMF was intended to maintain and coordinate currency exchange rates through a centralized mechanism linked to the gold standard.[13] However, today, having gone off the gold standard, currency rates change, or float, depending on their relative value. The IMF continues to make loans to countries facing financial stress and has stepped in to assist in stabilizing the Euro during the financial crisis that hit Europe beginning in 2009.

The policies of the two loaning institutions have often come under criticism as conflicting with the humanitarian goals of the broader UN system, particularly regarding debt payments by developing countries when interest rates began to rise and the structural adjustment requirements imposed by the institutions. The Bank and IMF wanted to be confident that the borrowing country would be able to pay back the funds in order to qualify for loans. Therefore, strict provisions were put in place to keep spending in line with income. What transpired is that many countries eliminated subsidies for daily items like bread and cut back on social services in order to meet spending limits, thus hurting those most vulnerable. However, both institutions have made it possible for developing countries to fund important development projects and have made policy changes by offering debt forgiveness.

UNICEF, created in 1946 by the UN General Assembly at first to meet the emergency needs of children in postwar Europe, now serves children in need all over the world, often following a natural disaster or when families and children are fleeing conflict. Considered a "fund" and not a specialized agency, it is supported by voluntary contributions from governmental and nongovernmental sources and its own fundraising activities. Awarded the Nobel Peace Prize in 1965, UNICEF provides healthcare and nutrition for children and mothers and funds water supply and sanitation projects that affect children. Emergency relief for children during crises caused by civil wars or natural disasters takes about 20 percent of the budget. UNICEF is governed by its thirty-six-member executive board, composed of government representatives elected in rotation for three years by ECOSOC.

The UNDP, established in 1965, has offices in 170 countries and territories around the world and coordinates the development activities of the UN. The thirty-six-nation executive board sets the policies for the programs. UNDP relies entirely on voluntary contributions from UN member states, multilateral organizations, the private sector, and other sources. The annual budget for 2020 was US$4.56 billion.[14] The primary goal for UNDP right now is to assist and support the 2030 Agenda and its Sustainable Development Goals (SDGs).

Also, UNDP publishes the *Human Development Report,* which provides a narrative and a statistical assessment of development around the world and ranks nations using UNDP's Human Development Index on their capacity to provide not only income for their citizens but also education, health, sanitation, and so forth. Nations like Norway and Canada tend to rank highest in providing the best conditions in their home countries, with life expectancy in the high 70s and low 80s and low infant-mortality rates. Countries like Sierra Leone, Zimbabwe, and Niger tend to rank at the bottom, with life expectancy in the 40s and 50s and very high infant-mortality rates. The huge gap between rich and poor is a constant issue within the United Nations. Under Annan, the UN created the MDGs to address issues of poverty, human rights, and health. In 2015, under the direction of Ban, member states, and civil society, the MDGs were replaced by the more expansive and complex SDGs, which the UN member states hope to achieve by 2030.

The World Health Organization (WHO), established in 1948, is governed by a thirty-one-nation executive board. All members of the UN are also members of WHO, which is headquartered in Geneva. Its annual budget is supported through voluntary contributions. Its primary purpose is to promote global health, and it has been very successful in collaborating with UNICEF and national governments to eradicate smallpox and polio. In developing countries, it has also worked hard to control malaria and other diseases, such as river blindness in West Africa, outbreaks of Ebola, and cholera. WHO also coordinates the UN's program on HIV/AIDS (human immunodeficiency virus and acquired immunodeficiency syndrome). While WHO has undertaken some specific health issue campaigns, its central strategy is based on primary healthcare, including health education, food supply and nutrition, safe water, sanitation, immunization, disease prevention, and the provision of essential drugs. Because of overlapping goals, WHO works closely with other UN bodies such as UNICEF (as mentioned), the UN High Commissioner for Refugees (UNHCR, also known as the Refugee Agency), OCHA, the World Food Program (WFP), and others to coordinate their activities as they relate to health. Since the outbreak of the Covid-19 virus in 2019/2020, the WHO has been under criticism for its slow reaction to the crisis and has been under pressure to reassess its working methods.

The UNHCR was originally founded in 1950 by the General Assembly to help with the 1.2 million refugees left homeless after World War II as well as other refugee issues. It is headquartered in Geneva, is governed by a forty-six-nation executive committee, and depends entirely on voluntary contributions from governments, nongovernmental organizations, and individuals. The 1951 Refugee Convention acts as the key legal document defining who is a refugee, the rights of refugees, and the legal obligations of states. The purpose is to safeguard the rights and well-being of refugees and their needs around the world. The organization strives to guarantee the right to seek asylum and find safe refuge with the option to return home voluntarily or resettle in another country. Legally, a refugee is defined as someone who has had to leave his or her country to find refuge. This refugee definition does not account for the many others who are displaced within their own countries but are nevertheless left homeless. UNHCR, with no mandate to help internally displaced persons (IDPs), does however assist those who are displaced due to conflict, natural disaster, and ethnic cleansing, although it must be requested to do so by the UN and must also have the consent of the country involved.

With wars in Syria, Yemen, South Sudan, and Ethiopia, and the continuing conflict in Afghanistan in recent years, the number of refugees has exploded. By 2022, there were 96.9 million displaced persons, which includes some 39.1 million persons formally designated as refugees (those having left their country of origin) and 53 million IDPs, plus 4.1 million asylum seekers.[15] These numbers do include the more than 7.6 million Ukrainian refugees fleeing Russian attacks.

It has been a challenge for UNHCR to manage the refugee camps that have sprung up in many places and to provide food, water, shelter, and security to these vulnerable people. Host countries are struggling to support millions of people—families and children—who have fled violence, arriving most often with nothing but the clothes on their backs. During its some seventy years in operation, UNHCR has helped many millions of people and has faced challenges in raising enough funds to meet the current crisis.

The World Trade Organization (WTO) is considered part of the UN system but operates independently, with its own governing body and budget. Following the end of the Cold War, the WTO was established in 1995 as a permanent body to oversee international trade, replacing the General Agreement on Tariffs and Trade (GATT), which was serviced only by an ad hoc secretariat. Members of the GATT automatically became members of the WTO. Recent members are the People's Republic of China (mainland China) in 2001, Chinese Taipei (Taiwan) in 2002, and Russia in 2012. The WTO, with its 164 members headquartered in Geneva in a large modern building constructed specifically for the organization, is not considered a UN agency but undertakes cooperative arrangements and practices with the UN. "The WTO provides a forum for negotiating agreements aimed at reducing obstacles to international trade and ensuring a level playing field for all, thus contributing to economic growth and development."[16] The Ministerial Conference, where policy decisions are made, meets every two years, with the most recent taking place in June 2022. The WTO oversees sixteen different multilateral agreements where all WTO members are parties and two plurilateral agreements where only some members are parties.

Trade disputes among members are adjudicated under its Dispute Settlement Mechanism. If a member of the WTO believes that another member has violated WTO rules, that country can take the issue to the Dispute Settlement Mechanism, which creates a panel of experts established specifically for each dispute. When the panel has made a decision related to the case, the aggrieved party may then request the Appellate Body, which is a permanent body, to hear the case. The final decision then must be approved by the Dispute Settlement Body, which is made up of the whole membership and generally approves the decision. Punishment for breaking WTO rules is then exercised by the complainant through trade mechanisms either by imposing tariffs or trade-related activities on the guilty party.[17] In sum, the WTO provides a forum for organizing trade and providing a level playing field for all countries, small or large, so international relations can run smoothly. If countries decide to run around the WTO for their own self-interests, they can undermine the system and could send trade back to a state of unregulated competition and chaos.

These brief descriptions represent only a few of the many organizations affiliated with the UN family. The following list names the funds, programs, agencies, and other organizations within the UN system, most of which have websites or can be searched through the UN's homepage at www.un.org.

Funds, Programs, and Other Bodies

- UN Children's Fund (UNICEF)
- UN Conference on Trade and Development (UNCTAD)
- UN Development Programme (UNDP)
- UN Environment Programme (UNEP)
- UN Population Fund (UNFPA)
- UN Relief Works Agency for Palestine Refugees
- UN University (UNU)
- World Food Programme (WFP)
- UN High Commissioner for Refugees (UNHCR)
- UN High Commissioner for Human Rights (UNHCHR)
- UN Office on Drugs and Crime (UNODC)
- UN Women
- Commission on the Status of Women
- UN Institute for Disarmament Research (UNIDIR)
- UN Institute for Training and Research (UNITAR)
- UN Research Institute for Social Development

Specialized Agencies and Organizations

- International Labour Organization (ILO)
- International Atomic Energy Agency (IAEA)
- Food and Agriculture Organization (FAO)
- United Nations Educational, Scientific, and Cultural Organization (UNESCO)
- International Civil Aviation Organization (ICAO)
- World Health Organization (WHO)
- World Bank
- International Monetary Fund (IMF)
- Universal Postal Union
- International Telecommunication Union (ITU)
- World Meteorological Organization (WMO)
- International Maritime Organization (IMO)
- World Intellectual Property Organization (WIPO)
- International Fund for Agricultural Development (IFAD)
- United Nations Industrial Development Organization (UNIDO)
- International Seabed Authority
- International Criminal Tribunal for the Former Yugoslavia (ended 2017)
- International Criminal Tribunal for Rwanda (ended 2015)
- International Organization for Migration (IOM)
- International Residual Mechanism for Criminal Tribunals

Conclusion

The picture painted here is of a vast system with six principal organs at its center and a myriad of other loosely coordinated entities at its periphery. There is a great deal of overlap and duplication, but this is not necessarily bad in a world where so much needs to be done and the tasks are so complex. In some ways, almost every activity is connected to and dependent on others. Greater coordination and efficiency would be welcome, but the larger issue is more a lack of resources to implement the huge tasks assigned to the UN system. The UN regular budget for one year for 2022 is US$3.12 billion.[18] That sum appears meager when compared to the US Defense Department budget of some US$740 billion annually; yet the United Nations is expected to address most of the world's problems. Inevitably, there are expectations placed on the UN that it cannot fulfill. The tendency is to claim that the UN is not doing enough. However, the

UN does not have any resources of its own and cannot raise taxes or take out loans. It is completely dependent on the support of the member states and in some cases donors to carry out its missions. The UN can only become what the member states want it to become.

Nevertheless, the UN has continued to grow and adapt as the international environment changes. The world has been gradually carved into independent states, each with responsibilities within its boundaries and interests in the global community. But states are becoming more and more interdependent, and global problems like climate change and the spread of diseases will continue to require global solutions by a collective state system willing to address these challenges and supply the resources that are needed.

Notes

1. https://www.un.org/securitycouncil/content/countries-never-elected-members -security-council.

2. Loraine Sievers and Sam Daws, *The Procedure of the UN Security Council,* Table 4, "Vetoes of Draft Resolutions and Proposed Amendments Cast in Formal Security Council Meetings, 1946 to Present," April 12, 2022, SCProcedure.com.

3. United Nations Charter, Chapter XI, Article 73, paragraph b.

4. *Basic Facts About the United Nations* (New York: United Nations Department of Public Information, 1998), pp. 276–278.

5. United Nations Economic and Social Council, "ECOSOC Members," n.d., https://www.un.org/en/ecosoc/about/members.shtml.

6. Higgins, *Problems and Process,* pp. 187–188.

7. Ibid., p. 188.

8. International Court of Justice, "Cases," n.d., https://icj-cij.org/en/cases.

9. Ministry of Foreign Affairs, "Kosovo," August 8, 2021, www.mfa-ks.net /en/politika/483.

10. Jean E. Krasno and Mitushi Das, "The Uniting for Peace Resolution and Other Ways of Circumventing the Authority of the Security Council," in Cronin and Hurd, *The Security Council,* 2021, pp. 173–195.

11. UN General Assembly, Resolution A/66/253, February 16, 2010.

12. World Bank, "World Bank Group Finances—IBRD—Financial Statements 2021," accessed August 9, 2021, https://financesapp.worldbank.org/summaryinfo/ibrd.

13. Hurd, *International Organizations,* 2nd ed.

14. *UNDP Annual Report 2020,* p. 16, http://annualreport.undp.org/assets.

15. UNHCR, "Figures at a Glance," accessed November 13, 2022, www.unhcr .org/en-us/figures-at-a-glance.html.

16. World Trade Organization, www.wto.org, About WTO-Overview.

17. Hurd, *International Organizations*, pp. 53–55.

18. "General Assembly Approves $3.12 Billion UN Budget for 2022," *UN News,* https://news.un.org.en.story/2022.

3

Founding the United Nations

Jean E. Krasno

This discussion of the origins of the United Nations offers a glimpse into the some of the major issues and debates involved in the creation of the organization. The hope is that understanding the political climate when the Charter was written in 1945, during and just following the end of World War II, may shed light on the thinking that formed the basic need for a world organization that would work toward maintaining international peace and security. The fundamentals have been retained over time; however, the UN has evolved significantly since its founding. Much of the information in this chapter has been gathered from a series of interviews with those people who were present at the key conferences and who worked as members of the delegations and behind the scenes as witnesses to the history that was being made.[1]

Rationale for a World Body

To most of the world, the United Nations symbolizes the hope for international peace and security through global cooperation, dialogue, and collective responses to security threats. The UN flag, as it flies over UN offices and peace operations around the world, is a constant reminder of this aspiration. The flag's blue field holds a lonely planet Earth embraced by olive branches. The cloth was metaphorically woven from the last remaining threads of hope that had survived two devastating world wars.

In 1945, nations were emerging from a second world war in which millions had been killed and maimed, and much of Europe lay in rubble.

The truth of the horrific genocide perpetrated by the Nazis was coming to light. Yet, only two decades before the outbreak of this violence, the world had witnessed the close of what was thought to be "the war to end all wars." Modern war-fighting technology had demonstrated in these two global conflicts its efficiency at killing and destruction. In World War II, the bombing of innocent civilians and the razing of cities became a frequent military strategy. The inhumanity of humankind made the front pages of the news on a daily basis. Waves of fear and guilt, images of the very dark side of human nature, washed over the world as it witnessed accounts of each new atrocity. Even as the deaths mounted, many began to seek some positive solution out of this despair. As the war was drawing to an end, leaders began to hope that those nations that united to defeat the Axis powers might stay united to prevent another world war.

Historical Base

The founders of the United Nations had history to draw upon for their plan. Nations had come together at various times to respond to crises, but the concept of an ongoing global organization was still considered experimental. The United Nations, as an intergovernmental organization, is based on the unit of the state. The state had not evolved until well into the seventeenth century, as historically recorded by the Treaty of Westphalia, a set of agreements reached among several European nations that ended the Thirty Years' War in 1648 as these nations broke away from the Holy Roman Empire.

At the onset of statehood, bilateral diplomacy was the primary means of communication and conflict resolution between states, but in nineteenth-century Europe, that process began to change, and the concept of large-scale, multilateral conferences emerged as a tentative first step toward formulating a dialogue on cooperation. Four major conferences took place between 1815 and 1822 in response to the devastation brought about by the Napoleonic Wars. The first of these, the Congress of Vienna, marked the primary attempt to reach a broader peace through hammering out an agreement among stronger and weaker powers, through a balance of power, to deter future aggression like that of France under Napoleon. Over the next 100 years, leaders of Europe's greatest nations, referred to as the Concert of Europe, assembled some thirty times to discuss urgent political matters of the day. These resplendent gatherings took place in Berlin, Paris, London, and other cities throughout Europe. The most powerful countries became known as the "great powers," which formed a kind of executive committee of European affairs. The Concert gradually admitted new members, accepting Greece and Belgium in 1830 and Turkey in 1856. As UN scholar Inis Claude explains, "Diplomacy by conference became an established fact of life in the nineteenth century."[2]

At the same time, in addition to the focus on security issues addressed by the Concert, Europe was engaging in international efforts to organize across state territories on other issues. River commissions were created to manage navigation on the Rhine River in 1804 and the Danube River in 1856. The Universal Postal Union and the International Telegraph Union, institutions that still exist today, were created to address the increasing demand for intercommunications. Increased trade and migration brought the spread of diseases like cholera, which motivated a total of six international conferences dealing with health issues between 1851 and 1903. At the same time, two international "peace" conferences were held in The Hague in the Netherlands, the first in 1899 attended by twenty-six countries, and the second in 1907, which expanded to forty-four nations, including most of Latin America. The contribution of the Hague conferences was not only the introduction of non-European states, but also the sense of equality given to all those participating, in contrast to the "great power" hegemony of the Concert. In addition, the Hague conferences introduced the notion that international relations might be based on standard norms and the regular convening of members. While these conferences did not create new permanent institutions, they laid the groundwork for an established multilateral consultation process that eventually led to the formation of an international court (the Permanent Court of International Justice, which was located in The Hague) and the League of Nations following World War I.

Creation of the League of Nations

World War I brought an end to the Concert of Europe and a scheduled third Hague peace conference. But following the war, the concepts reappeared and were merged into the formation of the League of Nations, which retained the great power executive committee status of the Concert in combination with the egalitarian universality of the Hague idea. The League Council became the executive committee, granting permanent status to the five major powers, which would serve with a number of rotating members but which enjoyed greater power and influence. The League Council and League Assembly, reflecting the egalitarian ideal of the Hague concept, granted equal voting rights to all League members. The League not only merged the two earlier ideas but added another layer by establishing a permanent secretariat and regular meetings to further institutionalize the cooperation that had been initiated by the conferences, river commissions, and public unions.

However, the League experiment encountered a number of serious setbacks before its ultimate collapse at the outbreak of World War II, which it had failed to prevent. First, the United States, whose president, Woodrow Wilson, is credited with being the "father" of the League, never joined. Wilson, a Democrat, did not succeed in convincing the Republican-led Senate to give its consent to ratify the treaty that was required for membership. The permanent seat reserved for the United States was left unoccupied throughout the League's short life span. This comment about the absence of the United States was made by someone present at the first meeting of the League Council: "As the afternoon wore on, the sun which streamed across the Seine and through the windows cast the shadow of the empty chair across the table. The shadow lengthened that day and the days that followed until the League died."[3] State Department staff member Alger Hiss explains:

> Now it is true that in the early days of the League and up until World War II broke out, the State Department was so afraid of being identified with the League since the Senate had rejected the League, that we did not have a regular observer. We had Prentiss Gilbert in Geneva report unofficially; the League was hush-hush, but only for that reason; no real hostility to it.[4]

The other problem was that two of the permanent members on the League Council were Italy and Japan, which emerged as aggressor nations and formed an unholy union with Nazi Germany to ignite yet another global conflict. The League's rules of consensus gave everyone on the Council a veto, which deadlocked the organization. The procedures were clearly a stumbling block, but the will to act was also weak, leaving the League unable to effectively react when permanent member Japan invaded Manchuria and Italy invaded Ethiopia. While economic sanctions were imposed on Italy, in fact they were removed when Italy completed its occupation of the nation across the Mediterranean. The League's creators believed that war could be prevented through peaceful settlement and hoped to thwart aggression through collective action by its members. But the League Covenant, its founding charter, never condemned war and only asked its members to wait three months before resorting to war. The League had been built on the premise that war was a mistake and that dialogue and negotiation could resolve disputes that might arise among its members. Ultimately, League members lacked the will to deal with the purposeful aggression of the Axis powers.

The War Years

US president Franklin Roosevelt and his secretary of state, Cordell Hull, still believed in the Wilsonian concept of the League even though it had been discredited for failing to deal effectively with the aggressive tactics that eventually led to another worldwide conflict. During the war years, Roosevelt instructed his State Department staff to reconstitute a framework based on the League idea that would not only provide the means for consultation and peaceful settlement, but also give the organization enforcement powers, or "teeth" to prevent aggression. It was assumed that the new institution would have a plenary assembly and an "executive" council, much like the League. However, because the new organization was to have enforcement powers, a new strategy had to be devised. Under the League, the Council and the Assembly had concurrent responsibilities. The Council had enforcement authority but neither the will nor the effective means to carry it through. Ruth Russell, in her book on the drafting of the UN Charter, describes the thinking of the State Department and Roosevelt at the time: "Given the fundamental decision to clothe the new institution with some kind of enforcement power, it was natural to think of making the smaller organ more of an executive agent for the whole organization and of centering in it the control of the security function."[5]

Roosevelt had expressed enthusiasm for an enforcement mechanism based on the wartime alliance of the four major powers: Britain, China, the Soviet Union, and the United States. France, which had been occupied by Germany from the onset of the war, was not a part of these preliminary discussions. In the Moscow Declaration of October 1943, Roosevelt and Hull carefully orchestrated an agreement among the four foreign ministers to pledge their countries to continuing wartime cooperation through the establishment of an organization committed to the maintenance of international peace. The Chinese foreign minister did not attend the Moscow conference but signed the agreement later. The atmosphere at the 1943 Moscow conference was positive on the Soviet side as well. Alexei Roschin, who attended the meeting for the Soviets agreed: "Yes, it was positive at the Moscow conference on foreign affairs in 1943 when [Vyacheslav] Molotov, Hull, and Eden met. In principle it was decided that a [founding] conference should take place and the organization was set up."[6] However, in Washington, a State Department committee created to study these proposals did not favor the idea of providing such predominance for the major powers and suggested that there be a larger body more like the League Council in order to better balance the might of the "big four." These powers would still make up an executive committee, but any decision emanating from the body would require majority support of the whole council, including the votes of those holding nonpermanent seats.

It was felt that the consent of the major powers was necessary because they would be providing the military force required to give the organization the teeth it needed. These nations would not be willing to have their militaries conscripted into an enforcement action against their will. They would withdraw from the organization. On the other hand, unanimity of the whole council as had been required under the League was to be avoided. To ensure the solidity of the enforcement threat, the decisions of the council would have to be binding on all members of the United Nations.

When President Roosevelt addressed the United States over the radio on Christmas Eve 1943, he laid the groundwork for his case to the American people:

> Britain, Russia, China, and the United States and their allies represent more than three-quarters of the total population of the earth. As long as these four Nations with great military power stick together in determination to keep the peace there will be no possibility of an aggressor Nation arising to start another war.
>
> But those four powers must be united with and cooperate with all the freedom-loving peoples of Europe, and Asia, and Africa, and the Americas. The right of every Nation, large and small, must be respected and guarded as jealously as are the rights of every individual within our own Republic.[7]

The United States was the pivotal power and took the lead on the creation of this new organization. The fact that the United States was also a democracy is key to the evolution of the conceptual development underlying the structure and wording of the UN Charter. Roosevelt knew that the United States could not become a member of the new institution without Senate approval. He had learned from Wilson's experience that this could be difficult. He therefore set about early in the process to bring leaders of the Senate into the dialogue through a special committee headed by Republican senator Arthur Vandenberg and Democratic senator Tom Connally. Roosevelt invited another leading Republican to the delegation, Governor Harold Stassen, someone who had spoken out in favor of a United Nations and who at the time was serving on the staff of Admiral William Frederick Halsey Jr.:

> Then that message from President Roosevelt showed that he had remembered my advocacy and he named me as the third [member] of our party, the Republican Party. Senator Arthur Vandenberg was the Chairman of the Senate Foreign Relations Committee and the leading Republican in the United States Senate. Congressman Eaton was the Chairman of the House Foreign Affairs Committee, the leading Republican in the House. I was then the third Republican that he appointed. . . . As far as I know, I was the first one in active public life in the United States to advocate that there should be a United Nations.[8]

Senator Vandenberg was deeply concerned that the new organization would undertake to keep a "just" peace. In addition, the Senate Foreign Relations Committee noted a concern expressed by a number of civic groups for the position of smaller states within the organization. Secretary Hull and Roosevelt took very seriously the senators' concerns because in the US democratic system, they needed the concurrence of the Senate and the American people. Senate concerns prompted Roosevelt to make this statement on June 15, 1944:

> We are not thinking of a superstate with its own police forces and other paraphernalia of coercive power. We are seeking effective agreement and arrangements through which the nations would maintain, according to their capacities, adequate forces to meet the needs of preventing war and of making impossible deliberate preparations for war, and to have such forces available for joint action when necessary.[9]

Thus, Roosevelt worked out a strategy to sustain support for his proposal to create a multilateral permanent body. He carefully courted both political parties and the American people, while at the same time orchestrating his plan on a global level with the major powers.

The Meetings at Dumbarton Oaks and Yalta

When the presentations for a new international organization were ready for discussion by the major powers, Roosevelt called a meeting at a large estate named Dumbarton Oaks in Washington, DC. Secretary Hull was

ill and Edward Stettinius was placed in charge. The US team that had
contributed to the preparations included, among others, Ralph Bunche,
Alger Hiss, Grayson Kirk, and an American of Russian origin named
Leo Pasvolsky.[10] The creation of the United Nations was a US endeavor:

> What was done by that research group up until at least the Dumbarton
> Oaks talks makes it proper to say that the United States really was the
> architect of the UN. That phrase has been prated about. But it's accu-
> rate—the Russians had too many distractions, the British didn't have the
> manpower, and we did—we had an extraordinary group of academic
> talent to work on all manner of things; to indicate how much dedication
> was involved: when Ralph Bunche was invited to join, it was unusual at
> that time to have a black officer in a position of importance. Cordell
> Hull was the Secretary of State and was as interested in the UN as any,
> although the real father of the UN—almost an obsession—was Franklin
> Roosevelt. When those in charge of gathering staff, the research staff,
> wanted Ralph Bunche particularly because of his knowledge of Africa,
> Hull said OK, (remember he was from Tennessee).[11]

Hiss describes the attitude of the team toward the League experiment:

> The League was regarded as definitely our forerunner. There was no
> hostility toward it. There was a feeling that it had to be improved upon,
> that it had failed and that we could learn from its failure. It was not
> universal enough; it was too Euro-centered; and it didn't seem to us to
> have the necessary powers that an international organization should
> have. And also we knew we would in a literal sense succeed the
> League and take over its properties and its functions. But the UN in no
> sense was hostile. The League was considered a brave experiment and
> there was much we could learn from its few successes and failures.[12]

The team set about preparing for the Dumbarton Oaks meeting,
which took place in two sessions. The Soviets and the British met with
the Americans first, starting the discussions on August 21, 1944. The
Soviets left on September 28, and the next day the Chinese arrived for
a nine-day meeting with the British and Americans. This procedure was
a political necessity at the request of the Soviets, who had not entered
the war in the Pacific against Japan and did not want to appear to the
Japanese that they were in collusion with the Chinese. The meeting with
the Chinese was largely a formality, and Hiss claims that they were not
major participants in the process.

A significant outline of the UN Charter was produced at Dumbarton Oaks. It was agreed that there would be a Security Council, a General Assembly, a Secretariat, and an International Court of Justice.
Alger Hiss, who took the notes for the State Department at the meet-

ing, explains that the "Economic and Social Council was only barely sketched" and "trusteeship was not taken up at all."[13] The question of voting procedures within the Security Council, including the veto, was discussed but not settled at Dumbarton Oaks and was taken up again at Yalta. In Washington, the Soviet ambassador to the United States, Andrei Gromyko, headed the Soviet delegation. Alexander Cadogan represented the British, and Edward Stettinius headed the US delegation. The Chinese delegation was led by the Chinese ambassador to London, V. K. Wellington Koo. Certain politically sensitive issues like the veto and trusteeship had to wait until the meeting at Yalta, where the heads of state would take up these matters.

At Dumbarton Oaks, no agreement was reached on exactly what the membership of the new organization ought to be except that members should be "peace-loving" nations. Under instruction from Moscow, Ambassador Gromyko stated that the Soviet Union wanted a seat for each of the fifteen Soviet republics plus a seat for the Soviet Union itself, for a total of sixteen members. Hiss remembers Roosevelt telling the US team that if the Soviets insisted on this membership, "Tell him [Gromyko] the whole thing's off."[14] Roosevelt basically took Gromyko's statement as a bargaining position, but nevertheless this issue would go through various stages before it was finally settled. Both Stettinius and Cadogan found Gromyko quite "compatible" to work with, and they felt that he understood the US position on the fifteen republics. It was mentioned that if such memberships were allowed, the United States could invite all of its forty-eight states to join.

Another point of contention between the Soviets and the Western powers that surfaced at Dumbarton Oaks was the issue of what the competence of the organization should be. The British and the Americans both agreed that the organization should address economic and social issues as well as strictly security considerations. The belief was that hostilities in Europe that had contributed to conflict had in part arisen from economic and social problems and that any organization dealing with the prevention of war would have to also address those conditions that underlay the fundamental causes. The Soviets, on the contrary, felt vigorously that the new structure should only deal with security. Roschin, advisor to the Soviets, explains that they were "strongly against" any other competency for the organization. They were committed to the idea of collective enforcement even to the extent that they eagerly supported the creation of the UN Military Staff Committee, which would be made up of the military chiefs of staff of the five major powers. The Soviets also wanted the veto to apply to all decisions emanating from the Security Council even on procedural matters. Interestingly, Alger Hiss recounts that initially the British and most particularly Winston Churchill were not in favor of the veto and had to be convinced: "The initial attitude of Churchill, we understood to our surprise, was against the veto. . . . I think it's because he didn't fully understand the issue. We were told . . . that, Marshal Smuts had persuaded Churchill to accept and to insist upon, to be in favor of the veto for the Great Powers."[15]

A number of things that had been left unfinished at the Dumbarton Oaks meeting were resolved at Yalta a few months later. In contrast to the Washington meeting, the Yalta Conference took place at the level of heads of state. Roosevelt, Churchill, and Joseph Stalin met at Yalta from February 4 to 11, 1945. The idea of membership was essentially resolved even though some of the agreements unraveled by the time the delegates reached the San Francisco Conference in April. The term, "peace-loving nations" was defined at Yalta to mean those countries that had declared war on the Axis powers by March 1, 1945. Argentina had still not declared war and had been supporting Nazi Germany, to the anger of the Soviets particularly. The Soviets at Yalta felt that the agreement meant that Argentina would not become an original member and would not be invited to the San Francisco Conference, where the UN Charter would be finalized.

Regarding the controversy over the fifteen republics, Stalin suggested at Yalta the Soviet Union plus three republics—Lithuania, the Ukraine, and Byelorussia—should be original members. The US position was absolutely negative. These republics were constituent parts of the Soviet Union and not sovereign states. But every time the issue came up, the Soviets would say to the British, "And what about India?"[16] Churchill was adamant that India, which was still a colony under British control, had to become a member, whatever one's view on its sovereign status. This was the stalemate until a diplomatic mistake occurred that ironically cleared up the matter. Hiss, who again was the note-taker at Yalta, describes what happened. The foreign ministers (for Britain, Anthony Eden; for the Soviet Union, Vyacheslav Molotov; and for the United States, Edward Stettinius, who had taken over as secretary of state for the failing Cordell Hull on December 1, 1944) met in the morning at their dacha, and the heads of state met in the afternoon at another dacha:

> It was my duty to read the minutes as soon as they were completed, and to my surprise I saw that the minutes said that agreement had been reached, that votes would be given to White Russia [Byelorussia] and the Ukraine. So I rushed up to Eden and said, "Mr. Eden,

it's a mistake, we didn't agree." And he, quite testily—which wasn't his usual manner—said, "You don't know what's happened, speak to Ed." I went to Stettinius and he threw up his hands and said that after the meeting on which there was substantial agreement on many matters, he had reported to Roosevelt as he usually did and had started by saying, "Mr. President, it was a marvelous meeting. We reached general agreement."

At that moment, Bohlen brought Stalin in for a personal call on Roosevelt. Not a negotiating call, really just a courtesy call. Roosevelt in his expansive way said, "Marshal Stalin, I have just been getting a report from my Secretary of State on the morning meeting and he told me there was agreement on everything." Stettinius started to grab at Roosevelt's sleeve, but Stalin came back quickly "and the two republics too?" And Roosevelt said, "Yes."[17]

Once the error was made, Roosevelt later thought about saying to Stalin that it was a mistake but decided against it. He understood that Stalin was seeking a balance in what was heavily a Western organization. He did at one point ask Stalin if Hawaii and Alaska could be admitted as members and Stalin consented, but that would have been impossible under the US Constitution.[18] In the end, it was generally agreed that representatives from the Ukraine and Byelorussia could come to San Francisco, and once they were there they would be accepted as voting members. The other agreement on representation that was reached at Yalta was that Poland would be represented by a joint delegation made up of government members in exile in both London and Moscow.

Trusteeship was another contentious discussion at Yalta, but in this case Churchill was the one who bristled. At one of the plenary sessions, Stettinius read out the proposal for a Trusteeship Council. Churchill, who had apparently not been briefed beforehand, was caught completely off guard and blew up. Eden had not had time to clear it with Churchill before Yalta, even though Eden and Stettinius, with the UK and US delegations, had met first at Malta before going on to the Yalta Conference. Eden had said at Malta that he had not had time to clear it with the prime minister. Churchill shouted that he had not been elected the king's first minister "to preside over the liquidation of the British Empire."[19] Roosevelt, who was presiding, had to call for a recess. Churchill was simply fuming. Hiss was asked to write down in plain language what "trusteeship" stood for. So in longhand he wrote that "the territories in trusteeship shall be territories mandated under the League, territories detached from the Axis powers and such other territories as any member nation may wish to place in trusteeship."[20]

When Churchill read the statement, he said that, in this case, trustee-ship was all right. So the crisis passed. Of course, the Americans were well aware that after the war, with the weakened condition of both France and the UK, their colonies might in fact fall under UN decolonization. The Soviets were supportive of the trusteeship idea and held a very anti-colonialist position, which to some appeared like pure hypocrisy.

The other controversies that seemed to have been resolved at Yalta were the veto and the competency of the General Assembly. Stalin finally agreed to allow the General Assembly to deal with whatever subjects arose in the international arena, including economic and social problems. The Soviets accepted that the Council would be reserved for security concerns and would be the central mandatory body on security affairs. An important issue related to the veto was also met with general agreement. Gladwyn Jebb (UK) had served as Cadogan's assistant at Dumbarton Oaks and again at Yalta. Jebb and Cadogan had discussed at Dumbarton Oaks the idea that when decid-ing on peaceful means of settling disputes, which became Chapter VI of the UN Charter, the great powers would lose the right to veto, which was surprisingly accepted by Stalin at Yalta. As Jebb describes, "A permanent member would have a veto [on Chapter VII], but . . . they would not have a veto on the previous section, which dealt with the pacific settlement of disputes."[21] Stalin also consented that the veto could be limited to substantive issues and was not to be exercised on administrative matters or peaceful settlements. That agreement was later challenged by his foreign minister, Molotov, at San Francisco. But there was also general consensus at Yalta that there ought to be an Economic and Social Council.

Other ideas were floated during this period, some which were never taken up. Jebb describes a suggestion made by Churchill to create regional security councils:

> That was Churchill's idea, but I always thought that that was slightly dotty. He hadn't thought it out. The idea was that there was going to be a Council of Asia. . . . He thought that because we wanted a Council of Europe there should be a Council of Asia, but he hadn't thought it out. It was nuts. Even his idea of a Council of Europe, nobody knew—and he was quite incapable of explaining—whether the Russians should be in or out, whether we should be in or out, what our influence should be.[22]

These ideas, which seemed so outlandish at the time, are at the heart of current political debates over seventy-seven years later. Nevertheless, ideas that were deemed unusable at the time were left for another day, and the meeting at Yalta was generally congenial. It was felt by Hiss that Churchill, Stalin, and Roosevelt believed that they had achieved a cooperative arrangement and genuine consensus on the principles of the new organization. This spirit had begun well before Yalta at Dumbarton Oaks, where Stettinius, Gromyko, and Cadogan had cultivated a cooperative atmosphere.

The Chapultepec Conference

Revisions were made in the Dumbarton Oaks proposal after the Yalta gathering, and the document was then distributed to the nations that were invited to meet in San Francisco to write the final UN Charter. However, the Latin Americans, who would make up twenty-one of the original fifty-one members, convened a preliminary meeting in Chapultepec, outside Mexico City, in February and March 1945, called the Inter-American Conference on the Problems of Peace and War. Ambassador Manuel Pérez Guerrero and C. Parra Perez of Venezuela, among others, attended the conference. Luis Padilla Nervo and his assistant Alfonso Garcia Robles represented Mexico. Pérez Guerrero explained that US Secretary of State Edward Stettinius came to Mexico directly from Yalta. The Latin Americans had several concerns: they called for a stronger General Assembly, universality of membership, and assured representation for Latin America on the Security Council. The role of regional organizations was of particular importance, and this was discussed extensively in Mexico, as described by Pérez Guerrero: "The Pan-American Union was in existence, not the OAS [Organization of American States] as it became later on after the conference in Bogota. But there it was the opinion of Parra Perez among other people—others as well, and in the end it was the opinion that prevailed—that that organization should be called upon to [represent the] hemisphere."[23]

The Latin American countries were prepared to press for the role of regional organizations, which was later taken up in San Francisco and became a part of the UN Charter. Also, in Chapultepec there was support for Argentina to join the original members of the United Nations as well as support for issues like decolonization. The Latin Americans would take these ideas with them when they arrived in San Francisco the next month.

The San Francisco Conference

The San Francisco Conference was to finalize the structure and language of the Charter for the new organization, now to be called the United Nations, named after the title given to those nations that had united as allies to defeat the Axis powers. While the atmosphere was enthusiastic, as the war in Europe was drawing to a close, there were still a number of open issues to be debated and resolved. President Roosevelt, who had been the energy behind the creation of the UN, would not make it to San Francisco. He died of a massive cerebral hemorrhage on April 12, 1945, only days before the conference opened on April 25. He was succeeded by his vice president, Harry Truman.

Many of the delegates had arrived by train, crossing the vast plains and winding through the high mountains of the western United States before arriving in the "City by the Bay" in early spring 1945. They were impressed by the massive size of the United States, which in contrast to Europe had not been touched by the devastating destruction of the war. There was a sense of enthusiasm, and many had never been to such an international gathering. As Pérez Guerrero of Venezuela describes: "There was a genuine spirit of co-operation, I suggest. Some of the countries, like Saudi Arabia, were very new. My first conversations on oil with Saudi Arabia date from that time, from the train taking us to San Francisco with some of the younger chaps of the Saudi Arabian delegation."[24]

Spring in San Francisco was a welcome change from the bombing, fires, and rubble of the war. Plans were made to receive the international delegations with excitement and touches of elegance. The main plenary sessions were to take place in the opera house at the civic center and the adjacent veterans' memorial building. Special chefs were brought in to prepare the food and hotels made room to house these important guests.

In Washington, other preparations were being made. Oliver Lundquist, who was on loan to the State Department from the US Office of Strategic Services, was assigned to work on the graphic presentations for the San Francisco Conference. His team was in charge of designing an official delegate's badge as a credential to identify members of the conference. They did not really start out to design a logo for the UN:

> We were thinking in terms of getting a delegate button, badge and credential made for San Francisco and it was not any long range plan on our part. We had several ideas on it and had a little contest among ourselves in the agency and came up with this one which was designed by

a fellow named Donal McLaughlin—I have to give him primary credit for it—he was one of my assistants at the San Francisco Conference and he was more in charge of the actual graphic work there.[25]

Lundquist explains that the color blue was purposely selected, and that when the design was shown to Stettinius, the secretary of state responded, "'Oh that's fine and I like that color.' We had used the blue color as the opposite of red, the war color, and then peace. . . . So then we referred to it as Stettinius blue. It was a gray blue, a little different than the modern United Nations flag."[26] Lundquist relates that the symbol of the globe was slightly different in the original design:

> Well, actually, it looked superficially like the existing one except that the latest one has been changed slightly. We had originally based it on what's called an azimuthal north polar projection of the world, so that all the countries of the world were spun around this concentric circle and we had limited it in the southern sector to a parallel that cut off Argentina because Argentina was not to be a member of the United Nations. We centered the symbol on the United States as the host country. . . . Subsequently, in England our design was adapted as the official symbol of the United Nations, centered on Europe as more the epicenter I guess of the east-west world, and took into account the whole earth including Argentina. By then, of course, Argentina had been made a member of the United Nations so that it was no longer necessary to cut them off.[27]

Major Themes and Debates at San Francisco

At San Francisco the founders had to come to agreement on the major themes and language to be used in the UN Charter. While they had agreed upon the major purpose of the organization—to maintain international peace and security—they had to reach consensus on other points: membership in the organization; competency of the General Assembly and Security Council; trusteeship; self-defense; the role of the Security Council and the power of its members, including the use of the veto; the role of the Secretary-General; the framework for the use of force by the United Nations; and human rights.

Membership

Immediately, the debate over membership exploded. The American countries who had met in Mexico insisted at the San Francisco Conference that Argentina be accepted for original membership. Nelson Rockefeller, assistant secretary of state for Latin American affairs in the US State Department, had attended the Mexico meeting and supported the Latin American position on Argentina. The Latin Americans wanted universal membership, meaning that all countries would be eligible for member-ship, taking most of the delegations by surprise in San Francisco. Foreign Minister Molotov, leading the Soviet delegation, was furious that the Yalta agreement had been ignored. But the Latin Americans had twenty-one votes at the conference and refused to accept the membership of the Ukraine and Byelorussia. The US position taken by Truman was that while the Americans had agreed to admit the two republics as members, this did not necessarily mean that they could become original members and participate in the conference.

The conflict over the three candidates was sent to committee. Molo-tov tried unsuccessfully to have the Argentina discussion removed from the agenda altogether. As a gesture of good will, the Latin Americans agreed to vote in favor of the two republics and the motion was passed unanimously. But Molotov still refused to equate this with an accept-ance of Argentina, calling the Argentine government fascist and throw-ing himself into a tirade, which was captured by the press covering the conference. Senator Vandenberg thought that the entire episode had "done more in four days to solidify Pan America against Russia than anything else that happened."[28]

Molotov, apparently in retaliation on the Argentine issue and because Poland was still not represented, began to object to limitations on the veto and the broad competence of the General Assembly that had been resolved in Yalta. President Truman had to resort to sending a special envoy to Moscow to seek an audience with Stalin to clear things up. Roschin, who was among the Soviet delegation in San Fran-cisco, says that Stalin accepted the envoy's presentation of the matter and informed Molotov to adhere to the decisions taken at Yalta on the veto and the General Assembly. Argentina was accepted as a member, and the conference proceeded. Molotov eventually left San Francisco, and Ambassador Gromyko, to everyone's relief, took up the leadership of the Soviet delegation.

Competency of the General Assembly

Ambassador Garcia Robles of Mexico, who took part in the Chapulte-pec Conference and was also part of the Mexican delegation at San Francisco, recalls that the Latin Americans also emphasized the impor-tance of enhancing and making more specific the powers of the General Assembly. It was agreed that the General Assembly could take up any matter considered important to the members, but that when the Security Council was seized with a matter, the General Assembly would refrain from taking up the topic. The competency of regional organizations in relation to the UN as had been discussed in Mexico was also agreed upon, and this language was entered into the Charter. This provision recognized the right to resolve a local issue regionally before handing it over to the international body.[29] Importantly, it was eventually agreed not only that the General Assembly would be able to address economic, social, and security issues, but that it would have power over the budget.[30]

Trusteeship

The concept of trusteeship was taken up at the conference, but again not without controversy. Majid Khadduri, a member of the Iraqi delegation, recalls that the Arab countries were concerned about the status of Syria and Lebanon, which had been invited to participate in San Francisco. Both countries had been mandates of France before the war. But because France had been occupied by the Nazis, it was not able to function as a mandatory power during the war years, and Syria and Lebanon had been left on their own to govern their territories. They therefore considered themselves independent.

The Arab delegations wanted to make sure that countries that had been invited to become members of the United Nations would not fall into the category of trusteeship, which would throw Syria and Lebanon back under French control. Because the League mandates were still in force,[31] technically France was still the mandatory power over Syria and Lebanon. In response to the Arab proposal, France tried to force Syria to sign a treaty delineating certain demands that would maintain some French control. Syria refused, and in May 1945, during the San Francisco Conference, France began bombing Damascus. The United States and Britain protested the bombing and insisted that the French withdraw, highlighting that the world was trying to establish peaceful relations and ought not to resort to war tactics. When the French withdrew, the Syrians claimed their independence and refused to negotiate any further with the French.[32] Khadduri explains that the Arab nations wanted assurances that these countries would not fall under the Trusteeship Council:

> For this reason Arab countries proposed that there should be something mentioned in the Charter of the United Nations that these countries should never be considered under the Trusteeship system

of the United Nations but should be treated as independent since they had already been participating in the San Francisco Conference. This matter was taken to the steering committee. It was suggested to add a special Article (Article 78) which states that "The trusteeship shall not apply to territories which have become members of the United Nations."[33]

Colonial issues, as such, were not to be discussed at the conference, so as not to alienate the colonial powers. But there was another reason. The United States itself had been internally split on the idea. Lawrence Finkelstein, as a young member of the staff, witnessed the debate from inside the State Department:

> The thing that I wanted to emphasize that I think is fascinating is that the reason that the colonial agenda was not as far advanced by the time the San Francisco Conference began as were most of the other issues of the Charter is that there had been a deep split in the US government on the issue going back for years. This emerged sharply in the late spring of 1944 as planning for the Dumbarton Oaks conversations was moving into an advanced stage. There had been a lot of preparation in the State Department of drafts for a trusteeship plan and a declaration having to do with principles of colonial government. There had been some consultation with the British. Most thought that this plan was ready to proceed, but it was the military service which threw a monkey wrench into the works for two reasons. The first, they were very concerned that these questions would involve territorial issues which might open up disputes among the countries still conducting the war against the Axis powers. We are talking about 1944. Their main argument was that they didn't want to introduce any unnecessarily contentious issues that might cause splits particularly between us and the Russians. The second issue was we were winning island by island from the Japanese, some of which had been under League of Nations mandate after World War I but others which had not. So, the navy was against any concept of trusteeship which might internationalize those islands and thus deprive the navy of US sovereignty over them."[34]

Still the controversy was not completely settled, and a debate arose on whether to use the word "independence" in the Charter when talking about the goal of the administration of colonies or trusteeship territories. According to Finkelstein, Stassen did not want to use the word because he was worried about losing the approval of the colonial powers, mainly the British. His staff tried to dissuade him in his car on the way to making his speech, but ignoring them, he gave a powerful address against using the term, which received very negative headlines in the press. This was a massive embarrassment to the United States, itself a former colony. General Carlos Romulo, head of the Philippine delegation at San Francisco,[35] recalls the fight that ensued:

> And in the Trusteeship Committee, we were discussing a proposal of the superpowers or the colonial powers then, that the aspirations of non-self-governing peoples should be self-government. I opposed that. I said, "That's not complete. Their aspiration should be self-government or independence. Because self-government is not independence." Well we had a real fight on that. . . . We discussed the point for 2 nights. Finally, we won. It's "self-government or independence." And I don't remember the number of votes. But I think, in the committee, we won by 12 or 14 votes. So, I got a note from Stassen after my reply to the statement of Lord Cranborne [with Stassen saying]: "Congratulations. Well done."
>
> So that's why I always say that the contribution of the Philippines to the Charter [was] two words: or independence. But that opened the door for the non-self-governing peoples which were under trusteeship at the time, to enter the United Nations.[36]

Ultimately, a compromise was reached so that *independence* was included as a goal for the trust territories but was not included in the wording that dealt with all the other colonies. The concept of self-determination also met with some confusion during the conference. It did not signify, as is interpreted today, democracy. It simply meant self-rule, as opposed to colonial rule, be it monarchy, oligarchy, dictatorship, or democracy. The term *independence* was seen as interchangeable with self-government or self-determination. So, these ideas did not include the concept of democratic rule, just national self-rule by whatever authority might emerge. As Finkelstein says, "They put the word 'independence' in one part and not in the other. That's the compromise they consciously reached. Although self-determination was interpreted by Stassen and others as broad enough to incorporate independence."[37]

Self-Defense

Neither Dumbarton Oaks nor Yalta had addressed the idea of self-defense, and it was not included in the Dumbarton Oaks provisions. Self-defense, however, launched a heated debate in the Mexico meeting that carried over to San Francisco. While Stassen had been against the use of the term *independence*, he explains that he took a different stand on the issue of self-defense. Stassen recalls that he threatened to withdraw from the conference and let everyone know his reasons if the right to self-defense was not written into the Charter. Stassen states why he took such a strong stand:

> I was concerned as to the matter of self-defense in a circumstance if the Security Council was not acting and what effect that might have. So I originated the suggestion that there would be some kind of section about nothing in the Charter shall impair the inherent right of self-defense if an armed attack occurs. And this was at first pretty much rejected; of course there was a general sort of mind-set of those who had worked on the original Dumbarton Oaks draft of objecting to any change in it, especially in the early stages, but it soon became apparent that it needed changing. . . . I circulated it to our United States delegation, then after they agreed it ought to be in there, then [they] brought it up in the five-power meetings and talked it over and it finally stayed in.[38]

The Veto Debate

The principle that there should be a veto was settled at Yalta, but the debate opened up again in San Francisco. In fact, the word *veto* never appears in the Charter, and the San Francisco participants often referred to it as the *unanimity* clause. Nevertheless, the United States needed the veto in order to gain Senate ratification and also because it did not want to be put in a position of committing its resources and troops in enforcement action in all parts of the world against its will. The veto probably produced the most disagreement in San Francisco, and according to US participant Finkelstein it came very close to wrecking the Conference. Finkelstein relates: "So, the question was not whether there should be a veto but how far down in the process of decision making the veto should apply. Here the United States wanted to avoid the application of the veto to decisions that an issue should be discussed. The Russians were arguing that the decision to discuss should be subject to the veto as well."[39] Molotov was very outspoken on the veto, and it became a serious issue that divided the big five. The US delegation and the Republicans on the team were very concerned. Stassen describes the discussion:

> One of the crucial questions on the veto power was whether the veto could stop even a discussion and whether the veto could prevent any kind of action in the Assembly. There was a lot of earnest examination of just how that should be worked out. Really Senator Vandenberg and I, and I think the United States delegation, after a lot of discussion, concluded that if the veto could completely stop any kind of Assembly action, it would be better not to make a start under those

circumstances. That led to President Truman sending Harry Hopkins over to see Marshal Stalin. . . . Then out of those further negotiations and the further conference of Hopkins with Marshal Stalin came the revisions down to the point where the actual practice has followed since that time.[40]

President Truman sent Harry Hopkins to Moscow in May 1945, during the conference, and Hopkins went to see Stalin with Averell Harriman, US ambassador to the Soviet Union. Hopkins was able to get Stalin to overrule Molotov. At that point, then, there was agreement among the five on the extent of the veto, which was based on the chain of events theory.[41] The theory contended that once an item was on the agenda, a chain of events could take place that could lead to threats to the interests of the great powers, which the veto was established to protect. As Finkelstein explains:

So, it came out that, although there can be no veto on discussion as such or on a decision to put an item on the agenda of the Security Council, beyond that the veto is pretty pervasive. That statement of the five powers that I referred to, that they imposed upon the rest of the Conference, also included the so called double veto. Namely that if there were dispute as to whether the veto should apply or not, that decision itself would be subject to the veto.[42]

Khadduri states that during the debate on the veto the Arab countries were essentially pro-Western and therefore accepted the great powers' need for a veto in the Security Council.[43] The smaller countries were generally opposed to the veto, but the major powers, now joined by France, which had been liberated at the end of the war in Europe, presented a unified front. The Latin Americans were particularly resistant to the idea; along with General Romulo of the Philippines and Foreign Minister Herbert Evatt of Australia, they put up a valiant fight but in the end had to retreat.[44] The smaller powers, according to Finkelstein, "knew that they were going to have to swallow it because there would be no Charter without it and they couldn't afford not to have the Charter."[45] In the final vote on the veto, thirty-three nations supported it, two (Cuba and Colombia) voted against it, and fifteen countries chose to abstain.[46] Finkelstein relates an anecdote from the conference regarding the veto:

[Senator Tom] Connally was sent on behalf of the US delegation to read the law, the riot act, to the other smaller countries on the question of the veto. He was sent deliberately because everybody understood that he would control whether or not there could be Senate approval.

He was a large imposing man, a very memorable character. He always wore a black string tie and he had a twenty gallon hat. He was a Texan. He wore a sort of preacher's black coat. He was marvelous and he played it up. He built up this persona. He was a fourth of July orator, a stump orator with orotund rhetoric. He was a lot of fun. There he was and he went down to this committee III, 3, to tell them that "if you don't lay off this veto you're not going to have a Charter. You're going home without it."

The place next to the US place was occupied by the British, the UK next to the US in alphabetical order around the table. The British on this occasion were represented by a mild mannered, very distinguished professor of history who later became Sir Charles Webster. There was old Connally waving his arms as he spoke as though he was addressing 50 thousand people down there in Austin, Texas on the fourth of July. I watched this poor old Charles Webster slump lower and lower and lower to avoid having his head knocked off by this waving arm and finally you could barely see the top of his head over the table.[47]

The Role of the Secretary-General

In San Francisco, the role of the UN Secretary-General was considered primarily an administrative position. Ruth Russell's summary of the discussions on the election of the chief administrator demonstrates that a number of options were considered.[48] It was suggested that the General Assembly elect the Secretary-General on its own. Others proposed that the Security Council could nominate three candidates, from which the General Assembly could select one. It was also discussed whether or not a deputy secretary-general ought to be elected by the General Assembly as well. It was settled that the General Assembly would elect the Secretary-General upon the nomination of the Security Council. The Soviet delegate argued that the nomination of the Secretary-General was not a procedural matter and therefore was subject to the veto. The British and French supported this point, and the United States highlighted that the major powers had to have confidence in the chief administrator and therefore had to have some control over the selection. The United States also pointed out that the General Assembly had the power to reject an unsatisfactory candidate. The position was generally considered a bureaucratic function. Nevertheless, the Secretary-General was given the power under Article 99 of the Charter to bring any issue to the attention of the Security Council, thus adding a political competence to the office. Today, the nature of the position as global leader has evolved well beyond the original intent.

The Use of Force

Clearly the founders of the UN intended for the organization to be able to use force to deter aggression. This was carefully delineated in Chapter VII of the Charter, specifically in Article 42. Hiss, who was appointed secretary-general of the San Francisco Conference, recalls the attitude at the time:

> One reason why I feel confident that military force was foreseen from the beginning is that this was one of the strong reasons why the veto was insisted upon. Because otherwise, it would mean that American forces could be called out by non-American officials and this just wouldn't go down with the American Congress. So I think we oversimplified the idea of a military contingent that would be readily available. This is why the Military Staff Committee seemed important and of course when the Cold War began it fell into complete disuse, as we were assuming a unanimity of the Permanent Members on enforcement.[49]

The Allied powers had worked well together during the war to defeat the Axis powers, and the belief was this cooperation could continue in peacetime. The United States particularly had worked closely with the British through the Combined Chiefs. It was a model that seemed immediately available. The Soviets initially also concurred. Roschin explains that at Dumbarton Oaks,

> we insisted that the Military Staff Committee should function as a regular body and we even proposed the creation of [an] international army in order to mix in different parts of the world to establish a guarantee of security. Later we changed this position; we considered that our attitude concerning the presidency of Truman and his administration was rather complicated and here it was the beginning of the Cold War.[50]

Roschin asserts that the Soviets did not know about the US atomic bomb during the conference, which ended in June 1945, and that they only found out at the time of the bombing of Hiroshima in August. Roschin says that the bomb, of course, changed everything.[51] But during the San Francisco Conference, not even the US delegation knew about the bomb, which was top secret. As the Cold War became more evident and superpower cooperation less possible, no member state ever signed an agreement with the UN to provide troops as Article 43 of the Charter called for. In addition, tired of the war, the troops wanted to go home. Once this happened, it was difficult to remobilize.

Human Rights

The global community that gathered at San Francisco to work on the UN Charter and to observe and influence the proceedings had been deeply troubled by emerging evidence of the Holocaust and the contempt for human rights demonstrated by the Nazi regime. Human rights were considered important, but the Charter was primarily focused on collective action as a means of stopping aggression rather than dealing with individual suffering. Determining how to enforce respect for human rights was beyond the scope of the conference, but most felt the need to pay moral homage to the concept. As Claude observes, the founders were remarkable in their ability to both look back and look forward. They did not know exactly what they were creating, but they were determined to achieve a "just and lasting peace."[52]

Provisions on human rights brought up by the United States at Dumbarton Oaks had been opposed by the other leaders. But in Chapultepec, the issue came up again and was discussed with Stettinius. The Latin American delegations and some forty groups representing professional, labor, business, religious, and women's organizations strongly lobbied for the inclusion of human rights at San Francisco. Women delegates from several Latin American countries insisted that the phrase "to ensure respect for human rights without distinction as to race, sex, condition or creed" be incorporated.[53] Ultimately, provisions for a human rights commission were written into the Charter. That the great powers never intended to enforce these moral considerations is clear, particularly with respect to the equal sovereignty of the members and other elements in the Charter that specifically declare that the domestic policies and actions of member states are beyond the purview of the UN. However, those who lobbied for the inclusion of human rights were visionaries who knew, or at least hoped, that these words would take on greater impetus as the UN matured. At the first meeting of the UN General Assembly in 1946, Eleanor Roosevelt was asked to chair the human rights commission, which was charged with writing the Universal Declaration of Human Rights.

The United Nations Is Born

The Charter of the United Nations was signed by fifty members at San Francisco on July 26, 1945. Poland, which never arrived, was nevertheless allowed to sign as an original member in the months that followed, bringing the total of original members to fifty-one.[54] Hiss describes the euphoria as the final draft was signed. He explains that Truman placed tremendous importance on it, so much so that the original document was given its own parachute on the flight back to Washington, DC even though Hiss, who was carrying it, had to travel without one:

> It was decided that there was no proper—let's call it receptacle, place of safekeeping—for the Charter. The United Nations hadn't come into existence, and the conference Secretariat would be disbanded. And it was agreed that Truman would keep it in a safe in the White House. Since the US had been the host, this would be appropriate. I was therefore deputed to carry the Charter to the White House and deliver it to him for that kind of safekeeping. And the army put a plane at my disposal for that purpose. The humorous aspect of this was that since the Charter was so valuable it had a parachute attached to it—and I didn't.[55]

After signing, each nation undertook through its own procedure to ratify the Charter. On July 28, 1945, the US Senate approved the Charter by a vote of eighty-nine to two. The participation by the Senate throughout the process proved to be a very successful strategy. Never before had a treaty been so publicly debated. By October 24, 1945, twenty-nine countries had signed and ratified the Charter, constituting a majority of the original fifty-one signatories. October 24 continues to be celebrated as the birth date of the United Nations. On that day, the United Nations was officially constituted, and by December 27, all the original members had ratified the Charter. While there had been inklings of the Cold War during the negotiations, there was still a feeling of hope that this new international cooperation could be sustained. Delegates of the participating nations at San Francisco formed a preparatory commission and met in London to make arrangements for the first meeting of the United Nations and to plan for the transfer of certain activities from the League to the UN. Enthusiasm still filled the hall at the first opening session of the General Assembly in London on January 10, 1946.

The United Nations celebrated its seventy-seventh anniversary in 2022. In the course of its first three quarters of a century, the UN has withstood the pressures of the Cold War, decolonization, and numerous regional crises. The UN Secretariat has become more complex and grown into a competent international bureaucracy beyond that anticipated in 1945. The Secretary-General, once primarily considered to be an administrator, has become a major world leader. With the end of the Cold War and the era of globalization, the UN has been under pressure to reform. It has been suggested that the Security Council ought to reflect changes in the global power balance and should become more transparent. But the

Charter has proven to be a flexible instrument; it has been amended only three times, once to enlarge the Security Council from its original eleven members to its current fifteen, and twice to enlarge the Economic and Social Council, which at present has fifty-four members. The UN has grown from its original 51 member-signatories in 1945 to 193 members in 2022. Decolonization, including the independence of trust territories, so sensitive an issue at Yalta and San Francisco, was successfully over-seen by the General Assembly and the Trusteeship Council. All the for-mer colonies and trust territories are now independent members of the UN, and the Trusteeship Council no longer has any real function.

Any organization must adapt to the changing times, and the UN has continued to find ways to creatively shape itself to the challenges of its new environment. However, to remain relevant in the face of global crises like the effects of climate change, pandemics, cyberattacks, and the increasing number of refugees and migrants, it will need to continue to evolve and change as the political and security situation mutates around it. If for some reason it fails to adapt, it may be pushed aside by more forthcoming institutions or it may cease to exist, like the Concert of Europe and the League of Nations before it. An examination of the debates and ideas that have been discussed here around the birth of the UN can facilitate an understanding of how it may or may not need to change. Perhaps the concurrence of the major powers is needed to solid-ify enforcement and maintain a credible deterrence. But by what criteria do we measure which are the major powers of a given era? If we give them this power, will they share a sense of global responsibility and act in concert? In an era of globalized information sharing, the UN will inevitably be held accountable.

Carlos Romulo, one of the founders of the UN at the San Francisco Conference in 1945, said succinctly: "We have, in the United Nations, the only world forum that we will ever have. You abolish the United Nations and we'll have to create another one. Voltaire once said, the great French writer, 'if we didn't have a god, we'd have to create a god.' The same thing is true."[56]

Today, the United Nations occupies a political space at the center of the global dialogue. As UN members took up the Millennium Develop-ment Goals in 2000 and the Sustainable Development Goals in Agenda 2030, the world body acknowledged its shared responsibility to manage economic, social, gender, and environment challenges. Peace, security, and stability are still at the center of the organization, but it is evolving in ways that see the connection among all these factors in being good stewards of the global community.

Notes

1. For the full set of interviews, see the Yale-UN Oral History collection by James Sutterlin and Jean E. Krasno housed in the UN Dag Hammarskjöld Library, New York, and the Yale University Archives and Manuscripts Library, New Haven, CT.

2. Claude, *Swords Into Plowshares*, p. 25.

3. Ibid., p. 87. This comment by Edwin L. James was quoted in his obituary, *New York Times,* December 4, 1951.

4. Alger Hiss, Yale-UN Oral History interview, October 11, 1990, p. 25.

5. Russell, *History of the United Nations Charter*, pp. 228–229.

6. Alexei Roschin, Yale-UN Oral History interview, May 25, 1990, p. 3.

7. *Public Papers and Addresses of Franklin D. Roosevelt: The Tide Turns, 1943* (New York: Harper and Brothers, 1950), p. 562.

8. Harold Stassen, Yale-UN Oral History interview, April 29, 1983, p. 4.

9. *US Department of State Bulletin* 10 (June 17, 1944), pp. 552–553.

10. Leo Pasvolsky spoke Russian and worked with the Soviets on English-Russian language issues for the writing of the Charter in San Francisco. Ruth Russell dedicated her book *A History of the United Nations Charter* to him.

11. Alger Hiss, Yale-UN Oral History interview, February 13, 1990, pp. 1–2.

12. Ibid., p. 3.

13. Ibid.

14. Ibid., p. 6.

15. Ibid., p. 7.

16. Ibid., p. 16.

17. Ibid., pp. 11–12.

18. Ibid., p. 13.

19. Ibid.

20. Ibid.

21. Gladwyn Jebb, Yale-UN Oral History interview, June 21, 1983, p. 26.

22. Ibid, p. 35.

23. Ambassador Perez Guerrero, Yale-UN Oral History interview, April 22, 1983, p. 12.

24. Ibid., p. 19.

25. Oliver Lundquist, Yale-UN Oral History interview, April 19, 1990, pp. 5–6.

26. Ibid., p. 6.

27. Ibid., pp. 6–7.

28. Quoted in Russell, *History of the United Nations Charter,* p. 639.

29. Alfonso García Robles, Yale-UN Oral History interview, March 21, 1984.

30. Ruth Russell describes that there had been general agreement even in the earlier drafts that the General Assembly would decide the budget, but there continued to be discussion on what role the Council might also play in these decisions. Ultimately, it was agreed that the Assembly would have that authority. See Russell, *History of the United Nations Charter*, pp. 377–378.

31. The League was not officially terminated until early 1946, a few weeks after the UN General Assembly's first meeting.

32. Majid Khadduri, Yale-UN Oral History interview, March 20, 1997, pp. 12–13.

33. Ibid., p. 8.

34. Lawrence Finkelstein, Yale-UN Oral History interview, November 23, 1990, pp. 15–16.

35. The Philippines was not independent at the time.

36. General Carlos P. Romulo, Yale-UN Oral History interview, October 30, 1982, p. 8.

37. Finkelstein, interview, p. 19.

38. Stassen, interview, p. 26.

39. Finkelstein, interview, p. 23.

40. Stassen, interview, p. 10.

41. The chain of events theory was written into the minutes of the US delegation by Leo Pasvolsky in a volume of *Foreign Relations of the United States (1945)* in an official document series of the conference. "The United Nations Conference on International Organization, San Francisco, California, April 25–June 26, 1945" (see https://history.state.gov/historicaldocuments/frus1945v01/comp1).

42. Finkelstein, interview, p. 26.

43. Khadduri, interview, p. 22.

44. Romulo, interview, p. 4.

45. Finkelstein, interview, p. 23.

46. Russell, *History of the United Nations Charter,* p. 739.

47. Finkelstein, interview, pp. 27–28. In another version of the Connally story, it was rumored that while he was warning the delegates that killing the veto provision would kill the entire Charter, he calmly tore the draft Charter into shreds and, at the climactic moment of his theatrics, scattered the shreds on the floor (letter from Inis Claude to Jean E. Krasno, April 2001).

48. Russell, *History of the United Nations Charter,* pp. 854–859.

49. Hiss, October 11, 1990, p. 1.

50. Roschin, interview, p. 9.

51. Ibid., p. 10.

52. Claude, *Swords Into Plowshares,* p. 80.

53. Anne Winslow, ed., *Women, Politics, and the United Nations* (Westport, CT: Greenwood Press, 1995), pp. 6–7.

54. The Soviets had arrested the London Poles when they arrived in Moscow to meet with their counterparts, the Lublin faction. This was a clear violation of the Soviet's agreement to let them meet and select a joint delegation to go to San Francisco. This event took place during the conference, and the news headlines created quite a stir—a warning that the Cold War was not far off. Toward the end of the conference, an agreement was finally reached on a provisional government for Poland, but not in time to reach San Francisco. Russell, *History of the United Nations Charter,* p. 929.

55. Hiss, interview, October 11, 1990, pp. 8–9.

56. Romulo, interview, p. 11.

4

Promoting
Human Development

Jacques Fomerand

The maintenance of peace and security is the first purpose
assigned to the United Nations in Chapter I of the UN Charter, and no
fewer than five of its eighteen chapters deal with peace and security
issues. In contrast, only one chapter, Chapter IX, explicitly makes men-
tion of development, describing it as an objective that the United
Nations should merely promote. Development is included in the context of a list of other objectives, reflecting the then-prevailing ortho-
doxy in economic thinking—the achievement of higher standards of
living, full employment, and conditions of economic and social
progress.[1] In spite of this thin constitutional basis, for at least three
decades the United Nations expanded these responsibilities by leaps
and bounds in an uncoordinated process of growth, spawning a large
network of agencies and programs concerned with humanitarian, economic, and social development questions. However, with the onset of
the 1970s, and more markedly in the 1980s, the United Nations growth
and expansion in the economic and social fields slowly ground to a
halt. Increasingly frequent and pointed criticisms of excessive decen-
tralization and redundancies led to a greater emphasis on streamlining,
rationalizing, and consolidating an organization perceived by some of
its key stakeholders as having grown out of control. In sharp contrast
with the buoyant experience of the previous decades, only a handful of
new institutions came into existence in the 1990s. Since then, the system seems to have entered a cycle of controlled institutional inertia
punctuated by "reform" outbursts, the latest one being the significant
changes introduced by Secretary-General António Guterres in 2017 in
the field operations of the organization.

57

The UN development system can certainly boast of having contributed to substantial achievements in human welfare.[2] As shall be seen, its financial presence is not negligible.[3] Current expenditures on UN operational activities for development amount to some US$38 billion.[4] This does not mean that the international community has reached a state of earthly developmental nirvana. Major threats like climate change, conflict, inequality and pandemics threaten that progress. But these gains are testimony to the fact that development has evolved into one of the fundamental and durable tasks of the United Nations. Here I provide a broad-stroked description and assessment of the role of the UN in the promotion of development against the background of the organization's evolving geopolitical environment. The focus is primarily on the United Nations proper, including the UN Secretariat, and the funds and programs set up for specific functional needs identified by member states, which report to the General Assembly. The specialized agencies and the Bretton Woods Institutions will be touched upon but would warrant a separate study.

The foregoing analysis rests on a number of assumptions about the nature of international organizations and the United Nations. One, the present study draws from the insights of constructivist and liberal-institutionalist scholars who posit that international organizations do have "actorness," in the sense that they can be differentiated from their constitutive environment, enjoy a degree of identity, structural and functional autonomy, and have the capacity to influence the statist environment they spring from.[5] As facilitators of interstate cooperation, and in the language of global governance scholars, the United Nations acts as a linchpin institution at the center of a tattered patchwork of authority and polycentric, messy multi-actor interactive networks concerned with the trans-spatial management of global issues beyond the capacity of individual states to resolve.[6] Neither enjoying sovereign powers nor ruling the world, more modestly, the United Nations may exercise a broad degree of influence on a wide range of developmental policy objectives, and it participates in the creation, monitoring, and (occasionally) enforcing international norms, rules, and distributive, regulatory, and redistributive policies.[7] As shall be seen, most development system activities of the UN are primarily of a normative and redistributive nature.

Throughout the discussion, I use the terms *North, South, Global South,* or *developing countries*. The use of this generic terminology can be traced back to the middle of the last century and refers essentially to two groups of countries broadly defined in terms of differing levels of historical background, wealth, and economic development, it being understood that neither North nor South are monolithic entities in their political, economic, and demographic makeup and that globalization has eroded their divide.[8] By South, we also refer to the formal and more widely based political groups, such as the Group of 77, through which developing countries coalesce in the context of UN multilateral politics and processes to maximize their national interests.[9]

The Development System

The United Nations development system is the outgrowth as well as a vast expansion of the little known work of its predecessor organization, the League of Nations, in such areas as infectious diseases, slavery, drug trafficking, and labor. In fact, so successful were the League activities that a committee constituted in 1939 (the so-called Bruce Committee, after the name of its Australian chair) produced a report advocating a wide expansion of the League's economic and social functions. Many of the Bruce Committee's recommendations were incorporated into the UN Charter, including the creation of an Economic and Social Council (ECOSOC).[10]

Institutions and Structures

The work of the "other United Nations"[11] (development rather than security issues) now spans a vast range of activities that can be clustered into four broad categories: (1) policy and analytical work, which provides the underpinning for intergovernmental deliberations; (2) facilitation of the efforts of member states to set norms and standards and build consensus on a range of international issues; (3) global advocacy on development issues; and (4) support of national development efforts through technical cooperation activities in developing countries and countries with economies in transition. Specific tasks falling within these groupings include the compilation and standardization of statistical data, the setting of technical and legal standards in functional areas of global interaction, and policy-oriented research and analysis. This standard-setting includes the promotion of child survival, human rights and women's equality, improving the livelihood and security of the poor, and ensuring sustainable environmental management. The UN also addresses support of refugees and vulnerable social groups, the prevention of AIDS, the fight against illicit drug trafficking, and the provision of emergency relief to victims of war, flood, drought, and crop failure. The list is by no means comprehensive.

These multifaceted tasks are carried out through a complex maze of UN bodies, institutions, and departments. At the apex of the system stands the General Assembly (and its Second and Third Committees, which deal with economic and social and humanitarian questions, respectively) as its supreme policymaking organ. In that role, the Assembly has convened global conferences (discussed below) and established a number of distinct funds and programs over the years that all report to the Assembly and carry out cross-sectoral work in such areas as children, gender equality, the environment, and humanitarian action. These entities, headed by senior officials appointed by the Secretary-General, have their own budgets and governing bodies. Another cluster of subsidiary institutions deal with research, policy analysis, and training, such as the United Nations Institute for Training and Research (UNITAR) and the United Nations University (UNU). They also have their own governing bodies, report to the Assembly, but enjoy varying but significant degrees of autonomy. Under the authority of the General Assembly, ECOSOC acts as a forum for the discussion of economic and social issues, the coordination of UN activities in the economic and social fields, humanitarian questions, and the governance of the UN's operational activities. ECOSOC has "functional commissions" on social development, human rights, narcotic drugs, crime prevention and criminal justice, women, population, statistics, and (up until 2012) sustainable development that report to it. Five regional commissions (Latin America and the Caribbean, Europe, Asia and the Pacific, Africa, and Western Asia) also report to the Council, as do a large number of session-specific and standing committees and expert ad hoc bodies. In accordance with Article 71 of the Charter, more than 6,000 nongovernmental organizations (NGOs) enjoy consultative status with ECOSOC, a standing that gives them access to the Council proceedings and its subsidiary bodies and to special events organized by the president of the General Assembly. NGOs must apply for consultative status to a committee of the UN established to review applications. Once an organization is approved, it can designate representatives, who then apply for UN ground passes to enter the UN and observe meetings open to civil society.

The UN development system further comprises a set of organizations based on separate founding documents and treaties that fulfill a wide variety of functions in such socioeconomic areas as health, employment, agriculture, and education. Some date back to the nineteenth century, others to the League of Nations. Those that have been incorporated into the UN system by ECOSOC under Articles 57 and 63 of the Charter are known as specialized agencies, such as the Food and Agriculture Organization (FAO), the International Fund for Agricultural Development (IFAD), the International Labour Organization (ILO), and the United Nations Educational, Scientific, and Cultural Organization (UNESCO). Formally, ECOSOC may make recommendations to the specialized agencies. In practice, the Council exerts only a loose degree of coordination because the agencies have their own governing bodies and separate budgets.

Finally, the Bretton Woods group (formally, the International Bank for Reconstruction and Development, IBRD) and its affiliates (the International Development Association [IDA], the International Finance Corporation [IFC], and the Multilateral Investment Guarantee Agency [MIGA]) are together known as the World Bank. The World Bank as well as the IMF do play an important role in development. They are technically part of the UN system, but they by and large operate separately, with an even more tenuous relationship to ECOSOC. A number of related organizations are active in development but not formally linked to the UN, such as the World Trade Organization (WTO). The International Atomic Energy Agency (IAEA) reports to the Security Council and the General Assembly. In 2016, the General Assembly agreed to make the International Organization for Migration (IOM) a related organization.

In terms of staffing and finances, the UN development enterprise is impressive in its own right. As of December 31, 2019, the staff of the Secretariat and related UN entities included a total of 77,620 personnel, with one-third of the Secretariat staff working in development-related fields. Factoring in the staff of the funds and programs of the UN, all in all, more than half of UN employees are involved in economic, social, and humanitarian affairs.[12] Contributions to UN operational activities for development have been steadily increasing, amounting in 2019 alone to US$38.1 billion, which equaled 23 percent of all official development assistance. In effect, the UN has established itself as the largest channel of multilateral aid. Peace operations at that time accounted for just a fifth of total expenditures, while global norm setting, standard setting, and policy advocacy make up the remaining 10 percent.[13] If the World Bank is brought into the analysis, the scope of the UN system activities devoted to development becomes even more striking. The World Bank made four loans totaling US$497 million in 1947. Between 2016 and 2020, it loaned close to US$100 billion, a figure that does not include IDA, IFC, and MIGA commitments.[14]

Partnerships for Development

In a narrow sense of the term, *partnerships* refers to civil society organizations. In this regard, as provided for in Article 71 of the UN Charter, ECOSOC can make "suitable arrangements for consultation with nongovernmental organizations which are concerned with matters within its competence," therefore, legitimizing a limited degree of participation by NGOs in UN proceedings. A standing committee of the Council (the Committee on Non-Governmental Organizations) grants them three different types of status based on their degree of interest and competence, and NGOs may contribute to the deliberations of ECOSOC. In 1946, when the system was put in place, forty-one NGOs were granted consultative status. There are currently slightly more than 6,000 organizations in consultative status with ECOSOC. Consultative relations have been more extensive with the specialized agencies (notably the ILO), but governments and, to a lesser extent, UN officials have resisted a further institutionalization of NGO involvement in UN work. NGOs have occasionally been allowed to address special sessions of the General Assembly. However, with the exception of the Red Cross, and in spite of their repeated demands, they are not authorized to participate in the regular sessions of the Assembly. A 2004 set of proposals by a panel of eminent persons that sought to broaden the engagement of civil society in multilateral decisionmaking elicited a virtually unanimous disapproval and promptly fell into oblivion.[15] In this regard, it should also be noted that the Charter does not grant any formal role to NGOs in meetings of the Security Council.

Behind these formal arrangements, the praxis conveys a significantly more nuanced picture as civil society institutions have, in effect, progressively enlarged the scope of their activities in all UN processes. Changing concepts of development and governance and, in particular, the emphasis increasingly being placed on the grassroots ownership of the development agenda have fed this trend. UN-sponsored global conferences, roughly speaking since the 1972 Stockholm conference, have also considerably broadened the political space available to NGOs. The 1992 Rio conference had no fewer that 2,400 accredited NGOs, and 17,000 attended its unofficial Global Forum. Close to 10,000 NGOs participated in the 2012 Rio Summit. Clearly, the existence of transnational NGO networks is a reality that can no longer be ignored and reflects the emergence of more pluralistic forms of governance and decisionmaking. Either formally or informally, NGOs help influence the process of multilateral diplomacy, participate in the drafting of UN resolutions and the preparation of the programs of UN global conferences, and act as indispensable partners in the field implementation of UN projects, all in so-called "informal participatory spaces."[16]

The United Nations Department of Economic and Social Affairs manages an online database of partnerships for the UN's more recent SDGs and lists over 5,000 partnerships and other voluntary initiatives and commitments to achieve them.[17] The Global Compact, which invites the business community to work with the UN, is perhaps the most visible manifestation of the organization's embrace of the private sector. First introduced by Secretary-General Kofi Annan in 1999, the Compact has since evolved into a global network of several hundred private companies, international trade unions, dozens of international NGOs, and business schools. Its prime task is to prod businesses to make globalization more inclusive. Entirely voluntary and relying on public accountability, transparency, and self-interest as catalysts toward responsible global corporate responsibility, the Compact has been joined by more than 13,000 companies.

An Uncertain Mandate in Shifting Tectonics

The UN development enterprise is no minor operation. Yet, it rests on shaky political foundations as neither its raison d'être nor its legitimacy has been durably agreed upon by its main stakeholders. The most critical factor in this regard has been and remains the widely differing views of member states about the very concept of development and the role of the United Nations. From the inception of the organization, two competing visions have been vying with each other over the ways and means to achieve the conditions of economic and social progress. One view is largely espoused by industrial powers and the United States, the North, and the other is shaped by the demands and concerns of countries of the Global South.

The North assigns only limited functions to the United Nations in economic and social affairs. From this vantage point, the United Nations is a voluntary association of sovereign states with no discretionary regulatory and legislative functions, but a forum for public dialogue. It is no more than a center for the harmonization of national policies, a catalyst, a facilitator, and a conveyor. Conversely, the more powerful and effective governance of economic and social development and the management of the world economy are the province of the Bretton Woods Institutions and other non-UN institutions such as the Group of 20 and the Organisation for Economic Co-operation and Development (OECD).

In contrast, countries of the South give priority to the resolution of the structural problems—internal and international—that hamper their drive toward modernization, industrialization, or in today's parlance, sustainable development. Thus, development cannot be left to the vagaries of international financial, monetary, and commercial markets. The state has an essential role in the definition of the development agenda and in the allocation of scarce resources required for development. Regulatory mechanisms and agencies must be put in place at the international and national levels to ensure that markets operate in such ways as to promote rather than hinder the resolution of developmental issues. For developing countries, the UN as the embodiment of a compact among sovereign and equal states, should be the keystone of the governance architecture of the world economy and development cooperation. It should have authoritative decisionmaking power, notably over the Bretton Woods Institutions.

In this polarized setting in which the North uses the language of effectiveness, and the South the normative rhetoric of equity and democracy, any agreement on governance has proved elusive. The creation of the UN Conference on Trade and Development (UNCTAD) in 1964 and the calls for a new international economic order and a Charter of Economic Rights and Duties of States in the 1970s all originated from the South.[18] But the more third world leaders dreamed of turning the UN into a world development authority, the more inclined developed countries were to shun the organization and to limit the scope of its activities to those originally envisaged in San Francisco. The United States led the counterattack against the "tyranny of the majority" through selective disengagement and the use of its financial weapon. Within the span of a few years, this objective was by and large achieved. Crushed by the weight of its debt crisis and locked in a debilitating lost decade of development in the 1980s, the third world coalition collapsed as an organized political force. At the same time, the demise of the Soviet Union at the end of 1991 discredited the intellectual foundations of hitherto prevailing development strategies, allowing some to proclaim the triumph of liberalism as heralding an "end of history."[19] A new ambiguous development paradigm lending itself to a wide range of interpretations has thus taken hold of the UN agenda.

The uncertainty and the risks associated with such changing global geopolitical conditions have been compounded by the sudden and unexpected outbreak of the Covid-19 pandemic. Covid-19 is in the first place a human catastrophe. The duration and scope of the pandemic hinge on a wide range of critical factors, some of them poorly understood. The true number of fatalities due to the virus may never be known, but at the time of this writing, it has already exceeded five million deaths in over two hundred countries and territories, and the number of deaths in the United States (over one million to date) has surpassed the total from the 1918 influenza pandemic.

The full economic impact of Covid-19 is equally difficult to fully appreciate, but the available data strongly suggest that decades of relative progress in the fight against global poverty may have been rolled back.[20] It may be far too early to confidently ascertain how and to what extent these developments will impact North-South relations in the UN, shape development policy outcomes in the organization, and more generally affect multilateralism.[21] But the pandemic has exacerbated high levels of inequality between and within countries and may lend further credence to the notion that the Western-led international liberal economic order is a poor instrument for national development and integration in the world economy. In any case, the current focus on rolling back and controlling the Covid-19 pandemic should not distract from the muted but real tensions that have arisen as a result of the North's overwhelming intellectual property rights control of existing vaccines and supplies and the glaring (and counterproductive) inequities in their distribution.[22] An intensification of the North-South political fault lines as sketched out here may not altogether be an unrealistic scenario of things to come.

Normative Policies:
Fabianism Through Expertise, Targeting,
Global Summits, and Commemorations

Policy Analysis in Support of
Internationally Managed Capitalism

Like any other national or international institution, the United Nations has its own distinctive organizational culture, a self-image, expectations, a philosophy, and values which operate as guideposts for its members in defining problems and solutions and in structuring their interaction with the outside world. Free markets and neoliberalism mark one perspective countered by a Fabian vision of socialism that would be established through gradual reforms within the law. The North-South cleavage, the evolving balance of power between groups of countries, and the gyrations of prevailing conventional wisdoms about the development process that accompany these shifts have been prominent factors in shaping the UN development organizational culture. Inevitably, those mental maps have been fluid over time. The discourse of the 1970s was overshadowed by the South's political demand for the establishment of a new international economic order accompanied by structural and regime changes. That language has given way to a discourse highlighting the need for new partnerships and new structures of cooperation of policies designed to strengthen institutional transformations for democratic governance, to create an enabling environment, and to increase equity of opportunities through access to productive assets.

This does not mean, however, that the United Nations has evolved into an unconditional mouthpiece of neoliberal economic policy prescriptions. The organization's culture remains embedded in the norms of universality, justice, equity, and equality, which provided the foundations of its earliest developmental concerns. These values derive from the broad injunctions of Article 55 of the Charter that calls for conditions of economic progress and development that have been reaffirmed in all UN-sponsored international conferences. The 2000 Millennium Declaration and the 2030 Sustainable Development Agenda have only amplified this normative message by adding the new layers of fundamental values, solidarity, respect for nature, and shared responsibility.

With these moral beacons as policy guideposts, the UN's desirable order of things has much in common with a Fabian vision of an internationally managed, reformist, and mildly redistributive capitalism. Its axiomatic foundation is that social systems should be inclusive and that all groups in society should enjoy the fruits of development. The same logic applies to the international society where the moral imperative of inclusiveness makes inequalities among nations no less acceptable than inequalities within them. Hence the insistence of UN discourse on the need for policies designed to reduce disparities between have and have-not nations, to promote equality of opportunity, to remove factors conducive to dependency, and more generally to protect the global commons for the benefit of mankind. The development decades launched by the United Nations in the 1960s, the Millennium Development Goals (MDGs) that emerged from the Millennium Declaration in 2000, the Sustainable Development Goals (SDGs) that followed in 2016, and the

Declarations and Programmes of Action produced by UN global conferences discussed below have all been grounded on these assumptions. Macroeconomic stability, deregulation, the privatization of large chunks of national economies, and the liberalization of international trade may be important, but to be both sustainable and human, development requires corrective public interventions in the operation of national and international markets.

The UN Development Programme (UNDP), created in 1965, produced its very first *Human Development Report* in 1990 in which it stated: "peoples must be free to exercise their choices in *properly functioning* markets" (emphasis mine).[23] The report emphasizes *human* development in contrast to the World Bank reports that focus primarily on gross domestic product or per capita income, overlooking the human condition. Hence, in the language of UNICEF and the ILO, the international community needed to give structural adjustment and globalization a human face.[24]

One of the major functions of the United Nations in development is to collect and disseminate economic and social information, monitor economic and social progress, and identify emerging issues of global concern. The UN thus produces a plethora of reports, studies, and monographs on an endless string of subjects. Some examples are natural resources, agriculture, industry, labor markets, the environment, population, human settlement, refugees, displaced persons, public health, and gender issues.

Providing guidance to intergovernmental bodies is the prime objective of these flagship reports of the UN. Such reports have made important contributions to international discussions on the international economy, trade and finance, and the reports' interactions with both long-term development issues and short-term microeconomic issues. The *World Economic Survey* and the *Human Development Report* are striking instances of the normatively oriented policy research work of the United Nations, where the focus is on such human conditions as health, education, infant mortality, and so forth.

The Global Summits

Global conferences are a long-standing feature of multilateral diplomacy, but it was not until the creation of the United Nations that they began to assume an important role in the formulation of policies on a global scale. The development-related issues that UN global conferences have focused on are listed in Table 4.1.

Table 4.1   Global Conferences

Topic	City and Date
Aging	Vienna, 1982
Agrarian reform	Rome, 1979; Porto Alegre, Brazil, 2006
Desertification	Nairobi, 1979
Disabled persons	New York, 2013
Disarmament and development	New York, 1987
Drug abuse and trafficking	Vienna, 1987 and 2019
Education	Jomtien, Thailand, 1990
Employment	Geneva, 1976
Food	Rome, 1974, 1996, 2002, 2009
Forests	Istanbul, 2013
HIV/AIDS	New York, 2001, 2006, 2011, 2016
Housing and urban development	Vancouver, 1976; Istanbul, 1996; Quito, 2016
Human rights	Tehran, 1968; Vienna, 1993
Human settlement	Vancouver, 1976; Istanbul, 1996; Quito, Ecuador, 2016
Information technology	Geneva, 2003; Tunis, 2005; New York, 2015
Law of the sea and oceans	1973–1982, 2017
Least-developed and landlocked countries	Paris, 1981, 1991; Brussels, 2001; Istanbul, 2011; Vienna, 2014; New York, 2019
Money and finance	Monterrey, Mexico, 2002; Doha, 2008; Addis Ababa, 2015
Natural disaster prevention	Yokohama, 1994; Kobe, 2005; Sendai, 2015
New sources of energy	Rome, 1961; Nairobi, 1981
Population	Rome, 1954; Belgrade, 1965; Bucharest, 1974; Mexico, 1984; Cairo, 1994; New York, 1999
Primary health care	Alma Ata, Kazakhstan, 1978
Science and technology for development	Vienna, 1979
Social welfare and development	Vienna, 1987; Copenhagen, 1995
Sustainable development	Stockholm, 1972; Rio, 1992; Johannesburg, 2002; Rio, 2012; New York, 2015
Technical cooperation among developing countries	Buenos Aires, 1978
Transnational crime	Every five years since 1947
Trade and employment	New York, 1947; Geneva, 1948
Racism and racial discrimination	Geneva, 1983; Durban, South Africa, 2001; Geneva, 2009
Refugees and migrants	New York, 2006, 2016; Istanbul, 2016
Small island developing countries	Barbados, 1995; Samoa, 2014
Transport	Ashgabat, Turkmenistan, 2016
Water	Mar del Plata, Argentina, 1977; Dublin, 1992
Women	Mexico, 1975; Copenhagen, 1980; Nairobi, 1985; Beijing, 1995; at five-year intervals thereafter

The proliferation of such global meetings has been accompanied by increasing controversy. Northern governments portray them as lavish, costly talk shows, too large to achieve meaningful results, while Southern countries complain that most of the policy objectives and developmental targets in the declarations and action plans of global conferences have been rarely matched by adequate policy responses and commensurate financial commitments. Conference fatigue may prevail for the time being, but scaled-down versions of them still continue at the South's insistence in the guise of "high-level meetings or dialogues," "special sessions," "reviews," and other "plenary" meetings taking place within the regular scheduling of the General Assembly yearly sessions. Whatever their format, UN global gatherings will continue to operate as town meetings of the world, not as instruments of authoritative decisionmaking, but as arenas for discussion and the production and exchange of information, as incubators of ideas and the normative agenda. These global conferences and gatherings include input from civil society and educate the public through the media attention they attract, enhancing their democratic appeal.

Commemorations: Days, Weeks, Years, Decades

In conjunction with global conferences, the United Nations designates special "days," "weeks," "years," and "decades" to promote causes that it stands for and advocates. Their basic objectives are, broadly speaking, to raise the level of knowledge and concern for emerging or current issues through public information campaigns and statements by UN senior officials, to mobilize and nurture grassroots support through a variety of activities at the local, regional, and international levels, and to promote policy solutions. Most of these observances are established or sanctioned by the General Assembly at the initiative of one of its member states. The specialized agencies, through their own policymaking bodies, have joined the fray in their own domains of activities.

Decades are more rare, but they can be far more ambitious undertakings to the extent that they often define specific time-framed goals, targets, and policies and provide for their periodic review and evaluation of progress achieved in meeting them. Perhaps the most extensively scrutinized were the UN Development Decades which were launched in 1961 and extended into the 1990s. Their demise, which was triggered by sharp North-South conflicting views about their objectives and policy prescriptions, was nevertheless followed by the subsequent normatively driven eight MDGs (to be achieved by 2015) and replaced by the seventeen SDGs of the 2030 Agenda. All three schemes strikingly rely on the same methodology: quantitative targets embedded in specified time frames, with ongoing systems of oversight and monitoring.

Redistributive Policies

Capacity Development

One of the most prominent and concrete manifestations of the UN's work in development is its large field presence within the countless technical-assistance activities that it carries out in developing countries. Problems of coordination and competition among implementing agencies in the field and at headquarters led in 1965 to the creation of the UNDP. Since that time, the basic architecture of the operational UN development system has remained basically the same. It was, and is still, funded on an entirely voluntary basis. Resources earmarked for operational activities for development currently exceed US$38 billion and account for 71 percent of all UN system activities (of which 33 percent relate to development and 38 percent to humanitarian assistance).[25] Three-quarters of the funding is provided by governments.

At the outset, technical assistance was operationally understood simply as the provision of expert advice, training and demonstration, the pooling of particular know-how developed in individual countries, and the application of that know-how to the problems of underdeveloped countries.[26] Services to be rendered were supposed to be decided by the governments concerned. With the establishment of UNDP, the UN expanded its operational work in pre-investment activities.[27] Changing concepts of development have since led to novel definitions of the purposes and modalities of technical assistance as needing to be locally owned and aimed at sustainability. In the past two decades, efforts have been made to embed UN operational activities within the framework of the multidimensional normative targets of the Millennium Development Goals and the 2030 Sustainable Development Agenda. Meanwhile, UNDP has drastically altered its capacity in development activities with a greater focus on aspects of poverty eradication, gender equity, the environment, and good governance in post-conflict rehabilitation and reconstruction situations.

The planning, programming, and implementation of UN operational activities raise the thorny question of coordination, a long-standing issue that has yet to receive a satisfactory answer. The creation of UNDP itself in 1965 was an effort to put an end to the scrambling for technical assistance funds among UN agencies, both at headquarters and in the field, and to ensure more unified and coherent programming. The system had indeed many built-in weaknesses, the most salient of them being the role of UNDP in coordinating the various agencies of the UN within the 170 countries and territories where it operates. This function was the responsibility of a UN resident coordinator who was also the UNDP representative. The dual functions of UNDP officials as representatives of their agency and of the UN system created operational difficulties, caught as they were between their role as coordinator/facilitator and defender of the interests of their own agency. In emergency situations, the growing presence of NGOs with their own agendas and priorities added another layer of complexity.

By 2017, incoming Secretary-General Guterres called for a "repositioning," or reorganization, of the UN development system.[28] His proposals were anchored in three basic ideas: (1) The Deputy Secretary-General would, within the Secretariat, oversee the UN Sustainable Development Group (UNSDG)[29] and lead a steering committee to strengthen coherence between the UN humanitarian and development agendas. (2) The effectiveness of UN Country Teams in the field would be enhanced by delinking the functions of UN Resident Coordinators from the UNDP. (3) The number of country-level offices would be decreased and the UN regional offices would be strengthened. This repositioning, reorganization exercise is still a work in progress and much remains to be done in actualizing "the ambitious strategic and policy guidance on how Member States wish to leverage a stronger United Nations development system in their transformative journey"— a hardly veiled reference to the political divisions of governments over how to achieve a more cohesive UN and for what purpose.[30]

Humanitarianism

Traditionally, humanitarian aid, development aid, and disaster relief were only loosely tied, in the sense that they were predominantly destined for developing countries. On the one hand, disaster relief was considered short-term; involved the provision of food aid, shelter, education, healthcare, or protection activities; and was designed to save lives and alleviate suffering in the immediate aftermath of manmade or natural catastrophic events. On the other hand, development aid addressed underlying socioeconomic factors and long-term structural issues, particularly systemic poverty hindering economic, institutional, and social development. It was also intended to build capacity and was thus a process that could take years, if not decades to complete. Both types of aid are related, and different forms of aid commonly have both humanitarian and development components. Distinguishing between them has been made challenging by the increasing salience of the need to protect civilians in internal conflicts, in particular in the context of UN integrated peace operations and the surge in the number of refugees and internally displaced persons in recent years.

Over the years, humanitarian assistance provided through bilateral channels has thus become much more important relative to multilateral aid. Humanitarian aid accounted for roughly 10.5 percent of all official development assistance in 2000, up steeply from the 5.8 percent seen between 1989 and 1993.[31] More recent data confirm that the trend continues unabated. Funding for development activity from 2010 to 2019 increased by 17 percent, whereas resources targeted for humanitarian work expanded by 135 percent.[32] The growth in humanitarian assistance appears to be driven by year-on-year increases in funding from wealthier nations to countries in protracted crises.[33] In addition, as is well known, humanitarian aid is doled out haphazardly and targeted to a few high-profile cases and favored countries. Contributing to the perpetuation of forgotten tragedies, countries with no perceived strategic value such as Eritrea, Yemen, South Sudan, and Sudan (Darfur) have fallen by the wayside.

Not surprisingly, humanitarian assistance has always been overshadowed by North-South tensions. Donor states talk of sovereignty as less a right than a responsibility, triggering developing countries' suspicions that man-made or natural disasters can be used as a pretext for intrusions in what they consider to be internal affairs. Against this political background, the dichotomy between development and humanitarian aid has to a large extent come full circle. That humanitarian assistance and development are two sides of the same coin is increasingly clear. It is understood that, on the one hand, conditions of underdevelopment allow disasters to occur or worsen their impact, and it is in responding to disasters that the seeds of development need to be planted. On the other hand, it is increasingly less clear what the term *humanitarian* assistance means. The 1990s dominant thinking of a relief-development continuum that underlined the complementary objectives and strategies in humanitarian and development aid was criticized for overlooking the structural or chronic factors that predate or outlast the outbreak of crises. It has been replaced by another focused on long-term solutions as well as immediate needs. More-recent debates have placed emphasis on linking humanitarian and development aid to the political and security agenda in fragile states or to a rights-based approach in order to overcome the dichotomy between humanitarianism and development. Climate change adaptation and the increasingly salient issue of protracted refugee displacement have more recently influenced the debate about the working principles, values, and assumptions of humanitarian and development actors.[34]

From an operational viewpoint, the centrifugal and often competitive nature of the current UN humanitarian architecture/regime adds another layer of complexity.[35] In the first place, there is no single intergovernmental body overseeing the elaboration, coordination, governance, and strategic management of humanitarian-related matters across the UN system. In the Secretariat of the UN, the role of the Office for the Coordination of Humanitarian Affairs (OCHA) is limited to bringing together humanitarian actors to promote a coherent response to emergencies among a hair-raising number of national ministerial entities and a multiplicity of national and international NGOs. Bilateral funding by governments and private donors is supplemented by several trust funds, including a Central Emergency Response Fund at Headquarters and an Expanded Humanitarian Response Fund in the field. Both are managed by OCHA and fed by voluntary contributions.[36]

Critiques of the system still abound. Critics also point to the fact that humanitarian assistance mainly goes to a small number of countries (42 percent of the total in 2019 went to two countries, Yemen and Syria) and mainly flows through big aid organizations, with international NGOs receiving 20 percent of the total, and local and national NGOs receiving only 2 to 3 percent of the total. At the same time, the source of humanitarian finance remains perilously narrow and vulnerable to political winds. In 2019, five donors (the United States, Germany, the UK, the European Commission, and Saudi Arabia) provided more than half of total assistance.[37] Over the next few years, it is probable that the humanitarian regime will continue to evolve incrementally as the conflicting notions of sovereignty, impartiality, and humanitarianism continue to vie for dominance in the UN system.[38]

Regulatory Policies and the Sustainable Development Goals

Both the MDGs and the SDGs in practice have become frames of reference for governments and international organizations for the formulation and implementation of their regulatory development policies.[39] These frames of reference have drawn heavily on treaties and agreements in other issue areas, primarily those regarding the environment. The 2012 Rio Summit was actually supposed to be focused on the environment as it had been twenty years before in 1992 at the Rio Earth Summit. However, with constant pressure from the developing world, the concept had evolved into sustainable development, meaning that the environment needed to be protected and its sustainability maintained if you wanted long-term development.

The outcome document of the Rio 2012 United Nations Conference on Sustainable Development titled "The Future We Want" explicitly recognizes the contributions of multilateral environmental agreements to sustainable development. The same document also stresses the need to deal with biodiversity issues in order to achieve the objectives of the 2030 Agenda. The participants in Rio created an action plan that would build on the MDGs, soon to expire in 2015, and expand their reach. The mood and cooperative atmosphere at Rio energized the formation of the seventeen interrelated SDGs as a "roadmap for our time."[40]

The list is impressive, if aspirational in nature. Goal 1: End poverty in all its forms everywhere. Goal 2: End hunger, achieve food security, improve nutrition, and promote sustainable agriculture. Goal 3: Ensure healthy lives and promote well-being for all at all ages. Goal 4: Ensure inclusive and equitable quality education and promote lifelong learning opportunities for all. Goal 5: Achieve gender equality and empower all women and girls. Goal 6: Ensure availability and sustainable management of water and sanitation for all. Goal 7: Ensure access to affordable, reliable, sustainable, and modern energy for all. Goal 8: Promote sustained, inclusive, and sustainable economic growth; full and productive employment; and decent work for all. Goal 9: Build resilient infrastructure, promote inclusive and sustainable industrialization, and foster innovation. Goal 10: Reduce inequality within and among countries. Goal 11: Make cities and human settlements inclusive, safe, resilient, and sustainable. Goal 12: Ensure sustainable consumption and production patterns. Goal 13: Take urgent action to combat climate change and its impacts. Goal 14: Conserve and sustainably use the oceans, seas, and marine resources for sustainable development. Goal 15: Protect, restore, and promote sustainable use of terrestrial ecosystems; sustainably manage forests; combat desertification; halt and reverse land degradation; and halt biodiversity loss. Goal 16: Promote peaceful and inclusive societies for sustainable development; provide access to justice for all; and build effective, accountable, and inclusive institutions at all levels. Goal 17: Strengthen the means of implementation and revitalize the Global Partnerships for Sustainable Development.[41] Each goal has multiple targets to be reached, some 169 in total with an additional 232 unique indicators—a huge task. If these issue areas look familiar to you, they should. They represent ideas from all the years of conferences, global summits, decades, and UN human development reports over the UN's history.

Included are a number of purposeful overlaps. For example, Goals 12 and 17 across the board and Goal 12 on chemicals and wastes, Goal 13 on climate change, and Goals 14 and 15 on ecosystems and biological diversity make direct or indirect reference to environmental agreements as important instruments in achieving the 2030 Development Agenda. To make the goals more concrete and operational, action plans with targets and indicators to measure progress toward the 2030 Agenda were developed along the lines of the structure of the UN Framework Convention on Climate Change (UNFCCC) and other conventions.

The Question of Reform

The image of the United Nations as an unwieldy and unmanageable organization has become a cliché. In this view, unholy coalitions of international civil servants, government representatives, and NGOs are tied together in webs of patronage.[42] Turf battles among status quo or imperial organizations and sheer bureaucratic viscosity have been factors contributing to the inertia of the system. For many, the United Nations suffers from an institutional deficit attributable to a process of structural growth and the devolution of an increasing number of functional tasks that proceeded on an ad hoc basis, driven more by the vagaries of the political process than by preestablished organizational blueprints for change.

From the very outset, reforming and adapting the UN has thus been an insatiable intellectual industry. All incoming executive heads of the organization feel compelled to come up with reform proposals, and the unkind observer will immediately note that a rich and deep strata of reform proposals has developed over time, providing an inexhaustible source of ideas, novel or recycled, to would-be reformers. But in the absence of a genuine political consensus among member states on the purpose and modalities of development, change has remained conservative and incremental. Suggestions to establish an Economic Security Council, to abolish ECOSOC, to merge the Assembly's Second and Third Committees or to abolish them altogether and transfer their functions to a revitalized ECOSOC, to bring the Bretton Woods Institutions under the authority of the General Assembly may all have intellectual merits within university and think-tank walls, but they have had little traction in the politically constrained and divided environment of the United Nations.

Developing countries temporarily prevailed in the General Assembly, and its resolution 32/197 of December 20, 1977, triggered a vast expansion of the intergovernmental and Secretariat structures concerned with development. A decade later, these reforms were rolled back by developed countries. In subsequent years and with the notable exceptions of the establishment of the Human Rights Council, which replaced the Commission on Human Rights, and the creation of the Peacebuilding Commission, the task of reforming the United Nations has by and large fallen on the Secretary-General, whose proposals have been more managerial than institutional in nature. The consequence is that UN governance structures have by and large been left unattended.

In this regard, the key issue facing the United Nations is that it is structurally ill-suited to deal with developmental issues in a holistic and integrated manner. The United Nations was set up and developed essentially along separate vertical and sectoral lines, mirroring national governmental structures. But changing conceptions of development have evolved from approaches that focused on discrete activities to an understanding that stresses horizontal linkages and underlines the necessity of concerted policy actions. Secretary-General Guterres, in terms of development, made the decision to place the implementation of the SDGs under the office of the dynamic Deputy Secretary-General, Amina Mohammed. Having done so may provide the holistic glue that will make the achievement of these aspirational goals moderately possible, despite the Covid-19 pandemic.

The reform changes may very well be cosmetic and rhetorical, but under the unrelenting Fabian and Keynesian pressures of the United Nations, the market-oriented Bretton Woods Institutions have shown a greater sensitivity to the social implications of their policies and given higher priority to poverty-eradication concerns. They embraced the MDGs and integrated them, often together with other UN organizations, into country-level planning instruments, including the so-called poverty reduction strategy papers. Since 2013, the eradication of poverty and the attainment of shared prosperity are the basic goals of the World Bank and coincide with SDGs 1 and 8. In the field with client countries, its projects focus on finance, data, and implementation—all designed to support country-led and country-owned policies to attain the SDGs.[43] Concurrently, even the Security Council has shown a greater sensitivity to the economic, social, and development dimensions of security issues within the framework of its growing concern for prevention.

In the field, UN activities in developing countries traditionally took place under UNDP's aegis. Broadly speaking, a Resident Coordinator (RC) was the designated representative of the Secretary-General for development cooperation and the leader of the UN country team. All RCs used to be UNDP Resident Representatives, but the RC pool progressively opened to staff from other UN agencies and, in several cases, from NGOs or the Red Cross Movement. The exact modalities of coordination through the RCs vary from country to country, but in terms of substantive policy issues, they have been increasingly linked to fulfilling the MDGs and now the SDGs through two key management tools: the UN Development Assistance Frameworks, now rechristened the United Nations Sustainable Development Cooperation Framework, and Standard Operative Procedures in line with the injunctions of the "Delivering as One" initiative.[44]

These reforms unquestionably contributed to lower transaction costs and competition among UN agencies, but they have not altogether eliminated organizational proliferation, competition for increasingly tight funds among agencies, and disparate business practices.[45] A new train of reforms proposed in 2017 by Secretary-General Guterres, reelected to a second five-year term that started in 2022, acknowledged the problems and were crafted to achieve a more "joined up" approach and stronger cross-pillar coordination. The proposals were clearly part of a broader scheme to connect UN prevention, conflict resolution, peacebuilding and peacekeeping efforts, and its long-term development work. The Secretary-General's proposals were formally approved by the General Assembly in May 2018. Their most radical departure from the status quo is the delinking of the functions of the RC system from UNDP. Field coordination has been removed from UNDP and given to RCs, who as UN officials report solely to the Deputy Secretary-General in charge of a revitalized UN Development Operation Coordination Office, now rechristened the UN Sustainable Development Group. The RCs are to be given more staff and resources, in part as a result of a reduction in the number of national offices and consolidation in regional bureaus. In addition, the Secretary-General requested the investment of US$225 million of assessed funding to structure the new resident coordinator system. In the meantime, a new funding compact has been drawn up for the purpose of increasing core funding and more pooling of resources.

Concluding Thoughts: The Issue of Leadership

The United Nations is an intergovernmental organization. This led Inis Claude, long ago, to opine that "the UN has no purposes—and can have none—of its own. It is a *tool* and, like other tools, that it has possibilities and limitations. . . . Its *Members* however, have purposes, changing and sometimes conflicting, that they would like it to serve." In brief, the changing purposes of the organization are simply a reflection of the changing balance of power among member states or groups of states that vie for its control.[46] The United Nations has certainly not lost its statist birthmark, and its state-centered basis cannot be overlooked as it still sets the broad parameters of its legitimacy and functioning. But neither should the capacity of the organization to shape the political process be underestimated. States may not be ready to abdicate any power to the United Nations, but as Inis Claude himself acknowledged, member states take seriously the UN's normative function even if it is inversely correlated to its executive functioning.[47] This does give to the organization a modicum of influence in the political process, reinforced by the vagueness of the Charter provisions on development, the lack of consensus among member states over its meaning and operationalization, and their widespread tendency to lean on the United Nations whenever their major interests are not at stake. That political vacuum paved the way toward an active and continuing involvement of the organization in development, enabling it to place development at the heart of the agenda of the international community and to keep it in the forefront of its concerns through its convening power, policy research, and field activities.

The concept of a United Nations merely responding to and acting on behalf of its stakeholders is thus only partially correct. In today's parlance, pundits would refer to the normative role of the United Nations that we stressed throughout this chapter. A critical variable in this process is the leadership of the Secretary-General and the Secretariat. The Global Compact, the Millennium Development Goals, and the Sustainable Development Goals around which the Secretary-General has mobilized the entire UN system, were all initiatives hatched within the walls of the organization, with the support and orchestration of coalitions for change. The Secretary-General's leadership may be fraught with political dangers and uncertainties, one of them being the perennial question of finance for development,[48] but he (or she one day) does have a considerable degree of latitude in shaping the political process and the development dialogue that cannot be underestimated. This is especially true in the context of an increasingly pluralized international society, major power rivalries, and a global order being shaken up by the Covid-19 pandemic. The corrosive impact of the Covid-19 pandemic on development makes it plain that development as a normative and operational priority of the United Nations will remain high on its agenda, thus providing the Secretary-General with ample opportunities to articulate and press for its Fabian values. Table 4.2 lists the regular UN flagship reports.

Table 4.2 UN Flagship Reports

Name of the Report	Substantive Focus	Issuing Institution	Year Publication Began
UNITED NATIONS			
World Economic and Social Survey	Socioeconomic development issues and policies	DESA	1947
World Economic Situation and Prospects	Biennial updates on the world economy	DESA, UNCTAD, and the Regional Commissions	1999
World Investment Report	Latest trends in foreign direct investment	UNCTAD	1991
Human Development Report	Exploration of different themes each year from a human development perspective	UNDP	1990
State of the World's Children	Analysis of key issues affecting children	UNICEF	1996
State of the World Population	Coverage and analysis of developments and trends in world population and specific regions, countries, and population groups	UNFPA	1978
Global Environment Outlook	Outline of current state of the environment with critical analyses of the effectiveness of policies	UNEP	1997 (irregular)
World Cities Report	Focus on urban development as affected by globalization, rural-urban inequalities, and sustainability	UN-Habitat	2008 (biennial)
World Drug Report	Overview of major developments in drug markets ranging from production to trafficking	UNODC	1997

continues

Table 4.2 Continued

Name of the Report	Substantive Focus	Issuing Institution	Year Publication Began
United Nations			
Progress of the World's Women	Review of the impact of changing socioeconomic and political circumstances on women	UN-Women (irregular)	2000
World Survey on the Role of Women in Development	Gender perspective on economic and development issues	UN-Women (every five years)	1999
UN Agencies and Bretton Woods Institutions			
World Development Report	Economic, social, and environmental state of the world, each report focusing on specific aspects of development	World Bank	1978
World Economic Outlook	Analyses of global near- and medium-term economic developments affecting industrial countries, developing countries, and economies in transition	IMF (biennial)	1993
State of Food and Agriculture Rural Development Report	Assessments of issues affecting food security Focus on processes or structural transformations intended to bring poor rural populations into the economic mainstream	FAO IFAD	1947 2001
World Health Report	Expert assessments of global health, including statistics with focus on a particular theme	WHO	1995
World Employment and Social Outlook (WESA)	Work issues and policies, with a different theme each year	ILO	2015 (WESA replaced previous *World of Work*)

continues

Table 4.2 Continued

Name of the Report	Substantive Focus	Issuing Institution	Year Publication Began
UN AGENCIES AND BRETTON WOODS INSTITUTIONS			
Global Report on Adult Learning and Education	Overview of trends and challenges in adult education	UNESCO	2010 (triennial)
UN World Water Development Report	Focus on a different water and sanitation theme each year	UNESCO (as leading interagency group)	2003
Industrial Development Report	Latest developments and trends in industrial development in a global context, with thematic and/or regional focus	UNIDO	2003
Measuring the Information Society Report	Global data and analyses on the state of global information and communication technologies development	ITU	2009
World Intellectual Property Report	Insights into the role of innovation in market economies on various specific trends in an area of intellectual property	WIPO	2011 (biennial)
State of the Global Climate Report	Documentation of physical signs of climate change and impact of weather and climate events on socioeconomic development, human health, migration and displacement, food security, and land and marine ecosystems	WMO	1993
World Migration Report	Latest data and information on global migration trends and policy issues	IOM	2000

Note: Reports are yearly, unless otherwise noted.
Source: The author and Dag Hammarskjöld Library, "UN Documentation: Overview," available at https://research.un.org/en/docs/reports.

Notes

1. United Nations Charter, Chapter IX, Article 55.

2. For details, see United Nations, *Millennium Development Goals Report 2015.*

3. Some reckon that in seventy years, half a trillion US dollars have been channeled through the United Nations. See "70 Years and Half a Trillion Dollars Later; What Has the UN Achieved?" *The Guardian,* September 7, 2015, https://www.theguardian.com/world/2015/sep/07/what-has-the-un-achieved-united-nations.

4. For further details, see Report of the Secretary-General on the Implementation of General Assembly Resolution 71/233 on the Quadrennial Comprehensive Policy Review of Operational Activities for Development of the United Nations System Funding of the United Nations Development System, Document A/76/75/Add.1-E/2021/57/Add.1 (2021).

5. As noted by Jacques Fomerand in "The Evolution of International Organizations as Institutional Forms and Historical Processes Since 1945: '*Quis Custodiet ipsos custodies*?'" *Oxford Research Encyclopedia of International Studies* (a peer reviewed publication of the International Studies Association) (2017), https://oxfordre.com/internationalstudies/view/10.1093/acrefore/9780190846626.001.0001/acrefore-9780190846626-e-87.

6. Weiss and Wilkinson, *International Organization and Global Governance,* pp. 3–12.

7. These concepts are drawn from Lowi, "Four Systems of Policy, Politics, and Choice," pp. 298–310, and Rittberger, Zangl, and Staisch, *International Organization.*

8. For an elaboration of the concepts of "North" and "South" in the international development arena, see Nayyar, *Catch Up,* and Reuveny and Thompson, *North and South.*

9. For a full discussion of the phenomenon of group politics in multilateral settings with particular attention to the United Nations, see Smith and Laatikaiden, *Group Politics in UN Multilateralism.*

10. As rightly noted by William Martin Hill in *The Economic and Financial Organisation of the League of Nations,* pp. 11–12.

11. To use the term of Robert W. Gregg who contrasted the lack of visibility of the UN economic and social work relative to the glare of public coverage of UN peace operations in "UN Economic, Social, and Technical Activities," in Barros, *The United Nations,* pp. 218–266.

12. These data are from the Report of the Secretary-General on the Composition of the Secretariat, Document A/75/591 of November 9, 2020, p. 20.

13. United Nations A/76/75/Add.1-E/2021/57/Add.1, pp. 2–3.

14. World Bank, *Annual Report 2020: Supporting Countries in Unprecedented Times,* p. 13, https://www.worldbank.org/en/about/annual-report.

15. Willetts, "The Cardoso Report." For a more general discussion of the role of NGOs in international affairs and the United Nations in particular, see Willetts, *Non-governmental Organizations in World Politics.*

16. Sénit, "Leaving No One Behind?"

17. For details, see "Partnerships for the SDGs" in the website of the Department of Economic and Social Affairs, https://sdgs.un.org/partnerships.

18. Declaration and Programme of Action on the Establishment of a New International Economic Order A/Res/3201 and 3202 (S-VI) and Resolution 3281 (XXIX) of December 12, 1974, "Charter of Economic Rights and Duties of States."

19. Fukuyama, *The End of History and the Last Man.*

20. World Bank, *Annual Report 2020.*

21. For thought-provoking reflections on the subject, Alhashimi et al., *The Future of Diplomacy After COVID-19.*

22. Priti Krishtel and Rohit Malpani, "Suspend Intellectual Property Rights for COVID-19 Vaccines," *BMJ* (2021), https://www.bmj.com/content/373/bmj.n1344.

23. *Human Development Report, 1990,* p. 1.

24. As argued by UNICEF in Cornia, Jolly, and Stewart, *Adjustment with a Human Face,* and the International Labour Organization in *Giving Globalization a Human Face.*

25. See Report of the Secretary-General on the Implementation of General Assembly Resolution 71/243 on the Quadrennial Comprehensive Policy Review of Operational Activities for Development of the United Nations System, Document A/76/75/Add.1-E/2021/57/Add.1, p. 2.

26. As noted by Narasimhan, "Technical Assistance for Economic Development."

27. For a full discussion of these early changes in UNDP activities, see Kirdar, *The Structure of United Nations Economic Aid.*

28. "Repositioning the UN Development System to Deliver on the 20130 Agenda—Ensuring a Better Future for All," Document A/72/124-/2018/3 of July 11, 2017.

29. Previously known as the United Nations Development Group (UNDG), the UNSDG was set by Secretary-General Kofi Annan to strengthen the activities of the UN at the country level. Composed of thirty-six United Nations funds, programs, specialized agencies, departments, and offices that play a role in development, the Group was supposed to identify the strategic development priorities of the system in response to initially triennial and now quadrennial policy reviews by ECOSOC and to enhance the focus and coherence of the UN field actions in support of countries seeking to attain internationally agreed development goals.

30. Report of the Secretary-General, Implementation of General Assembly Resolution 71/243 on the Quadrennial Comprehensive Policy Review of Operational Activities for Development of the United Nations System, Document A/75/79-E/2020/55, Para 271, https://digitallibrary.un.org/record/1298793?ln=en. For the latest on the views of the Secretary-General on his reform measures, see A/76/-E/2021/XX.

31. Margie Buchanan-Smith and Judith Randel, *Financing International Humanitarian Action: A Review of Key Trends,* HGP Briefing 4 (London: ODI, November 2002), pp. 1–2.

32. Joint Inspection Unit, *Financing for Humanitarian Operations in the United Nations System,* Document JIU/REP/2012/11, Geneva, 2012, pp. 12–13, and Report of the Secretary-General. Implementation of General Assembly Resolution 75/233 on the Quadrennial Comprehensive Policy Review of Operational Activities of the United Nations System: Funding of the United Nations Development System, A/76/75/Add 1.-E/2021/57/Add 1, p. 2–3.

33. Paul Knox Clarke, *State of the Humanitarian System,* 2018 edition (London: ALNAP/ODI, 2018), pp. 46–48, https://www.alnap.org/help-library/the-state-of-the-humanitarian-system-sohs-2018-full-report. This is consistent with the findings of an OECD study which documents the mounting significance of humanitarian assistance to "fragile" states. See OECD, *States of Fragility Report 2018* (Paris: OECD, 2018), Chapter 4.

34. For a fuller discussion of these intellectual and political trends, see the 2015 short but enlightening piece of Róisín Hinds, "Relationship Between Humanitarian and Development Aid," GSDRC Applied Knowledge Services, February 16, 2015, https://gsdrc.org/publications/relationship-between-humanitarian-and-development-aid.

35. The total personnel involved in the humanitarian sector had climbed to 647,000 in 2017. Of that number, 79,000 were fielded by UN agencies, including 68,000 national and 11,000 international staff; 330,000 by NGOs; and 159,000 by the Red Cross. Knox Clark, *State of the Humanitarian System,* pp. 16–17.

36. Since its creation in 2006, the Central Emergency Response Fund has provided more than US$6 billion in humanitarian assistance. In 2019, it distributed US$494 million to some thirteen million people caught up in twenty underfunded and neglected crises around the world. For details, see OCHA, *Global Humanitarian Overview 2020,* https://www.unocha.org/sites/unocha/files/GHO-2020_v9.1.pdf.

37. *Global Humanitarian Overview 2020,* chapter 3.

38. For an instance of such stirrings, see World Health Organization, *The New Way of Working: Strengthening the Humanitarian, Development, Peace Nexus,* 2021.

39. As emphasized by Sakiko Fukuda-Parr in *Millennium Development Goals.*

40. Caballero and Londoño, *Redefining Development,* p. 1.

41. For a fuller discussion, see *Transforming Our World: The 2030 Agenda for Sustainable Development,* UN Department of Economic and Social Affairs, 2015, https://sdgs.un.org/2030agenda.

42. A point emphasized by Stephen Browne and Thomas G. Weiss throughout their recent *Routledge Handbook on the UN and Development.*

43. "The World Bank Group's Twin Goals, the SDGs, and the 2030 Development Agenda," n.d., https://www.worldbank.org/en/programs/sdgs-2030-agenda.

44. For details, see United Nations Development Operations Coordination Office, "Building Blocks Towards 2030: UNDG Standard Operating Procedures for 'Delivering as One,'" *2022 Progress Report,* https://undg.org.

45. Browne, *Sustainable Development Goals and UN Goal-Setting,* especially chapters 1 and 4.

46. Claude, *The Changing United Nations,* p. xvii.

47. Ibid., pp. 88–89.

48. Implementation of the SDGs might cost US$5 to 7 trillion a year through 2030, which according to UN estimates would still leave a financing gap to achieve the SDGs in developing countries amounting to US$2.5 to 3 trillion a year. See *UN Secretary-General's Roadmap for Financing of the 2030 Agenda for Development 2019–2021,* 2020, pp. 1–2, https://www.un.org/sustainabledevelopment/wp-content/uploads/2019/07/UN-SG-Roadmap-Financing-the-SDGs-July-2019.pdf.

5

Supporting
Human Rights

Bertrand Ramcharan

In this overview of the United Nations and its support for human rights, I take a look at humanity's current earnest quest for survival in the face of climate change and other threats to human existence. The chapter draws into focus humanity's search for dignity and equal treatment for every person. The United Nations strives for a social and international order conducive to human survival, human dignity, and human rights; the organization represents the struggles against gross violations of human rights that, alas, continue to be rampant in the world.

The United Nations human rights system[1] consists of its normative and jurisprudential architecture anchored in the International Bill of Rights: the UN Charter, the Universal Declaration of Human Rights, and the two International Covenants on Human Rights.[2] Supervisory organs established under the Charter of the United Nations play a key role, notably the Security Council[3], the General Assembly,[4] and the Human Rights Council.[5] In addition, there are supervisory organs established under ten core human rights treaties,[6] an important one being the Human Rights Committee[7] established under the International Covenant on Civil and Political Rights. Cooperation with human rights NGOs such as Amnesty International, Human Rights Watch, the International Commission of Jurists, and many others sets up essential partnerships in monitoring and promoting human rights.[8] The UN's principal judicial organ, the International Court of Justice, is also an important player, as it has heard several cases involving human rights.[9] While not a part of the UN per se, the International Criminal Court that went into effect in July 2002 is also a key actor, with the ability to hold individuals accountable for human rights violations.

The supervisory organs established under the UN Charter and the supervisory organs established under the human rights treaties are all impacted by the increasing assertiveness and push for political control by governments in a geopolitical environment characterized by great power competition or conflict and by doctrinal or philosophical challenges to the content of human rights. For the time being, the universality of human rights has held up tenuously in this environment, but the UN's supervisory organs come under increasing pressure in the form of financial control and overt efforts by powerful governments to control them.[10] It would not be rash to suggest that the UN human rights edifice faces existential challenges.[11] In this environment, the following question arises for reflection: Which part of the United Nations could perform the role of an international arbiter on the content of international human rights law and on the human rights responsibilities of governments, including their responsibility to protect human rights? This should be the International Court of Justice, the principal judicial organ of the United Nations, which has undoubtedly contributed to clarifying the content of international human rights law, to the development of international customary law in the area of human rights, and to clarifying the responsibility of governments to protect human rights—for example, the responsibility to prevent the commission of genocide, a crime against humanity.

In what follows, I submit that the United Nations has developed a solid and noble normative and jurisprudential architecture of human rights, enshrined the protection of the right to life, highlighted the importance of respect for human dignity and equality, and promoted a social and international order conductive to human survival and human rights. While the UN has clarified the content of human rights through its treaty supervisory bodies and the International Court of Justice, it has struggled to protect human rights in the face of widespread gross violations of those rights and has operated imperfect institutions such as the Security Council, the General Assembly, and the Human Rights Council. Nevertheless, it has fortunately benefited from the continuing heroic efforts of NGOs, against great odds, for a more just world anchored in the protection of human rights.

The UN's Normative and Jurisprudential Architecture of Human Rights

A great contribution of the United Nations has been its development of rules of international law for governing the conduct of governments and others in diverse areas of international relations.[12] The UN's normative and jurisprudential architecture of human rights takes pride of place in this endeavor. Global norms for the promotion and protection of human rights are contained in the UN Charter, the Universal Declaration of Human Rights, the two International Covenants on human rights, a broad range of international treaties, and in normative statements adopted by the UN General Assembly.[13] These have various titles, such as Declarations, Bodies of Principles, and Codes of Conduct.[14] Through optional petition procedures under human rights treaties, a solid body of jurisprudence has been established clarifying the content and thrust of core provisions of international human rights law.[15]

The UN's normative and jurisprudential architecture of human rights have firmly established the following:

- There are universal norms of human rights binding on all countries, regardless of political, economic, or social systems, philosophies, beliefs, or customs. This settled a debate going back to Socrates and Greek pre-Socratic philosophers.
- It is impermissible in any circumstance to engage in acts such as genocide, ethnic cleansing, torture, crimes against humanity, war crimes, slavery, or human trafficking. Crimes such as these are international crimes that may be prosecuted before national, regional, or international courts.
- Every government has a responsibility to protect human rights, and this responsibility is buttressed by a corresponding responsibility on the part of regional and international organs such as the Security Council and the Human Rights Council.

What the UN's architecture on human rights has established is that every government is required, under international law, to pursue strategies of governance that are inspired in their conception and guided in their implementation by international norms on human rights. It was the UN General Assembly, in resolution 217 (3) of December 10, 1948, that proclaimed the Universal Declaration of Human Rights (UDHR)

as a common standard of achievement for all peoples and all nations, to the end that every individual and every organ of society, keeping this Declaration constantly in mind, shall strive by teaching and education to promote respect for these rights and freedoms and by progressive measures, national and international, to secure their universal and effective recognition and observance, both among the Member States themselves and among the peoples of territories under their jurisdiction.[16]

Importantly, the UDHR subsequently inspired the adoption of some seventy treaties in the area of human rights at the international and regional levels.[17] The UDHR has been translated into over 500 languages.

Prior to the establishment of the United Nations, it used to be asserted that how a government treated its inhabitants was a matter within its internal affairs. Under the UN this is no more. In 1948, shortly after the adoption of the Universal Declaration, there was a historic debate on this matter in the UN General Assembly over the then–South African government's claim that its apartheid policies were a matter purely within its internal domain. The General Assembly decisively rejected this claim.[18] The United Nations, in virtue of its Charter, has exercised the right to investigate allegations of gross violations of human rights in any part of the world, to document those violations, to condemn where warranted, to call for justice for the victims, and to accompany the victims in their hour of tribulations. In 2005, at the UN's sixtieth anniversary, the UN General Assembly agreed as per paragraph 138 of the World Summit Outcome Document:

> Each individual State has the responsibility to protect its populations from genocide, war crimes, ethnic cleansing and crimes against humanity. This responsibility entails the prevention of such crimes, including their incitement, through appropriate and necessary means. We accept that responsibility and will act in accordance with it. The international community should, as appropriate, encourage and help States to exercise this responsibility and support the Organisation in establishing an early warning capability.[19]

United Nations human rights norms have sought to provide protection of the human rights of large swathes of humanity, such as women, children, indigenous populations, and minorities. The UN had to pioneer the development of norms in these areas. The UN has also made historic pronouncements on the protection of women from genital mutilation, the protection of persons who have suffered from leprosy, and the protection of albinos, to give some examples.

The jurisprudence laid down by human rights treaty organs and by the International Court of Justice has helped establish limits on such actions as the declaration of a state of emergency, the use of force by law-enforcement authorities, and upholding the equality of treatment for women. This body of jurisprudence includes the prohibition of discrimination; impermissible forms of torture; and cruel, inhuman, or degrading treatment or punishment. Although there is still a long way to go, the normative and jurisprudential architecture of the United Nations is helping to humanize societies and their governance.

As this is being written, international law is under challenge from the great powers and from other quarters, calling into issue the content of international law and of international human rights law. The war in Ukraine has demonstrated that major powers can be guilty of human rights violations and has challenged the role of the Security Council. United Nations processes have established that international law, and international human rights law, are laid down and upheld in consensual processes within organs such as the Human Rights Council, the General Assembly, and the Security Council. In other words, it is for the authoritative organs of the United Nations to decide on the content of international human rights law rather than for individual governments to do so. As the International Law Commission famously said at the start of the UN, the content of international law is determined internationally.[20] Nevertheless, governments must conform to international human rights law nationally, regionally, and internationally.

Protection of the Right to Life

Humanity is faced with threats of extinction because of climate change, pandemics such as Covid-19, and threats from nuclear, chemical, biological, and other weapons of mass destruction. The Security Council, the General Assembly, and the Human Rights Council have all sought to address these dangers as best they can.[21] But this is patently not good enough.

The General Assembly has, in the past, articulated the responsibility to protect in a 2009 resolution about genocide, ethnic cleansing, crimes against humanity, and war crimes.[22] Despite heated debate among member states since then, a recent UN General Assembly resolution of May 18, 2021, decided "to include in its annual agenda the item titled 'The responsibility to protect and the prevention of genocide, war crimes, ethnic cleansing and crimes against humanity.'"[23]

The 2022 war of aggression by Russia in Ukraine has presented challenges to the UN human rights system. When the Security Council was blocked by the Russian veto, the General Assembly in March 2022 condemned Russian aggression in Ukraine and expressed "grave concern at reports of attacks on civilian facilities, such as residences, schools, and hospitals,"[24] all of which would be grave violations of human rights under humanitarian law and the Geneva Conventions. On February 26, 2022, Ukraine also took its case to the International Court of Justice, making claims against Russia on the grounds of the perpetration of genocide. The ICJ took up the case, and it began hearings and to accept country declarations related to the case in October and November of 2022. Ukraine, along with several other countries, also requested the Prosecutor of the International Criminal Court to launch an investigation into Russian attacks in Ukraine, claiming genocide, crimes against humanity, and war crimes.[25] All these efforts utilized various UN avenues, but the war continued.

Faced with existential threats to human existence from wars, climate change, and pandemics, the responsibility to protect must first and foremost apply to protection of the right to life of humanity as a whole. Here, UN international human rights norms provide a policy framework for action in the form of the UN's articulation of the right to life: humanity's right, nations' rights, individuals' rights, group rights. A Human Rights Council resolution of July 8, 2021, on climate change noted in its preambular section that

> the adverse effects of climate change have a range of implications, both direct and indirect, that can increase with greater global warming, for the effective enjoyment of human rights, including, inter alia, the right to life, the right to adequate food, the right to the enjoyment of the highest attainable standard of physical and mental health, the right to adequate housing, the right to self-determination, the rights to safe drinking water and sanitation, the right to work and the right to development, and recalling that in no case may a people be deprived of its own means of subsistence.[26]

Article 3 of the Universal Declaration of Human Rights has a nifty provision: "Everyone has the right to life, liberty and security of person." Building on this provision, Article 6 of the International Covenant on Civil and Political Rights states: "Every human being has the inherent right to life. This right shall be protected by law. No one shall be arbitrarily deprived of his life."

Article 12 of the International Covenant on Economic, Social, and Cultural Rights added: "The States Parties to the present Covenant recognize the right of everyone to the enjoyment of the highest attainable standard of physical and mental health." The steps to be taken to achieve the full realization of this right include "the improvement of all aspects of environmental and industrial hygiene" and "the prevention, treatment and control of epidemic, endemic, occupational and other diseases."

UN supervisory bodies have given a dynamic interpretation to the right to life: they have affirmed that governments have a legal duty to act preventively to head off threats to human life, threats to the lives of their peoples, or to particular lives under threat.[27] This means that governments should have in place national prevention and protection systems, and so should regional organizations and the United Nations.

In its general comment No. 6 (16) (1982), the Human Rights Committee, which monitors the Covenant on Civil and Political Rights, elaborated on the right to life. In general comment No. 14 (23) (1984), the Committee stated that the designing, testing, manufacture, possession, and deployment of nuclear weapons are among the greatest threats to the right to life that confront mankind today. The production, testing, possession, deployment, and use of nuclear weapons should be prohibited and recognized as crimes against humanity. The Committee accordingly, in the interest of mankind, called upon all states to take urgent steps, unilaterally and by agreement, to rid the world of this menace.

Governance is changing before our very eyes in the face of risks to humanity from climate change and pandemics such as Covid-19. The rationale of this change is that governments must act for the protection of human life—for the practical implementation of the right to life. In inserting the right to life in the Universal Declaration of Human Rights and in the International Covenants, the United Nations was both far-sighted and justice-oriented. Henceforth, every government will be judged by whether it is acting effectively to protect the right to life—for humanity, for individuals, and for groups.

Promotion of Human Dignity and Equality

The United Nations was established in the wake of the Holocaust and in the midst of colonialism; apartheid; slavery; widespread poverty and inequality; pervasive discrimination on the grounds of race, sex, language, and religion; and with millions of indigenous populations and minorities treated in a degrading and offensive manner. Women were the victims of widespread abuses and ill-treatment. In the face of such a global situation, the Charter of the UN proudly proclaimed a philosophy of dignity and freedom and a commitment to a world of equality and nondiscrimination.

The opening article of the Universal Declaration of Human Rights contained the ringing affirmation that all human beings are born free and equal in dignity and rights. They are endowed with reason and conscience and should act toward one another in a spirit of fellowship. Human dignity had been singled out for special emphasis by the philosopher Immanuel Kant; the Universal Declaration of Human Rights made it a global norm of universal application.[28]

The universal realization of human dignity is still a far way off in a world of widespread poverty, want, inequality, and discrimination. Yet, in the promotion of human dignity and equality the United Nations has made some of its most noble endeavors and achieved spectacular successes. Colonialism and apartheid are largely no more. Although slavery has not disappeared totally, it is adamantly prohibited and is largely a phenomenon of the past.

The United Nations has adopted treaties for the prevention of discrimination and for the protection of women and children. United Nations norms have also been established for the protection of indigenous populations and minorities. The very raison d'être of the UN human rights program is to promote human dignity and equality. The world, these days, is echoing chants of "Black Lives Matter." Already at the 2001 Durban world conference on racism and racial discrimination, the final documents highlighted the importance of acting for the dignity and equality of persons of African descent, and the UN Human Rights Council has a dedicated expert working group considering this issue on an ongoing basis.

When the International Covenants on Human Rights were adopted in 1966, Secretary-General U Thant commented that "in the philosophy of the United Nations, respect for human rights is one of the main foundations of freedom, justice and peace in the world. . . . peace, and respect for human rights go hand in hand."[29] At the heart of this UN philosophy stand the principles of human dignity and equality.

Promotion of a Social and International Order Conducive to Human Survival, Dignity, and Rights

The very mission of the United Nations, according to its Charter, is to strive for a world of peace, development, justice, and universal respect for human rights. Although the UN has made some progress in each of these areas, there is still a long way to go on all four fronts. The key to this challenge lies in two seminal provisions of the Universal Declaration of Human Rights, Articles 21 and 28.

"The will of the people," Article 21 declares, "shall be the basis of the authority of government: this will shall be expressed in periodic and genuine elections which shall be by universal and equal suffrage and shall be held by secret vote or by equivalent free voting procedures." Article 28 adds, with a poetic touch: "Everyone is entitled to a social and international order in which the rights and freedoms set forth in this Declaration can be fully realized."

Alas, the human rights organization Freedom House reported in 2021 that the number of countries with truly democratic governments has been in decline. The result has been more misery in the human condition and extensive gross violations of human rights in numerous countries of the world.

In the face of heavy odds, the UN human rights program has nevertheless been endeavoring to promote—nationally, regionally, and internationally—social and international orders conducive to human survival, dignity, and rights. The UN has led the struggle against climate change. The World Health Organization (WHO) leads the fight against pandemics. The UN strives for the international rule of law, including international human rights law. The Universal Periodic Review process operated by the UN Human Rights Council engages in an ongoing dialogue with governments on their efforts to implement international human rights norms. Supervisory organs established under human rights treaties consider reports, engage in dialogue, and—in respect of countries that have so accepted—consider and deliver their views on individual petitions submitted to them.

The UN High Commissioner for Human Rights (UNHCHR) cooperates with governments on their efforts to establish national protection systems. Conceptually, a national human rights system should have at least six components: constitutional, legal, judicial, institutional, educational, and preventive. National constitutions should reflect international human rights law. The provisions of international human rights treaties should be incorporated into national law. A national human rights commission or similar institution, for example an ombudsperson, can help promote and protect human rights inside countries. Human rights should be taught in institutions of primary, secondary, and tertiary education. In multiethnic countries, especially, monitoring arrangements should be in place that can help detect grievances before they break out into disputes or conflict.

Adequate and effective national protection systems are still lacking in many countries. But the UN continues to strive valiantly. This effort is spearheaded by the Office of the UN High Commissioner for Human Rights. Led by a High Commissioner, it engages in efforts to help promote the implementation of international human rights law and provides advisory services and technical assistance to governments that request them. OHCHR undertakes research and studies into new human rights problems such as climate change; supports the efforts of the Human

Rights Council, the human rights treaty bodies, and human rights investigators looking into gross violations of human rights; and issues public statements in the name of the High Commissioner in reaction to situations of gross violations of human rights.

The UN is striving on an ongoing basis for a world fashioned in the image of the Universal Declaration of Human Rights.

Clarification of the Content of International Human Rights Law Through the Human Rights Treaty Organs and the International Court of Justice

The Human Rights Committee has significantly influenced the human rights jurisprudence of the world.[30] Of equal significance, the Committee has held in a landmark case that the foremost United Nations organ, the Security Council, must comply with international human rights norms when its actions affect individuals. This is a breathtaking decision of the Human Rights Committee in the case of *Sayadi and Vinck v. Belgium* (2008).

Among the legal precepts developed by the Human Rights Committee are the following:

- Governments are legally bound to take reasonable and appropriate measures to protect people within their jurisdiction or control.
- The law must strictly control and limit the circumstances in which a person may be deprived of his or her life by the authorities of the state.
- A state, by invoking the existence of exceptional circumstances, cannot evade the obligations it has undertaken under international human rights law by ratifying the Covenant.
- A situation in which the functions and competences of the judiciary and the executive are not clearly distinguishable or where the executive is able to control or direct the judiciary is incompatible with the notion of an independent and impartial judiciary.
- Governments are under a legal obligation to ensure that remedies for violations are effective. Expedition and effectiveness are particularly important in the adjudication of cases involving torture.
- Where violations have taken place, governments must take measures to ensure that similar violations do not take place in the future.
- Governments should take specific and effective measures to prevent the disappearance of individuals and establish effective facil-

ities and procedures to investigate thoroughly by an appropriate and impartial body, cases of missing and disappeared persons.

- Being subjected to incommunicado detention in an unknown location constitutes cruel and inhuman treatment.
- Women and men are entitled to equal treatment in the application of laws.
- The Committee has made landmark contributions in the area of state responsibility for violations of human rights.[31]

The International Court of Justice has also made important contributions that clarify the content of international human rights law. As Vera Gowlland-Debbas has noted, nothing bars the ICJ under the UN Charter from handling disputes over human rights. Over time, the Court could not remain impervious to an "increasingly individually oriented international law and has been solicited in a growing number of cases raising serious violations of human rights as well as humanitarian law." These cases have involved the right to self-determination, racial discrimination, human rights in armed conflict, grave breaches of the Geneva Conventions, torture and genocide, among others.[32] She concludes that "it has played a non-negligible and on occasion a significant role in the development of international human rights law and the place it occupies within general international law."[33] A seminal moment in the Court's consideration of treaties of a humanitarian character is its 1951 Advisory Opinion on Reservations to the Genocide Convention:

> In such a convention the contracting states do not have any interests of their own; they merely have, one and all, a common interest, namely, the accomplishment of those high purposes which are the raison d'etre of the convention. Consequently, in a convention of this type one cannot speak of individual advantages or disadvantages to states, or of the maintenance of a perfect contractual balance between rights and duties.[34]

Its pronouncements in various cases (including the *Barcelona Traction* case, 1970) have given rise to "obligations *erga omnes*" in which all States had a legal interest in their protection. A purposive or teleological, rather than a strict positivist, approach to interpretation has led to jurisprudence that UN treaty bodies and human rights have relied on.

The continued expectation of a normative role of the court in the development of international human rights law was reflected in Thomas Burri's call for the Court to consider the *Chagos Islands* case not as a matter of sovereignty but instead as a human rights matter, that is, the denial of the Chagosians, under UK rule, of their human rights.[35] Burri cites the "*erga omnes* obligations, [that emerged out of] *Barcelona Traction* . . . as a means for the Court to do just that, address human rights."[36]

Struggling Against Widespread Violations of Human Rights

Gross violations of human rights remain rampant in the world: extrajudicial executions, torture, enforced and involuntary disappearances, religious intolerance, violence against women, and trafficking in human beings. The UN is an organization controlled by governments, and quite often it is the very governments that are grossly violating human rights that sit in judgment of themselves and their peers. Struggling against gross violations of human rights is thus no easy matter at the UN.

Nevertheless, public discussions of gross violations do take place in UN human rights organs, and resolutions are passed criticizing governments for gross violations—although selectively, it must be admitted. UN human rights fact finders, known collectively as "special procedures," investigate allegations of gross violations either on a national basis or a thematic, global basis. The work of these special procedures is invaluable. But, alas, they are coming under increasing pressure to engage more in dialogue and cooperation rather than in confrontation. Confrontation here means openly criticizing governments for gross violations. This gives rise to wrenching issues of conscience when it comes to acting for the protection of those being killed, tortured, or made to disappear.

International Criminal Tribunals

The establishment and operations of the ad hoc criminal tribunals and of the International Criminal Court, taken together, represent an important positive chapter in the strengthening of the international protection of human rights. This is true for at least three reasons: first, as a matter of justice, it is important to victims of gross violations of human rights and their families that those accused are brought to account; second, the tribunals and the International Criminal Court have helped clarify and further develop international human rights law; and third, taken together, they represent worthwhile additions to the international architecture of protection and of justice.

On the first issue, UN Basic Principles adopted by the UN General Assembly call for remedies and compensation for victims of gross violations of human rights.[37] This is an important declaration and a foundational part of international human rights law. On the second issue, one thinks of the International Criminal Tribunal for Rwanda holding that rape in conflict can constitute crimes against humanity. On the third issue, the international protection of human rights has three dimensions: preventive, mitigatory, and remedial. International criminal tribunals and the International Criminal Court contribute to all three dimensions. Once perpetrators of gross violations hear that they are under the gaze of prosecutors, they run to their lawyers. And they always have to be aware that after their hold on power is over, they may be brought to account before the law for their depredations.[38]

Operating Imperfect Bodies:
The Security Council, the General Assembly,
and the Human Rights Council

As we have seen, UN international norms prescribe ground rules for all governments on how they must protect human rights. The foundation of these norms includes the UN Charter, the Universal Declaration, and the International Covenants. These are universal norms applicable to all countries.

Every country should have in place an adequate and effective national protection system inspired by and reflecting international norms.[39] This includes national constitutional provisions reflecting the Universal Declaration and the Covenants and legislative provisions reflecting international human rights treaties accepted by the government. These actions include judicial enforcement of human rights; formation of a national human rights institution charged with promoting and protecting human rights, education, and dissemination of human rights norms; and arrangements to help prevent violations of human rights from taking place.

The Universal Periodic Review (UPR), which is operated by the UN Human Rights Council can help countries develop or enhance their national protection systems.[40] It can also provide an opportunity to air concerns about human rights problems within a country. Human rights leaders should familiarize themselves with the UPR process and how it operates in the Human Rights Council. Human rights NGOs, such as Amnesty International or Human Rights Watch, can make written submissions into the process, as well. To a limited extent, they are also able to take the floor in the plenary of the Human Rights Council.

The special procedures of the UN Human Rights Council are the strongest protection actors have within the United Nations.[41] They investigate and publish reports about human rights problems such as extrajudicial executions, torture, enforced and involuntary disappearances, racism and racial discrimination, violence against women, trafficking in human beings, and similar problems. Leaders should be aware of them, send them information, and try to get the relevant mandate-holder to visit their country in the event that there are problems of human rights violations inside the country. The special procedures can also issue urgent appeals where people are at risk of imminent violations of their human rights.

There is an international complaints procedure that petitioners can activate by submitting reliably attested information about gross violations of human rights. Unfortunately, it is heavily politicized by governments, which control it. Human rights advocates should be aware of this complaints procedure so that they can consider using it to submit complaints about allegations of gross violations of human rights.

There are some individual petition procedures established under particular treaties, which advocates may be able to use.[42] Prominent among these is the procedure under the Optional Protocol to the Covenant on Civil and Political Rights. There is also a rich international jurisprudence that has been developed from the case law of the human rights treaty bodies.

Several prominent international human rights NGOs operate at the United Nations, and they can help advance human rights causes at the United Nations. These include Amnesty International, Human Rights Watch, the International Commission of Jurists, the International Service for Human Rights, and Geneva for Human Rights. In addition, the UN Secretary-General, the High Commissioner for Human Rights, and the president of the UN Human Rights Council are international personalities of moral stature who are able to help publicize and respond to specific cases.

The UN Human Rights Council, initially called the Human Rights Commission, was created at the first UN meeting in January 1946. Eleanor Roosevelt was named as its chair and was asked to form a committee to write the UN Universal Declaration of Human Rights. The Council discusses and prepares new human rights norms and works to promote human rights generally. It meets in three sessions per year and sometimes holds special sessions to discuss human rights emergencies. Its record of actually protecting human rights is not even-handed because of political influences by governments; yet, the Council can be used as a forum to help air grievances and to publicize causes. NGOs are given limited space to speak in the Council, but they can organize parallel meetings to help air their grievances. Unfortunately, the Human Rights Council today is essentially a political body and often does not act on the principle of justice. Rather, for the most part it acts on the basis of political expediency. The Council has a record of establishing international commissions of inquiry when it is faced with situations of severe violations of human rights. As an example, the Council recently announced an investigation into human rights violations undertaken by the Taliban in Afghanistan.

The Social and Humanitarian Committee of the UN General Assembly sometimes discusses human rights problems inside countries. NGOs are not allowed to speak in the Committee, but their concerns can be raised by a government or governments. The prominent international human rights NGOs can assist in briefing governmental representatives on the Committee about human rights problems that deserve United Nations attention.[43]

Struggling for a Wise Arrangement on the Role of Treaty Supervisory Organs

At the time of this writing, ten supervisory bodies[44] have been established under the principal UN human rights treaties to support the implementation of those treaties. For example, the Committee on Human Rights monitors the implementation of the International Covenant on Civil and Political Rights; the Committee Against Torture oversees the Convention Against Torture and Other Cruel, Inhuman, or Degrading Treatments or Punishment; and the Committee on the Rights of the Child monitors compliance with the Convention on the Rights of the Child. Taken all together, they discuss national reports with the submitting governments, offer advice, make comments and recommendations, consider petitions, and in some instances, make country visits. Their role is a valuable one.

In recent times, the human rights treaty bodies have come under pressure from governments for allegedly pursuing "confrontational policies"; for using up too much time, resources, and documentation; and for not pooling their efforts optimally. The UN General Assembly has been pursuing a process of rationalization and reform, and the UN High Commissioner for Human Rights kick-started this discussion in 2012.[45]

In favor of the existing system is the fact that each treaty benefits from the targeted attention of a supervisory body. In a world of serious problems when it comes to the implementation of human rights, this must surely be a good thing. And the resources expended are well spent. Various ideas have been floated to "rationalize" the system. Most are unworkable or inefficient. The human rights movement is striving valiantly to keep the system so that the world can benefit from it. Whether they will succeed remains to be seen.

Grudgingly Benefiting from the Contributions of NGOs

From the inception of the United Nations, NGOs have played a crucial role in the drafting of norms and in the global promotion and protection of human rights.[46] NGOs identify new problems that require the drafting of new norms. They suggest the text of such new norms and work for the emplacement of national human rights institutions inside countries. They provide information and advice to bodies such as the Human Rights Council and to the human rights treaty bodies. Put simply, the UN's human rights program would be distinctly poorer without the inputs of NGOs.

At the beginning of the UN, NGOs were allowed more space to make their contributions. They still do so, but with the changing attitudes of governments they have come under increasing pressure when it comes to the allocation of time to make their statements, to criticize governments for gross violations of human rights, and to tender recommendations for the consideration of UN human rights bodies. Today, they are permitted to make very short oral interventions. Video submissions of 90 seconds are permissible! Many autocratic governments actively seek to prevent NGOs from their respective countries from participating in human rights meetings in Geneva.[47]

A former UN human rights leader once wrote an essay on the NGO contribution with the apt title "Partners in the Promotion and Protection of Human Rights."[48] Written by Theo van Boven shortly before he became head of the UN human rights program, it summarizes the UN-NGO relationship: one of partnership in the cause of human rights. Van Boven noted then:

> Whatever the status (or the lack thereof) of private persons, groups and nongovernmental organizations within the framework of international organizations and certain formalized international procedures, their capability and competence to act as partners and partisans in the promotion and protection of human rights—against their own State or even against other States—is clearly established in human rights law itself.[49]

He noted also that, in addition to the proclamation in resolution 217 (3) cited above, the partnership role for NGOs is also contained in the preambles of both Covenants, which state: "the individual, having duties to other individuals and to the community to which he belongs, is under a responsibility, to strive for the promotion and observance of the rights recognized in the present Covenant."[50]

Conclusion

The story of the UN and Human Rights can be represented graphically: At the core of three concentric circles there is *the principle of commitment* to a world of universal human rights as reflected in the UN Charter and its sister document the Universal Declaration of Human Rights. Outside of this center of commitment there is first, a small *circle of progress*—the norms and institutions established internationally, regionally, and nationally to help uphold human rights. Beyond this first circle there is a second circle of what may be termed the *circle of possibilities* to take forward the cause of human rights. Into this circle may be put issues on which international cooperation may be achievable—for example, a respect for human rights while combating climate change. Then, in the outer sphere, there is a wide, wide, *circle of problems* to address—the numerous crises adversely affecting the universal realization of human rights, including poor governance, inequitable development and sharing of resources, and shocking gross violations of human rights. The challenge before the UN is to strive constantly to help widen the circle of progress, a truly daunting challenge in the circumstances of the world of 2022.

It could help, though, to see the UN and human rights in terms of the principle of commitment, the circle of progress, the circle of opportunities, and, alas, the daunting circle of problems in a world of climatic, geopolitical, and philosophical change. At the end of the day, the following question provides a crucial test of what would be wise for the future: What works best to advance human rights in the various treaties and to protect people from suffering violations of those rights? The UN should be ready to devote the time and resources to this essential cause.

Notes

1. Samarsinghe, "Human Rights: Norms and Machinery."
2. The International Covenant on Economic, Social and Cultural Rights and the International Covenant on Civil and Political Rights and their Optional Protocols.

3. Mégret, "The Security Council," in Alston and Mégret, *The UN and Human Rights*.

4. Clapham, "The General Assembly (August 4, 2012)," in Alston and Mégret, *The UN and Human Rights*.

5. Freedman, "The Council and Commission on Human Rights," in Alston and Mégret, *The UN and Human Rights*.

6. See chapters 9–17 in Alston and Mégret, *The UN and Human Rights*.

7. Hennebel, "The Human Rights Committee," in Alston and Mégret, *The UN and Human Rights*.

8. See generally, McGaughey, *Non-governmental Organisations*.

9. Simma, "The International Court of Justice," in Alston and Mégret, *The UN and Human Rights*.

10. UN News, "'Eyes and Ears' of UN Human Rights Council Facing Funding Crisis," September 20, 2020, https://news.un.org/en/story/2020/09/1074042. Ted Piccone, "UN Human Rights Council: As the US Returns, It Will Have to Deal with China and Its Friends," Brookings blog, February 25, 2021, https://www.brookings.edu/blog/order-from-chaos/2021/02/25/un-human-rights-council-as-the-us-returns-it-will-have-to-deal-with-china-and-its-friends/.

11. For an insight on the wider, evolving context see Zeid Ra'ad Al Hussein, former UN High Commissioner for Human Rights, "Is International Human Rights Law Under Threat?" BIICL Annual Grotius Lecture at the Law Society, London, June 26, 2017, https://www.biicl.org/documents/1680_is_international_human_rights_law_under_threat_speech_260617.pdf?showdocument. See also, Hopgood, *End Times of Human Rights*.

12. Shelton, *United Nations System for Protecting Human Rights*.

13. Scott Meyer, "The Changing Role of the UN General Assembly," International Bar Notes, The International Bar Association, October 31, 2012, https://ssrn.com/abstract=2169161.

14. See, for example, Fikentscher, "United Nations Codes of Conduct."

15. Moller and Zayas, *United Nations Human Rights Committee Case Law*.

16. United Nations, Resolution 217 (3), Universal Declaration of Human Rights (December 10, 1948), OHCHR website, https://www.un.org/en/ga/search/view_doc.asp?symbol=A/RES/217(III).

17. "The Universal Declaration of Human Rights," United Nations website, n.d., https://www.un.org/en/about-us/universal-declaration-of-human-rights.

18. Sohn and Buergenthal, *International Protection of Human Rights*.

19. UN General Assembly, Resolution A/RES/60/1, 2005 World Summit Outcome (September 16, 2005), https://www.un.org/en/development/desa/population/migration/generalassembly/docs/ global compact /A/RES_60_1.pdf.

20. See International Law Commission, *Survey of International Law in Relation to the Work of Codification of the International Law Commission: Preparatory Work Within the Purview of Article 18, Paragraph 1, of the of the International Law Commission—Memorandum Submitted by the Secretary-General*, A/CN.4/1/Rev.1, Extract from the Yearbook of the International Law Commission, 1949, https://legal.un.org/ilc/documentation/english/a_cn4_1_rev1.pdf.

21. Ramcharan, *UN Protection of Humanity*.

22. UN General Assembly, Resolution 63/308, The Responsibility to Protect (September 14, 2009). For a background note, see Global Centre for the Responsibility to Protect, *The Responsibility to Protect: A Background Briefing*, October 7, 2009, https://reliefweb.int/sites/reliefweb.int/files/resources/the-responsibility-to-protect-background-briefing.pdf.

23. UN General Assembly, Resolution 75/277, The Responsibility to Protect and the Prevention of Genocide, War Crimes, Ethnic Cleansing and Crimes Against Humanity (May 21, 2021).

24. UN General Assembly, Resolution A/ES-11/L.I, Aggression Against Ukraine (March 1, 2022).

25. "Ukraine: Countries Request ICC War Crimes Inquiry," Human Rights Watch, https://www.hrw.org/news/2022/03/02/ukraine-countries-request-icc-war-crimes -inquiry.

26. UN General Assembly, Resolution A/HRC/47/L.19, Human Rights and Climate Change (July 8, 2021).

27. Ramcharan, *Right to Life in International Law.*

28. Kateb, *Human Dignity.*

29. UN General Assembly Official Records, Twenty-First Session, 1966, 1496th meeting, p. 8, para. 74.

30. Conte and Burchill, *Defining Civil and Political Rights.*

31. A. Mavrommatis, "Foreword," in Moller and de Zayas, *United Nations Human Rights Committee Case Law,* pp. xix–xxi.

32. Gowlland-Debbas, "The ICJ and the Challenges of Human Rights Law."

33. Ibid., p. 110.

34. Ibid., p. 114.

35. Burri, "Two Points for the International Court of Justice in 'Chagos,'" http://dx.doi.org/10.2139/ssrn.3309228.

36. Ibid., p. 105.

37. See UN General Assembly, Resolution 60/147, Basic Principles and Guidelines on the Right to a Remedy and Reparation for Victims of Gross Violations of International Human Rights Law and Serious Violations of International Humanitarian Law (December 16, 2005).

38. See, generally, Meron, *The Humanization of International Law*; Răduleţu, "The Role of International Criminal Tribunals"; and Frulli, "The Contribution of International Criminal Tribunals."

39. See European Union Agency for Fundamental Rights, *Strong and Effective National Human Rights Institutions: Challenges, Promising Practices and Opportunities,* 2021, https://fra.europa.eu/sites/default/files/fra_uploads/fra-2020-strong -effective-nhris-summary_en.pdf. For a useful learning tool, see Danish Institute for Human Rights, "The National Human Rights System: An Introduction to Actors, Policies and Processes in the National Human Rights System," Course 4/5 of the Basics of International Human Rights course collection, https://www.humanrights .dk/learning-hub/national-human-rights-system.

40. Tistounet, *UN Human Rights Council.*

41. Nolan, Freedman, and Murphy, *United Nations Special Procedures System.*

42. Office of the High Commissioner for Human Rights (OHCHR), "Individual Communications: Human Rights Treaty Bodies," 2021, https://www.ohchr.org/en /hrbodies/tbpetitions/Pages/IndividualCommunications.aspx. OHCHR, "23 Frequently Asked Questions About Treaty Body Complaints Procedures," 2021, https:// www.ohchr.org/sites/default/files/Documents/HRBodies/TB/23FAQ.pdf.

43. Mertus, *The UN and Human Rights.*

44. See OHCHR, "Videos about the Treaty Bodies," 2021, https://www.ohch r.org/EN/HRBodies/Pages/TreatyBodies.aspx.

45. Navenethem Pillay, *Strengthening the United Nations Human Rights Treaty Body System,* A Report by the UN High Commissioner for Human Rights, June 2012, https://www.refworld.org/pdfid/4fe8291a2.pdf.

46. Korey, *NGOs and the Universal Declaration of Human Rights*. Weeramantry, *The Slumbering Sentinels*.

47. See UN Human Rights Council, "NGO and NHRI Information," 2021, https://www.ohchr.org/EN/HRBodies/HRC/Pages/NgoNhriInfo.aspx.

48. Van Boven, "Partners in the Promotion and Protection."

49. Ibid.

50. Ibid.

6

The Evolution of Peacekeeping Operations

Jean E. Krasno

Hundreds of soldiers descend the metal stairs hastily anchored in place at the side of a transport plane, ship, or helicopter. They wear the blue cloth berets or caps, some with blue painted helmets, symbolizing the United Nations as they step onto uncertain soil. On their sleeves are the insignias of the nations, their homelands, from which they embarked days before. They represent their countries' contributions to a larger cause brought together by the United Nations to promote global peace.

Who are these peacekeeping soldiers, and what is peacekeeping? Peacekeeping is never mentioned in the UN Charter, which lays down the goals and guidelines of the United Nations. The Charter in Article 43, in fact, spells out a plan for each of the member nations to enter into agreement with the UN to provide permanent national contingents to the UN for use when needed, a kind of UN army for collective security. But no nation followed through by signing an Article 43 agreement to provide such troops. With no UN army to deter aggression, the organization was left to improvise. Countries would lend trained units of soldiers to the UN for short periods of time on a case-by-case basis, always reserving the right to say no.

A far cry from the force envisioned by the founders, countries have continued to volunteer peacekeepers to assist in monitoring cease-fire arrangements, guarding buffer zones, observing compliance with human rights accords or border agreements, providing UN civilian police, and more. When troop rotation is taken into account, over a million military and civilian personnel have taken part in UN operations since they began in 1948. By 2022, there have been seventy-one different peacekeeping missions sent into the field, with twelve currently in operation. The budget authorized by the General Assembly's Fifth Committee for the year July 2021 through June 2022 was US$6.38 billion,[1] a sum that is dwarfed by the US defense budget of some $740 billion in 2022.

Peace Operations During the League of Nations

Like most innovative ideas, the concept of peacekeeping, sending multilateral troops to secure a peace arrangement, did not emerge in a vacuum. In fact, before the term *peacekeeping* was created in 1956, the UN had already sent unarmed observers to stabilize tense situations. Now those observer missions of 1948 are counted as peacekeeping operations. The theory was that observers would provide a kind of transparency to deter provocative acts of violence that could induce conflict.

A little-known fact, however, is that the League of Nations had also employed this practice well before the UN was created.[2] The League was formed after World War I as an initial attempt to create a permanent multilateral body to preserve peace. Established as a part of the Treaty of Versailles, which set the terms for the end of the war, the League was tasked with ongoing issues of international dispute. It was the first international body to set the precedent of deploying military personnel drawn from member nations for the purpose of peaceful settlement of disputes. League missions consisted of numbers anywhere from a few military officers to a few hundred or a few thousand soldiers. These personnel engaged in investigating activities, reporting, and monitoring the separation of conflicting forces. They oversaw adherence to boundary agreements or neutral zones and administered territories that found themselves with no governance structures after the war.[3]

The following examples illustrate the League precursors to later UN peacekeeping activities. For fifteen years, from 1920 to 1935, the League Council established a five-member commission to administer the Saar Basin, a province of ethnic Germans located on the border with France. At the end of World War I, France had been granted the coal rights to the region, but the League had the responsibility of governing the region for the fifteen-year period. At the end of that period, the League was to administer a referendum for the Saar citizens to decide whether to become a part of Germany or to join France. During this time, the commission consulted occasionally with the Saar people and reported regularly to the League. In 1934, the League Council organized a plebiscite with 1,000 League officials to carry out voter registration and the final balloting. The League also established a military force to ensure order during the registration and voting process, calling on 3,300 troops from Italy, the UK, Sweden, and the Netherlands. This marked the first multilateral military operation under the auspices of an international organization. The citizens of Saar voted to reunite with Germany.[4]

Another example of the League's work took place in Danzig, now called Gdansk. Danzig was a German enclave on Poland's Baltic coast that had been a part of West Prussia before World War I. The Treaty of Versailles had removed it from German control and created Danzig as a "Free City," under the protection of the League. The League did not govern Danzig as it had Saar but had two key responsibilities: to draw up and guarantee Danzig's constitution, and to deal with disputes between Danzig and Poland. The League also appointed a High Commissioner for Danzig to mediate the frequent issues that emerged with Poland. The first ten years of the "Free City" worked well, but by 1938, Germany had reasserted its influence and Danzig was annexed by the Nazis on the first days of World War II.[5]

Other cases in Europe involving the League were Upper Silesia, a border area between Poland and Germany, Vilna (Vilnius), and Memel, the latter two in Lithuania. In Upper Silesia, League personnel administered a plebiscite to determine its status, decided the boundary between Germany and Poland, and heard complaints by minorities to reduce tensions. In Lithuania, the League helped administer the area called Memel until Germany occupied it in 1939. The League was less successful in Vilna, where the organization tried to establish a plebiscite and mediate a solution but failed due to power politics. Russia took over Vilna when the Nazis occupied Poland in World War II.

Outside the European theater, the League was also asked to settle other disputes. In the Middle East, through a commission of inquiry into the area around the city of Mosul, the League established the boundary between Iraq and Turkey, granting Mosul to Iraq, thus splitting up the Kurdish population. In Alexandretta, a small territory that had been a part of Syria, the League designated a peace plan to carry out elections. But France, the League mandate power in Syria, and Turkey did not cooperate with the plan, and the area fell to Turkey.

In Latin America, the League assisted in settling a dispute between Peru and Colombia that had erupted during the interwar period. In 1933, Peru seized Leticia, a territory on the Amazon River between the two countries. The League demanded the withdrawal of Peru and later took control of the region. Three League commissioners and a seventy-five-man military contingent of the League governed Leticia for one year, after which the League returned Leticia to Colombia.[6]

Enter the United Nations

Many of the ambassadors to the League also served in the early delegations to the United Nations beginning in 1946 when the UN met for the first time. Henri Vigier served as a member of the League's staff as well as a political officer on the staff of the UN in its early years. These diplomats were able to use their experiences with the League and the deployment of peace missions during the interwar years. Therefore, when complaints were received that trouble was brewing in the northern part of Greece, the UN delegates had history to draw upon. In 1947, the UN created the United Nations Special Committee on the Balkans (UNSCOB), which was the first UN deployment of an observer mission. UN observers were sent to northern Greece to investigate and monitor allegations of outside support from Albania, Yugoslavia, and Bulgaria (then all part of the Communist bloc) for Greek Communist guerrillas in their insurgency attempts to oust the Greek government endorsed by the West. Along with the investigations, UNSCOB was asked to assist the four countries in restoring normal relations after the war. To avoid continued Soviet vetoes that had thwarted the creation of the mission, the United States maneuvered the issue onto the agenda of the General Assembly through a procedural vote in the Security Council. A General Assembly resolution established UNSCOB on October 21, 1947, and called upon Albania, Yugoslavia, and Bulgaria not to furnish aid to the guerrillas and to find a peaceful solution to the problem. Reports of the committee were submitted to the General Assembly, not the Security Council. Nevertheless, the committee included nine of the eleven countries serving on the Security Council at the time. The Soviet Union and Poland declined to serve on the committee. UNSCOB, which terminated in 1951, was funded at a cost of US$3 million under the UN regular budget. The crisis dissolved, which marked the first UN observer mission a success.[7]

While the term *peacekeeping* does not appear until the 1956 Suez crisis, the year 1948 is generally cited as the first official date for the deployment of a UN peacekeeping operation, even though unarmed UN observers had already been sent to northern Greece in 1947 and would also be sent to the India- and Pakistan-disputed area of Kashmir in 1949. Because this is an evolutionary process built on a number of previous experiences, like other inventions, it is hard to determine the exact beginning. The first recognized precursor of peacekeeping is the UN Truce Supervision Organization (UNTSO), created by the Security Council in June 1948. Unarmed UNTSO observers were sent to the Middle East to monitor the truce agreements established at the end of fighting in 1948 between Arabs and the State of Israel, newly created on May 15, 1948. UNTSO, which reports to the Security Council, has continued to adapt to changes on the ground and operates today to observe and report violations of peace agreements. Headquartered in Jerusalem, UNTSO maintains observers in the Golan Heights, Lebanon, Egypt, and Jordan. Unarmed, their only protection is the symbolic legitimacy of the blue UN berets and insignias they wear on their uniforms.

The Creation of UN Peacekeeping

When the Suez crisis erupted in 1956, the United Nations could draw on past experience and the building momentum that laid the groundwork for the next innovative step: UN peacekeeping as it is thought of today. In July 1956, Egyptian leader Gamal Abdel Nasser had nationalized the Suez Canal, taking the lucrative revenues out of the hands of the former colonial powers in order to pay for building the Aswan Dam. To regain the canal, the United Kingdom and France met secretly with the Israelis to formulate what in retrospect appears to have been a bizarre plan to take the canal out of the hands of Nasser. Israel, which had been denied access to the canal and the Straits of Tiran by Egypt, was to attack Egypt from the east through the Sinai and move toward the Suez. France and the United Kingdom would then heroically announce that they would attack from the north at Port Said to save the canal from Israeli capture. They would then move in to retake control. The covert operation was put into action on October 29, 1956. Israel launched its attack as planned, followed two days later by British/French bombing in the north. The US Eisenhower administration immediately condemned the action by its European allies, who were both permanent members of the UN Security Council. Brian Urquhart, political advisor to UN Secretary-General Dag Hammarskjöld, explained the event this way:

> The scenario was that the Israelis would invade the Sinai and get down to the Canal and the British and French would then give an ultimatum to Israel and Egypt, saying that unless they both withdrew their

forces 10 miles back from the Canal the British and French would intervene to separate them and thereby keep the peace. It was one of the most self-serving pieces of bullshit ever created by anyone and no one believed it.[8]

Repeated attempts by the UN Security Council to pass resolutions demanding a halt to attacks were vetoed by France and the UK. "In fact, it was at that point that Macmillan, the British Chancellor of the Exchequer, was told the financial assistance from the United States would cease, thereby threatening the British pound."[9] The United States then orchestrated the use of the mechanism first tentatively utilized for UNSCOB and more formally introduced for the Korean conflict to move the issue out of the Security Council and onto the agenda of the UN General Assembly through a special session of the Assembly convened on November 1, 1956. The mechanism had been formalized in 1950 during the Korean crisis in General Assembly resolution 377 (V), termed the "Uniting for Peace" resolution. According to "Uniting for Peace," the General Assembly can take up an issue if the Security Council is unable to act. The Soviets, who were preoccupied in 1956 with the Hungarian uprising, were delighted to see France and the UK humiliated before the international body by the maneuver. In 1947 and again in 1950, it had been the Soviets who had been denied their veto privileges by the shift to the General Assembly.

Secretary-General Hammarskjöld was called upon to mediate a cease-fire.[10] The original idea put forth by Canada's foreign minister and delegate to the UN, Lester Bowles Pearson, was to subsume the British and French into a UN-authorized international force, but Hammarskjöld knew that was a nonstarter: "You could never get the Security Council, not even the United States, to vote for the British and French staying on under the UN flag after what had happened."[11] The UN had to come up with something completely different but had to do it before the British and French naval ships were to land on Egypt's Mediterranean coast on November 5, 1956. Then Pearson, who had served as president of the UN General Assembly in 1952 and was well respected in the international forum, devised the idea of an armed UN peacekeeping force made up of soldiers drawn from member states through voluntary contributions to secure a buffer zone between the parties. There was not enough time to ask for a cease-fire, and unarmed observers were not going to be enough of a deterrent. The concept of having actual armed UN troops was new.[12]

According to Urquhart, Hammarskjöld at first was not enthusiastic about the idea and had to be convinced. Once he saw how it could be orchestrated successfully, he worked to solidify the concept.[13] Pearson's Canadian proposal was adopted by the General Assembly on November 4, 1956. Urquhart, Ralph Bunche, and other UN staff worked around the clock to implement the plan. The Egyptians were against the Canadians being a part of the force. The regiment the Canadians had earmarked for deployment was the Queen's Own Canadian Dragoons, whose uniforms were identical to those of the British. Something had to be done to identify the multinational UN troops, who would be wearing their own uniforms. It was decided that the only clear way to distinguish them would be by their hats because that is what you see first on the battlefield.[14] The team decided that the hats should be blue, and Urquhart remembered saying, "you know the United States helmet liner, which is made of plastic, is a wonderfully light, perfectly comfortable hat once you take the metal part off of it, and surely it must be possible to dip it into a bucket of blue paint . . . this is what we finally did . . . and that is where the blue helmet started."[15]

After consultation with Egypt, Hammarskjöld accepted contingents from ten countries, including finally the Canadians, and the assistance of three additional nations. The Canadians covered transport, medical, and dental units. UNTSO provided the first set of observers, who arrived on November 12, followed by the first UN Emergency Force (UNEF) units on November 15 and 16. The target strength of about 6,000 troops was reached by February 1957.[16]

Hammarskjöld established several principles by which UNEF would operate to ensure the safety of the multinational force and to provide assurances to Egypt. Israel refused to allow UN troops on its soil, and so negotiations were primarily with Nasser. Hammarskjöld's principles included the following: (1) peacekeeping forces could only be deployed after a cease-fire had been reached; (2) the consent of the host country had to be granted before deployment; (3) UN troops could only fire in self-defense; and (4) the UN had to remain impartial. Hammarskjöld wanted to be sure that the UN troops would not become embroiled in the dispute and place themselves in danger. Troop-contributing countries would withdraw their soldiers if they suddenly became a part of the conflict. Urquhart explained that the Secretary-General knew that they were setting a precedent and wanted to be careful to get it right.[17]

UNEF is important not only for its contribution to peace but also because of the precedent established by the deployment of multinational armed troops to preserve the peace, the introduction of Hammarskjöld's principles, and the creation of the UNEF Advisory Committee, which was constituted of the troop-contributing countries, to advise the Secretary-General from time to time. Pearson won the Nobel Peace Prize in 1957 for this innovative concept. Pearson, Hammarskjöld, Urquhart, Bunche, and the troop-contributing countries are to be congratulated for their inventive spirit in creating what has been termed "chapter six and a half" of the UN Charter, somewhere between Chapter VI (peaceful dialogue and mediation) and Chapter VII (the use of force). UNEF not only established the first armed peacekeeping operation, but it is the reference point for what later was to be called "classic or traditional peacekeeping," meaning the type that provided security for a buffer zone between warring parties and adhered to Hammarskjöld's principles.

UNEF I lasted about eleven years until the 1967 Six-Day War. On May 16, 1967, Nasser had his chief of staff, General Mohammed Fawzi, send a letter to UN Force Commander Indar Rikhye stating that Egypt was withdrawing its consent to host the UN peacekeepers, and UNEF began leaving on May 29 under orders by Secretary-General U Thant, who succeeded Hammarskjöld. Some have criticized Thant for removing the UN troops without first calling for debate of the issue in the Security Council or the General Assembly, where the peacekeeping operation was first authorized. However, Thant traveled to Cairo to discuss the matter with Nasser but failed to convince him to reverse his decision. Thant had consulted with the UNEF Advisory Committee, which was split on the issue, and troop-contributing countries were already withdrawing their forces, fearing the worst if they overstayed their welcome.[18]

Nasser had been under political pressure at home to retake the territory occupied by the Israelis. On May 22, Egypt closed the Straits of Tiran at Sharm el Sheikh to Israeli passage, which the Israelis considered an act of war, as they had already warned Nasser. When war erupted on June 5, 1967, some UNEF troops were caught in the cross-fire, and fifteen UN personnel were killed. Thus began the Six-Day War, during which Israel expanded its territory. UNEF II did not return to the Middle East until October 1973, after the October War, called the Yom Kippur War by the Israelis because Egypt launched its surprise attack on the Jewish holy day. UNEF II was removed in 1979 after the signing of the US-mediated Camp David Accords, ending the conflict between Egypt and Israel and returning the Sinai to Egypt.[19]

The Belgian Congo: A Glimpse of the Future

In January 1960, Hammarskjöld toured Africa as decolonization was beginning to take root. Belgium had agreed in January to give independence in six months to its colony, the Belgian Congo,[20] with its capital in Leopoldville (now Kinshasa). The Secretary-General feared the precipitous handover would not go smoothly and asked Bunche to go to Leopoldville in May 1960, about a month before independence. A few weeks after his arrival in the Congo, Bunche wrote a confidential note to Hammarskjöld, describing the Belgians' condescending treatment of the Congolese as "downright embarrassing."[21]

Only days before the independence ceremonies were to take place, a compromise was reached whereby rival dominant Congolese leaders from two of the larger tribal groups would share power: Joseph Kasavubu as president and Patrice Lumumba as prime minister. While this compromise lifted some of the internal unease, other tensions emerged during the independence ceremonies on June 30, when the new prime minister, Lumumba, denounced Belgium for its racist colonial rule. After independence, law and order was to be kept by the Force Publique, a Congolese army that still maintained its white Belgian officers. When it became clear to the low-paid Congolese soldiers that they would continue to be subjected to the harsh authority of the white officers, the central garrison at Thysville mutinied on July 5. The chaos, looting, and violence that followed quickly spread like wildfire to other cities and towns. The Congolese threw out all the Belgian officers, which meant that no officers were left.[22]

On July 9, some Europeans were killed in the attacks, and by the next day Brussels ordered the return of Belgian troops to protect the white population. The troops landed in Leopoldville, Elizabethville, Matadi, and Luluabourg. In some cases, heavy fighting broke out between the Belgians and the Congolese forces. Panic led to the exodus of most of the Belgian population—roughly 100,000 Belgians had stayed on after independence—which included government administrators, technicians, and medical personnel, all of whom had agreed to stay initially for the transition. This left the country in a security crisis with a breakdown of essential services.[23] "There was nobody in the power station to do the switching; there wasn't anybody in the telephone exchange; there was nobody in the police station; there wasn't anybody in the whole transport system on which the country depended."[24] The lack of preparation for independence astounded the international community. Only about seventeen Congolese had university degrees. Practically no black person had a medical degree or had even been in the white-run hospitals.

For the first time invoking Article 99 of the UN Charter, which gives the Secretary-General the authority to bring a matter to the attention of the Security Council, Hammarskjöld requested on July 13 an urgent meeting of the Council on the Congo crisis. "Hammarskjöld had taken the precaution of talking beforehand to all the members of the Council privately."[25] In its resolution 143, the Council called upon Belgium to withdraw its troops and authorized the Secretary-General to establish a peacekeeping force to meet the needed tasks.[26] This marked the second deployment of armed UN peacekeepers.

The UN Operation in the Congo (ONUC) was beset with complications from the onset. This time, peacekeepers were not going to be monitoring a buffer zone between two states, a relatively clear-cut task, but were going to be interposed in a situation of civil strife with no obvious boundaries. Nevertheless, they did have the consent of the Leopoldville government. The Congolese cabinet, with the assistance of Bunche, had sent a letter to the UN requesting assistance of a technical nature. However, that consent was compromised when Katanga province declared secession on July 11, 1960, only six days after the mutiny. The Congo not only faced a state of anarchy, but now became embroiled in a civil war. Lumumba wanted the UN to take the side of the government to end the secession, but the UN was reluctant to abandon the principle of impartiality. Thus the UN embarked on a very messy endeavor of trying to balance mediation and impartiality, with the deployment of UN troops in Katanga without full consent. These imponderables were to appear again in later years in Somalia and the former Yugoslavia.

While the risks of getting involved were great, UN members also realized that the risks posed by not becoming involved could be even greater. With each day that went by, the country was sinking into a worsening crisis. One of the largest and richest countries in Africa, with gold, diamonds, uranium, and other mineral deposits, the Congo was also strategically located in the center of the African continent, with two key airfields in Kamina and Kitona occupied through agreement with Belgium, a member of the North Atlantic Treaty Organization (NATO). If the international body did not intervene, the United States or the Soviet Union would naturally jump in to fill the void, and the Congo would be enmeshed in the Cold War conflict.

Urquhart offers his firsthand description of what happened immediately after the Security Council met to pass resolution 143 on July 13 and into the early hours of July 14:

> The moment the Council meeting ended we all went up to the Secretary-General's conference room on the thirty-eighth floor and sat down for another three hours to figure out the rudiments of that operation. Hammarskjöld ran the meeting, occasionally taking the telephone to call up various countries to get the first troops, and by 6:30 that morning we

had, I think, four countries with the troops actually standing by; we had the United States Military Air Transport Command getting ready to go and pick them up and, incidentally, the Russians who flew in Ghanaian contingents from Accra. We had a name for the operation [ONUC]; we had the beginnings of a logistical system; we had a commander. . . . Bunche, who was in Leopoldville anyway having quite a difficult time in one way or another, was made the temporary Commander of Operations until Von Horn could arrive from Jerusalem where he was Chief of Staff of UNTSO.[27]

Ultimately, not only did the UN deploy troops to provide security, retrain the Congolese army, and carry out police duties, the whole UN system became involved. Air controllers were supplied by the International Civil Aviation Organization (ICAO); the World Health Organization (WHO) provided doctors; and the UN International Children's Emergency Fund (UNICEF, now the UN Children's Fund) delivered emergency food supplies. Although the UN had not wanted to become embroiled in the civil war, it became impossible to remain impartial. Lumumba believed that the UN should support unification of the country against the Katangese secession, and when that was not forthcoming, he turned to the Soviets for assistance. In an attempt to deter all-out civil war, the UN shut down the airport so Soviet planes could not land. The Security Council continued to debate the matter but failed to reach any conclusion because of East-West differences. Utilizing the "Uniting for Peace" resolution yet another time, the General Assembly took up the issue in an emergency special session September 17–20, 1960.

Violence continued, with UN troops frequently under attack. In addition, Lumumba was kidnapped and on January 17, 1961, was taken to Katanga and assassinated under mysterious circumstances.[28] The Soviets blamed Hammarskjöld for the situation and demanded his resignation.[29] Nevertheless, Hammarskjöld flew to Leopoldville to try to reach a peaceful agreement on the Katangese secession and scheduled a meeting with Katanga's president, Moise Tshombe, outside the Congo at Ndola, Northern Rhodesia (now Zambia). Hammarskjöld, who had given so much to the UN, was tragically killed along with seven other staff members and the Swedish crew when his plane mysteriously crashed on the night of September 17, 1961, shortly before arriving at the Ndola airport.[30] Some suspected sabotage, but so far reports have been inconclusive.

U Thant of Burma (now Myanmar), who had been a vice president of the General Assembly and ambassador of Burma to the UN, was named Secretary-General to replace Hammarskjöld. Conflict continued with Katangese forces, primarily made up of Belgian mercenaries. Finally, due to the ongoing conflagration, the Security Council met in November 1961 and passed resolution 169, which authorized the Secretary-General and UN troops to use force to end the secession. This was a landmark decision by the Council. The principles of having a cease-fire in place, consent of the parties, impartiality, and a policy of firing only in self-defense were now out the window. The policy of only firing in self-defense only encouraged Tshombe and his mercenary army to run circles around the ONUC. The UN finally went on the offensive, and by January 4, 1963, UN troops had secured the Katangese capital of Elizabethville and other key points. With the civil war ended, the UN was able to draw down its troops and authorized a reduced force of 3,000 to stay on through the first half of 1964 to complete the transition.[31]

The crisis in the Congo threw the UN into its own parallel crises. Some 250 UN soldiers had been killed; a revered Secretary-General had died tragically trying to resolve the conflict, and some US$500 million had been poured into the operation (US$120 million a year) at a time when the entire UN regular budget was only about US$75 million annually. The UN was also caught up in the tensions of the Cold War, with the Soviet condemnation of Hammarskjöld and claims that the UN was siding with the West. For years, the Soviets refused to pay their share of the costs of the Congo operation. In addition, the French, who also withheld their dues on the Congo, had sided with Belgian interests in the mineral-rich Katanga region. The UN General Assembly ultimately requested an advisory opinion of the International Court of Justice as to whether peacekeeping dues were mandatory. "On July 20, 1962, the Court affirmed that peacekeeping costs were legitimate 'expenses of the Organization' to be borne by the members as apportioned by the General Assembly."[32] Severely burned by the Congo, the UN did not fund another armed peacekeeping operation for ten years and kept peacekeeping missions at the level of observers.

From the Congo Crisis to the End of the Cold War

Still licking its wounds following the Congo-invoked institutional crisis, the UN took on a more cautious profile with two exceptions: Cyprus and Lebanon. The major powers on the Security Council, especially the United States, considered these two situations too important to let them fester and threaten further destabilization to the bipolar status quo. In Cyprus (1964 to present), tensions broke out between Greek and Turkish Cypriots throughout the island. The mission of the United Nations

Peacekeeping Force in Cyprus (UNFICYP) was primarily to reduce tensions between the two communities, but in 1974, when Turkey invaded from the north to protect its Turkish compatriots from escalating events, the mission took a new direction. The conflict between the two communal groups appeared irreconcilable, and Turks from the south of the island were encouraged to move north and vice versa. The UN then established a buffer zone, dividing the north from the south that cut through the capital city of Nicosia. Since 1974, UN troops have patrolled the cease-fire buffer zone successfully with no return to violence.[33] The UN has continued to offer its good offices to mediate the dispute, and several Secretaries-General from Kofi Annan, Ban Ki-moon, and now António Guterres have offered comprehensive plans to resolve the impasse, but the island remains divided today.

UN missions to Lebanon took place in two phases. The first, the UN Observer Group in Lebanon, was a small observer mission undertaken in May 1958 launched shortly after the Suez crisis. The Lebanese government requested the operation due to a threat from Syria to destabilize the country. The UN observers were able to deter illegal arms from coming across the border and established a calm enough environment so that peaceful elections of a new president could take place. A UN withdrawal plan was in place by October 1958 and completed by December 9.[34]

The second UN operation in Lebanon, the UN Interim Force in Lebanon (UNIFIL) began in 1978 and, with several changing mandates, remains in place today. A new wave of refugees had washed into Lebanon after the Palestine Liberation Organization (PLO) had been tossed out of Jordan in 1970, following Black September when the PLO had hijacked several passenger airliners and held them at the airport in Amman. By 1978, heavily armed PLO forces had control over most of southern Lebanon. Armed by Syria, Libya, Iraq, and Egypt, the PLO used its bases in Lebanon to attack Israel along its northern border.[35] In 1978, the PLO launched an attack in an area near Tel Aviv, and the Israelis retaliated by sending troops into Lebanon, occupying the country south of the Litani River and destroying villages and homes.[36] Lebanese ambassador to the United Nations, Ghassan Tueni, protested to the Security Council, saying that Lebanon was not responsible for the PLO bases and had no connection with the commando operations. By March 19, 1978, the Council had quickly passed resolution 425, calling for the withdrawal of Israeli forces and the establishment of a UN interim force for the purpose of confirming the withdrawal of Israeli troops, which was completed by June 1978.[37]

The United States, with President Jimmy Carter personally in the lead, was deeply embroiled in peace negotiations between the Egyptians and the Israelis at the time and did not want the embarrassment of an Israeli invasion on another border to threaten the Camp David process. The United States wanted the issue off the international agenda as soon as possible, and others on the Council were willing to go along. Ambassador Tueni achieved his resolution, which called for restoring peace and removing Israeli troops, effectively a win-win victory.[38]

Nevertheless, the PLO and some forty other guerrilla groups remained in Lebanon, and Israel invaded again in 1982 to stop these new attacks. Eventually, the international community forced the PLO out of Lebanon, and it moved its headquarters to Tunisia. While UNIFIL has been able to patrol the border area, Hezbollah and other groups replaced the PLO. In 2006, following Hezbollah attacks from across the border, Israel once again retaliated by targeting Hezbollah strongholds within Lebanon. At first, the international community and the Security Council were slow to respond, seeing Israel's response as self-defense. But when Israel started using cluster bombs, causing the deaths of innocent civilians, the UN stepped in. UN Secretary-General Annan took on the task of mediating a peaceful solution to the conflict, which was later endorsed by the Security Council.[39]

Thawing of the Cold War: Complexities, Successes, and Failures

The demise of the Cold War, which formally took place in the final days of December 1991 when the Soviet Union collapsed, brought with it an opening in what had been a divided East versus West world, with Communist and Western spheres of influence jostling for power. Hints of this détente emerged in the mid-1980s with the rise of Mikhail Gorbachev as leader of the Soviet Union. The UN, which had been to a great extent frozen out of playing an intermediary role by Cold War vetoes in the Security Council, was now about to enter center stage. The Council met for the first time at the level of heads of state in January 1992 and a new-world-order euphoria filled the chamber. On the one hand, conflicts that had festered during the Cold War as proxy wars—each side supplied with unending weaponry by one or the other superpower—were now ripe for resolution, as the West and East no longer had to fight over carving up the world. On the other hand, regions where dictators backed by a superpower had maintained total control over any form of opposition began to break apart. The UN Security Council, with its five permanent members, was now eager to take action. But the success or failure of a UN operation depends on whether the parties to the conflict believe there is more to be gained through a peaceful, negotiated settlement; if not, they may decide to prolong the fight with the hope of winning, thus thwarting any attempts at a peaceful resolution. The world saw this play out in El Salvador and in Mozambique, where the parties who were tired of years of fighting through proxy wars became ready for a mediated peace. Whereas, in Somalia and the former Yugoslavia, competing national identities and clan loyalties drove these conflicts deep into a dark and violent abyss.

The other dramatic shift was that conflicts were no longer between states but emerged as intrastate civil wars, affecting not only a single nation but regional neighbors as well. The UN was asked to address all these new challenges, some resulting in success, others in failure, but forcing the organization to find new ways to adapt. For the most part, buffer zones to keep the parties separated were replaced by multidimensional peace operations. Now able to promote democratization, UN peacekeepers were called on to provide security for transitional processes that included voter registration, elections, new constitutions, humanitarian assistance, and police and judicial reform. The former ad hoc manner in which peace operations were constituted was no longer feasible. Therefore, in 1992 following the collapse of the Soviet Union and under the leadership of Secretary-General Boutros-Ghali, the Department of Peacekeeping Operations (DPKO) was first created to handle these new challenges. Where conflicts were ripe for resolution, the UN was able to maintain consent of the parties, remain impartial, uphold a cease-fire, and retain a policy of firing only in self-defense. As Hammarskjöld had envisioned, adhering to these principles would ensure greater success. However, in regions where new conflicts were erupting and nations were breaking apart, there was no peace to keep, no consent, and no cease-fire, yet the UN was tossed into these vexing quagmires by member states who optimistically envisioned success. In these cases, renewed turmoil began to resemble the Congo crisis of the 1960s. As an example, the creation of the UN Assistance Mission for Rwanda (UNIMIR) in 1993 as a traditional Chapter VI peacekeeping operation turned out to be totally inadequate when the violent genocide broke out a few months later.

Along with these complexities, the number of peace operations grew dramatically. During the forty-year period from 1948 when

UNTSO was dispatched to the Middle East to January 1988 as the Cold War was winding down, the UN had deployed thirteen UN peacekeeping operations. In contrast, by 2022 the UN had undertaken a total of seventy-one operations, which means that fifty-eight have been instituted in the last twenty-four years. Over 4,000 UN peacekeepers have died since peacekeeping began.[40] When DPKO was first formed in 1992, there were about thirty staff members, all fitting around a single conference table. As demands proliferated, the department had to increase the numbers of desk officers and support staff, adding hundreds of new personnel. Under Secretary-General Ban, DPKO split off the logistics and procurement work to create a new department: the Department of Field Support.

Additional adjustments and adaptations have been added under current Secretary-General Guterres. The new department is more accurately named the Department of Peace Operations (DPO), reflecting the reality that there is often no peace to keep. Political affairs, which had been under the Department of Political Affairs, is now handled by the Department of Political and Peacebuilding Affairs (DPPA). Each newly named department is led by an under-secretary-general. The other new innovation is that DPO and DPPA now share information and reporting in a joint unit, instead of duplicating these efforts between the two departments. The new information-gathering body is divided into regions, each headed by an assistant secretary-general. The regions include the Middle East, Asia, and the Pacific with two subdivisions (Middle East and Asia Pacific); Africa with five subdivisions (African Union Partnerships, Western Africa, Central and Southern Africa, Northern Africa, and Eastern Africa); and Europe, Central Asia, and the Americas with two subdivisions (Europe and Central Asia, and the Americas). The unit also has a director for coordination and shared services.[41]

Early Successes at the End of the Cold War

Some key successes following the end of the Cold War set the tone within the Security Council and the member states that the United Nations could achieve peaceful solutions to old, long-term conflicts. I include a few samples of how UN peacekeeping operations began to establish some of the initial tools the UN would carry forward into future operations as it learned on the job. Here I briefly describe Namibia and El Salvador as important examples, but others include Cambodia, Mozambique, and East Timor, to name a few.

Namibia

The independence of Namibia from South Africa in 1989–1990 is often cited as a UN success story. Namibia, called South West Africa before its independence, had been a colony, beginning in 1884, of Germany, known for its brutal rule and the genocide perpetrated against the Herrero and Nama peoples. During World War I, as Germany was on the brink of defeat, the British occupied the territory, and when the League of Nations was created at the end of the war, South West Africa was established as a mandate to be administered by South Africa and prepared for independence. However, South Africa refused to fulfill its obligations and incorporated the territory into its control. A few years after the United Nations was created, by 1949, it began the frustrating struggle of demanding Namibia's independence, twice unsuccessfully taking the issue to the International Court of Justice. The apartheid system imposed in South Africa also became a part of South Africa's rule in Namibia, something the General Assembly abhorred. Fed up, ultimately, the UN established the Council for Namibia that continued to pressure South Africa, bring representatives of Namibia as observers to the UN General Assembly, and set up a school in Arusha, Zambia, to train selected Namibians to run the country and be ready for independence when it arrived.[42]

In 1989, four decades after the UN's initial call for Namibia's independence, the UN Transition Assistance Group for Namibia (UNTAG) was implemented under Security Council resolution 435 to oversee free and fair elections, assist in writing a new constitution, and guarantee the rights of all the people of Namibia. Coming at the same time as the fall of the Berlin Wall, cooperation on the Security Council was a clear side effect of the thaw between the East and West. The UN had the consent of the South African leadership, but on the ground the white South Africans who had tightly controlled the indigenous population resisted the transition, and the UN was challenged on all fronts. UNTAG Special Representative Martti Ahtisaari (Finland) and the Deputy Joseph Legwaila (Botswana) had to make frequent trips to Pretoria to speak with President F. W. de Klerk and his staff and have them pressure those still running Namibia to cooperate with the UN mission. The UN oversaw security and the registration of voters, the protection of political parties, and the vote count in order to declare the election free and fair. On November 14, 1989, the counting of ballots was completed, and the Namibian peoples movement turned political party South West Africa People's Organisation had won about 57 percent of the seats in the newly created constituent assembly charged with writing the new constitution.

Approving the constitution required a two-thirds vote, so the smaller parties were satisfied that they would have input in the final document.[43] UNTAG Deputy Special Representative Legwaila stated: "To tell you the truth, I think UNTAG was a trailblazer for United Nations peacekeeping and peacemaking."[44]

El Salvador

The UN Observer Mission in El Salvador built upon the multidimensional activities begun in Namibia, going beyond the monitoring of a buffer zone—such as what separated the parties in UNEF I and II—to mediate a cease-fire and work within the country to create a fair system of governance. The UN began a mediation process, creating a dialogue between the Salvadoran government and the rebel movement, the Farabundo Martí National Liberation Front (FMLN), at the end of 1989. A preliminary agreement was reached in Geneva on April 4, 1990, followed in May by the Caracas Agreement, which established an agenda of items for negotiation.[45]

A civil war had ravaged the country for over twelve years, killing some 75,000 people with one million displaced. A classic proxy war, the United States supported the government, while the Soviet Union through Cuba and Nicaragua supplied the FMLN with weapons and financial backing. In November 1989, the FMLN had launched the largest attack of its campaign, again at about the same time as the fall of the Berlin Wall, hoping to take the capital San Salvador and prove that it was strong enough on its own even if the USSR were to withdraw its support. It succeeded in capturing much of the capital, but failed to inspire the uprising it had expected. Nevertheless, the government had to accept that it could not end the war through military force. With a clear military stalemate, both sides decided independently to request the UN to intervene, and UN Secretary-General Pérez de Cuéllar appointed his political advisor Alvaro de Soto to mediate a solution.

El Salvador is a key operation to study because of all the "firsts" that were established within the agreement ushered through by de Soto. At a critical moment when the parties were deadlocked on even where to begin, de Soto introduced the concept of human rights. Both sides had been complaining about human rights violations, and de Soto had found the key to reopening the dialogue. This would be the first time the UN would establish a human rights verification component within a peace operation, and the UN deployed human rights monitors even before the parties had a cease-fire in place. The peace plan was complex and multidimensional in several ways. It included converting the FMLN into a political party that could propose candidates for election to the National Assembly. The plan also included reform of the military and government security forces that had been used as death squads. Another first was the creation of a civilian police force that would be trained by a UN-supervised police academy. Electoral assistance, reform of the justice system, and the first demobilization, disarmament, and reintegration (DDR) program was introduced where both government and FMLN troops demobilized in camps set up by the UN, disarmed and turned in their weapons to the UN, and were then given a small package to enable these former fighters to reintegrate into civil society. The UN also established the National Commission for the Consolidation of Peace, which was made up of representatives of both sides and chaired by the UN and was successful in hearing complaints and finding solutions before they escalated into conflict.[46] Another first in a UN peace operation was the formation of a truth commission to examine past human rights violations and list the perpetrators, revealing the truth and bringing an end to unanswered questions. All of these innovations have become normal aspects of UN peace operations going forward.

Recent Successes

Although it is beyond the limitations of this chapter to discuss all fifty-eight new peace operations, I will focus on a few examples.[47] There are many more successes than failures, and therefore I will start with those.

With lessons learned from both its successes and failures, the United Nations now recognizes that peacekeeping is a core activity of the organization. The UN began to accept that under certain circumstances peace operations had to be given Chapter VII mandates, enabling the use of force, which meant that at times the UN had to abandon impartiality when one party was violating the conditions of a peace agreement. The capacity of the UN also had to be increased and reformed to meet demands. At its height, the UN had some seventeen peace missions in the field at the same time, involving over 100,000 troops. As explained earlier in the chapter, Secretary-General Guterres has reformed the DPO to include a broader perspective of its work where there may be no peace to keep, and bringing about stability within a country may call for Chapter VII, political advisement, the protection of civilians, conflict resolution, and ongoing mediation.

Some recent successes demonstrate how much the UN has learned over the years. Examples are Sierra Leone, Liberia, Ivory Coast (Côte d'Ivoire), Kosovo, and East Timor.

Sierra Leone

The experience in Sierra Leone is worthy of analysis here due to its multidimensional complexity and because of the willingness of key member states to rescue the mission when it fell into crisis in May 2000. The UN operation in Sierra Leone (UNAMSIL) began in 1999 with Security Council resolution 1270. When war in Sierra Leone started, the rebels, the Revolutionary United Front (RUF), intended to overturn a government that profited from corruption, benefiting a few select groups and not distributing resources equitably. But those motives quickly deteriorated into greed and control over rich diamond areas in the eastern part of the country, reinforced by Charles Taylor, who exchanged the diamonds for weapons to support his own rebellion in neighboring Liberia. The RUF burned villages, raped women and girls, kidnapped children to become child soldiers, and amputated at first fingers, then hands and arms in an effort to prevent people from voting.[48]

However, UN troops arrived slowly, and by May 2000, the RUF took advantage of UNAMSIL's weak presence to return to its warring tactics and regain territory almost all the way to the capital of Freetown on the coast. Not wanting to repeat the horrific humanitarian crisis of Rwanda, the UN called on well-armed British troops to confront the RUF and force them to honor the peace agreement. The UN provided security during the transition, oversaw free and fair elections, established a truth and reconciliation commission, carried out DDR, assisted the return of child soldiers to their families, set up a UN radio station (Radio UNAMSIL) to provide accurate information to people, educated people on their human rights, and formed the Sierra Leone Special Court to hold those accountable who bore the greatest responsibility for war crimes and crimes against humanity during the conflict.[49] UNAMSIL successfully completed its mission in December 2005 and was replaced by a UN office to help consolidate peace. Other UN agencies and programs have stayed to provide broad assistance to Sierra Leone, and it was one of the first to receive ongoing support from the newly created Peacebuilding Commission.

Liberia

Getting off to a rocky start, the United Nations Mission in Liberia (UNMIL), established in September 2003 by Security Council resolution 1509, once again undertook a multidimensional role in order to implement a cease-fire and stabilize the country. Some 250,000 people had died with another 800,000 displaced during a civil war that had plagued Liberia for fourteen years. Taylor, the person most responsible for the violence, was forced to flee the country in 2003. While its neighbor, Sierra Leone, had been a British colony, historically Liberia had become the destination of many African Americans following the abolition of slavery at the end of the US civil war during the nineteenth century. With that history, the United States had an interest in guaranteeing the success of the new UN mission and had stationed over 14,000 troops off the coast of Liberia in the early months of the mission.[50] As Sierra Leone was stabilizing in 2003, several UN troops from Sierra Leone were quickly moved across the border into Liberia to jump-start the mission. The UN was tasked with multiple activities, including police and military reform, the delivery of humanitarian assistance, DDR of former combatants, protection of human rights, and ultimately the oversight of both parliamentary and presidential elections in 2005.[51] The UN established the first all-female police unit to encourage women to come forward to report sexual abuse and rape and to help protect their human rights. Ellen Johnson Sirleaf was elected president in 2005 and was later awarded the Nobel Peace Prize for her work to rebuild Liberia. In 2016, UNMIL transferred the security responsibilities to the Liberian government, and on March 30, 2018, was able to successfully complete its mandate.[52]

Ivory Coast (Côte d'Ivoire)

Once admired as an economically strong and stable nation following its independence in 1960 from French colonial rule, Côte d'Ivoire fell into disarray after the death of its founding president, Félix Houphouët-Boigny in 1993. As a result of a coup six years later, the country descended into a deadly armed conflict. The UN first became involved as a small monitoring mission, but in February 2004, the Security Council established the UN Operation in Côte d'Ivoire to facilitate the implementation of a peace agreement signed the previous year. The UN was to monitor presidential elections to take place in 2010 and declare them free and fair. However, the incumbent president, Laurent Gbagbo, refused to accept the election results and allow his competitor, Alassane Ouattara, to take office. With the French and under Chapter VII, the UN mission forcefully removed Gbagbo from office. Under the new President Ouattara, Gbagbo was arrested and delivered to the International Criminal Court (ICC) to stand trial for war crimes and crimes against humanity. The Operation in Côte d'Ivoire provided security during the transition and undertook the DDR of former combatants. With Côte d'Ivoire stabilized, the UN successfully completed its mission in 2017.[53] However, tensions could erupt again. Gbagbo was acquitted by the ICC in 2018 and released. He had been living in Belgium but returned to Côte d'Ivoire in June 2021.[54]

Kosovo and East Timor (Timor Leste)

Kosovo and East Timor have many aspects in common. Both were provinces that broke away from a larger country (Kosovo from Serbia and East Timor from Indonesia) and both began that transition in 1999. Violence and human rights atrocities had gone on for years against the local populations in each territory. Because the people had not been allowed to govern themselves in these cases, the UN had to step in and administer the newly independent nations and prepare them for self-governance. In both peace operations, the UN successfully handed over governance responsibilities to the people.

Kosovo emerged as a remnant of the dissolution of the former Yugoslavia. Serbia, which inherited the former Yugoslav army, was intent on retaining the province of Kosovo after experiencing the loss of its republics through violent conflict ultimately ended by the 1995 Dayton Accords. After reports of genocide in 1999 against the Kosovar Albanian people that made up some 90 percent of the population, NATO forces came in to end the genocide. A multinational force called Kosovo Force (KFOR) monitored security in the territory while the UN Mission in Kosovo (UNMIK) administered the governance system. By 2008, Kosovo, having achieved complete self-governance, declared itself independent. The International Court of Justice stated in an advisory opinion that Kosovo had the right to unilaterally declare its independence. However, Serbia backed by Russia has never recognized Kosovo's independence. Therefore, due to a Russian veto, Kosovo is not a member of the United Nations.

However, East Timor became an independent country and joined the UN as a member state in 2002, the difference being that Indonesia, under President B. J. Habibie, had allowed the residents of East Timor to vote on whether they would like to stay as a part of Indonesia or to become independent. The voters overwhelmingly voted for independence. Violence, backed by the Indonesian military, broke out immediately following the results. However, within a few weeks, the Security Council authorized under Chapter VII a peacekeeping force led by Australia that brought an end to the conflict. The UN stayed on to administer the country but its independence had already been decided.

Failures

Somalia

With the end of the Cold War, the dictator Said Barre, no longer supported by the West as a bulwark against the Communist threat and facing a newly emboldened opposition, fled the country, leaving a power vacuum as Somalia descended into clan warfare and anarchy. As warring clans forced people off their lands, people were no longer able to raise their own food, and a drought further complicated the situation. Images of starvation were viewed around the world through globalized media coverage, referred to as "the CNN factor." Some 200,000 Somalis had starved to death, and an additional 30,000 to 50,000 had died in fighting by March 1992.[55] The international community was calling for humanitarian intervention, but there were no legitimate leaders with whom to negotiate in order to garner consent, and the most powerful clan leader, Mohamed Farah Aideed, never offered his consent.[56]

Nevertheless, US President George H. W. Bush, after losing his bid for a second term in 1992, decided on humanitarian grounds to send American troops (the Unified Task Force, not a UN mission) to protect the delivery of food and humanitarian assistance, which they did successfully. The bulk of the troops, having completed their mission, left the country in May 1993 under the new US president Bill Clinton. A small contingent, US Rangers Delta Force, stayed on, intending to capture and defeat Aideed, whose followers were killing UN peacekeepers and thwarting the delivery of humanitarian assistance after the United States departed. But in October 1993, Delta Force carried out what turned out to be a fumbled, catastrophic mission, and eighteen US soldiers were killed. One was dragged naked through the streets of the capital, Mogadishu, by Aideed supporters, all caught on camera. Americans watched this on television over and over again in horror. Why were American soldiers being slaughtered in a far-off country like Somalia where there were no US interests? Clinton withdrew the US forces a few months later and worked to revise US policies on American involvement in humanitarian assistance in the midst of a civil war where there were no US interests.[57] After months of review, the memorandum termed Presidential Decision Directive 25 (PDD-25) was released on May 3, 1994.[58] The new policy that limited US involvement in civil wars was to have a devastating effect on the catastrophic events in Rwanda. UN efforts in Somalia with United Nations Operation in Somalia—UNOSOM I from April 1992 to March 1993 and UNOSOM II from March 1993 to May 1995—failed to halt the fighting. The Security Council, deciding that too many peacekeepers had lost their lives in a fruitless effort to bring stability when the parties to the conflict were not interested in a peaceful solution, pulled out of Somalia, cutting the UN's losses.

The African Union (AU), through the African Union Mission in Somalia (AMISOM), was authorized by the UN Security Council to provide security to the Somali government in January 2007 with some 20,600 troops. Having stabilized the government, with political assistance from the UN, AMISOM had planned to leave Somalia at the end of 2021 and transfer security responsibilities to the Somalia Security Forces prior to its exit, thus implementing UN Security Council resolution 2568 (2021).[59] However, the terrorist group al-Shabaab still provides a threat to stability, and therefore the AU, UN, and Somali government decided that on April 1, 2022, "AMISOM will be replaced by the AU Transition Mission in Somalia (ATMIS). The new mission will operate until the end of 2024, after which all responsibilities will be handed to the Somali Security Forces."

Rwanda

The failures in Somalia and the resulting Clinton PDD-25 policy are linked to the devastating genocide in Rwanda and the unwillingness of the UN Security Council to step in to halt the killing. "But with the Somalia debacle, enthusiasm to continue the wave of new, large, multi-dimensional peacekeeping operations quickly subsided."[60] The devastating events in Somalia that had unfolded in 1993 contributed to the humiliating failure of the UN to respond some six months later to the breakout of genocide in Rwanda in spring 1994. Conflict between the two ethnic groups, the Hutu and Tutsi, had gone on for decades; however, the long-negotiated, power-sharing Arusha Agreement had reached a successful conclusion, and the UN Security Council authorized UNIMIR on October 5, 1993, to oversee the accord. The agreement was intended to end the attacks by the Tutsis, led by the Rwanda Patriotic Front, who had lived in exile in camps over the border in Uganda.

UNIMIR, which deployed some 2,500 troops with Roméo Dallaire of Canada as the force commander, was under Chapter VI of the Charter, meaning no use of force. While the Arusha Agreement had the consent of Rwanda's Hutu president Juvénal Habyarimana, internal support was weak. Hutu militia groups such as the Interahamwe were against any power sharing with their Tutsi rivals and were planning a strategy to sabotage the accord. On January 11, 1994, a few months before the outbreak of genocide, Commander Dallaire sent a code cable to UN headquarters addressed to Maurice Baril, military advisor to Secretary-General Boutros-Ghali. Because these two men were unavailable at the time, the cable went to Kofi Annan, Under-Secretary-General for Peacekeeping. In the cable, Dallaire related to the UN that an informer had confided in him that a "cadre of Interahamwe-armed militia of MRND (the ruling Hutu political party)"[61] was planning to provoke a civil war, including attacks on Belgian peacekeepers to cause their departure from Rwanda. The informant also told Dallaire of a cache of weapons stored by the militias in preparation, and Dallaire states in his note that he plans to raid the armed cache. He ends the cable with "Allons-Y," in French meaning "Let's Go."[62] Annan replies to Dallaire that under the Chapter VI Security Council mandate, this action was not allowed. He further told the force commander to inform the Rwandan president and other key ambassadors in the capital of this information.[63] Some felt in retrospect that Annan had acted too cautiously, but it was this kind of raid by the Delta Force in Somalia that had led to the catastrophe just a few months before. Furthermore, under Boutros-Ghali, Annan would not have been allowed to take the issue to the Security Council. Boutros-Ghali only allowed himself and one advisor to meet with the Council.

The Interahamwe launched their strategy on April 6, 1994, shooting down the president's aircraft on its return from peace talks, thus assassinating President Habyarimana. From there they killed Belgian UN troops, as planned, and moved on, using hate radio to mobilize others to kill nearly one million Tutsis and moderate Hutus within 100 days. Dallaire immediately requested assistance, but instead Belgian troops were withdrawn and the UN force was reduced from the original 2,500 to just 270. The UN Security Council ignored pleas for help, claiming that they could not intervene in another civil war. They would not even use the word *genocide*, even though the international press displayed headlines reporting on the Rwandan genocide. Dallaire has claimed that if the Security Council had sent him even 5,000 well-trained troops, he could have ended the violence.[64] In his book on Rwanda, Dallaire clearly states: "If UNIMIR had received the modest increase of troops and capabilities we requested in the first week, could we have stopped the killings? Yes, absolutely."[65]

Bosnia

The United Nations is only capable of implementing what the member states are willing to do. The UN does not have an army or resources of its own and is therefore completely dependent on the will of its members. Lack of will and consensus of purpose, particularly within the Security Council, were clearly illustrated in the case of Rwanda and soon thereafter again in Bosnia. Mats Berdal explains: "The confused, hesitant, and reactive nature of the international community's response to the disintegration of Yugoslavia provides the essential backdrop against which the history of United Nations operations in the Balkans" unfolded.[66] The breakup of Yugoslavia following the end of the Cold War resulted in major conflicts between its regions: first Serbia and Croatia and then progressing into Bosnia and Herzegovina. The UN Protection Force, mandated under Chapter VI—no use of force—to deliver humanitarian aid in the midst of war, was unable to prevent the ongoing violence.

The whole history is complex and beyond the limitations of this chapter, but the failure to protect the safe areas is clearly the greatest failure of the operation. In an attempt to respond to calls for action, the Security Council decided to create seven "safe areas." The Secretariat recommended a force of some 35,000 troops to protect the seven areas, but the Council authorized in resolution 836 only 7,500 and then only delivered about 3,700 soldiers.[67] Underequipped and under-forced, UN troops were easily overrun in the summer of 1995 by Serb fighters who called their bluff. By July, in one of the safe areas, Srebrenica, some 8,000 Bosnian Muslims were slaughtered within a few days, and in the same month the Bosnian Serb army took control of the Zepa safe area and attacked Goradze and Sarajevo. UN peacekeepers were also taken hostage during the conflict. The Dutch battalion responsible for protecting Srebrenica was too small and too weak to resist the Serb attack and could only stand by and watch as innocent civilians were raped, tortured, and murdered. A Dutch parliamentary inquiry was so scathing that that entire government was forced to resign. The signing of the Dayton Accords in November 1995 orchestrated by President Clinton brought an end to the fighting, but only after thousands had lost their lives.

Current and Ongoing UN Peace Operations

There are twelve current and ongoing UN peace operations, some of which this chapter has already discussed. These include the following (abbreviations are defined in the List of Acronyms section at end of book): MINURSO in Western Sahara; MINUSCA in Central African Republic; MINUSMA in Mali; MONUSCO in the Democratic Republic of Congo; UNDOF in Golan Heights; UNFICYP in Cyprus; UNIFIL in Lebanon; UNISFA in Abyei Sudan/South Sudan border area; UNMIK in Kosovo; UNMISS in South Sudan; UNMOGIP on the Pakistan/India border in Jammu and Kashmir; and UNTSO in the Middle East. While there are a number of UN political missions, such as in Colombia, those are not covered here. I will describe three of the larger peacekeeping missions and one, Western Sahara, that still follows the traditional type of peacekeeping by monitoring a buffer zone.

Western Sahara

The territory of Western Sahara had been a colony of Spain, but in 1975, after the death of Spain's dictator, Francisco Franco, the territory was given its independence. However, shortly thereafter, Morocco to the north and Mauritania to the east invaded and occupied the area. In what was called the "Green March," some 150,000 Moroccans were sent across the border in the name of Islam. Intense fighting broke out when the people of Western Sahara, represented by the Polisario Front, resisted this invasion. In 1979, Mauritania signed a peace agreement with the Polisario and withdrew from the territory. In 1991, the UN brokered a cease-fire and by 1992 established United Nations Mission for the Referendum in Western Sahara (MINURSO) headquartered in Western Sahara.

The agreement included a UN-led referendum that would allow the people of Western Sahara, the Sahrawi people, to vote on whether to become completely independent or be considered an autonomous region of Morocco. The stumbling block to holding the referendum has been determining who is eligible to vote. MINURSO has worked diligently to compile a list of eligible voters, but that comprehensive database has undergone constant dispute, primarily by Morocco who wants to include many Moroccans instead of keeping the list strictly to the Sahrawi people. Nevertheless, during this time, the UN-monitored cease-fire has held, substantially due to the 1,500 kilometer sand berm riddled with landmines built by Morocco as a buffer zone to keep the Polisario at bay. Several UN Secretaries-General have tried unsuccessfully to mediate a solution.[68] After decades of continued stalemate, in November 2020, the Polisario Front declared an end to the cease-fire, which portends a return to fighting.[69]

Democratic Republic of Congo

The UN operation in the Democratic Republic of Congo (DRC), MINUSCO, was established in July 2010 to replace an earlier mission MONUC (UN Organization Mission in Democratic Republic of the Congo). Fighting had broken out in 1994 after the genocide in Rwanda when refugees flocked into eastern Congo to flee the slaughter, destabilizing the ruling authority in what was then called Zaire. Seven African countries who had entered the fighting in the DRC negotiated a peace agreement in Lusaka, Zambia, but the agreement failed to stop the conflict. In November 1999, the UN Security Council established MONUC to bring peace and monitor the Lusaka agreement.[70] Although some stability had returned to the country by 2010, the UN stayed on, replacing MONUC with MINUSCO, mandated to protect civilians and consolidate the peace. More accurately, MONUC was renamed MINUSCO, in great part as a concession to the DRC authorities who wanted the mission to depart or at least to start withdrawing because they viewed continued presence as a stain on the country that did not reflect the evolution on the ground from a tense conflict to some level of peace and stability by 2010. Nevertheless, militia forces continued to wreak havoc in eastern Congo, gaining control of rich mineral deposits, attacking villages, and carrying out humanitarian atrocities. African countries requested the UN Security Council in 2013 to authorize the Intervention Brigade, made up of all African troops, to bring an end to this violence. This request was prompted by the takeover of key cities, including Goma, by an armed group supported by neighboring Rwanda, the M23. While the actions of other armed groups had not launched such a reaction, the attacks by the M23 invoked memories of the previous Congo conflagrations and the risk of a major regional conflict. Authorized under Chapter VII, the Intervention Brigade deployed in 2014 and in a few weeks defeated the militias.

MINUSCO is currently composed of 17,783 personnel, which includes UN troops, police, staff, and other civilians. As of July 2022, the top troop contributors were Pakistan with 1,928 soldiers, India with 1,834, and Bangladesh with 1,599.[71] There have been 230 deaths suffered by the UN in the DRC.[72] The UN had been involved in the Congo in the early 1960s, as described earlier in this chapter. It is a very large country strategically located in the center of the African continent; therefore, containing the conflict from spreading throughout the region has continued to be a priority of the United Nations.

Mali

The UN Multidimensional Integrated Stabilization Mission in Mali (MINUSMA), established in 2013 and reinforced by the Security Council in 2014, was given the mandate to support the political process and the transition in Mali to stabilize the country. The Council further decided the peace operation should ensure security, protect civilians, support a national dialogue and reconciliation, reestablish state authority, rebuild the security sector, and protect human rights. France, the former colonial power in Mali, entered the process authorized by the Council under Chapter VII to use force, addressing the rebel uprising particularly in the north. The Economic Community of West African States (ECOWAS) has also supported the UN efforts there.

Adding to the complexity, MINUSMA has been deployed in an area of active terrorism. Counterterrorism operations led by France and the G5 Sahel countries, something unique for UN peacekeeping, have worked together to address the problem of terrorist groups. There is also the divide among members of the Security Council on what the mission should take on. Some argue in favor of a more robust mission, whereas others defend a more traditional force.[73] Unfortunately, instability continues to define the situation in Mali. Despite the presence of UN peacekeepers, a number of coups have taken place within twelve months, and fighting has been perpetual. The total number of UN personnel in Mali, which include troops, police, staff, and civilians is 17,609, of which 1,722 are police. The top troop-contributing countries are Bangladesh, France, and Chad. A record number of deaths, 275 since its inception, marked the tenuous environment in the country as of July 2022.[74]

Central African Republic

The UN peace operation in the Central African Republic (CAR)—UN Multidimensional Integrated Stabilization Mission in the CAR (MINUSCA)—was established in 2014 with a mandate to protect civilians and support the governmental transition process. The protection of civilians is the mission's highest priority. MINUSCA replaced the African-led mission, which transferred its authority to the UN operation on September 15, 2014. Violence in CAR first erupted in 2012. The brutal conflict has affected all aspects of society—including closing schools and weakening the healthcare system. Some 57 percent of the population are food insecure in an increasingly volatile security environment as reported in September 2021.[75]

The Security Council, with its internal divisions and major power politics, also has an effect in CAR. Russia and France have been clashing within the Council as Russia became a close ally of the authorities in Bangui, the capital, and France lost influence. On the ground, France as the former colonial power, was considered to have the upper hand. However, its loss of influence has complicated France's relations with the local leaders. A similar Council dynamics may play out in Mali as Russia could be sending soldiers there as well.[76] The total number of UN personnel deployed in CAR as of July 2022 is 15,663, including troops, police, staff, and civilians. The top three contributing countries are Rwanda with 1,360, Bangladesh with 1,283, and Pakistan with 1,212. The high number of UN deaths reached 160 by 2022, and the spread of violence and humanitarian suffering continues to challenge the mission.[77]

Concluding Thoughts

This chapter has described the evolving progress in deploying peace operations in crisis situations, examining this history from the League of Nations, through the early years of the United Nations, and finally in current peace operations. UN involvement has grown from creating traditional peacekeeping that monitored buffer zones between warring parties to the multidimensional, complex peace operations deployed today. Member states understood the UN had to address the root causes of instability to prevent a return to conflict. Therefore, the Peacebuilding Commission was created in 2005 to provide funding and support to countries emerging from crises. The Peacebuilding Fund has provided some US$1.47 billion to 24 countries, which includes support for recovery efforts amid the Covid-19 pandemic.[78]

In 2022, the UN had deployed more than 87,000 peacekeeping personnel in twelve missions in four regions: Africa, the Middle East, Europe, and Asia. There are some 121 countries that contribute personnel to peace operations, many from the developing world. The UN pays these countries US$1,428 per soldier each month. Then the country pays their troops according to their military standards. The UN recognizes that peace operations are a core activity of the organization, a change from the early ad hoc reaction to crises before the end of the Cold War. The UN also realized that it must work with partners in the field in hybrid missions, including the African Union, ECOWAS, and the EU, to name a few. The challenges are enormous, but allowing violence to spread uncontained is clearly a threat to international peace and security, and the UN Security Council as well as the General Assembly have an obligation to do what they can to protect peace and security in the world.

Notes

1. United Nations, "Global Peacekeeping Data," July 9, 2022, http://peacekeeping .un.org/en/data.

2. For an examination of peace operations conducted by the League of Nations and the early days of the UN, see James, *The Politics of Peacekeeping*.

3. Ratner, *The New UN Peacekeeping*; see chapter 4, "Fits and Starts: The League's and UN's Early Efforts at the New Peacekeeping," pp. 89–116.

4. Ibid.

5. Ibid., p. 95.

6. Ibid., p. 97.

7. Birgisson, "United Nations Special Committee on the Balkans," pp. 77–83.

8. Brian Urquhart, Yale-UN Oral History interview, October 15, 1984, p. 17. The Yale-UN Oral History collection is housed in the UN Dag Hammarskjöld Library, New York, and the Yale University Archives and Manuscripts Library, New Haven, CT.

9. Ibid.

10. Brian Urquhart, Yale-UN Oral History interview, July 20, 1984, p. 6.

11. Urquhart, interview, October 15, 1984, p. 17.

12. Urquhart, interview, July 20, 1984, p. 9.

13. Ibid.

14. Ibid., p. 10.

15. Brian Urquhart, interview by Jean E. Krasno, January 21, 2003, at UN head-quarters, New York. Yale-UN Oral History interviews.

16. *Blue Helmets*, pp. 42–43.

17. Urquhart, interview, July 20, 1984, p. 13.

18. Brian Urquhart, Yale-UN Oral History interview, June 27, 1984, p. 9.

19. Mona Ghali, "United Nations Emergency Force I" and "United Nations Emergency Force II," in Durch, *Evolution of UN Peacekeeping*.

20. The Belgian Congo after independence in 1960 was named Congo, then was renamed Zaire in later years, and is now called the Democratic Republic of Congo (DRC).

21. Ralph Bunche, confidential letter written to Dag Hammarskjöld, June 27, 1969, UN Archives Library, S-216-1-2, RJB-trip to Congo, Bunche's letter/report to S-G, June 27–July 4, 1960.

22. Higgins, *United Nations Peacekeeping, 1946–67*, p. 12.

23. Ibid., p. 395.

24. Brian Urquhart, Yale-UN Oral History interview, October 19, 1984, p. 3.

25. Ibid. p. 2.

26. *Blue Helmets*, p. 177.

27. Urquhart, interview, October 19, 1984, p. 5.

28. *Blue Helmets*, p. 184.

29. Durch, "The UN Operation in the Congo," in Durch, *Evolution of UN Peacekeeping*, pp. 323–324.

30. *Blue Helmets*, p. 192.

31. Ibid., pp. 194–195

32. Ghali, "United Nations Emergency Force I: 1956–1967, in Durch, *Evolution of UN Peacekeeping,* p. 114.

33. Birgisson, "United Nations Peacekeeping Force in Cyprus," in Durch, *Evolution of UN Peacekeeping,* pp. 219–236.

34. Mona Ghali, "United Nations Observer Group in Lebanon: 1958," in Durch, *Evolution of UN Peacekeeping,* pp. 163–164.

35. Ghassan Tueni, Yale-UN Oral History interview, Beirut, Lebanon, March 17–18, 1998.

36. Ibid.

37. Ibid.

38. Ibid.

39. Daily Press Briefing by the office of the Spokesman for the Secretary-General, August 16, 2006, Middle East trip, in Krasno, *Collected Papers of Kofi Annan,* pp. 4153–4154.

40. "Honouring the Fallen," August 18, 2021, news.un.org/en/story/2021/08 /1098072, and "Global Peacekeeping Data," August 29, 2021, https://peacekeeping .un.org/en/data. As of Februrary 28, 2022, 4,183 UN peacekeepers had been killed.

41. DPPA-DPO Information Management Unit, found at "UN Reform: Two New Departments for the Peace and Security Pillar," August 23, 2018, www.un.it /news/un-reform-two-new-departments-peace-and-security-pillar.

42. Hage Geingob, Yale-UN Oral History interview by Jean E. Krasno, March 10, 1999, Windhoek, Namibia, p. 14.

43. For a more complete description of the struggle for Namibia's independence, see Krasno, "Namibian Independence," in Shapiro and Lampert, *Charter of the United Nations,* pp. 174–192.

44. Joseph Legwaila (ambassador to the UN from Botswana), Yale-UN Oral History interview by Jean E. Krasno, May 11, 1999, New York, p. 17.

45. Johnstone, *Rights and Reconciliation,* p. 18.

46. Ibid., p. 14.

47. For a complete list and brief summaries of all UN peace operations, see the homepage of the Department of Peace Operations under historical timelines, https:// peacekeeping.un.org/en/historical-timeline-of-un-peacekeeping.

48. *Sierra Leone: Rebuilding a Torn Society,* documentary film directed and edited by Jean E. Krasno, filmed in Sierra Leone and released in 2004. Available on YouTube: "Sierra Leone Chapter 1," https://youtu.be/r_7Aanmt2Fo, and "Sierra Leone Chapter 2," https://youtu.be/XrFIiCWMH3A.

49. Ibid.

50. Howard, *UN Peacekeeping in Civil Wars,* p. 312.

51. Ibid.

52. "UNMIL Fact Sheet: United Nations Mission in Liberia; Headquarters, Monrovia," UN Peacekeeping, September 4, 2021, https://peacekeeping.un.org/en /mission/unmil.

53. "ONUCI Fact Sheet: United Nations Operation in Côte d'Ivoire, Duration: 2000–2017," UN Peacekeeping, September 4, 2021, https://peacekeeping.un.org/en /mission/onuci.

54. "Ivory Coast's Ex-President Gbagbo Returns Home After ICC Acquittal," BBC News, June 17, 2021, www.bbc.com/news/world-africa-57471468.

55. Howard, *UN Peacekeeping in Civil Wars,* p. 23.

56. Ibid., pp. 22–23.

57. Durch, *UN Peacekeeping, American Policy,* pp. 347–348.

58. Clinton Presidential Decision Directive PDD-25, May 3, 1994, Clinton Digital Library, https://Clinton.presidentiallibraries.us/items/show/12749.

59. "AMISOM Military Commanders Meet to Plan on Speeding up Operations," Africanews, August 28, 2021, www.africanews.com/2021/08/28/amisom-military-commanders-meet.

60. Howard, *UN Peacekeeping in Civil Wars,* p. 29.

61. Annan, *Interventions,* pp. 16–17.

62. Ibid., p. 17.

63. Ibid.

64. Ken Shiffman, "Scream Bloody Murder: As Genocide Raged, General's Pleas for Help Ignored," CNN, 2008, https://www.cnn.com/2008/WORLD/africa/11/13/sbm.dallaire.profile/.

65. Dallaire, *Shake Hands with the Devil,* p. 514.

66. Berdal, "The United Nations in Bosnia," p. 3.

67. Howard, *UN Peacekeeping in Civil Wars,* p. 46.

68. William Lacy Swing (Special Representative of the Secretary-General for MINURSO), interview by Jean E. Krasno, November 12, 2003, in New York.

69. Houda Chograni, "The Polisario Front, Morocco, and the Western Sahara Conflict," Arab Center, Washington, DC, June 22, 2021, https://arabcenterdc.org/resources/the-polisario-front-morocco-and-the-western-sahara-conflict.

70. "DR Congo: Chronology," Human Rights Watch, August 21, 2009, https://www.hrw.org/news/2009/08/21/dr-congo-chronology.

71. "MONUSCO Fact Sheet: United Nations Organization Stabilization Mission in the Democratic Republic of the Congo, July 2010," UN Peacekeeping, July 2022, https://peacekeeping.un.org/en/mission/monusco.

72. Ibid.

73. Interview with a member of the UN Secretariat who covers African peace operations, September 17, 2021.

74. "MINUSMA Fact Sheet: United Nations Multidimensional Integrated Stabilization Mission in Mali, April 2013 to Present," UN Peacekeeping, July 9, 2022, https://peacekeeping.un.org/en/mission/minusma.

75. United Nations Office for the Coordination of Humanitarian Assistance (OCHA), "Central African Republic Situation Report," September 3, 2021, https://reports.unocha.org/en/country/car.

76. Interview with a member of the UN Secretariat who covers African peace operations, September 17, 2021.

77. "MINUSCA Fact Sheet: United Nations Multidimensional Integrated Stabilization Mission in the Central African Republic, April 2014," UN Peacekeeping, https://peacekeeping.un.org/en/mission/minusca.

78. Data compiled from United Nations Peacebuilding Commission website, September 5, 2021, https://www.un.org/peacebuilding.

7

Democratization and Electoral Assistance

Massimo Tommasoli and
Therese Pearce Laanela

As with the topics discussed in other chapters, internal dynamics and global trends have shaped the UN's involvement in democracy building and electoral assistance, cutting across its pillars of human rights, peace and security, and sustainable development. Whether framed as self-determination, civil-rights protection, or political participation, UN engagement has shaped the way elections are seen and conducted globally. From initially being part of its decolonization work, UN electoral assistance has in recent decades moved from the centerpiece of high-visibility peacebuilding operations to an under-the-radar yet meaningful piece of broader global agendas, like the SDGs.[1]

In this chapter, we explain how and why the UN engages in electoral processes, where electoral assistance fits in a broader narrative about democracy and multilateralism, and how global shifts in the democratization trajectory bring new challenges to the policies and practices of the UN's work. The chapter explores the considerable potential and occasional drawbacks of the UN system—including its membership—to deal with democratic erosion and threats to the integrity of electoral processes.

Trajectory of UN Involvement in Democratization and Electoral Assistance

That electoral assistance would become a central part of the UN's portfolio of work was not a matter of careful consideration but rather the result of interplay between unfolding global events, an evolving interpretation of UN mandates, and the UN capacity and ambition to deliver.

The earliest iteration of this process was the imperative to secure international peace after World War II and the principle of self-determination that accompanied the realigning of postwar global order. In 1945, the UN Charter affirmed self-determination from two perspectives: the right of a state to choose freely its political, economic, and social system, and the right of a people to constitute itself in a state.

This duality was put to the test quickly. Horacio Boneo, the first director of the Electoral Assistance Division, gives two examples that may be interpreted as foundational for each of the two perspectives on self-determination. As regards the former, the first electoral mandate of the UN was established by General Assembly resolution 112(II) issued in November 1947. It noted that "the Korean question was primarily a matter for the Korean people itself, invited elected representatives of the Korean people to take part in consideration of the question and established a UN Temporary Commission on Korea (UNTCOK) to facilitate such participation."[2] With respect to the latter, in addressing the disputes in Jammu and Kashmir, the UN Security Council again turned to elections as the means to operationalize self-determination, as expressed in its resolution of April 21, 1948,[3] which stated that "both India and Pakistan desire that the question of the accession of Jammu and Kashmir to India or Pakistan should be decided through the democratic method of a free and impartial plebiscite, following withdrawal of their respective military forces."[4] For the Jammu-Kashmir crisis, although the plebiscite was never held due to continued conflict over the issue by India and Pakistan, the UN role would have expanded beyond observation to organizing the elections.[5]

The Korean and Jammu-Kashmir cases established important precedents to understand, and justify, why the international community would engage in an ostensibly sovereign process such as a domestic election. Opportunities for UN engagement in the electoral field grew in the 1950s with modest interventions. As Maarten Halff points out, the Somaliland mission with a three-member advisory council supported by a small secretariat was "typical of assistance activities at the time," with its mission to supervise and assist Somalia's transition to independence through advice on electoral preparations, registration of parties and voters, and the drafting of electoral legislation.[6]

Under the stewardship of the Trusteeship Council, the UN supervised and observed plebiscites, referenda, and elections as steps toward independence. The Trusteeship Council was established by the UN Charter to prepare non-self-governing territories for self-government or independence. In Article 77 of the Charter, this supervision only applied to the following: "a. territories now held under mandate; b. territories which may be detached from enemy states as a result of World War II; and c. territories voluntarily placed under the system by states responsible for their administration."[7] The Trusteeship Council was not tasked with overseeing decolonization. That process was taken up and overseen by the UN General Assembly. Nevertheless, optimism was widespread for these exercises, with "near universal approval of UN involvement among Member States."[8] The intense global wave of decolonization in the 1960s brought the principle of self-determination to the fore, demanding, in turn, ways and means to gain the views of the citizens of the colonial territories.

The late 1980s and early 1990s—in conjunction with the collapse of the Soviet Union and the end of single-party rule in Central and Eastern Europe and elsewhere—saw the size of missions increase dramatically. For example, Namibia in 1989, Cambodia in 1993, and Mozambique in 1994 exemplify the shift in scope. The 1989 UN operation in Namibia (UNTAG) involved "1,758 electoral supervisors from the UN system"[9] and resulted in the successful election of a constituent assembly that wrote a new constitution, enabling Namibia to declare its independence from South Africa in the spring 1990. The 1992 UN Verification Mission in Angola (UNAVEM II)[10] included only 400 electoral monitors,[11] which emerged unsuccessful as the opposition movement led by Jonas Savimbi returned to war immediately following the elections. The 1992 Security Council resolution 745 that established the United Nations Transitional Authority in Cambodia (UNTAC) set in motion not only the largest electoral operation to date, but also the first time that the UN was entrusted with the entire organization and conduct of elections in a member state, which took place in May 1993.[12] These large-scale consultations built in-house electoral experience and capacity for major operational exercises.

A second shift was the move from major peace operations to member state–requested electoral assistance, in tandem with transitions from authoritarian rule to democracy. The UN experience was put to good use in the next wave of electoral involvement, in the wake of the democratization in Portugal, where UN involvement was not linked to decolonization.[13] The Portuguese experience shaped and informed subsequent democratization waves in southern Europe from the 1970s and onward to Latin America. The post–Cold War dynamics symbolized by the fall of the Berlin Wall brought a new wave of transitions on all continents, particularly Central and Eastern Europe. Guyana in 1992 is one example of this shift of UN assistance beyond peacebuilding missions to developing or democratizing countries more broadly.[14] This post-peacekeeping role for UN electoral work was different in nature, leaning toward development support to build political institutions and the legitimacy that the UN could bestow on these institutions—that is, the focus shifted from the election event to institutional infrastructure.

This change was in part due to the growing hegemony in donor approaches of the US-influenced post–Cold War notion of *conditionality* of aid, whereby development assistance became linked with good governance and "free and fair" elections. Stephen Brown explains how promoting democratic institutions abroad became an explicit goal of US development aid, beginning with the Foreign Assistance Act of 1961:

> From the early 1960s to the late 1980s, an era of intense superpower competition, strategic alliance was the most common condition for development assistance. Security imperatives dominated the choice of aid recipients. While the USSR supported strategic allies, especially Marxist-Leninist regimes, the US and other Western donors provided economic assistance to developing countries that helped contain communism and Soviet "expansionism." For the US and, to a lesser extent, other bilateral donors, recipient allegiance usually eclipsed concern about the nature of internal political arrangements. A formal semblance of democracy was deemed sufficient; often, not even that was of import. Still, donors sometimes used aid as leverage to pressure a developing country to carry out certain political and social reforms. The US, especially after the Cuban revolution in 1959, worried that conspicuous inequality in poor countries increased the chances of socialist revolutions paving the way for alignment with Moscow.[15]

This demand to deliver and provide proof of credible elections in the early and mid-1990s opened up a machinery of support to mid-level emerging democracies and a plethora of electoral assistance and electoral observation actors in addition to UN agencies.[16]

This shift from peacebuilding to development had implications for the scope, scale, and skill sets needed to respond. Boneo describes this change in scope as follows:

> The requests received in the early '90s came from countries lacking experience in the organization of elections, either because elections had not taken place in the recent past or because they took place in the context of single-party systems. Therefore, most countries required support in establishing and sustaining the basic electoral institutions,

which resulted in increasingly complex situations and demands. The Secretariat did not have, at the time, specific structures or relevant expertise in handling those requests, with the exceptions of the experience accumulated in Namibia, Nicaragua and Haiti.[17]

The International Covenant on Civil and Political Rights was an important vehicle to move UN involvement in electoral processes from the first entry point of the "self-determination" narrative to a second entry point centered on the "democratic entitlement" narrative. A human rights–anchored approach privileges the political rights of a people in any given country alongside the government of the day.

In the 1960s, the growth of UNDP contributed to the stabilization of a democracy and elections portfolio within the UN. Through UNDP country offices, the UN established a more regularized presence in developing member states that included governance as part of a commitment to institutional development, economic growth, and social stability in developing countries. This trend consolidated in the late 1980s and early 1990s, when the end of the Cold War marked the emergence of a democratic governance agenda, strictly related to the recognition of the role of electoral processes for strengthening and legitimizing governance institutions. This was epitomized in the UN General Assembly resolutions on *Enhancing the Effectiveness of the Principle of Periodic and Genuine Elections* issued since 1988.[18] A third entry point, building on its role as supervisor during the decolonization period, was the UN as a provider of legitimacy to sovereign governments through a continued supervisory role.

While the entry points of decolonization, institutional development, and bestowing of legitimacy explain the "demand" side of UN involvement in electoral processes, the "supply" side of UN agency interest in engaging can be explained in terms of the relative ease of mobilizing resources and support for electoral work in cases that are of high profile or high geopolitical importance. Whether for self-determination as in Namibia in 1989, and similarly twenty years later in Timor Leste; for peacebuilding in Cambodia in 1992–1993; or because of the imperative of avoiding failed elections or collapsed states in the Solomon Islands, Iraq, Afghanistan, or Libya, there has been donor willingness to fund costly electoral processes. International assistance in this area often has been framed within the context of "exit strategies" in postconflict situations and has aimed at settling issues of internal and external legitimacy. Technical triumph is not always matched by political success, which depends on a broader range of factors than technical perfection.[19]

Special Characteristics of Electoral Assistance

While the UN gained electoral operational capacity through experience, certain features made electoral assistance a distinct and complex category of UN work. First, at the turn of the century, electoral assistance shifted from event-driven endeavors influenced by the prominence of a political crisis in the geopolitical environment to a process-oriented approach framed within the concept of the election management cycle. This included an increased emphasis on the notion of the integrity of the whole electoral process, with important implications for the design, implementation, and longer-term sustainability of international assistance. Second, as many of the UN officials working in the democratization space quickly understood, elections are at once both technical and political, demanding different internal mechanisms and skill sets—from legal to procurement to diplomatic. Third, in terms of programming horizons, electoral assistance can form part of long-term governance and institution building or it may demand rapid responses to navigate an immediate political impasse and avert a crisis. Elections may be exhilarating and historically momentous, such as Nelson Mandela's election in 1994 or the popular consultation that brought independence to Timor Leste. Or they may be potentially divisive if results are delayed, contested, or have an unexpected outcome such as in Kenya in 2008, the United States in 2020, or Myanmar in 2020–2021. Elections are time-bound, whether linked to a peacebuilding timetable or a constitutional or legal electoral calendar—complex logistical events demanding both transportation and communication infrastructure, as well as the mobilization of an "army" of temporary staff.

The Cambodia example highlights the operational complexity of the UN's involvement but also the political dimensions. From peace agreement mandates, such as Cambodia or Mozambique, to the design of interventions—every decision point has implications for power and influence. Keeping factions in the tent and on the ballot paper is sensitive behind-the-scenes work requiring top diplomatic skills of UN officials and key member states. The closer to an electoral event—and a binding electoral result—the starker the political stakes for domestic actors.

These dynamics of stakes and power explain one of the key differences between UN work in this sector compared to those covered in the other chapters. Moreover, these dynamics explain why the UN's role in bestowing legitimacy and credibility on elections is key to its electoral-assistance work. The point of an election is not just to be held, but that the results be accepted, at least by a critical mass of stakeholders, including political parties, civil society organizations, and citizens at large, and often the international community. This "acceptance" needs to be built and fostered from an early moment—political opponents need to be convinced to stay "in the game" even when the outlook for victory is weak. They may need to be convinced to accept results even if unexpected or not in their favor. These incentives can be related to recognition and international standing—but can also be more tenuous from a democratic viewpoint—such as campaign funding, power-sharing arrangements, amnesty, or alternative pathways for obstinate leaders. In Mozambique in 1994, key UN officials worked tirelessly and creatively behind the scenes to arrange incentives to ensure that the Renamo opposition movement stayed within the electoral tent rather than outside.[20]

This combination of operational and legitimacy-oriented imperatives explains why the UN has continuously emphasized the importance of long-term and capacity-building support to electoral management bodies in its programming and guidance. While election administration can be under the radar for several years, during an election year or as part of a peace process, elections are high-profile, high-risk, and carry high geopolitical importance. On the operational side, stable, trusted, and competent electoral management bodies are better placed to deliver the orderly elections necessary for a peaceful transfer of power and stability in governance. The risks of the converse—that the competence of the election commission to hold fair elections is in doubt—are anathema to all other UN economic and social policy goals.[21]

The UN has turned to key member states for advice and secondment to reinforce the full panoply of skills to design and implement programs encompassing these multiple dimensions of electoral-assistance work. Initially, Elections Canada (Namibia) and the Australia Electoral Commission (Namibia, Cambodia, Timor Leste), and subsequently also Mexico electoral authorities (Instituto Nacional Electoral, formerly Instituto Federal Electoral), stand out in this regard as stable and reliable partners, willing to second staff or support the United Nations efforts with expertise and design advice. These three electoral management bodies also serve as partners to the United Nations on global cooperative projects for electoral capacity building and electoral knowledge sharing.[22]

A final point about the special characteristics of electoral assistance is the costs of organizing or supporting elections, particularly in post-conflict environments where infrastructure is lacking, citizen identification lists are inaccurate, or where security is at risk. Election-related costs can include helicopters, security forces, or full voter registration costs. For this reason, the United Nations has developed mechanisms to mobilize resources with reliable partners. These mechanisms include basket funds with interested bilateral donors managed by the relevant UNDP office at the country level and a special arrangement with the European Union via a joint task force to develop rapid response election-financing arrangements to meet European Commission and UNDP criteria.[23]

Shaping of UN Election Fieldwork Choices

Experiences on the ground shaped the UN electoral imprint. Understandably, successes begot confidence, consolidation, and expansion of the UN appetite for involvement in elections, while quagmires and ordeals begot caution and risk aversion. These tendencies and tensions between caution and ambition weaved, waxed, and waned as events played out concurrently in different parts of the world. Overall, the trajectory of UN operational size can be thought of as a curve from small and few interventions to major large-scale operations to many and modest. At the same time, the support for electoral work has moved from "near universal" to a contested space for the United Nations.[24]

The optimistic and expansive trajectories are starkly visible in the Namibian case. Even though South West Africa (Namibia) was given as a mandate to South Africa by the League of Nations to prepare for independence, when South Africa refused to carry out its responsibility, the UN began a decades-long resolute involvement in Namibia that became part and parcel of the independence and decolonization movement. In 1967, the United Nations Council for Namibia was established, placing Namibia under the direct responsibility of the United Nations. In 1978, the Secretary-General submitted a plan to ensure the orderly transition to independence whereby a Secretary-General's Special Representative would work closely with an Administrator-General appointed by the South African Government. Unfortunately, this plan did not go into effect until 1989, after the Cuban troops had been removed from neighboring Angola, eliminating the threat of Communist influence in Namibia. Importantly, this plan included the administration of elections, as stated earlier, for a constituent assembly where an independence referendum was protected by a large-scale peacekeeping force.[25]

Taking advantage of this long-awaited real opening in Namibia, the UN scaled up dramatically via the "hands-on" United Nations Transition Assistance Group mechanism. As Horacio Boneo explains,

UNTAG was essentially a political operation, the basic mandate of which was that free and fair elections were to be held in Namibia. Its task consisted of the creation of the conditions necessary for the conduct of such an election, which required a profound change in the political atmosphere in the territory, such that the electoral campaign could develop in a democratic climate.[26]

To support this mandate, the UN pulled in advisors from strong member-state electoral commissions, notably Australia and Canada, to design the conduct of elections and legitimize the polls through a large-scale observation mission. This active and large-scale Namibian electoral support model influenced subsequent UN choices for decolonization elections and post-conflict elections more broadly.

Meanwhile, the experiences in preparation for the Nicaraguan 1989 elections similarly affected the UN models of electoral assistance. Under the Esquipulas II Agreement of August 7, 1987, the presidents of Costa Rica, El Salvador, Guatemala, Honduras, and Nicaragua undertook

to promote in their own countries an "authentic democratic process" that was "pluralistic and participatory." They further agreed to "invite . . . the United Nations . . . to send observers to verify that the electoral process (in each country) be governed by the strictest rules of equal access for all political parties to media and ample opportunities for organizing public demonstrations and any other type of political propaganda.[27]

In 1989, Nicaragua "requested that the Secretary-General establish a group of international observers to verify the electoral process so as to ensure that it was genuine during every stage."[28]

The emphasis was on verification rather than conduct—the idea being that the most important role the international community via the UN could play would be to instill a sense of legitimacy to the electoral event and trust in its conduct in the context of deep societal divides. Without this legitimization, the acceptance of the results and stability of government would be in peril. The Observation Mission to Nicaragua was mandated to check and verify all aspects of the electoral process, "ranging from the composition of the Supreme Electoral Council to the processing of complaints received or interferences detected. In that context, the mission could also, where appropriate, request information on any remedial action that might be required."[29]

Along with Nicaragua, Haiti was the second election in which the UN monitored elections in an independent member state. As Jon Ebersole pointed out: "These missions engendered heated debate in the UN between those Member States concerned about protecting state sovereignty and those advocating the critical importance of free and fair elections to meeting the goals of development, human rights and the maintenance of global stability and security."[30]

The Paris Peace Accords gave the United Nations the sweeping electoral mandate to fully conceptualize and implement the Cambodia elections of 1993. Informed by lessons learned in the design of the Namibian mission, the UNTAC Electoral Component deployed UN Volunteers throughout the country a year in advance to decentralize election preparation. No expense was spared to deliver credible elections, from the security features on the ballot paper to the security and air operations that ensured materials arrived on time. While elections were held with great domestic and international excitement, the enthusiasm waned when democracy failed to take hold and when the local capacity to organize and protect subsequent elections was weak. These lessons on sustainability, capacity building, and local ownership influenced the design of subsequent electoral missions.

The design of the electoral support component for Mozambique (General Peace Agreement for Mozambique, 1992) which created the UN Operation in Mozambique (UNOMOZ) was much more focused on local control, with the UN playing two key roles. First, informed by the setbacks of support to the Angolan elections in 1992, which plunged Angola back into civil war, a more politically oriented electoral component of UNOMOZ worked hard behind the scenes to keep potential spoilers in the electoral process. This careful, sensitive, and often creative work paid dividends in Mozambique in 1994, where Renamo and its leader Afonso Dhlakama accepted their electoral loss, allowing a peaceful transition. Meanwhile, a second shift for the UN in Mozambique was the commitment to institution building of the electoral management body known as the Commissão National de Eleições. This long-term orientation, focusing on the institute's capacity rather than just the elections, marked the beginnings of UNDP engagement in electoral work. The structure of UNDP support to the Mozambican elections was designed to quietly complement and support the Mozambican election officers in their work, whereby international staff were embedded in normal operations for trust-building and support.

The importance of capacity building and local ownership successfully and powerfully influenced the design of UN support to the popular consultation and subsequent elections in Timor Leste from 1999 onward. A comprehensive curriculum on elections—subsequently adopted worldwide—was developed by and for the Timorese fledgling electoral authorities, as were processes for twinning with international counterparts and archiving all election materials and information for posterity.[31] This approach gave dividends in the form of robust electoral capacity and high rankings on electoral lists for decades following the interventions.

The UN dominance in electoral support broke in conjunction with the many post–Cold War elections held in Central and Eastern Europe and with the rise of specialized organizations such as the International Foundation for Electoral Systems. For peace processes held in Bosnia and Kosovo, the Organization for Security and Cooperation in Europe (OSCE), the European Commission, and the United Nations divided the workstreams into distinct "pillars" to avoid duplication. The OSCE took the larger responsibility for elections. The Bosnian example echoes a broader trend of electoral units with existing global and regional intergovernmental organizations as well as stand-alone institutions with capacity for electoral support and observation.[32]

A similar model for sharing responsibilities was deployed in Afghanistan. The Joint Electoral Management Body[33] was used for a cooperative approach to fund and support the ambitious efforts from the presidential 2004 elections onward.[34] The UN, through the UN Office for Project Services, was uniquely able to handle complex and large-scale procurement. The capacity-building methods that had proved so successful in Timor Leste were challenged in the Afghanistan context—the attrition rates of staff, corruption, security risks, and political interference were some of the elements that made sustainable institution building difficult.

The Afghanistan and Iraq interventions mark the apex of managing complex funding and operations, including ambition levels for voting services. The UNDP-ELECT I 2006–2011 project and related programs had costs estimated to US$380 million with UNDP as implementor.[35] The US Agency for International Development (USAID) had a US$20 million contingency fund used to rapidly deploy a complex electoral audit for a disputed election. The International Organization for Migration (IOM) acted as a player to ensure diaspora voting.[36]

While other organizations were arguably more agile than the United Nations, the UN retained relevance and importance in many areas; on the one hand, it convened power and bestowed legitimacy, but on the other hand, it provided operational capabilities for deploying to difficult areas, managed complicated financial donor baskets, and conducted large-scale procurement. In combination with the complex financing and operations, the time-bound nature of elections led to delays in many cases, with knock-on effects on electoral quality when materials or personnel arrived late.

For this reason, toward the 2000s, with USAID as the largest donor to UNDP, and UNDP as the largest electoral-assistance provider, this created mechanisms to ease and simplify the transactions. The EC-UNDP Joint Task Force (a partnership between the European Union and the UNDP) codified and ordered modalities through standardized project structures, forecasting of potential areas of work, and joint training of desk officers and beneficiaries.[37]

Expanding Web of UN Agency Engagement on Elections

The complexity and geographical reach of the electoral field operations and engagement drew on many skill-set sources within the UN. By 2017, Halff identified seven UN actors as directly implicated, performing many different functions, including the organization and conduct of elections, election supervision, and technical assistance.[38] These clusters of roles waxed and waned over time and were devolved variously to different entities throughout the United Nations.[39] The DPPA is the home of the Electoral Assistance Division (EAD), which serves as the focal point for the UN and where difficult political assessments are made as to the scope, feasibility, and appropriateness of UN interventions. Ebersole describes how the idea of a system-wide focal point came about, with leadership to ensure coherence and consistency across UN entities involved in electoral activities:

> The United States led, and numerous other countries supported, the effort to increase UN involvement and to establish an administrative center for these activities in the UN Secretariat. In his speech before the United Nations General Assembly in 1990, George Bush strongly advocated greater UN electoral assistance and proposed that "the United Nations establish a Special Coordinator for Electoral Assistance, to be assisted by a UN Electoral Commission comprised of distinguished experts from around the world."[40]

UNDP takes prime responsibility for longer-term, holistic engagement focused on democratic institution-building. For shorter-term peacekeeping elections, the Department of Peace Operations (DPO) serves as central coordinator for establishing missions that often include an elections component. Field operations will rely on the UN Office for Project Services for complex and large-scale procurement, deployment, and recruitment support. Meanwhile, influencing the electoral support agenda on the normative side with specialist expertise, the OHCHR is engaged in setting UN expectations and direction on political rights, UN

Women is involved in providing evidence-based knowledge networking work to promote women's political participation, and UNESCO participates in the civic education space.

This multi-agency engagement marks a significant shift from the early days of UN electoral assistance. From the first plebiscite observation mission to Togoland in 1956, the UN Trusteeship Council played the critical UN role. During the 1950s and 1960s, the Trusteeship Council had the support of the UN member states to supervise and observe plebiscites, referenda, and elections in non-sovereign territories that had been placed under the Trusteeship system. Later, with the undertaking of decolonization, this work morphed into the Special Committee on the Situation with regard to the Implementation of the Declaration on the Granting of Independence to Colonial Countries and Peoples.[41] Once the UN began to initiate a referendum or consultation on self-determination, a legal framework had to be developed to ensure that the conduct of the consultations was free and fair. Missions were small, reaching a peak number of members, between five and thirty on an election day, responsible for oversight and reporting back to both UN member states and the territory's administering authority.[42]

The shift from decolonization as the main entry point for elections changed who at the UN would be involved. A series of small, inexpensive, and agile electoral-assistance missions to Haiti and Nicaragua in the decade shift from the 1980s to 1990s mark the transition. Eyewitness reports speak of designing interventions at airports and airplanes for the small-scale but highly effective interventions in Haiti and Nicaragua. These early successes were critical for the willingness to establish a UN focal point on elections and explain the establishment of the Electoral Assistance Division within the Department of Political Affairs (now the Department of Political and Peacebuilding Affairs).

Not all the designated UN agencies are involved in implementation, and not all UN electoral work is costly. In addition to the supervisory, political, and developmental roles (described above), one key area of UN electoral work has been normative, shaping a globally shared understanding of how elections are understood and conducted. This normative work has many shapes—of a large scale in the form of global declarations and international obligations, and of a smaller scale in codes of conduct, handbooks,[43] and statements.[44] An example is the Declaration of Principles for international election observation and UNDP handbooks.

The multiple entry points meant the engagement of a wider range of actors within the UN family. Whether focusing on reform (EAD focus); institution building (UNDP); support for women's empowerment, political participation, and representation (UN Women); or support to civil society organizations (UN Democracy Fund), each intervention has strengthened internal knowledge and capacities within the UN. DPPA and DPO honed expertise on the role of elections in peacekeeping space. At the same time, UNDP and UN Office for Project Services gained valuable experience conducting large-scale or complex field support and procurement for elections. Through hands-on experience with Iraqi diaspora voting, IOM gained experience and expertise on the voting of migrants and out-of-country voting that informed subsequent support for Kosovo and Afghanistan. The longer-term development-oriented interventions allowed a conduit for discussing gender equality and the participation and representation of women, increasing the role of what would become UN Women in the elections space.

No longer confined to one part of the UN system, we can see UN engagement in elections system-wide, albeit with UNDPPA/EAD as the focal point. A system-wide approach is recognized as important—delivering "as one" as in other policy areas—and much is under review.

UN Membership and Democracy

The strength and the vulnerability of the UN's democracy work are in its membership. Through formal mechanisms and funding patterns, member states have influenced the UN's ability to engage and its modes of engagement. Formally, election work falls under the Third Committee as part of its remit on human rights, guiding the "regular" electoral assistance work of the main UN bodies and General Assembly. Meanwhile, the Security Council addresses elections related to major crises, where elections may be included as a mechanism for reestablishing a legitimate government after conflict. While the Security Council is not always in agreement, Iraq and Timor Leste are examples of where action was enabled. The Peacebuilding Commission reports to both the General Assembly and the Security Council. It is an intergovernmental advisory body that supports peace efforts in conflict-affected countries, mostly in Africa. The Peacebuilding Fund is a financial instrument that may mobilize short-term resources to sustain peace in countries. While most activities are about dialogue and are political in nature, the mandate of sustaining peace can also be about ensuring that elections occur and are seen as legitimate, thus linking democratization, peacebuilding, and electoral processes.

Making those same connections, the process of the International Conference for New and Restored Democracies (ICNRD) launched in 1988 was an example of an inclusive approach to sharing experiences and lessons learned among the UN member states on national efforts at strengthening democracy. The conference was structured as a tripartite event (governments, parliamentarians, and civil society) and was held on a shift basis in different regions. However, the design to be as inclusive in membership as possible proved to be its downfall. After Qatar was host in 2006, the next in line, Venezuela, indefinitely postponed the organization of the subsequent conference, and this indetermination caused the mechanism to freeze. On a positive note, the ICNRD process led to the establishment of the UN International Democracy Day, celebrated on September 15 each year. The date was chosen following the adoption by the General Assembly of the Interparliamentary Union of a Universal Declaration on Democracy in September 1997 in Cairo.

The cost of electoral operations opens another type of influence, namely willingness to fund projects or interventions. Support for post-crisis interventions tend to follow geopolitical interest lines: as in Australia's support to UNDP programs in the Solomon Islands, European support to programs in Libya, or US and Canadian support to programs in Haiti or Latin America.[45] Sweden's long-term and consistent assistance to UNDP-supported Arab elections network and electoral work has created a space for creativity and professional growth, while Sweden's support to UN Women has allowed for a holistic and global approach to women's participation and gender work.[46] Spain's generous funding of the General Corporation for Environmental Protection program, which emphasized capacity building and regional electoral networks in elections, allowed UNDP to significantly scale up and expand knowledge and networking election work for several years. When the global financial crisis hit Spain deeply, this program was significantly impacted and discontinued.[47] These examples demonstrate how the ability for UN agencies to engage in particular types of democracy and electoral work, whether in a particular country or at the global level, can depend on a sympathetic or interested donor. The impact on Spain caused by the sudden curtailment of the General Corporation for Environmental Protection's funding due to the global financial crisis demonstrates the programming vulnerability that donor reliance brings and the impact of global economic trends on programming.[48]

The democratic credentials and enthusiasm for democracy among UN members complicate engagement in democracy. Gone are the days from the first era of UN involvement, with the near universal approval of UN engagement among member states described by Ebersole.[49] For UNDP, national-level programming is contingent on a host-country agreement and, in the case of middle-income and upper-middle-income countries, contingent on funding from the host country itself. This arrangement fosters buy-in and cooperation but can also lead to risk aversion and avoidance of governance-oriented programming—for example, judicial independence, in favor of other sectors of more interest to the host government such as food programs, education, or infrastructure. The influence of UN member states such as China and Russia, among others, that have traditionally considered UN engagement in this area as a sensitive issue, in consideration of its potential conflict with principles of state sovereignty and noninterference in matters within the domestic jurisdiction of any state, has led to a caution on overt democracy advocacy, favoring an emphasis on more widely palatable concepts such as election inclusiveness. Far from promoting any specific form of government, "the UN endorsement of democracy reflects a commitment to popular self-rule, guided by the principle of self-determination."[50]

Protecting Democracy—UN Global Role

Since the early days of UN electoral involvement, the UN has increased its capacity and knowledge exponentially but is at the same time dealing with a sharply different reality. Rather than organizing or monitoring elections conducted in good faith, the ubiquity and deliberate undermining of elections and institutions demand a different way of working: at once political *and* developmental. Political work is, for example, the behind-the-scenes work to facilitate acceptance of elections results and orderly transitions. Developmental work is the programming that builds resilient electoral institutions to navigate societal fault lines and political risks or crises. For UN agencies, the sensitivities of governance-oriented programming and a chronic lack of funds for work in lower-profile contexts, as well as the limited flexibility allowed by donors when providing targeted funding, demand leaner working methods. Recognizing its experience, structure, in-house knowledge, global reach, mandate, and limitations, the United Nations is well placed to contribute to much-needed democratization and election-focused work in the following roles: norm setting, providing leadership and defining agendas, providing assistance, and knowledge networking.

Norm Setting

The United Nations is uniquely placed for the cumbersome work of building consensus foundational to the instruments, conventions, and treaties regarding civil and political rights. Once set and adopted by the United Nations, global norms provide cogency, common language, and lasting impact as benchmarks and global understandings of expected government behaviors. As public international law, these instruments influence national legislation and shift power dynamics to citizens as rights holders and with their governments as bearers of the duty to uphold these rights. New norms are continually emerging to meet new global challenges. One example is the norm of international election observation; once controversial, it is now seen as normal.

Reinforcing democratic norms demands keeping discussion channels open, continuously placing key issues on the agenda, and regular recommitment to mechanisms such as the Declaration of Principles for International Election Observation.[51] The United Nations can define the norms needed at the global level to increase multilateral action regarding electoral processes and reinforce the important interplay between global and regional norm setting. Regional norm setting is the natural precursor to global norms, as more acceptable initially to individual countries. The strong incremental value of building regional norms is that the more countries are brought into a conversation to discuss specific issues within specific regional and subregional contexts, the more highly polarized discourses can be demystified and normalized in global policy forums.

Leadership Role and Defining Agendas

Through its mandate and decades of peacekeeping experience, the United Nations is uniquely placed for agenda setting in complex situations. As has been well established, in crises rooted in societal cleavages, elections can serve as arenas both for channeling conflict and triggering conflict.[52] Well-designed electoral assistance can support a "prevention" agenda, and UN convening power can support the design of institution-building and development pathways.

While the UN is well known as the institution of last resort in a crisis with its blue helmets and frontline humanitarian workers, its leadership role often falls short of its ambition, particularly with hindsight from its potential as a sole global convening actor in the early interventions. While the rise of other regionally based organizations makes for a more crowded field, the United Nations remains uniquely placed to take its proper role as a global champion of transformative change from within its member states in line with the global norms and universal principles to which they have committed and using tools such as dialogue and incentives for them to "stay" in the democratic tent.

Providing Assistance

Through UNDP and other agencies, the UN is an experienced and reliable electoral-assistance provider, showing leadership and self-correction in its move from quick-fix event-focused modalities of the 1990s to the current modus operandi of a smaller footprint in terms of visibility and longer-term institution and capacity-building goals. The Timor Leste example described in this chapter exemplifies this shift.

Knowledge Networking

A shared knowledge base is a prerequisite for effective work: for example, what worked well where, how, and why? What is transferable? What shared words do we use for this concept? (This is a particularly important endeavor as the meanings of concepts in the highly contested field of democracy are constantly shifting and need continued negotiation.) With its convening power and global reach, the United Nations has access to knowledge that can provide an evidence base and has the convening power to design modalities to share that knowledge within the UN system, but it also has access to networks of actors around the world. The active involvement of the United Nations in knowledge networking initiatives such as the ACE Electoral Knowledge Network, the BRIDGE curriculum on elections, the iKNOW Politics site initiated by UN Women, and the Declaration of Principles community on international election observation are examples of this knowledge sharing and actor empowerment role. Similarly, support to programming that encourages knowledge sharing and South-South cooperation is another way in which the UN contributes—linking, for example, institutes that work on national statistical capacities and voter registration. Another way the UN can and does counter asymmetry in knowledge (and the power that comes with knowledge) is through its emphasis on and capabilities in translation. The program on Arab electoral networks is an example of where knowledge is generated regionally and adapted and translated from international sources to provide rich Arabic-language sources of evidence and research for policy and practice decisions for the region.

The global conditions for democracy and election-focused work are shifting and complex. Therefore, the UN is needed as much as at any previous point in its history. The United Nations and its agencies are uniquely placed to contribute, not only for in-country programming of electoral assistance, but also more broadly in setting norms, defining agendas, and sharing knowledge. The UN is needed in a leadership role, not only as an institution of last resort in a crisis but also as a champion of transformative change.

Notes

1. For previous reviews and analysis of UN electoral assistance work, see the following: Boneo, "Elections and the United Nations," in Banerjee and Sharma, *Reinventing the United Nations*; Ludwig, "Free and Fair Elections," in Krasno, *United Nations*; Ludwig, "Democratization and the UN"; Ludwig, "The UN's Electoral Assistance: Challenges, Accomplishments, Prospects," in Newman and Rich, *UN Role in Promoting Democracy*, pp. 169–187; Lübermann, *UN Electoral Assistance*.

2. Banerjee and Sharma, *Reinventing the United Nations*, p. 96.

3. United Nations Security Council Resolution 47, April 21, 1948. "The security council . . . recommends to the Governments of India and Pakistan the following measures as those which in the opinion of the Council are appropriate to bring about a cessation of the fighting and to create proper conditions for a free and impartial plebiscite to decide whether the State of Jammu and Kashmir is to accede to India or Pakistan, https://digitallibrary.un.org.

4. Lauwaars et al. *International Organisation and Integration.*

5. Banerjee and Sharma, *Reinventing the United Nations*, p. 97.

6. Maarten Halff, "The United Nations Approach to Electoral Management Support," Paper presented at the Annual Conference of the European Consortium for Political Research (ECPR), Oslo, September 2017, p. 2, http://www.electoralmanagement .com/wp-content/uploads/2017/01/MHallf-ECPR-UN-electoral-management-2017.pdf.

7. United Nations Charter, Chapter XII, Article 77, paragraphs 1: a, b, and c.

8. Ebersole, "The United Nations' Response."

9. Howard, *UN Peacekeeping in Civil Wars,* p. 83.

10. UNAVEM I of 1988 involved UN peacekeepers to oversee the removal of some 50,000 Cuban troops from Angola and did not include elections. See Howard, *UN Peacekeeping in Civil Wars,* p. 37.

11. Ibid.

12. Ludwig, "Free and Fair Elections," in Krasno, *United Nations,* p. 125. See also Lyons, "Post-conflict Elections," p. 52. Also see: Newman and Rich, *UN Role in Promoting Democracy,* pp. 258–281.

13. Foresti and Harris, *Democracy Support Through the United Nations,* p. 24.

14. Inken von Borzyskowski, "Peacebuilding Beyond Civil Wars: UN Election Assistance and Election Violence," January 20, 2015, p. 4, https://www.peio.me/wp -content/uploads/PEIO8.

15. Brown, "Foreign Aid and Democracy Promotion," pp. 180–181.

16. Leterme, "Elections in International Democracy Assistance."

17. Boneo, "Elections and the United Nations," p. 104.

18. Haack, *United Nations Democracy Agenda,* p. 62.

19. Chesterman, *You, The People,* pp. 204–235.

20. Kumar and Ottaway, *From Bullets to Ballots.*

21. UNDP, *UNDP Electoral Assistance Implementation Guide,* ACE Electoral Knowledge Network, 2007, pp. 37–39, https://aceproject.org/ero-en/misc/undp-and -electoral-assistance.

22. See websites for the BRIDGE (Building Resources in Democracy, Governance and Elections) project, www.bridge-project.org, and the ACE Electoral Knowledge Network, www.aceproject.org.

23. See the EC-UNDP Joint Task Force on Electoral Assistance website, https:// www.ec-undp-electoralassistance.org/en.

24. Ebersole, "The United Nations' Response," pp. 91–121.

25. Boneo, "Elections and the United Nations," p. 99.

26. Ibid.

27. Ibid., p. 100.

28. Ibid.

29. Ibid., p. 101.

30. Ebersole, "The United Nations' Response," p. 91.

31. Arghiros et al., *Making It Count.*

32. Leterme, "Elections in International Democracy Assistance," pp. 81–95.

33. "Afghanistan: Joint Electoral Management Body (JEMB) Organizational Structure,"ACE Electoral Knowledge Network, https://aceproject.org/ero-en/regions /asia/AF/JEMB%20ORG%20Chart.doc/view.

34. Ponzio, *Democratic Peacebuilding,* pp. 134–137.

35. UNDP Election Assistance Projects, United Nations Development Program, Washington Representation Office (October 2015).

. 36. "On 21 July 2004, the United Nations Assistance Mission in Afghanistan (UNAMA) and the International Organization for Migration (IOM) entered into agreement on the conduct of the Out of Country 2004 Afghan Presidential elections in Pakistan and Iran. The task of conducting this exercise was entrusted to IOM who implemented the Program on behalf of the Afghan Joint Electoral Management Body (JEMB) and UNAMA." International Organization for Migration, Out-of-Country Voting, Election Support Unit, Geneva, Switzerland, 2007. See Hess, Pearce Laanela, and Maley, *Preparing for Elections in Afghanistan.*

37. See EC-UNDP Joint Task Force on Electoral Assistance, https://www.ec -undp-electoralassistance.org/en.

38. Halff, "United Nations Approach to Electoral Management Support," p. 3.

39. Ludwig, "Free and Fair Elections," p. 119.

40. Ebersole, "The United Nations' Response," p. 9.

41. Boneo, "Elections and the United Nations," p. 97.

42. Ibid., p. 100.

43. UNDP, *Handbook on Planning, Monitoring and Evaluating for Development Results,* 2009.

44. Carroll and Davis-Roberts. "The Carter Center and Election Observation," p. 90.

45. Arghiros et al., *Making It Count. UNDP, Evaluation of UNDP Contribution to Strengthening Electoral Systems and Processes,* December 2017.

46. Pearce Laanela et al., *Supporting Elections Effectively.*

47. Ibid.

48. Ibid.

49. Ebersole, "The United Nations' Response," p. 1.

50. Joyner, "The United Nations and Democracy," p. 350.

51. United Nations, Declaration of Principles for International Elections Obser- vation, 2005, https://www.osce.org/files/f/documents/e/c/215556.pdf.

52. Sead Alihodžić and Nicholas Matatu, *Timing and Sequencing of Transitional Elections,* International IDEA Policy Paper No. 18, April 2019.

8

Addressing
Human Security

*Kimberly Gamble-Payne and
Jean E. Krasno*

Historically, security exclusively referred to national security—defending sovereign borders and addressing conflict. Today, human security represents a shift away from a sole focus on national security to include the safety and well-being of people and is therefore viewed as a "nontraditional" concept of security. Human security includes the protection of individuals who may be suffering from conflict, displacement, poverty, compromised health, environmental degradation, human rights violations, or other concerns. The three issues of global health, climate change, and migration are linked to security through this evolving nontraditional shift from thinking about security as exclusively "national security" to including the concept of "human security." This normative paradigm shift opens the door to a conceptual framework that focuses on the quality of the human condition as a security priority. In this chapter, we examine security through these two open doorways: (1) national security, defending the stability and territorial integrity of the nation-state, and (2) human security, protecting the quality of human life. Here we concentrate on the interaction among the Covid-19 pandemic, climate change, and migration.

In spring 2020, a massive and devastating pandemic exploded across the world. First discovered in late 2019 (hence the name Covid-19), the coronavirus has been reported by scientists to have originated in Wuhan, China, although the exact source is still unknown. The 2022 report of the International Organization for Migration states that Covid-19 "has been the most severe pandemic in a century, with its combination of high transmission, virus strains and the severity of the disease forcing policymakers into previously uncharted territory."[1]

Some 222 countries and territories have been affected, and while the numbers continue to rise, there were some 570 million cases and 6.4 million deaths worldwide as of the end of June 2022.[2] The United States alone had over 90 million cases and over 1 million deaths. The World Health Organization found that Covid-19 deaths were most likely even higher. The organization estimated that "nearly 15 million more people died during the pandemic than would have in normal times."[3] Global travel immediately contributed to the rapid spread of the disease. Governments closed borders and barred travel from certain countries, but to no avail as community contagions began to account for the geometric growth in cases.

While challenges to global health, the threat of climate change, and the rise in migration seem like separate issues, they are intrinsically intermingled. Millions of people have been forced to leave their homes due to conflict and the effects of climate change, such as intense weather events, drought, and flooding. These migration and extreme climate change events have erupted simultaneously while the world is desperately trying to cope with an elusive, deadly virus that continues to mutate. A 2021 UN report on the rise in migration titled "A Paradox Not Seen Before in Human History" stated:

> This rise was coupled with a drop in global mobility overall due to stricter travel rules, prompting the Director General of the UN migration agency (IOM), António Vitorino, to declare that the world was "witnessing a paradox not seen before in human history."
> "While billions of people have been effectively grounded by Covid-19, tens of millions of others have been displaced within their own countries," he said, at the launch of the agency's 2021 World Migration Report.[4]

The migration agency also warned that refugees, and migrants who move out of necessity, have been particularly hard-hit by Covid-related travel restrictions, and millions have found themselves stranded away from home and in danger.[5] The 2022 IOM report states: "Some countries stopped all entry of foreign citizens, some banned citizens of specific countries, while even further, some countries completely closed borders to stop departure and entry of all people, including their own citizens."[6]

The Global Health Governance System: Is It "Fit for Purpose"?

Former UN Secretary-General Kofi Annan, near the end of his second term, stated that we must disabuse ourselves of the notion that health is either exclusively a "development issue," or exclusively a "security issue." It transcends compartmentalized policies and responses. We must abandon traditional bureaucratic thinking, and work across ministries and departments to forge a holistic approach equal to such an all-encompassing challenge.[7]

In the history of the UN's role in global health, 2005 was a special year. It was the sixtieth anniversary of the UN. Annan was the first Secretary-General to have come from inside the UN system, and, in fact, his first job at the UN was in the World Health Organization (WHO). Therefore, population health had a strong champion at the head of the international system. He made it clear that health is central to every aspect of the mission of the UN—security, development, and human rights.

He was also conscious of the political nature of the emergent global health enterprise and the essential role of the UN to ensure that through the Millennium Development Goals (MDGs), progress would be made to fulfill the promise of "Health for All," giving special attention to low- and middle-income countries and vulnerable populations everywhere. The lessons from the outbreak of HIV/AIDS highlighted the glaring failures of the international response to the most affected countries and populations. The Secretary-General was acutely aware of the fact that health systems worldwide were ill-equipped to respond to global health crises. Somehow, health had to capture the sustained attention of the world's political leaders in order to strengthen every component of the global health sector. This would mean marshaling and coordinating human, technical, and financial resources on a large scale. A step in that direction was taken when the ministers of health of every country in the world agreed to update and strengthen the International Health Regulations—the rules of the road for coordinating an international response to outbreaks of infectious disease.

The HIV/AIDS epidemic demonstrated in the most horrific way the linkages of global health to the security, development, and human rights agendas of the United Nations. The international political and technical response to HIV/AIDS revealed how ill-prepared the system was to mount a robust, coordinated, and effective effort to contain and control that disease. Today, in 2022, nearly thirty-eight million people are living with the virus.[8] While effective treatment is now widely available forty years after the outbreak began, a safe and effective vaccine and other prevention measures remain out of reach. Thousands of new infections occur daily.

With the Covid-19 pandemic, once again the international system has been challenged to lead an effective response. The International

Health Regulations of 2005 have proved to be a weak instrument for mobilizing the kind of multipronged effort that is required to prevent an outbreak from becoming a pandemic. Within the WHO, national and regional interests have been placed ahead of the interests of public health. Weaknesses in the right to accurate and timely information plus inequitable access to life-saving information, testing, vaccination, and treatment undermine public trust in the international system and national health systems as well. The Covid-19 pandemic has pushed even the most well-funded and well-managed health systems to the brink of collapse. The world is no better prepared for global pandemics, and their social and economic consequences, today than it was in 1918 when the "Spanish" flu hit the world.

Emergence of Global Health

Trade and travel are associated with the spread of infectious disease.[9] Robust trade and travel, by land and sea, among Europe, the Middle East, and Asia goes back to ancient Greece.[10] With the advent of the steamship and the steam-powered train in the mid-nineteenth century, trade and travel were greatly increased, exposing people to new pathogens and moving new vectors—fleas, mosquitos, and rats—around the world, contributing to the spread of deadly disease.[11]

In 1851, the imperial powers of Europe met in the first of fourteen International Sanitary Conferences to agree on a common response to outbreaks of infectious diseases that originated outside of their territories.[12] The objective was to protect global trade and business activities and to protect their populations from epidemic diseases such as the yellow fever, plague, and what they called "Asiatic cholera"—which is just cholera. The worldview at the time was that infectious disease originated *outside* of their region, *external* and menacing. In order to prevent the spread of these foreign diseases, the Europeans adopted common practices of quarantine, isolation, and travel bans. These policies, and the political and commercial interests that support them, remain in place today.

By the mid-twentieth century, in the aftermath of World War II, the WHO was established as the highest technical resource for national governments and as a forum for states to negotiate cooperation to prevent and combat disease. The WHO constitution is a legally binding agreement based on the principles of the UN Charter. It calls on all states to take measures to achieve the highest attainable standards of health for all.

The WHO and its governing body, the World Health Assembly, has led the most successful improvements in population health in history, including the first and only eradication of a disease—smallpox. WHO is mandated to coordinate the international response to outbreaks of infectious disease with the aim of preventing outbreaks from becoming epidemics and preventing epidemics from becoming pandemics. The World Health Assembly and Executive Council that oversee the work of the organization are governmental bodies, and the government delegations include both technical and foreign policy experts. Therefore, national foreign policy interests inevitably enter into negotiations about the allocation of resources and in priority-setting deliberations.

During the last few decades, WHO's leadership position has been eroded by a combination of geopolitical forces and the entrance into global health work of an array of influential nongovernmental actors, including global philanthropies, international nongovernmental organizations, the global biopharmaceutical industry, and highly influential social movements.

The critiques of WHO's performance during the HIV/AIDS crisis and subsequent outbreaks of infectious disease, including the Ebola outbreak and the Covid-19 pandemic, are well documented. In response to the Ebola outbreak in 2014, the UN Security Council and the UN General Assembly endorsed the Secretary-General's proposal to create a special UN Mission for Ebola Emergency Response to coordinate the international response, including the participation of peacekeeping operations.[13]

In this same period, the geopolitical and economic landscape has shifted, revealing a multipolar world with national groupings and upper-middle-income countries like China and India beginning to exercise significant political and economic power. This shift has implications for the leadership and operations of multilateral organizations like WHO and other international health organizations.[14] For example, China has reestablished the ancient Silk Road strategy, called the Belt and Road Initiative. Some 144 countries from every region of the world—except, for example, countries such as Canada, Germany, Mexico, the United States, and the UK—have entered into agreements that involve economic cooperation on infrastructure development, expansion of manufacturing, and exchange of technology.[15] In 2017, China signed a memorandum of understanding (MOU) with the World Health Organization to cooperate on Collaboration in Health with the new Belt and Road Initiative, signaling a strategic alliance with Beijing.[16]

Reimaging Global Health Governance:
An International Relations Agenda

The twenty-first century is witnessing another acceleration in trade and travel. Digital technology and communication is bringing opportunities for trade and commerce to every part of every continent. Yet, the rapid growth of crowded urban settings, population growth, climate change, and trade agreements can be detrimental to health, and taken together, all threaten collective and individual health security.

Global health challenges are complex, requiring active engagement at the highest levels of political and civil society leadership and the global private sector. Coordinating worldwide responses to twenty-first-century global health challenges requires multisectoral approaches and the engagement of diverse stakeholders. Threats to global health are driven by factors and conditions that lie outside the reach of public health policy and the practice of medicine. In the case of the spread of infectious disease, spillovers happen all the time, but for a spillover to become an outbreak and an outbreak to become an epidemic or a pandemic, certain conditions must be present. Those conditions are largely due to patterns of inequality, neglect, and the failure of governments to protect human rights. Global health justice advocates, including the UN Secretary-General, are calling for a global health system that is based on the fundamental right to health and principles of inclusion and solidarity.

In response, global health policy advocates are calling for global health diplomacy to be integrated into the training of public health practitioners and into studies of global public health policy in order to ensure that, moving forward, a "health in all" policy approach is a core strategy in global health governance for the future.[17] Many observers of international relations and global health suggest that to address the multifaceted nature of global health challenges today, especially in this time of profound sociopolitical uncertainty, the world needs more multilateralism, not less.

The emerging age of pandemics, beginning roughly with the HIV/AIDS outbreak in the late 1980s and continuing through subsequent events (dengue in 2000, SARS 2003, H1N1 2009, MERS 2012, Ebola 2014, Zika 2015, and now Covid-19 and its variants) has triggered a steady uptake of interest and analysis about the implications of global health in international relations.[18] Colin McInnes and Kelley Lee point out three reasons why health has now become an agenda item in international relations scholarship and the practice of diplomacy.

First, and probably the leading motive, is the threat of bioterrorism and infectious disease to peace and security. A second aspect is the fact that population health issues transcend borders, and their control requires international cooperation. The third factor is that the international cooperation that is required includes negotiated agreements at the highest political level, beyond the technical work among international health policymakers and managers of health systems. In particular, effective pandemic preparedness and response is a whole-of-government and a whole-of-society effort.[19]

UN Secretary-General António Guterres addressed the World Health Assembly after the second full year of the Covid-19 pandemic with an endorsement of calls for a reform of the pandemic response arrangement but noted that a much broader range of action is needed: "The pandemic demonstrated how poorly we are prepared for crises. . . . Global security and preparedness need to be strengthened through sustained political commitment and leadership."[20]

A systematic review and redesign of the International Health Regulations is underway. Historically international negotiations on health issues have been considered "low politics," in the realm of "soft power" and the work in human development. However, moving forward, in addition to the social and commercial determinants of health, the political dimension of the conditions that give rise to infectious and chronic diseases will need to be addressed, bringing the global health agenda squarely into the arena of national and regional self-interests. In the wake of the Covid-19 pandemic, calls have been renewed for a robust international pandemic treaty to add rigor and political accountability. Such an agreement would need to be developed with the full participation of nonstate actors, including the biopharmaceutical industry, independent panels of health scientists, and transnational social justice movements.[21]

In addition, the UN Development System reforms aim to streamline the intergovernmental support to low- and middle-income countries. A consortium of thirteen international organizations has adopted a Global Action Plan for Healthy Lives and Well-Being for All to better coordinate technical and financial support to national governments "towards an equitable and resilient recovery from the Covid-19 pandemic and further progress towards the health-related SDGs."[22]

As the second decade of the twenty-first century gets underway, the geopolitical landscape is changing and the "world order" is being reimagined. The United Nations remains a critical forum for mobilizing the leadership, the technical expertise, and the financial resources from both the public and private sectors that are required to prevent and control catastrophic global health crises.[23]

The Threat of Climate Change

Along with global health, one of the biggest challenges threatening the entire planet today is global warming, brought about by greenhouse gas (GHG) emissions. Global warming has already caused oceans to warm, water levels to rise, and extreme weather conditions to proliferate, leading to floods, droughts, and massive wildfires. However, this looming crisis had been ignored for years. As far back as 1896, the "Swedish chemist Svante Arrhenius first hypothesized the warming potential of industrial gases."[24] Yet, it was not until more than half a century later in 1958 that Charles Keeling, who began measuring atmospheric concentrations of CO_2, demonstrated that the gas was, in fact, accumulating in the atmosphere. "This was significant because the more CO_2 there is in the atmosphere, the more it will trap the incoming energy from the sun, leading to a warmer planet."[25] By the year 2006, it was reported that the "average global temperature has increased .74 degrees Celsius" above preindustrial levels, and in the more recent decade, the world has witnessed the warmest years on record.[26] Sea levels are also rising at about 3.8 millimeters per year.[27]

In December 1988, the UN General Assembly passed a resolution calling upon the World Meteorological Organization and the UN Environmental Programme to create the Intergovernmental Panel on Climate Change (IPCC), which was an important political acknowledgment that climate change had become a significant global challenge and placed the United Nations at the center of the issue.[28] The IPCC is an expert, independent advisory, policy-neutral body whose regular reports enable science to inform policymakers. Its first assessment report of 1990 spurred the creation of the UN Framework Convention on Climate Change (UNFCCC), which was agreed to in 1992.[29] Thus, the UN has become the focal point for efforts to address climate change through the formation of the UNFCCC and through the regular scientific assessments on global warming by the IPCC. In 2007, the IPCC and Al Gore were awarded the Nobel Peace Prize.

The UNFCCC is a framework convention that lays out the general goals and standards to be achieved without concrete regulations in order to garner more signatories, with the intention of strengthening the regime down the road. The US president at the time, George H. W. Bush, signed the Convention in Rio in 1992, after insisting that it was only a framework, thus enabling the Senate to ratify the agreement.[30] The next step was to create the 1997 Kyoto Protocol under the UNFCCC, which strengthened the Convention by clarifying emission standards and binding reductions. However, Kyoto divided countries into two groups: Annex I industrialized countries and Annex II developing countries. Annex II countries included China and India as developing countries and therefore exempt from binding reductions. Because these countries were already giant emitters of greenhouse gases, the US Senate refused to ratify Kyoto. Nevertheless, the Protocol went into force in 2005 once the number of those ratifying constituted 55 percent of total GHG emissions.[31]

The UNFCCC Conference of Parties (COP15) met in Copenhagen in 2009 and bore witness to a heated debate, representing differing points of view. With the election of US President Barack Obama, the United States attempted to take a leading role but met opposition from a split European Union and a fragmented G-77 (alliance of developing countries). China, Brazil, India, and South Africa took on the role of dissenting states because of their desire to remain exempt from emissions regulations. These countries considered these regulations a threat to their economic security. Small island and low-lying states among others were in favor of binding regulations, considering the rise in sea levels as a security threat to their very existence. However, the United States wanted commitments by both the industrialized and developing countries. A strategic debate arose over whether to hold the negotiations under the Kyoto Protocol, which would require ratification, or under the UNFCCC, which would not include that requirement. Copenhagen ended in an inconclusive deadlock. However, two achievements were reached: negotiations would be held only under UNFCCC and Kyoto would be extended beyond its end date of 2012 until 2020.[32]

When he first came into office in 2007, Secretary-General Ban Ki-moon stated that his main goal was to reach a global agreement on climate change, and he worked constantly to keep the issue alive.[33]

> My proudest accomplishment in ten years of public service at the United Nations is the international accord to slow the global havoc of man-made global warming. I championed what would become the 2015 Paris Climate Agreement long before anyone thought the world's governments could agree to limit greenhouse gas emissions.[34]

Many conferences on the issue had come and gone with no consensus. However, in December 2015, the Paris Agreement on climate change was signed by 197 countries. The biggest breakthrough had occurred months before when President Obama met with Chinese leader Xi Jinping, and they announced a public pledge committing the two nations to a successful climate agreement in Paris and a transition to green, low-carbon, climate-resilient economies.[35] With the two leading emitters of GHG now in agreement, the strategy going into Paris was established with a common agenda. The parties to the Paris Agreement made some very significant steps forward: (1) they all agreed that climate change was happening; (2) they agreed that it was in part man-made; and (3) they agreed that all countries must work together to limit global warming to 2 degrees Celsius or even 1.5 degrees from the pre-industrialized era. Those three understandings had never been achieved before. Each country was asked for the first time to prepare a strategy and national plan for the reduction of greenhouse gases. Paris, as stated, was conducted under the UNFCCC, which the United States had already ratified; thus, the US Senate was not required to ratify the Paris Agreement—an important strategy undertaken by Obama at a time when the Senate was under Republican control.

US President Donald Trump, a climate-change denier, pulled the United States out of the accord, but that did not stop countries, and cities for that matter, from moving forward. The election of President Joseph Biden brought the country back into the Paris Agreement just in time for the 2021 UNFCCC Conference of Parties. The Conference of Parties 26 (COP26) that met in Glasgow, Scotland, in November 2021, demonstrated mixed results as a follow-up to Paris. Country plans fell short of what was needed, and some nations, like India, flatly refused to lower the number of coal-fired power plants, claiming they had a right to economic development.[36] Yet, on a positive note, a greater sense of urgency filled the meeting rooms, and agreements were reached on curbing methane gas emissions, limiting deforestation, and changing the ultimate goal from 2 degrees Celsius to the lower rate of 1.5 degrees. Nevertheless, many criticized the conference for not providing any means of enforcement because all of these agreements and commitments are voluntary. Yet, if countries believe that the danger has already arrived and there must be a global response with every country playing its part, then reports from future COP meetings may indicate some relative success.

Despite the lack of enforcement, global attention to the urgency of the crisis has brought some relief. Pre-Paris policies would have projected an increase in global warming by 3.6 degrees Celsius to 4.2 degrees Celsius. "In 2014, before the Paris climate agreement, the world was on track to heat up *nearly 4 degrees Celsius* (7.2 degrees Fahrenheit) by the end of the century, an outcome widely seen as catastrophic."[37]

However, forecasts by the end of 2021, thanks to increases in clean energy such as solar and wind, put the world on pace to achieve about 3 degrees Celsius global warming by the year 2100. This is better but still not enough. After COP26, if countries stick with their commitments to cut emissions even faster, "the world could potentially limit total warming to around *2 to 2.4 degrees Celsius* by 2100."[38] Scientists agree that even that much is too risky, however. Holding the rise in global temperatures down to a safer 1.5 degrees Celsius will require much greater action on these commitments.

The discussion here has focused on international agreements and support for climate change remedies, however, action is also taking place in national litigation forums. Historically, these cases were often disposed of by national courts, but that is changing and more lawsuits against governments and business have been successful. For example, in May 2021, the District Court of the Hague ordered Royal Dutch Shell to "drastically cut its emissions."[39] In March 2021, the German Federal Constitutional Court pronounced on a series of cases brought by diverse groups as challenges to the German Climate Protection Act. While the court rejected the claims on technical grounds, it asked the parliament and administration to work together to take such actions, specifically addressing the consequences of inaction on climate change for future generations. Importantly, the court took up the cases instead of dismissing them, noting their importance. It went on to state that there is an obligation to protect the Earth's climate and ultimately to require climate neutrality, "meaning a true balance between emissions and mitigation."[40] The language of the court fell under the concept of respect for fundamental rights protection. The court also noted Article 9 of the Paris Agreement that developed states are expected to provide financial aid to developing countries in assisting their adaptation to climate change.[41] The approaches of these courts could inspire other national and international legal bodies to engage and take action.

These commitments are not just talk. Extreme weather conditions are already bringing about drought and desertification. Fresh water is under stress, which may leave certain populations threatened by a lack of water for drinking or agriculture. Glaciers, which have provided storage systems for the gradual release of water, are melting at an alarming rate because of global warming, and mountain snow caps that melt in summer to offer water to the lands below are likewise diminishing. Crop irrigation consumes 70 percent of global water, and this level is growing in the developing world. Forests, which provide habitats for biodiversity as well as carbon sinks for the absorption of CO_2, are disappearing at a rate of 6.6 million hectares a year.[42] Other consequences from global warming threaten human security. Warmer temperatures cause higher evaporation in soils and plants, leaving areas vulnerable to fires. Rising sea levels bring about the erosion of coastal areas and deltas, destroying homes, farmland, and villages. Acidification of oceans by CO_2 emissions affects marine life and shellfish because GHG emission impedes the formation of calcium carbonate shells.[43]

Global warming also affects sustainable food supplies. Drought, flooding, and extreme weather events can destroy farmland, which takes up only about 10 percent of the 130 million square kilometers of the earth's land mass.[44] The remaining land is taken up by deserts, mountainous areas, and cities, where food is not generally produced. Lack of food can cause people to migrate in search of sustenance. Food insecurity already leads to high levels of malnutrition, affecting some 40 percent of the world's population or about three billion people, while some 900 million face chronic hunger, defined as an insufficient intake of calories, proteins, vitamins, and mineral nutrients. These deficiencies can impair brain development as well as physical growth. *Stunting* (not reaching the normal growth in height) and *wasting* (very low body weight) are caused by poor diet, parasites, and a lack of access to safe water and sanitation. Shortages of food cause rising prices on food, which hurt the poor, leading to regional food crises. Lack of food security can bring about poor health, a weak immune system, and the inability to fight off infections like SARS, Ebola, HIV/AIDS, and now Covid-19. When people become desperate, they may resort to violence or migration because they have nothing to lose.[45] While the quality of human life and security are clearly threatened by global warming, the consequences of the loss of needed life-giving resources can also erupt into volatile disputes between nations over conflicting territorial claims.

Migration

The migration of peoples moving from one geographic region to another has been the norm for centuries. Humans have migrated throughout history to every continent in pursuit of survival, food, water, shelter, and a better quality of life. Anthropological research has demonstrated that the human species, as we know it today, first appeared in East Africa and from there moved all over the world, finding new homes and developing trade routes up and down Africa, through the Middle East to Asia, to Europe, and on to the Western Hemisphere.

The Universal Declaration of Human Rights (UDHR), approved by the UN General Assembly in 1948, lays out the right to the freedom of movement in several of its articles:

Article 13
1. Everyone has the right to freedom of movement and residence within the borders of each State.
2. Everyone has the right to leave any country, including his own, and to return to his country.

Article 14
1. Everyone has the right to seek and to enjoy in other countries asylum from persecution.
2. This right may not be invoked in the case of prosecution genuinely arising from non-political crimes or from acts contrary to the purposes and principles of the United Nations.

Article 15
1. Everyone has a right to a nationality.
2. No one shall be arbitrarily deprived of his nationality nor denied the right to change his nationality.

Nevertheless, while the UDHR offers the freedom of movement to everyone, in today's legal terms, these rights are different for migrants than for legally defined refugees. Officially, a refugee is defined as "any person who . . . owing to well-founded fear of being persecuted for reasons of race, religion, nationality, membership of a particular social group or political opinion, is outside the country of his nationality and is unable or, owing to such, to return."[46] The rights of refugees include, as examples, the right to protection from refoulement (forced return to the country of origin), the right to freedom of movement, the right to seek asylum, the right to equality and nondiscrimination, and the right to liberty and security of the person.[47] The 1951 Convention, which applied only to refugees who fled their country due to the events of World War II, added a Protocol in 1967 that now applies to all refugees. The Convention is overseen by the UN refugee agency UNHCR.

Migrants, however, are defined as person leaving their country of origin to seek a better life, either for personal or economic reasons. There is no convention offering the same rights to migrants as are guaranteed to refugees. Often the difference between the two categories is unclear; migrants and refugees are mixed together, or the precise definitions of the two groups are broadly misinterpreted by the media. To attempt to remedy this confusion, in 2018 the UN undertook to create a Global Compact for Refugees and adopted the Global Compact for Safe, Orderly and Regular Migration (the Global Compact), which in the Preamble clearly states in paragraph 7 that it is a non-legally-binding framework.

The Global Compact acknowledges that "migrants and refugees may face many common challenges and similar vulnerabilities."[48] Paragraph 4 states the following:

> Refugees and migrants are entitled to the same universal human rights and fundamental freedoms, which must be respected, protected and fulfilled at all times. However, migrants and refugees are distinct groups governed by separate legal frameworks. Only refugees are entitled to the specific international protection as defined by international refugee law. This Global Compact refers to migrants and presents a cooperative framework addressing migration in all its dimensions.[49]

The Global Compact on Migration is based on the concept that migration is a normal part of history and that a comprehensive approach is needed so that people are treated humanely in a safe and orderly manner. "It intends to reduce the risks and vulnerabilities migrants face at different stages of migration by respecting, protecting and fulfilling their human rights."[50] The Compact calls for providing migrants with care and assistance and also aims to address the drivers that lead to migration. Its success rests on trust and the mutual solidarity of states in a spirit of reaching a win-win situation.

The need for such a compact was brought about by the maltreatment of migrants and refugees during the mass movements of people into Europe beginning in 2015 and continuing today. Migrants desperately fleeing adversity drowned at sea trying to reach parts of Europe and safety, their travails captured by the media. They were denied entrance by governments that erected barbed-wire barriers. Abandoned in the cold, many were deprived of food and water for days. Women gave birth during their attempts to reach safety with no medical treatment available. Accounts show that 1.3 million refugees and migrants flooded into Europe in 2015.[51] Taken by surprise, countries were left to find their own solutions, some denying entrance to any "outsiders," as they were called. The EU eventually stepped in to provide some common order and policy, asking each member to accept people in relation to the country's population and capacity to care for them. But many nations ignored these requests.

The International Centre for Migration Policy Development (ICMPD) estimated that there were 272 million international migrants in 2020, and the numbers grow each year.[52] By 2022, the IOM reported the total to be 281 million.[53] In 2019, 68 percent of refugees came from five countries: Syria, Venezuela, Afghanistan, South Sudan, and Myanmar.[54] Many of those moved within their own region or continent. Host countries with the largest numbers of refugees and migrants are Turkey with 3.7 million, Colombia with 1.7 million, Pakistan with 1.4 million, Uganda with 1.4 million, and Germany hosting 1.2 million.[55] During 2020, irregular migration arrivals to Europe shifted away from the Eastern Mediterranean route, which decreased by a dramatic 75 percent. Instead, migration into Europe moved to other routes, including by Central Mediterranean, Western Balkan, and Western African routes, the latter of which increased by some 900 percent over 2019.[56] Nevertheless, the Covid-19 pandemic cut off mobility, "stranded migrants, destroyed jobs and income, reduced remittances and pushed millions of migrants and vulnerable populations into poverty. It has, however, not put an end to migration."[57]

Europe is not the only region witnessing an influx of migrants. By 2019, UNHCR estimated some 15 million persons were migrating within Latin America, including 8.2 million internally displaced and about 3.6 million Venezuelans who had left their country of origin, flowing primarily to other Latin American nations. The causes for these high numbers are a combination of crime, food insecurity, state failure, and the inability to earn a decent livelihood.[58] Africa faces even stronger numbers of displacement. The number of refugees in Africa rose to 7.3 million in 2020, while at the same time the number of internally displaced persons increased to 18.5 million.[59] The Sahel is a growing region of concern. "Between 2018 and 2020 an estimated 1.8 million people were internally displaced and 845,000 had to flee across borders."[60] Actually, contrary to popular views, asylum seekers going from Africa to the EU rank below those from Asia, the Middle East, and Latin America.[61] The flow of African migrants tends to remain within the African continent. This is also true for parts of Asia. Within the eleven countries of Southeast Asia, which include among others Myanmar, the Philippines, Vietnam, and Thailand, there continues to be large-scale population movements. Yet the majority of the about 23.6 million migrants remain on the continent or in the subregion. In this case, more than half are female due to the demand for domestic care workers.[62]

While the data appear daunting, global and regional efforts are underway to meet these challenges. The Global Compact on Migration, discussed earlier, offers twenty-three objectives for safe, orderly, and regular migration. They include such goals as improving the collection of accurate data, facilitating fair and ethical treatment, curbing human trafficking, ensuring all migrants have proof of legal identity, saving lives, and providing access to basic services, to name a few. The Compact also calls for the strengthening of "international cooperation and

global partnerships of safe, orderly and regular migration."[63] In support
of worldwide cooperation to implement the Compact, the UN established
the Network on Migration, which is led by an executive committee of
nine UN bodies: the International Labour Organization (ILO), IOM
(which acts as the coordinator and secretariat for the Network), Office of
the High Commissioner for Human Rights (OHCHR), UN Department
for Economic and Social Affairs, UN Development Programme (UNDP),
UNHCR, the UN Children's Fund (UNICEF), UN Office on Drugs and
Crime (UNODC), and the WHO. The objectives of the Network are to
"ensure effective, timely, coordinated UN system-wide support to member states in their implementation, follow-up and review of the GCM
[Global Compact on Migration], for the rights and well-being of all
migrants and their communities of destination, origin, and transit."[64]

The Global Compact, however, is silent on standards for undocumented or irregular migrants. Therefore, the Platform for International
Cooperation on Undocumented Migrants (PICUM) was established as a
network of organizations who work together to provide justice for
undocumented migrants within Europe. The Platform is based in Brussels, Belgium, but works across Europe to provide support for individuals who may have migrated outside conventional methods, perhaps as
victims of human trafficking.[65] Adding to these efforts, the EU in 2021
enhanced its 2008 EU Pact on Migration and Asylum:

> The Commission welcomes the agreement that the European Parlia-
> ment and the Council have just found to transform the European Asy-
> lum Support Office into a European Union Agency of Asylum. It is a
> key initiative under the New Pact on Migration and Asylum. The new
> agency will help make asylum procedures in member states of higher
> quality, more uniform and faster. Its new reserve of 500 experts will
> also provide more effective support to national asylum systems facing
> a high caseload, making the overall EU migration management system
> more efficient and sustainable.[66]

In addition to these global and European initiatives, Latin Americans are coming together to address issues related to migrants fleeing
the crisis in Venezuela. As of October 2021, due to a combination of
violence, lack of food and medicine, and a fundamentally failed state in
Venezuela, more than 5.9 million people had fled the country, creating
one of the greatest displacement crises in the world.[67] The Friends of the
Quito Process, which includes Latin American countries, is a new group
established in 2018. The group has thirteen member states, all from
Latin America and the Caribbean, and was created to promote cooperation among countries receiving Venezuelan migrants and refugees. It

aims "to specifically address this humanitarian situation separate and apart from political questions about Venezuela's future."[68] The aim of the group is to effectively, in a cooperative manner, address the needs of migrants and the host countries receiving these people on the move, while remaining neutral and without interfering with, or commenting on, the political difficulties in Venezuela.

Concluding Thoughts

In sum, global efforts have emerged to address the intermingled challenges of climate change, migration, and global health, which taken together affect the quality of the human condition and human security. Migrants flee many types of situations—including drought, floods, rising sea levels, and food insecurity—all caused by climate change. Global health also impacts migrants who may be forced to live in crowded conditions as they wait to enter countries that have closed down their borders. The Covid-19 pandemic forced businesses and factories to shut down, causing major shortages in needed food, medicine, and other essentials. All this continues to cause tensions as costs rise. Disputes that emerge over competing interests and desperation can also lead to violence, affecting national security concerns. Only through cooperation across countries and the formation of humanitarian norms that promote respect and protection for all human beings in the areas of health, climate change, and the movement of people can the world begin to better these conditions.

Notes

1. *World Migration Report 2022,* published by the International Organization for Migration, 2022.

2. "Countries Where COVID-19 Has Spread," *Worldometer,* July 10, 2022, https://www.worldometers.info/coronavirus.

3. Benjamin Mueller and Stephanie Nolen, "W.H.O. Finds Covid Deaths Vastly Higher," *New York Times,* May 6, 2022, page A1.

4. "A Paradox Not Seen Before in Human History," International Organization for Migration, Migrants and Refugees, December 29, 2021, https://news.un.org/en/story/2021/12/1108472.

5. Ibid.

6. *World Migration Report 2022.*

7. Kofi Annan, "Secretary-General's Remarks at the Doctors of the World Health and Human Rights Leadership Awards Dinner (As Prepared for Delivery)," United Nations, New York, June 16, 2005.

8. UNAIDS Fact Sheet, "Global HIV & AIDs Statistics," World AIDS Day 2021, www.unaids.org/en/resources/fact-sheet.

9. Knobler et al., *Impact of Globalization on Infectious Disease,* https://www.ncbi.nlm.nih.gov/books/NBK56579.

10. Trade between Europe and Asia expanded considerably during the Greek era (about the fourth century BCE), by which time various land routes had been well established connecting Greece, via Anatolia (Asia Minor), with the northwestern part of the Indian subcontinent. "Trade of Asia," Britannica, n.d., https://www.britannica.com/place/Asia/Trade.

11. "A World in Motion: The Global Movement of Peoples, Products, Pathogens, and Power," chapter 1 in Knobler et al., *Impact of Globalization on Infectious Disease.*

12. "International Sanitary Conferences [1851]," Contagion: Historical Views of Diseases and Epidemics, Curiosity Collections, Harvard Library, n.d., https://curiosity.lib.harvard.edu/contagion/feature/international-sanitary-conferences.

13. UN General Assembly, Resolution A/Res/69/1, September 2014.

14. UN Health Consortium includes FAO, UNFPA, UNICEF, WFP, UNDP, and the World Bank Group.

15. David Sacks, "Countries in China's Belt and Road Initiative: Who's In and Who's Out," Council on Foreign Relations, Asia Unbound blog, March 24, 2021, https://www.cfr.org/blog/countries-chinas-belt-and-road-initiative-whos-and-whos-out.

16. World Health Organization, "Cooperating Globally to Respond to Health Crisis and Disease Outbreaks," China memorandum of understanding on Belt and Road Initiative, 2017, https://www.who.int/china/activities/cooperating-globally-to-respond-to-health-crisis-and-disease-outbreaks.

17. Ariansen et al., "Time for Global Health Diplomacy," *Lancet* 395 (May 30, 2020), https://doi.org/10.1016/S0140-6736(20)30490-6.

18. Council on Foreign Relations, "Major Epidemics in the Modern Era, 1899–2021," n.d., https://www.cfr.org/timeline/major-epidemics-modern-era.

19. "Constructing a New Agenda: Global Health and International Relations," chapter 2 in McInnes and Lee, *Global Health and International Relations.*

20. Guterres calls for "sustained political commitment" for a healthier world. UN News, https://news.un.org/en/story/2022/10/1129577.

21. Suerie Moon and Ilona Kickbusch, "A Pandemic Treaty for a Fragmented Global Polity," *Lancet Public Health* 6, no. 6 (May 5, 2021), https://doi.org/10.1016/S2468-2667(21)00103-1. See also: Johnathan H. Duff et al., "A Global Public Health Convention for the 21st Century," *Lancet Public Health* 6, no. 6 (May 5, 2021), https://doi.org/10.1016/S2468-2667(21)00070-0.

22. WHO, *Stronger Collaboration for an Equitable and Resilient Recovery Towards the Health-Related Sustainable Development Goals: 2021 Progress Report on the Global Action Plan for Healthy Lives and Well-Being for All* (Geneva: World Health Organization, 2021), https://www.who.int/publications/i/item/9789240026209.

23. Independent Panel for Pandemic Preparedness and Response, *COVID-19: Make It the Last Pandemic,* May 2021, https://theindependentpanel.org/wp-content/uploads/2021/05/COVID-19-Make-it-the-Last-Pandemic_final.pdf

24. Joseph Lampert, "Science and Politics on a Warming Planet: The IPCC and the Representation of Future Generations," in Shapiro and Lampert, *Charter of the United Nations,* p. 226.

25. Ibid.

26. Ibid., pp. 226–227.

27. Ibid., p. 231.

28. Ibid., p. 225.

29. Ibid., p. 231.

30. Chasek, Downing, and Brown, *Global Environmental Politics,* pp. 166–167.

31. Ibid., p. 171.

32. Ibid., pp. 171–177.

33. Krasno, *The Collected Papers of Secretary-General Ban Ki-moon.*

34. Ban Ki-moon, *Resolved,* p. 265.

35. The White House, "U.S.-China Joint Presidential Statement on Climate Change," press release, September 25, 2015, www.whitehouse,gov/the-press-office /2015/09/25/us-china-joint-presidential-statement-climate-change.

36. David Stringer and Rajesh Kumar Singh, "At 14 Million Tons a Day, India and China Still Addicted to Coal," *Bloomberg Green,* November 15, 2021, www .bloomberg.com/news.

37. Nadia Popovich and Bill Marsh, "The World Has Bent the Emissions Curve. But Not Enough," *New York Times,* October 27, 2021, p. A1; emphasis in original.

38. Ibid.

39. Helmut Philipp Aust, "Climate Protection Act Case, Order of the First Senate" published online January 14, 2022 (Cambridge, UK: Cambridge University Press).

40. Ibid.

41. Ibid.

42. Chasek, Downing, and Brown, *Global Environmental Politics,* pp. 7–8.

43. Sachs, *Age of Sustainable Development,* pp. 334–335.

44. Ibid., p. 328.

45. Ibid., pp. 318–328.

46. UNHCR, https://www.unhcr.org/what-is-a-refugee.html.

47. UNHCR, 1951 Convention and 1967 Protocol Relating to the Status of Refugees, https://www.unhcr.org/en-us/1951-refugee-convention.html.

48. Global Compact for Safe, Orderly, and Regular Migration, Final Draft, July 11, 2018, Preamble, paragraph 3.

49. Ibid., paragraph 4.

50. Ibid., paragraph 12.

51. Pew Research Center, "Number of Refugees to Europe Surges to Record 1.3 million in 2015," August 2, 2016, www.pewresearch.org/global/2016/08/02.

52. International Centre for Migration Policy Development, "Introduction," in *ICMPD Migration Outlook 2021: Seven Things to Look Out for in 2021, Origins, Key Events and Priorities for Europe,* January 7, 2021, https://www.icmpd.org/file /download/50542/file/ICMPD_Migration_Outlook_2021_final.pdf.

53. *World Migration Report 2022.*

54. International Centre for Migration Policy Development, "Introduction," in *ICMPD Migration Outlook 2021.*

55. UNHCR, *Global Trends: Forced Displacement in 2020,* June 18, 2021, https:// www.unhcr.org/statistics/unhcrstats/60b638e37/global-trends-forced-displacement -2020.html.

56. Ibid., p. 3.

57. Ibid., p. 2.

58. Ibid., p. 9.

59. Ibid., p. 8.

60. Ibid., p. 3.

61. Ibid.

62. Migration Data Portal, "Migration Data in South-eastern Asia," midyear 2020 report, accessed January 9, 2022, https://migrationdataportal.org/regional -data-overview/south-eastern-asia.

63. "Objectives for Safe, Orderly and Regular Migration," in Global Compact for Migration, pp. 5–6.

64. UN Network on Migration, "About Us," January 9, 2022, https://www
.migrationnetwork.un.org/about#.

65. Platform for International Cooperation on Undocumented Migrants, home-page, January 9, 2022, https://picum.org.

66. European Commission, "New Pact on Migration and Asylum: Agreement Reached on the New European Union Agency for Asylum," press release, June 29, 2021, Brussels, www.ec.europa.eu/commission.presscorner.

67. UNHCR Staff, "Data Reveals Plight of Venezuelan Refugees and Migrants Evicted in Pandemic," October 25, 2021, https://www.unhcr.org/en-us/news/latest /2021/10/61769bea4/data-reveals-plight-venezuelan-refugees-migrants-evicted -pandemic.html.

68. "International Technical Meeting on Human Mobility of Venezuelan Citizens in the Region (Quito Process)," UN International Organization on Migration (IOM), accessed November 20, 2021, https://iom.int/node/103049.

9

Disarmament and Arms Control

Randy Rydell

Disarmament and arms control efforts at the United Nations remain among its most important activities to keep the organization relevant in a shifting global environment, especially one characterized by frequent wars and arms races. While many may question the effectiveness of these efforts in meeting such challenges, few can dispute the degree that disarmament has become part of the UN's identity. As Inis Claude once wrote, "The assertion that disarmament is the key to peace and that its promotion is the foremost task of the world organization has become a central tenet of the orthodox ideology of the United Nations speech-making and resolution-drafting."[1] In this chapter, I argue that the UN's work on disarmament has produced far more than words alone and that it continues to confirm not just the UN's relevance but also its indispensability in fulfilling its core mandate to maintain international peace and security.

The UN's "Hardy Perennial" and Humanity's Elusive Goal

Over 2,000 years ago, Prince Rama in the Sanskrit epic *Ramayana* prohibited his generals from using a massively destructive weapon against his evil enemy Ravana because any such use would violate what were *even then* viewed as the "ancient" laws of war.[2] References to disarmament and defense conversion can be found in the Bible, including the memorable line from Isaiah (2.4) calling on people to "beat their swords

179

into plowshares," which has fittingly been inscribed on a wall in Ralph Bunche Park outside UN headquarters.

While the history of disarmament clearly predates the appearance of the nation-state, it has taken on new significance with the rapid advance of weapon technology in the modern era and what would soon become the potential of armed conflicts to expand to a global scale. The deadly combined growth of nationalism and militarism in the nineteenth century inspired early efforts to conclude international treaties to prohibit or limit certain weapons, like poison gas, incendiaries, and dum-dum bullets. The Hague Peace Conventions of 1899 and 1907 deliberated various commitments both to disarmament and to limiting the conduct of warfare.

After World War I, the Covenant of the League of Nations required "the reduction of national armaments to the lowest point consistent with national safety and the enforcement by common action of international obligations," and the parties also agreed that "the manufacture by private enterprise of munitions and implements of war is open to grave objections" (Article 8). The League of Nations also established a disarmament section in its Secretariat. Yet interwar disarmament efforts came to naught.

Despite or largely because of World War II, disarmament once again was on the global agenda. It explicitly appeared twice in the UN Charter, in Articles 11 and 47, relating respectively to the deliberative roles of the General Assembly and Security Council mandates to plan and adopt measures to maintain international peace and security. In language reminiscent of the League Covenant, Article 26 also addressed "the establishment and maintenance of international peace and security with the least diversion for armaments of the world's human and economic resources." The history of the UN's work in disarmament reveals the evolution of these mandates to include the establishment of new institutions and new mandates, including for the UN Secretary-General.[3]

The United Nations has been pursuing two fundamental goals in this field since its creation, as symbolized by two of its earliest resolutions. Resolution 1(I) of January 24, 1946—the General Assembly's first resolution—established the goal of eliminating all "weapons adaptable to mass destruction" (WMDs) including specifically "atomic weapons"; it also created a UN Atomic Energy Commission under the Security Council to consider both the elimination of such weapons and peaceful uses of nuclear technology.[4] On December 14, 1946, the General Assembly adopted resolution 41(I) dealing more broadly with the "general regulation and reduction of armaments and armed forces"; the

Security Council echoed this regulatory goal on February 13, 1947, by adopting resolution 18, which established a UN Commission on Conventional Armaments.[5] Thus, by 1947, the two primary mandates of disarmament (i.e., the *elimination* of WMDs and the *regulation* of conventional arms) emerged as the foundation for the UN's basic approach to dealing with weapons. Facing the realities of the emerging Cold War and its resulting stalemate in the commissions, the General Assembly combined both commissions into a new UN Disarmament Commission in 1952, but the basic goals remained.

These twin goals have proven to be remarkably durable. By 1955, Secretary-General Dag Hammarskjöld was already referring to disarmament as the UN's "hardy perennial," an apt description to the present day.[6]

It is noteworthy that the UN has never sought just to "regulate" nuclear weapons or to "eliminate" all conventional arms. The Charter, for example, also has language requiring states to contribute armed forces to assist in maintaining international peace and security[7] while also allowing states under certain specific circumstances to use force in self-defense.[8]

The dialectic at the UN between disarmament and arms control—with both being pursued on parallel but separate tracks—has historically yielded a mixed record. While it has remained a kind of de facto "double helix" encompassing virtually all UN activities to control weaponry, this evolution has been uneven at best, as discussed below. Its persistence has yielded some impressive achievements, but also some major setbacks, as the UN has institutionally sought to adapt to changing political and technological circumstances. This ongoing evolution has shaped both the functions and structures of the UN in disarmament.

Primary Functions

The work of the UN in disarmament centers on certain specific functions that together relate to the creation, maintenance, and adaptation of multilateral norms, that is, norms that apply to all UN member states. Various regional arrangements—such as nuclear-weapon-free zones—supplement such norms, as do an assortment of bilateral or plurilateral treaties and gentlemen's agreements that apply to disarmament. These functions derive from an assumption—often unspoken but widely held throughout the UN—that the world community can best pursue international peace and security and global prosperity within a framework of shared expectations of state behavior. Together, these norms—especially those that states regard as legally binding—constitute "the rule of law" as it applies to disarmament, a field that has grown significantly, especially in recent years.

While the Charter is at the heart of disarmament's international rule of law, the UN performs its normative functions by a variety of means. It offers states a unique global forum for the *deliberation* of both existing and evolving norms. It provides a forum for the maintenance of some *accountability* for the performance of international legal and political commitments. It embraces the norm of *universality* in ensuring that even the smallest of states (consistent with the "principle of sovereign equality" of member states in Article 2.1 of the Charter) has an opportunity to participate in the creation and maintenance of norms. It functions (or at least seeks) to ensure that the agreed multilateral norms are *equitable* in the sense that they do not convey privileged benefits to one state or group of states over another. On rare occasions not involving a great power, it has also served to *enforce* disarmament norms, as, for example, through its activities to address WMD issues in Libya and Iraq and its disarmament-related activities performed by agreement after local armed conflicts. It recognizes the importance of *representation* through participation by civil society in the deliberation of such norms and makes available opportunities for groups to monitor and contribute to this norm-building and norm-maintenance process. Its debates, resolutions, and publications help to *educate* the public both about the UN and the importance of disarmament issues. All together, these functions serve to preserve the priority and relevance of disarmament within the UN system as a primary means to strengthen international peace and security.

Evolving Structures of the "United Nations Disarmament Machinery"

The history of UN activities in disarmament reveals a continuous process of organizational growth and adaptation, as seen in the proliferation of UN offices and institutions with disarmament functions since the days of the early commissions. Together these entities constitute the UN's "disarmament machinery," the collective name for its organizations that serve as a de facto "assembly line" for creating and maintaining multilateral disarmament norms.[9] Former Secretary-General Kofi Annan once noted that the many divisions among member states have hampered the operation of this machinery. "Quite frankly," he said, "much of the established multilateral disarmament machinery has started to rust—a problem due not to the machinery itself but to the apparent lack of political will to use it."[10] The following description builds on this well-founded proposition.

After the demise of the first two commissions in 1952, the General Assembly created the UN Disarmament Commission (UNDC) to prepare a comprehensive disarmament and arms control treaty.[11] Yet the UNDC was also unable to make progress, again due to the Cold War, and the next major (system-wide) organizational change came in 1978 with the General Assembly's first Special Session on Disarmament (SSOD-I). At that event, the General Assembly adopted the blueprint for the present-day configuration of this machinery, along with a declaration of principles, a "programme of action," and an agreement that the UN's "ultimate goal" shall be "general and complete disarmament under effective international control" (GCD),[12] a term encompassing both WMD disarmament and conventional arms control—another distant echo of the two earlier postwar commissions.[13]

Recalling that a primary function of the General Assembly under the Charter is debate, SSOD-I made the First Committee (which covers disarmament and international security) responsible for preparing and deliberating disarmament resolutions, the next stage of the norm-building process. In 2020, the General Assembly adopted sixty-one disarmament-related resolutions and ten decisions; twenty-two resolutions dealt with nuclear weapons and most of these required a vote. This illustrates a familiar pattern in the General Assembly voting: the lack of consensus on nuclear disarmament issues. Only three regionally focused resolutions were adopted without a vote, indicating persisting divisions among member states, especially between nuclear-weapon and non-nuclear-weapon states.[14]

Although nonbinding, these resolutions have historically established or clarified international expectations for progress in achieving disarmament; such resolutions could also launch studies, request reports from the Secretary-General, or refer information to the Security Council. At its Special Session in 1978, the General Assembly reestablished the UNDC as its subsidiary body and (as later elaborated) endowed it with a mandate to deliberate two specific weapons issues—with one on nuclear disarmament—over a three-year period and prepare recommendations to the General Assembly for developing agreed standards and principles in those issue areas. Unlike its 1952 predecessor, the UNDC consists of all UN member states and is subordinate to the General Assembly, not the Security Council. From 1978 to 1999, it adopted unanimously sixteen

texts of principles, guidelines, and recommendations.[15] After a long stalemate, it was finally able in 2017 to adopt consensus recommendations on
"Practical Confidence-Building Measures in the Field of Conventional
Weapons."[16] Yet, persisting disagreements, especially between nuclear-
weapon and non-nuclear-weapon states, have prevented additional
progress in the UNDC; often, the mere agreement on an agenda has not
been possible, even in 2002, the year of its fiftieth anniversary.

Based in Geneva, the Conference on Disarmament (CD) is responsible for the third stage in the norm-building process: negotiating multilateral disarmament treaties. Its raison d'être is to establish legally
binding disarmament commitments that apply universally. The CD or
one of its predecessors was responsible for negotiating (or deliberating)
the Nuclear Non-Proliferation Treaty (NPT), the Chemical Weapons
Convention, the Biological Weapons Convention, the Comprehensive
Nuclear Test Ban Treaty (CTBT), and other accords. While the CD is
institutionally separate from the UN, it is customarily viewed as part of
the UN disarmament machinery and maintains a close relationship to
the UN: the Director-General of the UN's Geneva office serves as the
CD's Secretary-General and is also the UN Secretary-General's personal representative to the CD; the General Assembly approves its
budget and recommends agenda items; the UN Secretariat's office in
Geneva provides administrative and substantive assistance; and the CD
reports to the General Assembly. In addition, many representatives of
national delegations to the CD often represent their countries in deliberations at UN headquarters, notably in the First Committee and the meetings of state parties to the NPT.

Like the UNDC, the CD has also experienced long periods of institutional deadlock, largely due to its rules of procedure, which require a
consensus on substantive issues. Over the past two decades, the CD has
been deeply split among groups of states that seek a priority for nuclear
disarmament (developing countries), a ban on space weapons (Russia
and China), and a prohibition on the production of fissile material for
weapons (the nuclear-weapon states and NATO states). The last treaty
to emerge from the CD was the CTBT in 1996.

Yet the CD's uneven record of achievement and its gridlock have
certainly not discouraged additional states from seeking to join. Its earliest antecedent was a small "sub-group" in the original 1952 UNDC, consisting of key members of the Security Council. This evolved into several disarmament committees with negotiating mandates: the "ten-nation
committee" (1960); the "eighteen-nation committee" (1964); the thirty-
one-member "conference of the committee on disarmament" (1969); the

forty-member "committee on disarmament" (1979); and the CD in 1984, with its current membership of sixty-five, which SSOD-I formally identified as the world's "single multilateral disarmament negotiating forum." The CD's deliberations each year focus on variations of a long-standing official agenda originally called the "Decalogue"; its 2021 agenda contained eight items, including nuclear and WMD disarmament, conventional arms control, military spending, space weapons, transparency, and a "comprehensive programme of disarmament" (embodying key GCD themes).[17]

Other Key UN Disarmament Institutions

The roles of the UN Secretariat and the Secretary-General in advancing disarmament have evolved considerably since 1946.[18] This demonstrates the ability of the UN to respond to challenges not explicitly identified in the Charter—a document that never defined *disarmament,* never identified a role for the Secretary-General in disarmament, and never prescribed any role for the Secretariat in this field. These roles and functions developed through mandates that reflected the demands and expectations of the member states, as well as through the demonstration of some personal initiative. Hammarskjöld distinguished between two roles of the UN, as "static conference machinery" and "dynamic instrument."[19] In disarmament, these are reflected in the Secretariat's role in managing conferences and performing routine administrative functions, and in the Secretary-General's authority within the constraints of the Charter (and existing mandates) to initiate his own proposals, studies, major public addresses, and referrals to the Security Council, as well as to set disarmament priorities within the autonomous Office for Disarmament Affairs (UNODA) and the wider UN system.

All of these particular activities derive from a broad interpretation of the five articles of Chapter XV of the Charter, which established some guidelines for the activities of the Secretary-General (as "chief administrative officer") and the Secretariat. The classic "elastic clause" here is found in Article 98, which provides that the Secretary-General "shall perform such other functions" as the other UN organs may entrust to that office. The General Assembly and NPT Review Conferences have been most active in assigning new mandates to the Secretary-General and the Secretariat, typically in the form of requesting studies, appointing groups of governmental experts, creating and maintaining databases, educating the public, and approving and overseeing organizational reforms.

A *Secretary-General's Bulletin* describes the activities of the UNODA and its three regional centers in Latin America and the Caribbean, Africa, and Asia—led by a high representative with rank of under-secretary-general—that reports to the Secretary-General. The principal mandates of the UNODA are to assist the Secretary-General on both substantive and administrative issues, while also assisting member states and civil society on disarmament matters.[20] This includes managing the Programme of Fellowships on Disarmament (another product of SSOD-I), which has trained over 1,000 officials from 170 states, largely from developing countries.[21] In 2021, the office published a *Strategic Plan* for its activities over the next five years, which covers the full gamut of UN mandates in disarmament including, not surprisingly, those in Secretary-General António Guterres's "Agenda for Disarmament" (discussed later).[22]

While UNODA has always emphasized the priority of nuclear disarmament, it has also created three databases that serve to enhance transparency on several weapons issues; these include: (1) the United Nations Register of Conventional Arms[23] (which tracks official reports of arms transfers), (b) the United Nations Report on Military Expenditures[24] (based on data reported by states), and (c) the Repository of Information Provided by Nuclear-Weapon States[25] (with official descriptions of nuclear disarmament activities). The value of these databases as confidence-building measures will depend upon the continued growth of participation by member states, another UNODA goal.

The Secretary-General also has an Advisory Board on Disarmament Matters, consisting of fifteen senior diplomats, former officials, academics, and private researchers with expertise in disarmament. The board meets twice a year and issues a report to the Secretary-General on its activities to fulfill its official mandates—that is, advice on current or emerging arms control and disarmament issues, including ongoing studies under UN auspices; advice on the implementation of the UN Disarmament Information Programme, an initiative to educate the public about disarmament; and service as the Board of Trustees of the United Nations Institute for Disarmament Research (UNIDIR).[26]

Established after a mandate from SSOD-I, UNIDIR is an autonomous, independent UN think tank based in Geneva that produces in-depth studies on a wide range of disarmament issues, including nuclear weapons and all other WMD, conventional arms, as well as emerging issues such as artificial intelligence, cyber weapons, gender and disarmament, hypervelocity weapons, autonomous weapons, missiles and missile defense, space weapons, and initiatives to establish a Middle East WMD-Free Zone.

Contrary to its Charter mandates both in disarmament and in the maintenance of international peace and security, the Security Council's record in disarmament has been disappointing. It has, for example, never implemented its principal Charter mandates to formulate "plans to be submitted to the Members of the United Nations for the establishment of a system for the regulation of armaments" (Article 26) and to use its Military Staff Council to provide advice on (inter alia) "the regulation of armaments, and possible disarmament" (Article 47). On the rare occasions when it has tangentially addressed nuclear disarmament at its summit meetings of heads of state and government (most notably on January 31, 1992, and September 24, 2009), it has referred to the "proliferation" (though not the *existence*) of "weapons of mass destruction" as "a threat to international peace and security," while calling for compliance with existing nonproliferation and disarmament commitments.[27] Other Council resolutions on disarmament-related themes have focused on particular states (e.g., Libya, Iran, Iraq, and North Korea), the nonproliferation of WMD, controls over the illicit trade in small arms and light weapons, and activities in peacekeeping and peacebuilding operations.

Regarding the latter, the United Nations has for many years implemented several disarmament, demobilization, and reintegration (DDR) initiatives that seek to facilitate the transition from local armed conflicts to the restoration of peace and security. As described in a UN field manual, the standards and principles for conducting DDR missions are designed to take into account the unique circumstances of individual conflicts.[28] Current DDR standards specifically for "disarmament" include four activities: information gathering and operational planning; weapons collection or retrieval; stockpile management; and weapons destruction.[29] As of 2020, DDR activities have been part of UN peacekeeping operations in the Central African Republic, the Democratic Republic of Congo, Mali, and South Sudan, with related activities underway in several additional countries, largely in Africa.[30]

With respect to norm building, the UN's principal juridical organ—the International Court of Justice—has made a groundbreaking contribution that continues to have lasting effects on global disarmament efforts. At the request of the General Assembly, it issued its Advisory Opinion in 1996 on the "Legality of the Threat or Use of Nuclear Weapons."[31] The opinion followed six months of deliberations and submissions from forty states, including four nuclear-weapon states (China took no part), and was the focus of a worldwide network of peace activists, doctors, and lawyers organized as the World Court Project.[32]

While a divided court found that any threat or use of such weapons would "generally" be against international law (without addressing the legality of use when a state's survival was at stake), the Court agreed unanimously that any use of nuclear weapons must comply with the laws of war, in particular humanitarian law, and that there exists an obligation to undertake and bring to a conclusion negotiations leading to nuclear disarmament. Though the nuclear-weapons states and their allies never accepted this opinion, Costa Rica has twice circulated a Model Nuclear Weapons Convention in UN and NPT arenas, and annual General Assembly resolutions continue to endorse the ICJ's opinion.[33] It also helped to lay the legal foundation for the Treaty on the Prohibition of Nuclear Weapons, which entered into force in 2021.

The greatest contribution of the United Nations to disarmament has come in the area of establishing and strengthening global norms in this field, and the multilateral disarmament treaties that have emerged under UN auspices stand as perhaps its greatest contribution in bringing the "rule of law" to disarmament, given that these norms are legally binding. Table 9.1 identifies these key treaties and the prominent role of the Secretary-General as the Depositary for most of them (and all of them adopted after 1978).[34]

Table 9.1   Multilateral Disarmament Treaties Concluded Under UN Auspices

Treaty	Year of Entry into Force	Parties (as of July 2022)	UN Secretary-General as Depositary
Outer Space	1967	111	
Nuclear Nonproliferation	1970	191	
Seabed Convention	1972	94	
Biological Weapons Convention	1975	183	
Environmental Modification	1978	78	✓
Certain Conventional Weapons	1983	125	✓
Moon	1984	18	✓
Comprehensive Nuclear Test Ban	1996[a]	170	✓
Chemical Weapons Convention	1997	193	✓
Nuclear Terrorism Convention	2007	118	✓
Arms Trade Treaty	2014	110	✓
Prohibition of Nuclear Weapons	2021	65	✓

Source: UNODA, Disarmament Treaties Database; and UNODA, *Disarmament and Related Treaties.*

Note. a. Adopted at the UN in 1996 but not yet entered into force.

A Tale of Two Secretaries-General

All of the UN's Secretaries-General addressed disarmament and, with variations of emphasis, stressed its importance in the maintenance of international peace and security. On only two occasions, however, did they elaborate a comprehensive plan for the achievement of the UN's disarmament mandates. These initiatives served primarily as a call to action by member states, who remain the ultimate "decisionmakers" at the United Nations and on all disarmament issues. Yet, in addition to serving as a blueprint for global action, these proposals also constituted a managerial plan for the handling of disarmament within the UN system itself. In summary, their common goal was to strengthen the priority of disarmament both in the conduct of international relations and in the day-to-day work of the Secretariat and the UN disarmament machinery.

The first such comprehensive initiative came from Secretary-General Ban Ki-moon at a disarmament conference hosted by the EastWest Institute at the United Nations in 2008.[35] He began by explaining why he was making this proposal. He called WMDs and disarmament "one of the gravest challenges facing international peace and security" and said that a world free of nuclear weapons "would be a global public good of the highest order." He noted that the UN had pursued disarmament for so long that "it has become part of the Organization's very identity."[36] He also became the first Secretary-General to state that the doctrine of nuclear deterrence "has proven to be contagious" and has thus made nuclear nonproliferation more difficult to achieve.

The first item of his five-point proposal was a call on all NPT parties, especially the nuclear-weapon states, "to fulfill their obligation under the treaty to undertake negotiations on effective measures leading to nuclear disarmament"; he added that they "could pursue this goal by agreement on a framework of separate, mutually reinforcing instruments."[37] In addition, Secretary-General Ban specifically called for an alternative nuclear-weapons convention.

In his second point, he challenged the Security Council to focus on "security issues in the nuclear disarmament process." He urged its permanent members to "unambiguously assure non-nuclear-weapon states that they will not be the subject of the use or threat of use of nuclear weapons." He called on the Council "to convene a summit on nuclear disarmament." And he urged non-NPT states to freeze their own nuclear-weapon capabilities and make their own disarmament commitments.[38]

His third point sought to bring the "rule of law" to disarmament through the advancement of new multilateral disarmament treaties (entry into force of the CTBT and negotiation of a fissile material treaty) and the further advancement of regional nuclear-weapon-free zones, including in the Middle East. And he urged all NPT parties to conclude the most advanced safeguard agreements with the International Atomic Energy Agency.

For his fourth point, he called for improvements in transparency and accountability among the nuclear-weapon states, in terms of reporting more details about their arsenals and the measures they are taking to reduce and eliminate them. He urged these states to report such information to the UN Secretariat.

Finally, he addressed a number of what he called "complementary measures" outside the field of nuclear disarmament, including the elimination of other types of WMDs; new efforts against WMD terrorism; limits on the production and trade of conventional arms; and new weapons bans, including on missiles and space weapons. He also urged the General Assembly to convene a "World Summit on disarmament, non-proliferation and terrorist use of weapons of mass destruction."[39]

He concluded, "When disarmament advances, the world advances. That is why it has such strong support at the United Nations."[40]

The international response (most notably from the non-nuclear-weapon states and nongovernmental groups) was very positive, and it was even endorsed by former US secretary of state Henry Kissinger, who attended the EastWest Institute event. Yet the impact on the nuclear-weapon states was less apparent, as all such states proceeded with well-funded, long-term projects to "modernize" their nuclear weapons and their delivery systems. Global military spending continued to grow, and the stalemates in the UN disarmament machinery persisted.

This disappointing environment set the context for the second and more comprehensive disarmament proposal offered a decade later by Secretary-General Guterres.[41] He announced his "disarmament agenda" at the University of Geneva on May 18, 2018.[42] UNODA published simultaneously a seventy-three-page report, *Securing Our Common Future: An Agenda for Disarmament.*[43] In October 2018, UNODA issued its "Implementation Plan" for this initiative.[44] The Guterres proposal built upon Ban's earlier initiative in several respects. It significantly expanded the scope to include a number of nonnuclear initiatives. It dealt explicitly with the status of disarmament in the UN bureaucracy and stressed the relevance of disarmament to the work of the entire UN family.[45] It also contained a detailed plan of action to guide future work of the Secretariat (not just UNODA) in disarmament. In this sense, the Guterres agenda appears fully consistent with the lineage of the UN's comprehensive GCD approach. As with Ban's approach, the Guterres agenda also noted the deterioration of international security due to competition in weaponry, the waste of resources on nuclear arsenals as hindering economic development goals, and the specific contributions of disarmament to many dimensions of international peace and security. Both Secretaries-General stressed that humanitarian law and the laws of war set a compelling legal foundation for future progress in disarmament.

The Guterres agenda addressed three basic priorities: disarmament to "save humanity" (eliminating weapons of mass destruction), disarmament to "save lives" (advancing conventional arms control), and disarmament "for future generations" (addressing challenges posed by emerging issues and new technologies). For each of these priorities, he emphasized the importance of engagement, dialogue, diplomacy, and negotiations among member states as the path to future progress. He placed great emphasis on cooperation with diverse groups in civil society to advance disarmament and the need to include a gender dimension in all work in disarmament. He sought to broaden the base of political support for disarmament to include wider sectors of society that have not been previously active in this field, including the business community, engineers, and diverse professional associations, as well as an increased emphasis on disarmament partnerships with women and youth groups.

His initiatives for specific types of weapons reflected many activities that General Assembly resolutions have long underscored as needed for WMD disarmament and conventional arms control. His newer themes included controls over missiles, missile defense, emerging weapon technologies, and a wide variety of conventional arms.

While the Guterres agenda was widely welcomed, especially by non-nuclear-weapon states, it has not been widely or deeply reflected in General Assembly resolutions, statements, and comments or in papers from civil society. To a large extent, it has been overshadowed by the outpouring of support from non-nuclear-weapon states and civil society for the Treaty on the Prohibition of Nuclear Weapons (TPNW), which went into force on January 22, 2021, after having been adopted by the General Assembly by a vote of 122–1–1 on July 7, 2017. In contrast to the UN's GCD goal and the comprehensive approaches adopted by the two Secretaries-General, the TPNW is focused just on nuclear weapons.

Conclusion

Throughout the history of UN disarmament efforts, there has always been some tension between holistic (comprehensive) and piecemeal (incremental, step-by-step, or "partial") approaches. In recent years, the latter have prevailed over the former. This is apparent not only in the advent of the TPNW but also in a wide variety of initiatives and arrangements in the field of conventional arms, including the trade in small arms and light weapons, antipersonnel landmines, cluster munitions, uniquely "inhumane" weapons (laser blinders, medically invisible shrapnel, booby traps, etc.), transparency and reporting improvements, the arms trade, unmanned aerial vehicles, autonomous weapons ("killer robots"), and ammunition.

Yet when one views all these activities overall, the picture that emerges very closely resembles longstanding UN views on GCD, which integrates WMD disarmament; conventional arms control; reductions in military spending; improvements in peacebuilding, peacekeeping, and mechanisms for the peaceful settlement of disputes; transparency and verification; universal commitments; and the principle of irreversibility of disarmament commitments. Most of these goals are also reinforced by a strong foundation in international humanitarian law, another unifying factor joining all these various threads of UN activities in the field of disarmament.

The obstacles to disarmament are numerous, and although they are almost entirely related to the policies, practices, and priorities of states—which makes it outrageously unfair to blame "the UN" for lack of progress in disarmament—other obstacles have continued to hinder greater progress. There is an extraordinary lack of "congruence" between the solemn international legal and political commitments of states in the field of disarmament and the domestic laws, institutions, plans, budgets, and policies of states; with rare exceptions (e.g., New Zealand), multilateral disarmament norms have simply not been "internalized" by member states. Moreover, many NGOs have had trouble sustaining their work in disarmament given serious funding constraints and lack of domestic support from existing political parties and the national bureaucracies.[46] Even within the UN system itself there are obstacles to integrating disarmament into mainstream activities of the multitude of offices, departments, and programs in the Secretariat. Angela Kane, former UN High Representative for Disarmament Affairs, has cited the phenomenon of a "disarmament taboo," by which new actors—even within the UN system—are reluctant to get involved with disarmament issues, due to their alleged difficulty, controversiality, and impracticality.[47]

Thus, disarmament is not the only "hardy perennial" at the UN—so too are obstacles to disarmament from both inside and outside the organization. It will succeed or fail depending not on the end of the nation-state, but on the rehabilitation of the ends of the nation-state. As an example, in February 2022, Russia attacked Ukraine, and when many states, including the United States and even the UN General Assembly, condemned Russia's aggression, Russia responded with a veiled nuclear threat. The General Assembly states in its resolution that it condemns "the decision of the Russian Federation to increase the readiness of its nuclear forces."[48] This resolution is entirely dependent upon political will (of both states and civil society), which itself is a function of the level of security it provides and the depth of support for its fundamental moral and ethical roots. As Kane once put it, "Disarmament will survive for two reasons: it works, and it is the right thing to do. It fuses together into an integrated whole the two forces that make the world go round: self-interest and idealism. And it does so better than any other approach for dealing with weapons."[49]

This close relationship between the security and the moral dimensions of disarmament also provides grounds for some cautious optimism about the future, including the future relevance of the UN—the world's common meeting place—in promoting disarmament. While addressing nuclear disarmament, Sergio Duarte's words also explain what will advance disarmament more generally in the years ahead:

> Moral leadership in eliminating nuclear weapons requires a troubled conscience, a dissatisfaction with the status quo, and a profound sense of repugnance for these weapons of mass slaughter—but it also requires the hopeful vision of a better world, an awareness of the concrete and spiritual benefits of achieving a world free of such weapons, and an appreciation that we will together leave for future generations a world that is safer and more peaceful than the imperfect one we share today.[50]

Notes

1. Claude, *The Changing United Nations,* p. 7.

2. Judge Christopher Weeramantry, Dissenting Opinion, Advisory Opinion on the Legality of the Threat or Use of Nuclear Weapons, International Court of Justice, July 8, 1996, https://www.icj-cij.org/public/files/case-related/95/095-19960708 -ADV-01-12-EN.pdf, p. 479.

3. For a comprehensive history of UN disarmament activities, see *The United Nations and Disarmament: 1945–1970; The United Nations and Disarmament: 1970–1975*; and the annual editions (since 1975) of *The United Nations Disarmament Yearbook*. All are available at https://www.un.org/disarmament/publications /yearbook/.

4. UN General Assembly, Resolution 1(I), Establishment of a Commission to Deal with the Problems Raised by the Discovery of Atomic Energy, January 24, 1946, https://documents-dds-ny.un.org/doc/RESOLUTION/GEN/NR0/032/52/PDF/NR003252.pdf?OpenElement.

5. UN General Assembly, Resolution 41(I), Principles Governing the General Regulation and Reduction of Armaments, December 14, 1946, https://documents-dds-ny.un.org/doc/RESOLUTION/GEN/NR0/032/92/PDF/NR003292.pdf?OpenElement; and UN Security Council, Resolution 18, Armaments: Regulation and Reduction, February 13, 1947, https://documents-dds-ny.un.org/doc/RESOLUTION/GEN/NR0/042/14/PDF/NR004214.pdf?OpenElement.

6. For further discussion, see Rydell, *Explaining Hammarskjöld's "Hardy Perennial,"* https://unoda-web.s3-accelerate.amazonaws.com/wp-content/uploads/assets/content/speeches/oda-ny/rydell/2013-02-15_RR_Perennial.pdf.

7. Article 43 provides that member states "undertake to make available to the Security Council, on its call and in accordance with a special agreement or agreements, armed forces, assistance, and facilities, including rights of passage, necessary for the purpose of maintaining international peace and security."

8. Article 51 recognizes "the inherent right of individual or collective self-defence if an armed attack occurs."

9. This chapter only addresses issues relating to the UN and disarmament. Other international organizations outside the UN family also make important contributions in this field, including the International Atomic Energy Agency, the Preparatory Commission for the CTBT Organization, and the Organisation for the Prohibition of Chemical Weapons. There is no comparable organization for the Biological Weapons Convention.

10. Secretary-General Kofi Annan, opening statement, 2000 NPT Review Conference, New York, April 24, 2000, https://www.un.org/press/en/2000/20000424.sgsm7367.doc.html.

11. General Assembly, Resolution 502 (VI), Regulation, Limitation, and Balanced Reduction of All Armed Forces and All Armaments, 1952, https://documents-dds-ny.un.org/doc/RESOLUTION/GEN/NR0/067/57/PDF/NR006757.pdf?OpenElement.

12. For further discussion of GCD, see Dan Plesch (ed.), *Rethinking General and Complete Disarmament in the Twenty-First Century,* United Nations Office for Disarmament Affairs (UNODA) Occasional Paper No. 28, October 2016, https://unoda-web.s3-accelerate.amazonaws.com/wp-content/uploads/assets/publications/occasionalpapers/en/op28.pdf.

13. General Assembly, Resolution S-10/2, Final Document of the Tenth Special Session of the General Assembly, June 30, 1978, https://www.un.org/disarmament/wp-content/uploads/2017/05/A-S10-4.pdf. The GCD item had first appeared on the General Assembly's agenda via Resolution 1378 of November 20, 1959, https://documents-dds-ny.un.org/doc/RESOLUTION/GEN/NR0/142/01/PDF/NR014201.pdf?OpenElement. For further discussion of the Special Sessions, see Randy Rydell, *Bringing Democracy to Disarmament: A Historical Perspective on the Special Sessions of the General Assembly Devoted to Disarmament,* UNODA Occasional Paper No. 29, October 2016, https://www.un.org/disarmament/wp-content/uploads/2017/11/op29.pdf.

14. UNODA, *The United Nations Disarmament Yearbook* (New York: UNODA, published annually); it contains texts of these resolutions, votes, sponsors, and subjects.

15. Note by Secretary-General Kofi Annan, "A Compilation of All Texts of Principles, Standards or Recommendations on Subjects Adopted Unanimously by the Disarmament Commission," Document A/51/182/Rev.1, June 9, 1999, https://

documents-dds-ny.un.org/doc/UNDOC/GEN/N99/171/29/PDF/N9917129.pdf ?OpenElement.

16. United Nations Disarmament Commission, "Report of the Disarmament Commission for 2017," Document A/72/42, April 27, 2017, https://documents-dds -ny.un.org/doc/UNDOC/GEN/N17/115/24/PDF/N1711524.pdf?OpenElement.

17. Conference on Disarmament, "Agenda for the 2021 Session," Document CD/2209, February 1, 2021, https://documents-dds-ny.un.org/doc/UNDOC/GEN /G21/024/26/pdf/G2102426.pdf?OpenElement.

18. For further discussion, see Randy Rydell, "The Secretary-General and the Secretariat," in Boulden, Thakur, and Weiss, *The United Nations and Nuclear Orders,* 2009, https://unoda-web.s3-accelerate.amazonaws.com/wp-content/uploads /assets/content/speeches/oda-ny/rydell/2014-04-25_sg_secretariat.pdf.

19. Secretary-General Dag Hammarskjöld, "Introduction to the Annual Report of the Secretary-General on the Work of the Organization, 16 June 1960–15 June 1961," General Assembly Document A/4800/Add.1, https://digitallibrary.un.org /record/543627?ln=en#record-files-collapse-header.

20. *Secretary-General's Bulletin,* "Organization of the Office for Disarmament Affairs," Document ST/SGB/2008/8, June 27, 2008, https://documents-dds-ny.un .org/doc/UNDOC/GEN/N08/404/53/PDF/N0840453.pdf?OpenElement.

21. Further details are available at the United Nations Office for Disarmament Affairs (UNODA) webpage, https://www.un.org/disarmament/disarmament-fellowship.

22. *UNODA Strategic Plan 2021–2025,* February 2021, https://www.un.org /disarmament/unoda-strategic-plan-2021-2025/.

23. UNODA, "United Nations Register of Conventional Arms," n.d., https:// www.un.org/disarmament/convarms/register/.

24. UNODA, "United Nations Report on Military Expenditures," n.d., https:// www.un.org/disarmament/convarms/milex/.

25. UNODA, "Repository of Information Provided by Nuclear-Weapon States," n.d., https://www.un.org/disarmament/wmd/nuclear/repository/.

26. Further details about the Advisory Board are available at UNODA, "Advisory Board on Disarmament Matters," https://www.un.org/disarmament/institutions /advisoryboard/. UNIDIR's website is located at https://unidir.org.

27. United Nations Security Council, Statement of the President, January 31, 1992, Document S/23500, https://documents-dds-ny.un.org/doc/UNDOC/GEN/N92 /043/34/PDF/N9204334.pdf?OpenElement; and United Nations Security Council, Resolution 1887, September 24, 2009, https://documents-dds-ny.un.org/doc/UNDOC /GEN/N09/523/74/PDF/N0952374.pdf?OpenElement.

28. *Operational Guide to the Integrated Disarmament, Demobilization and Reintegration Standards,* https://peacekeeping.un.org/sites/default/files/operational -guide-rev-2010-web.pdf.

29. Ibid., p. 121.

30. United Nations Peacekeeping, "Disarmament, Demobilization and Reintegration," n.d., https://peacekeeping.un.org/en/disarmament-demobilization-and-reintegration.

31. The Advisory Opinion and relevant background and supporting documents are available at International Court of Justice, "Legality of the Threat or Use of Nuclear Weapons," https://www.icj-cij.org/en/case/95.

32. For further information, see "The World Court Project," Disarmament & vSecurity Centre (New Zealand), http://www.disarmsecure.org/nuclear-free-aotearoa -nz-resources/the-world-court-project.

33. Costa Rica first circulated a draft at the UN in 1997, and its updated 2007 version appears at https://digitallibrary.un.org/record/601411?ln=en.

34. UNODA, "Disarmament Treaties Database," https://treaties.unoda.org. UNODA, *Disarmament and Related Treaties,* UN Publication Sales No. E.15.IX.1 (New York: United Nations, 2015).

35. Secretary-General Ban Ki-moon, "The United Nations and Security in a Nuclear-Weapon-Free World," address to EastWest Institute, UN Headquarters, October 24, 2008, https://www.un.org/sg/en/content/sg/speeches/2008-10-24/address-east-west-institute-united-nations-and-security-nuclear. Quotes in this paragraph come from this speech.

36. Compare this with the following quote: "The total elimination of nuclear weapons is in the DNA of the United Nations." Secretary-General António Guterres, "Remarks at University of Geneva," Switzerland, May 24, 2018, https://www.un.org/sg/en/content/sg/speeches/2018-05-24/launch-disarmament-agenda-remarks.

37. Secretary-General Ban Ki-moon, "The United Nations and Security."

38. Ibid.

39. Ibid.

40. Ibid.

41. For further discussion, see Rydell, "The Guterres Disarmament Agenda," https://www.tandfonline.com/doi/full/10.1080/25751654.2020.1764259.

42. Guterres, Remarks in Geneva, May 24, 2018, in Secretary-General Ban Ki-moon, "The United Nations and Security."

43. UNODA, *Securing Our Common Future: An Agenda for Disarmament,* May 2018, https://s3.amazonaws.com/unoda-web/wp-content/uploads/2018/06/sg-disarmament-agenda-pubs-page.pdf#view=Fit.

44. The text is available at https://www.un.org/disarmament/sg-agenda/en/#actions.

45. Guterres stated, "My agenda . . . integrates disarmament into the priorities of the whole United Nations system, laying the foundations for new partnerships and greater collaboration between different parts of our organization and Governments, civil society, the private sector and others." (UNODA, *Securing Our Common Future,* p. viii). He later added, progress "requires a more general effort to reintegrate disarmament into the peace and security pillar of the organization, build effective partnerships and better deliver as one United Nations." (ibid., p. 34).

46. In 2021, the John D. and Catherine T. MacArthur Foundation, a major source of funds for disarmament and arms control groups, announced that it would cease funding projects in these fields. Daryl Kimball, Executive Director of the Arms Control Association, "A Blow to Efforts to Reduce Nuclear Risks," statement on July 20, 2021, https://www.armscontrol.org/blog/2021-07-20/blow-efforts-reduce-nuclear-risks. Also see Dave Lindorff, "Peace-Washing: Is a Network of Major Donors Neutralizing Activism in the Peace Movement?" Salon, June 2, 2021, https://www.salon.com/2021/06/02/peace-washing-is-a-network-of-major-donors-neutralizing-activism-in-the-peace-movement/.

47. Kane, *The New Zealand Lectures on Disarmament,* pp. 43–49, https://unoda-web.s3-accelerate.amazonaws.com/wp-content/uploads/assets/publications/occasionalpapers/en/op26.pdf.

48. UN General Assembly, Resolution A/ES-11/L.1, "Aggression Against Ukraine," March 1, 2022.

49. Ibid., p. 9.

50. Sergio Duarte, "Moral Leadership and Nuclear Weapons," lecture, Yale University Divinity School, New Haven, Connecticut, September 19, 2008, http://web.archive.org/web/20170703143111/https://unoda-web.s3-accelerate.amazonaws.com/wp-content/uploads/assets/HomePage/HR/docs/2008/2008Sept19_Yale_Divinity.pdf.

10

Financing the United Nations

Wannes Lint

It was the academic Aaron Wildavsky who noted in his seminal *Politics of the Budgetary Process* that when confronted with the vast array of figures in a budget, "one is likely to think of budgeting as an arid subject, the province of stodgy clerks and dull statisticians. Nothing could be more mistaken."[1] In 2004, Jeffrey Laurenti opened the chapter on UN finance in the predecessor of this book as follows:

> Far from being a dry, specialized subject of little interest outside the institution, the finances of the United Nations are the subject of high political drama, marked by conflicts among competing claims of global idealism, state sovereignty, international law, crass self-interest, and national power. The lifeblood of any political entity is cash flow: the financial resources it is able to devote to the priorities decided by its decision-makers. States enjoy broad authority to extract those resources by taxation, restrained only by the occasional constitutional limits, adverse consequences to their economic competitiveness, and the political rebellion of irate taxpayers. ... At the international level, governments have been chary of delegating taxing authority to international agencies (but) the political battles can be as contentious in global fora as in town meetings.[2]

I was lured into the world of intergovernmental negotiations and budgetary politics by an article in the *UN Chronicle* in which reference was made to a certain Collen Vixen Kelapile (currently the president of ECOSOC and a permanent representative), who as a young diplomat was told, "if you want to know the UN system, don't hesitate to take the Fifth Committee."[3]

This chapter takes a broad view of the budgetary process at the United Nations and identifies five different stages, which are discussed in turn, even if the stages are not necessarily sequential:

1. mandates, or how member states agree on what the United Nations will do, including instructions for the UN Secretariat;
2. program planning, or how mandates are translated into work plans;
3. budgeting, or how resources are budgeted to implement work plans;
4. assessing, or how the budget is divided between member states; and
5. contributing, or how and when member states pay the amount of money they are supposed to, as agreed.

Discussions on financing traditionally focus on stages 3 and 4, which indeed take center stage in the budgetary process. How much is paid collectively for the United Nations and what portion of the budget each state is responsible to pay for are questions that surely need to be answered. However, only rarely are proposals made by the Secretary-General without the prior adoption of a resolution that contains a mandate. And, even if it's important to answer the how and why of assessments, the current liquidity crisis has little to do with the actual scale, and much more with member states not paying their dues or only paying toward the end of a year. As stated above, one should not necessarily think of the above stages as sequential. For example, in resolution 72/266 A, member states made clear that the proposed program budget was to include both the proposed program plan (stage 2) and the post and non-post resources (stage 3).[4]

In 2014, a group of ambassadors and experts were asked to make an assessment of the overall budgetary process. In their report, titled *Because Process Matters,* they gave their own justification of a focus on procedural matters:

> Processes, as we all know, matter. They are especially important in the field of multilateral diplomacy. They affect how Member States interact with one another, and they affect the outcome of negotiations. The more straightforward, transparent, and rational a process, the better the outcome both for Member States and the Organization.[5]

It is for this reason that I offer a procedural review of the budgetary process, at the expense of a technical examination of budget tables, resource allocations, and recosting methodology. While I do not shy away from technical aspects, the focus of the chapter is how these technical matters influence both the overall process and the outcome of negotiations. Before we start this examination, it is important to note that there is no single UN budget. Within the UN system—which includes specialized agencies and UN funds, programs, and entities—as well as within the UN Secretariat, one can point to multiple "UN budgets," each with its own structures, approval processes, and local dynamics.

At the end of this chapter, the reader will have acquired an understanding of the balance found at each stage of this planning and budgeting process.

Budget Theory

This chapter opened with a quote from Wildavsky's *Politics,* which summarizes in a few lines the overall tenet of his seminal book. He concluded that budgeting is characterized by "extraordinary complexity."[6] Another academic, Irene Rubin, refers to it as a "unique" arena of politics, for almost all other decisions "have to take place in the context of budgeting."[7] At the United Nations, and pretty much anywhere else, work across all pillars of the organization is enabled, or constrained, by the budgetary space such work is given.

In addition to the pervasiveness of budgets, the expansiveness of budgets should be recognized—and the limited information processing capacity on the part of most, if not all actors. As the Secretary-General noted in one of his reports on the management reform agenda,[8] thousands of pages of program planning and budget information are written in all six official languages. There is limited capacity on the part of senior managers, expert review bodies, and representatives of member states to assess all the information that is furnished during budget negotiations. And clarifying questions trigger even more documentation.

As a result, squarely in keeping with ideas of bounded rationality first developed by R. A. Dahl and C. E. Lindblom in *Politics, Economics, and Welfare,*[9] Wildavsky arrives at a theory of budgetary incrementalism, in which "limited" human minds can in reality only zoom in on the marginal changes, while the "base"—the approved budget of a prior year—is oftentimes taken as a given. Even if in method a budget could be "zero-based"—that is, built from zero each budget period—the nature of the review process remains incremental in practice.

Wildavsky wrote about a national budgeting process. When considering the planning, budgeting, and financing of international organizations, one cannot limit oneself to national budgetary processes. It's hard to overstate the degree to which funding and budgetary processes are an essential part of the "institutional design" of international organizations. While questions of institutional design tend in many cases to focus on questions of membership and decisionmaking, budgeting is another area designed in a manner that allows member states to exercise their influence.

Similarly, if one thinks of a budget as a contract between "principal" (member states) and "agent" (the Secretariat), it would be good to emphasize that both principal and agent are more often than not heterogeneous, with different interests and positions for each of their parts. This departs from international relations literature, where a traditional principal-agent model is oftentimes premised on both principal and agent being singular entities.

Mandates

In the UN budgeting process, all resource requests find their origin in a mandate. Before the UN Secretariat engages in a particular activity, member states would have to collectively agree to request the Secretary-General to do so. In fact, mandates come in many forms and shapes, and whether a proposal confers a mandate is oftentimes the subject of serious exegesis in the context of negotiations. For purposes of this chapter, we will be mostly interested in those mandates that have financial implications (i.e., program budget implications), but of course there are also mandates that do not have budgetary implications.

In the traditional sense, a mandate is essentially an order or a request by a competent principal directing an agent to undertake a particular action, but normally with flexibility on how that order or request is carried out. At the United Nations, member states decide to undertake a particular course of action and entrust the Secretary-General to take certain actions (big and small) related to that decision, which is the mandate given to the Secretary-General. A big mandate could be the implementation of the establishment, continuation, or closure of a peace operation or the establishment of a new forum. Smaller mandates are requests to the Secretary-General to convene a conference or meeting on a specific subject matter on a certain date, or to provide a report to the General Assembly on a particular matter. Mandates can also be purely "substantive" in nature, in the sense that they do not trigger any separate action but inform the direction of existing activities.

Some mandates are specific in their order (e.g., a request to convene a conference on a specific subject matter on a certain date), and others are more vague (e.g., a request to operationalize for a mechanism

to continue to consider, in a coordinated manner, the impact of technological changes on the achievement of the Sustainable Development
Goals and to align this endeavor with the follow-up cycle of the high-
level political forum on sustainable development). Some mandates are
firm in their order and entail a clear decision or request; other mandates
are less committal, inviting the Secretary-General to consider a particular perspective or encouraging the Secretary-General to bring a matter
to the attention of the international community.

When discussing mandates, any intergovernmental body can be
thought of as the "principal" in the principal-agent relationship. In case of
the General Assembly and the Economic and Social Council (ECOSOC),
these principal organs confer mandates to the Secretary-General, in many
cases at the recommendation of their subsidiary bodies. For example, a
draft resolution would be discussed in a main committee of the General
Assembly and recommended to the General Assembly for final adoption.
Similarly, a draft decision from a regional commission would be recommended to ECOSOC for final adoption.

It's in the very early stages of this legislative process that most program plans, budgets, and assessments are conceived, for member states
collectively drive the program planning and budgeting process. And so
when the secretariat of an intergovernmental body receives a draft resolution or decision from a member state, this proposal is submitted to
the Program Planning and Budget Division of the Department for Management Strategy, Policy, and Compliance. This team coordinates the
formulation of both program plans and budgets and at this stage conducts what is called the review for "program budget implications."

Questions Relating to the Program Budget

Once a proposal is submitted to the Secretariat, discussions on the consideration of financial implications of draft resolutions and decisions
are governed by the Rules of Procedure of the General Assembly. Of
relevance is Rule 153,[10] which provides that

> no resolution involving expenditure shall be recommended by a com-
> mittee for approval by the General Assembly unless it is accompanied
> by an estimate of expenditures prepared by the Secretary-General. No
> resolution in respect of which expenditures are anticipated by the Sec-
> retary-General shall be voted by the General Assembly until the
> Administrative and Budgetary Committee (Fifth Committee) has had
> an opportunity of stating the effect of the proposal upon the budget
> estimates of the United Nations.[11]

In accordance with this rule, the General Assembly reaffirms at the beginning of each session that consideration by the Administrative and Budgetary Committee (Fifth Committee) of any proposal involving expenditure is mandatory before such a proposal is voted on by the Assembly and the rule as formulated does not provide for any exceptions.[12] In practice, this means that the General Assembly will not take action on a proposal until such time as the Fifth Committee has considered the related financial implications, following the examination of the proposal by the Advisory Committee on Administrative and Budgetary Questions. When proposals are recommended by a subsidiary organ, this rarely causes confusion because it is widely understood that the Fifth Committee considers such proposals before action is taken in the Assembly. However, the same holds when proposals are submitted directly to the plenary. While proposals can be issued as a document of the Assembly and a statement can even be made to "introduce" the proposal (i.e., to explain its rationale) in the Assembly before the Fifth Committee's consideration, the related action would in such cases be postponed to allow time for the review of the related program budget implications by the Fifth Committee.[13]

A similar provision exists in connection with action on decisions by councils, commissions, or other competent bodies. While action in such bodies is not held until such time as the General Assembly has had the opportunity to review any budgetary implications, Rule 5.9 of the Regulations and Rules Governing Program Planning, the Program Aspects of the Budget, the Monitoring of Implementation, and the Methods of Evaluation (also known as PPBME) provides that "no council, commission or other competent body shall take a decision involving either a change in the program budget approved by the General Assembly or the possible requirement of expenditure unless it has received and taken account of a report from the Secretary-General on the program budget implications of the proposal."[14] The clock starts ticking once a text is submitted to the Secretariat. General Assembly Decision 34/401[15] sets forth a minimum period of forty-eight hours before action is taken on a proposal so as to allow the Secretary-General to prepare the program budget implications of proposals before the Assembly. However, at the beginning of each session, the General Committee brings to the attention of the Assembly the fact that, in most cases, more than forty-eight hours are required for the Secretary-General to review the program budget implications of proposals. The General Committee also draws the attention of the General Assembly to the establishment of a deadline, no later than December 1, for the submission to the Fifth Committee of all draft resolutions with financial implications.

Upon conclusion of the review, the budget office would advise the relevant department or office whether the adoption of a proposal would entail program budget implications. In case there would be financial implications, an "oral statement" would be made to the body in question,[16] and if there are financial implications for a budget period of which the budget is already considered by the Fifth Committee, action would be postponed to a later date.[17]

The oral statement would indicate the paragraphs that, if adopted, would give rise to program budget implications and under which program and section of the program budget. Where possible, these would be accompanied by a price tag or a range, and assumptions made on the part of the Secretariat would be articulated. The latter is especially important when proposals have a degree of constructive ambiguity, so that member states are clear on the Secretariat's interpretation. For example, when a specific meeting is requested but no dates are mentioned, an oral statement could indicate that the dates are to be agreed upon in consultation with the Department for General Assembly and Conference Management, which maintains the calendar of conferences, so as to avoid overlap with peak periods.

Acting Without a Specific Mandate

The above emphasis on mandates was not meant to suggest that any budget proposals submitted by the Secretary-General can only be submitted if and when such proposals are linked to hard and specific mandates found in adopted resolutions. In fact, the regulations and rules governing the program planning and budgeting process make this quite clear:

> Financial Regulation 2.1. The proposed program budget for each budget period shall be prepared by the Secretary-General.
> Financial Rule 102.1 (a) The Secretary-General shall decide on the program content and resource allocation of the proposed program budget to be submitted to the General Assembly.[18]

As such, it's not uncommon for a proposed program budget to include so-called "other changes," a category separate from "new or expanded mandates." For example, the proposed program budget for 2022 provided an increase of US$2.8 million to strengthen the development pillar, including new technical cooperation activities, additional funding for a particular office, and to facilitate the progress of member states toward the achievement of the SDGs.[19] Such changes are proposed to the General Assembly based on the Secretary-General's decision on the program content and resource allocation of the proposed program budget.

Like budgets, mandates are incremental. They are in most cases entrusted only once. While there are repeat resolutions that occur on an annual basis, budgets are rarely mandated "anew," unless activities were budgeted for on a nonrecurrent basis. In such a case, a new resolution would be required prior to the initiation of the resource request.

Program Planning

Before delving into the financing of activities conducted in the implementation of mandates, one needs first to conceptually understand the process of "mandate translation"—that is, the process of reaching agreement on the activities that the Secretariat will conduct to implement its contribution to the achievement of objectives set out in a resolution. In the Secretariat, this process is commonly known as "program planning," which, per the existing PPBME, is done prior to the process of budgeting and financing.[20]

The origins of what is today known as program planning can be found in discussions in the 1970s, during which a number of "experimental cycles" of preparation and implementation of so-called medium-term planning had culminated in the seminal report prepared by Inspector Maurice Bertrand of the Joint Inspection Unit, in which he set out a number of recommendations to improve planning processes at the United Nations.[21] Prior to this, member states had expressed their interest in better understanding the relationship between mandates entrusted to the organization and the financing required for their implementation. In 1966, the General Assembly had endorsed in resolution 2150 (XXI) recommendations to establish an "integrated system" of longer-term planning, program formulation, and budget preparation. It was, however, not until the Bertrand report that we really started to see the contours of the present-day system emerging.

In chapter I, titled "The nature of the problems and possible approaches to solutions," Bertrand outlines a "state of crisis" in which he found medium-term planning at the United Nations. Not only did he point to the medium-term plan's "excessive bulk" (1,300 pages), but in his report he also demonstrated how articulating the contribution of planned activities to the attainment of precise objectives would increase the credibility of organizations. It is worth quoting his words directly:

No doubt everyone is aware that the resolutions of intergovernmental bodies, which are often couched in ambitious terms, are more a reflection of trends, aspirations or exhortations than of precise solutions to the problems mentioned. . . . No one expects that resolutions on literacy will immediately bring about the disappearance of illiteracy, nor does anyone imagine that the adoption of growth-rates will at once accelerate the pace of development. Member States would, on the other hand, have a right to hope that, in each of the areas under consideration, limited but reasonably effective action would be taken by international organizations within the framework thus established.[22]

His report then set the stage for a number of "handles" on which, in his view, an "objective-based program structure" should enable member states to make a number of informed choices. These choices would relate to (1) the general orientation of a program, (2) the establishment within each program of objectives, (3) the general definition of priorities, and (4) the maintenance, elimination, or verification of the usefulness and effectiveness of effective functions. In broad terms, the instruments that would enable such choices are, essentially, the ones that are in place today and include an overall "program policy" outlining the relationship between activities and objectives, which is currently reflected in the "program plan and performance information," and the establishment of priorities for the organization as a whole, currently reflected in the plan outline.

Committee for Program and Coordination

The interaction between member states and the Secretariat on issues of "mandate translation" and program planning is most visible in the Committee for Program and Coordination. The Committee, a subsidiary organ of ECOSOC and the General Assembly for planning, programming, and coordination, was established by ECOSOC. The Committee is called to review the programs of the United Nations, including "the totality of the Secretary-General's work program, giving particular attention to program changes arising out of decisions adopted by intergovernmental organs."[23] It also is expected to give guidance to the Secretariat on program design by interpreting legislative intent, so as to assist the Secretariat in translation of legislation into programs.

The report of the Committee provides some insight into matters discussed during the meetings of the body, which are restricted. For the proposed program budget for 2022, for example, a department made reference in its program plan[24] to it providing intergovernmental services in support of virtual meetings and planning to transform such services into new modalities that member states can use. In the report of the Committee,[25] reference is subsequently made to member states enquiring as to whether the department in question was planning to undertake that transformation, considering that the Assembly had at the time not taken a decision on such a new modality. Another member state sought confirmation that new working methods were not going to change the working methods recognized and established by member states and that the prerogative of the Assembly in terms of definition of working methods was not going to be undermined.

Program Plans and Performance Information

So how is information presented to the Committee for Program and Coordination? Before the Committee are so-called program plans and program performance information. In keeping with resolution 72/266,[26] the General Assembly requested that the Secretary-General include the program plan and program performance information in the proposed program budget. Previously, the information was presented in a separate document, the proposed biennial program plan.[27] In this connection, it's worth underlining that, while mandates and plans drive resourcing, since resolution 55/231[28] the Secretariat has been asked to base its budgets on results and indicators that demonstrate progress toward the attainment of objectives.

In the program plan, the Secretary-General proposes to member states how the Secretariat intends to make its contribution toward the attainment of objectives that member states have set. This is an iterative process whereby over time program plans that are carved out as new mandates are entrusted to the organization. Should member states give a new mandate to the organization in an area for which no program plan exists, the Secretary-General might state that the adoption of a resolution would lead to the inclusion of a new chapter in a subsequent program plan.

Objectives

In its most recent form, the program plan would set out the collective objectives, to which individual entities have planned to contribute. Strictly speaking, an objective refers to an overall desired achievement involving a process of change and aimed at meeting certain needs of identified end users within a given period of time. Objectives are derived from the policy orientations and goals set by intergovernmental organs. For example, in the case of the United Nations Office of Drugs and Crime (UNODC), work is done on countering corruption, for which the objective is stated as follows: "The objective, to which this subprogram contributes, is to prevent and counter corruption through the effective implementation of the United Nations Convention against Corruption."[29] Member states would subsequently review the rationale for selecting specific objectives to ascertain their completeness, balance, and also if the specific terms used are inter-governmentally agreed upon. In practice, objectives change only if there are significant changes to the overall policy orientations and goals set by intergovernmental organs. It's quite common for smaller changes in programming not to trigger any changes to the overall objective.

Activities and Outputs

The program plans also present information on planned activities and outputs. Over the years the format has evolved considerably, from lists and paragraphs to the current tabular form, but the building block has remained the same throughout. Outputs are final products or services delivered by a program or subprogram to end users, such as reports or publications, which an activity is expected to produce in order to achieve its objectives. Activities in turn are specific actions taken to transform inputs into outputs. For example, in the above case from UNODC, a tabular presentation of quantifiable outputs is presented in the same program plan, including lines as follows:

> Note by the Secretary-General on crime prevention and criminal justice: 1 [note]
>> Reports on the sessions of the Conference of the States Parties and its subsidiary bodies: 6 [reports]
>> Thematic reports on the Mechanism for the Review of Implementation of the United Nations Convention against Corruption: 2 [thematic reports][30]

While outputs lend themselves to bean-counting, they form the cornerstone of what in program management is known as a logical framework. Over the years, considerable efforts have been made to standardize outputs into different categories, while strengthening output-based variance analysis to explain why more or less of a certain output is deemed necessary. Member states have requested for there to be more focus on genuine results-based management and less on the measurement of output-based implementation rates.[31] Up to a few years ago, there was a practice of calculating so-called implementation rates, which would parse tens of thousands of outputs of various categories across various offices into a single, almost magical number—the implementation rate—essentially the percentage of planned outputs that were actually implemented, which could then be compared across offices and give a sense of managerial control and oversight.

Results

If one were to extend the logical framework analogy to the United Nations, then what is known as results and indicators would essentially form the middle layers between outputs and objectives. Results, including performance measures, track the extent to which the objective has been achieved, in both qualitative and quantitative terms. Over the years, the format of results has evolved quite considerably, more or less in sync with how different industries have also grappled with side effects of excessive quantification of metrics. In a number of reports and resolutions, member states concluded that qualitative aspects of indicators had to be improved, toward more of a holistic focus.[32] Efforts were made to introduce qualitative indicators and more concrete explanations of how outputs contributed to specific results. For example, in the case of UNODC, the office would provide both backward- and forward-looking narratives on planned and actual performance:

Result 1: member states developing policy responses to support the implementation of measures to respond to threats and vulnerabilities emerging during the Covid-19 pandemic

Result 2: review of the implementation of the United Nations Convention Against Corruption to spearhead national anticorruption reforms

Result 3: fast-tracking the implementation of the United Nations Convention Against Corruption by states parties, in terms of the number of country-level activities

Result 4: translation of political declaration adopted at the special session of the General Assembly against corruption in 2021 into actionable and practical measures to advance the global fight against corruption[33]

These result narratives are complemented by quantitative and qualitative performance measures over time. Different areas of work would offer different kinds of evidence—certain areas could lend themselves to quantification (number of member states launching a satellite into space) and other areas less so (confidence-building measures toward the resumption of a political process). Already within the span of a single area of work, a variety of results across different lines of work are presented, ranging from policy responses by member states to normative action in intergovernmental bodies. Across the entire Secretariat, the picture is even more diverse.

Plan Outline

In addition to the program plans that are prepared across the organization across twenty-eight different programs, resulting in thousands of pages of frameworks and committee reports, the Secretary-General is also requested to submit a plan outline, which is expected to highlight in a coordinated manner the policy orientation of the United Nations, the longer-term objectives and strategy, and the trends deduced from mandates that reflect priorities set by intergovernmental organs. Currently, the plan outline is submitted once every three years.

The most recent issuance of the plan outline included an identification of transformative agendas, including the 2030 Agenda for Sustainable Development; the Addis Ababa Action Agenda; the Women, Peace, and Security Agenda; and many others. The plan outline set out how the long-term objectives of the organization revolved around these transformative agendas across the eight priorities of the organization, such as sustainable development, the maintenance of international peace and security, human rights, and humanitarian assistance.

Relationship to "Local" Intergovernmental Bodies

The Committee for Program and Coordination is not the only body that reviews the program plans prepared by departments. In fact, Regulation 4.8 of the PPBME provides that:

> The programs and subprograms of the proposed strategic framework shall be reviewed by the relevant sectoral, functional and regional intergovernmental bodies, if possible during the regular cycle of their meetings, prior to their review by the Committee for Program

and Coordination, the Economic and Social Council and the General Assembly. The Committee for Program and Coordination shall consider the proposed strategic framework in accordance with its terms of reference.[34]

As was concluded in *Because Process Matters,* "one of the most important elements of the United Nations planning and budgetary process is the requirement for comprehensive and inclusive involvement of member states in all of the stages [...] of the process."[35] In addition to the Committee for Program and Coordination (CPC), other specialized intergovernmental bodies review program plans well before a proposal is before the CPC. As we will revisit in the last part of this chapter, the substantive experts, including on disarmament, drug control, and other subjects, are oftentimes represented in such local bodies—they are not necessarily in the CPC, which is composed of generalists. The CPC therefore receives a document from the Secretariat, which synthesizes any views that such "local" bodies might have expressed on the program plans.

Budgeting

The legal framework within which the budgetary process is conducted is clear. The Secretary-General, in his capacity as chief administrative officer of the organization, as per Article 97 of the United Nations Charter, prepares the proposed program budget of the organization. The General Assembly, in keeping with Article 17, paragraph 1, of the United Nations Charter, considers and approves the budget of the organization. Other players in the budget process are the Fifth Committee, the main committee to which the program budget–related agenda items are allocated, and the Advisory Committee on Administrative and Budgetary Questions, which, in keeping with Rules 155–157 of the Rules of Procedure of the General Assembly, is responsible for expert examination of the program budget and assists the Fifth Committee.[36]

While there is a clear legal framework within which budgets are proposed and approved, the diverse interests of member states oftentimes invite a degree of "constructive ambiguity," which helps ensure that member states can jointly decide on how the organization is financed. Although initially the budgetary requirements were limited to intergovernmental affairs and conference servicing, over the years the program budget of the United Nations has grown to include new activities in a number of other areas, including political affairs; drugs and crime; human rights; development at global, regional, and local levels; and public information. New mandates led to new program plans and new and increased budgets.

Is US$3.208 Billion a Lot of Money to Run the UN?

For the year 2021, in resolution 75/254 A,[37] the General Assembly appropriated on December 31, 2020, a program budget in the amount of US$3.208 billion, following an original proposal by the Secretary-General dated May 11, 2020, in the amount of US$2.987 billion.

People frequently ask if budgets in the range of US$3.208 billion is a lot for an organization like the United Nations. There are different ways to respond to such a question. One can respond by comparison to other organizations. For example, the proposed budget of the New York City Police Department for 2022 totaled US$5.44 billion.[38] One can also look for the total of contributions made by member states to one of the pillars of the United Nations. For example, total official development assistance by member countries of the OECD's Development Assistance Committee (twenty-nine member states of the United Nations and the European Union) amounted to US$161.2 billion in 2020.[39] Then one could assess how and where the UN actually contributes in specific locations. For example, in 2016, a report commissioned by the city of New York estimated that the UN community contributed an estimated US$3.69 billion in total output to the New York City economy in 2014.[40] And, finally, assessments are made of whether paying the UN is cost-effective from the perspective of individual member states. For example, in 2006, the Government Accountability Office of the United States issued a report comparing the then cost of actual UN operations and hypothetical US operations in Haiti. It found that it would cost the United States about twice as much as the UN to conduct a peacekeeping operation similar to the then mission in Haiti.[41]

Over the past ten years, most areas of the UN Secretariat's regular budget have not grown in real terms (the overall stated figure did not increase), only in nominal terms as a result of inflation and exchange rate factors. This was made possible by a continuous drive toward more efficiency, enabling the absorption of new mandates at zero cost to member states.

How Is a Budget Prepared?

The budgetary process begins well before a proposal is submitted to the General Assembly. Months before the submission, the Department for Management Strategy, Policy and Compliance (DMSPC) submits budget instructions to the various Heads of Department seeking their submissions, based on the vision pronounced by the Secretary-General. The memorandum with the budget instructions would outline policy guidelines—for example, how resources can be moved from one department to another or from one budget line (e.g., other staff costs) to another (e.g., general operating expenses), the establishment or abolition of specific posts, or the need to meet specific budgetary or staffing targets. These submissions would then be discussed with the Secretary-General and, in keeping with their guidance, consolidated into the overall proposed program budget. The Secretary-General would then decide on the final resource allocation and propose any inclusion of new resources.

In parallel, DMSPC would prepare and update various costing parameters—for example, for payroll and common staff costs for staff positions, currency exchange rates, or inflation. Such parameters are updated throughout the budget cycle and are also the subject of principled political discussions. In its resolution 68/246, the General Assembly requested an independent study on recosting and options for dealing with fluctuations in exchange rates and inflation, which led to a number of recommendations to address both pressures external to the organization, such as currency exchange rate fluctuation, and challenges internal to the organization, in terms of how this variation is managed.[42] In fact, finding a package of solutions, the subsequent panel concluded in its report, could free member states and the Secretariat to focus on other aspects of the work of the United Nations.[43] A number of significant changes regarding currency rates of exchange have been implemented since as detailed in a report by the Secretary-General, leveraging the new enterprise resource planning system, which addressed the current shortcomings regarding the visibility and the internal flow of information.[44]

How Can the Budget Be Broken Down?

There are multiple ways to break the US$3.208 billion down. One example is provided in Table 10.1, taken from the proposed program budget for 2022.[45] The table provides past expenditure, the current year budget, and any changes vis-à-vis the current year. What is included under "technical adjustments," "new and expanded mandates," and "other" is provided in the introduction of the proposed program budget.[46]

Table 10.1 Past and Present Breakdowns for 2022 Budget (US$ thousands)

Section	2020 Expenditure	2021 Appropriation	Changes					2022 Estimate (before recosting)	Recosting	2022 Estimate (after recosting)
			Technical Adjustments	New/Expanded Mandates	Other	Total	Percentage			
1. Overall policymaking, diretion and coordination	71,850.30	78,809.40	(91.10)	120.50	—	29.40	0.00	78,838.80	1,019.00	79,857.80
2. General Assembly and Economic and Social Council affairs and conference management	321,577.00	340,979.20	(6,550.60)	1,640.00	65.40	(4,845.20)	(1.40)	336,134.00	4,027.00	340,161.00
3. Political affairs	760,420.10	792,787.70	(6,991.80)	—	7,502.50	510.70	0.10	793,298.40	1,021.40	794,319.80
Special political missions	700,323.10	730,359.80	(7,080.50)	—	7,387.00	306.50	0.00	730,666.30	—	730,666.30
Other	60,097.00	62,427.90	88.70	—	115.50	204.20	0.30	62,632.10	1,021.40	63,653.50
4. Disarmament	12,428.70	12,859.20	(589.10)	372.00	—	(217.10)	(1.70)	12,642.10	190.10	12,832.20
5. Peacekeeping operations	49,757.00	55,113.30	—	—	(289.70)	(289.70)	(0.50)	54,823.60	2,603.30	57,426.90
6. Peaceful uses of outer space	3,876.60	4,493.60	—	—	—	—	—	4,493.60	52.60	4,546.20
7. International Court of Justice	25,742.30	30,778.80	(129.10)	—	136.80	7.70	0.00	30,786.50	310.40	31,096.90
8. Legal affairs	58,277.40	57,654.50	577.70	678.30	(1,103.00)	153.00	0.30	57,807.50	618.40	58,425.90
9. Economic and social affairs	81,412.50	83,857.30	—	—	(335.40)	(335.40)	(0.40)	83,521.90	1,315.80	84,837.70

continues

Table 10.1 Continued

Section	2020 Expenditure	2021 Appropriation	Changes					2022 Estimate (before recosting)	Recosting	2022 Estimate (after recosting)
			Technical Adjustments	New/Expanded Mandates	Other	Total	Percentage			
10. Least developed countries, landlocked developing countries and small island developing states	5,619.20	6,609.30	283.60	—	259.50	543.10	8.20	7,152.40	111.50	7,263.90
11. United Nations support for the New Partnership for Africa's Development	7,984.80	7,823.60	—	—	189.30	189.30	2.40	8,012.90	129.00	8,141.90
12. Trade and development	67,874.40	73,777.60	—	—	(474.80)	(474.80)	(0.60)	73,302.80	243.10	73,545.90
13. International Trade Centre	18,861.80	20,641.50	—	—	—	—	—	20,641.50	144.50	20,786.00
14. Environment	21,909.90	23,720.40	(406.30)	—	—	(406.30)	(1.70)	23,314.10	465.80	23,779.90
15. Human settlements	12,167.30	12,495.80	196.20	597.00	—	793.20	6.30	13,289.00	385.10	13,674.10
16. International drug control, crime and terrorism prevention, and criminal justice	21,616.50	23,363.10	(579.40)	—	(71.90)	(651.30)	(2.80)	22,711.80	215.20	22,927.00
17. UN-Women	9,692.10	9,719.90	—	—	—	—	—	9,719.90	145.80	9,865.70
18. Economic and social development in Africa	78,248.40	78,703.60	—	—	(523.80)	(523.80)	(0.70)	78,179.80	1,956.00	80,135.80
19. Economic and social development in Asia and the Pacific	54,615.50	59,071.70	(1,083.80)	—	(139.80)	(1,223.60)	(2.10)	57,848.10	908.70	58,756.80

Similarly, the proposal would include an overview of employment posts presented, which amounted to a total of 10,005 posts proposed for 2022. A key table in the proposed program budget (see Table 10.2) shows increases emanating from new or expanded mandates, which would reference both the included budgetary increases as well as the resolutions pursuant to which the inclusion was authorized.[47] In this category one also finds those changes proposed by the Secretary-General.

What Is the Role of the ACABQ?

The Advisory Committee on Administrative and Budgetary Questions (ACABQ) is an expert committee of twenty-one members elected by the General Assembly for a period of three years, on the basis of broad geographical representation. The Advisory Committee was enlarged in 2020 pursuant to resolution 74/267,[48] which revised Rule 155 of the Rules of Procedure.[49] The members do not serve as representatives of member states but in their personal capacity. As set forth in Rule 157, the ACABQ is responsible for expert nomination of the program budget of the United Nations and assists the Administrative and Budgetary Committee (Fifth Committee). It submits a report with recommendations on the proposed program budget before the Fifth Committee considers the Secretary-General's proposal.

What Is the Role of the Fifth Committee?

The Fifth Committee is the Main Committee of the General Assembly to which the administrative and budgetary agenda items of the United Nations are allocated by the General Assembly, including the program budget and program planning items. Together with the recommendations from the ACABQ, the Fifth Committee will have before it the proposals from the Secretary-General, will endorse the ACABQ's recommendations (or not), and will add language of its own to the draft resolution it would, at the end of its session, recommend to the General Assembly.

It was only following a budgetary crisis in the 1980s that resolution 41/213, the cornerstone of the current program budget process, saw the light of day.[50] The General Assembly considered it desirable that the Fifth Committee, before submitting its recommendations, should continue to make all possible efforts toward establishing the

Table 10.2 New and Expanded Mandates for 2022, by Budget Section (US$ thousands)

Section	Amount	Description
1. Overall policymaking direction, and coordination	120.50	Continuation of the investigation into the conditions and circumstances resulting in the tragic death of Dag Hammarskjöld and of the members of the party accompanying him, in accordance with General Assembly decision 75/542
2. General Assembly and Economic and Social Council Affairs and Conference Management	1,640.00	Conference services requirements pursuant to: (a) Resolutions and decisions of the General Assembly: (i) Nuclear disarmament verification (resolution 74150); (ii) Political declaration of the high-level meeting on universal health coverage: Universal health coverage: moving together to build a healthier world (resolution 7412); (iii) Sustainable fisheries, including through the 1995 Agreement for the Implementation of the Provisions of the United Nations Convention on the Law of the Sea of 10 December 1982 relating to the Conservation and Management of Straddling Fish Stocks and Highly Migratory Fish Stocks, and related instruments (resolution 75189); (iv) Oceans and the Law of the Sea (resolution 751239); (v) Investigation into the conditions and circumstances resulting in the tragic death of Dag Hammarskjöld and of the members of the party accompanying him (resolution 741248); (vi) Follow-up to the Fourth United Nations Conference on the Least Developed Countries (resolution 741232 B); (vii) Developments in the field of information and telecommunications in the context of international security (resolution 7S/240); (viii) Implementation of the outcome of the United Nations Conference on Housing and Sustainable Urban Development (Habitat 111) and strengthening of the United Nations Human Settlements Programme (UN Habitat) (resolution 711235); (b) Resolutions and decisions adopted by the Human Rights Council from its twenty-eighth through thirtieth sessions and from its fortieth through forty-fifth sessions (c) Review of the jurisdictional set-up of the United Nations common system (resolution 751245 B)
4. Disarmament	372.00	(a) Subvention to the United Nations Institute for Disarmament Research, pursuant to General Assembly resolution 75182; (b) Technical and substantive support in connection with the preparations for and substantive servicing of the work of the Open-ended Working Group on Developments in the Field of Information and Telecommunications in the Context of International Security, pursuant to General Assembly resolution 75/240
8. Legal affairs	678.30	(a) Attendance and support for the second year of the third cycle of the Regular Process for Global Reporting and Assessment of the State of the Marine Environment, including Socioeconomic Aspects, pursuant to General Assembly resolution 75/239; (b) Assistance to the Review Conference on the Agreement for the Implementation of the Provisions of the United Nations Convention on the Law of the Sea of December 10, 1982, relating to the Conservation and Management of Straddling Fish Stocks and Highly Migratory Fish Stocks in discharging its mandate, pursuant to General Assembly resolution 75189

broadest possible agreement. Although there are main committees in which more than a hundred recorded votes are taken per session, the Fifth Committee generally conducts its decisionmaking by consensus, so as not to impose collective financial contributions by majority vote.

While all meetings of the Fifth Committee, with the exception of the formal meetings, are restricted mostly to member states, a number of diplomats commented to an edition of the *UN Chronicle* in 2002 on the decisionmaking process in the Fifth Committee, and their comments continue to be of relevance to date.[51] At formal meetings, reports would be introduced by representatives of the Secretary-General, the chairperson of the ACABQ and others, while member states would outline their general positions on the issues before the Committee. Following formal meetings, a number of informal consultations would be convened in a smaller meeting room.

In informal consultations, forging a consensus rests on the shoulders of the Coordinator. "The first part is the question-and-answer session," says Thomas Schlesinger, a Fifth Committee delegate quoted in the article. "The Coordinator invites Member States to submit language proposals. If one wants result A, other Member States do not want result B, and only then does the role of the Coordinator really start."[52] Schlesinger says that the Coordinator has to work with the delegations to shape a consensus. "And this is the very tricky part. It is very difficult for the Coordinator to put something forward and not appear biased to either side. It does require negotiating and coordinating skills to bring together views that are very far apart."[53]

These sessions are followed by so-called informal informals:

> In the third level of negotiations—the Informal Informals—small drafting groups meet in a corner of Conference Room 5 or even outside it, while the Chairperson sits in the centre of the room. "Where you move to the corner of the room, you dispense with interpretation and hopefully stay in the corner with the most interested delegations," says Schlesinger, "then later come back to the centre, say if an agreement was reached—or go straight back to the formal informal for the chairperson or Secretariat officials to apprise the delegations of the agreement reached and ask if it can be formally announced."[54]

And the last level is a political meeting, oftentimes at ambassadorial level:

> The fourth level in informal negotiations is the political meeting. When diplomats cannot agree in the least formals, the Ambassadors themselves take over and agree on a compromise. "It involves also a

carrot-and-stick approach," says a Committee delegate who requested "diplomatic anonymity." "Normally, it takes the form of a reminder that 'I value the bilateral relation between us as much as you do.' It must give you the impression that someone speaks with my interest at heart, so you would revisit your position to meet it some place on the other side," explained the diplomat.[55]

How Is It Decided What Each Member State Contributes?

Once a program budget has been approved, the expenses of the organization are borne by member states as apportioned by the General Assembly, in keeping with Article 17, paragraph 2 of the United Nations Charter. Since the early days of the United Nations, this appointment has followed the principle of "capacity to pay," as codified in Rule 160 of the Rules of Procedure of the General Assembly.[56] The apportionment is set out in a scale of assessments, which, in keeping with the same Rule, when once fixed by the General Assembly, shall not be subject to a revision for at least three years. The scale distributes the overall budget.

While the finer details of the methodology have evolved quite considerably over the years, the overall approach taken has remained fairly constant.[57] As a basis, the methodology takes the gross national income of a member state, denominated in United States dollars. This income measure is taken as the first approximation of member states' capacity to pay. For purposes of comparison, the gross national income is converted to United States dollars using market exchange rates. In specific cases where no such exchange rates are available, United Nations operational rates of exchange are used instead. At times, in cases of extreme volatility, adjustments are made.

Subsequently, a number of standard adjustments are made. First, there is the debt burden adjustment, which serves to account for the impact of external debt repayment on the capacity to pay. The adjustment is applied to member states with a per capita gross national income (GNI) below a threshold. One-eighth of the total debt stock is discounted, on the assumption that external debt is repaid over a period of eight years. Second, an adjustment is made for those member states that have a low income per capita. A discount is given in the equivalent of 80 percent of the percentage by which a member state's per capita GNI is below the per capita GNI of all member states.

After the adjustments, three limits are imposed: a floor, in terms of a minimum assessment rate of 0.001 percent for all countries; a ceiling, which is a maximum rate of 22 percent for all countries; and another ceiling for least-developed countries of 0.01 percent. This overall methodology is then applied to both a three-year and a six-year base period, of which the average will constitute the new scale of assessments.

What Is the Role of the Committee on Contributions?

The Committee on Contributions advises the General Assembly on issues of apportionment, under Article 17 of the Charter, and the suspension of voting privileges as a consequence of a failure to pay, under Article 19. Like the Advisory Committee on Administrative and Budgetary Questions, the Committee on Contributions is composed of eighteen members, in keeping with resolution 31/95, who serve in their personal capacity, and it reports to the Fifth Committee.

What Happens If a Member State
Does Not Pay Its Contributions?

Article 19 is quite clear about the consequences of not paying member contributions:

> A Member of the United Nations which is in arrears in the payment of its financial contributions to the Organization shall have no vote in the General Assembly if the amount of its arrears equals or exceeds the due from it for the preceding two full years. The General Assembly may, nevertheless, permit such a member to vote if it is satisfied that the failure to pay is due to conditions beyond the control of the Member.

As reflected in Rule 160 of the Rules of Procedure of the General Assembly, the Committee on Contributions would discuss any such claims being made that the failure to pay is due to conditions beyond the control of the Member and make recommendations in its report in a chapter titled "Application of Article 19 of the Charter."[58] The General Assembly provided some general guidance to this effect in resolution 54/237 C,[59] in which it urged all member states in arrears requesting exemption to provide the fullest possible supporting information to support their claim. In its report it would set out those member states requesting an exemption under Article 19 of the Charter, as well as general information, such as the number of consecutive years that the state fell under Article 19. On the basis of such information, if the Committee is satisfied, it would then recommend that the member state in question be permitted to vote until the end of the session of the General Assembly.

Based on such a recommendation, the Fifth Committee would discuss, seek further clarification, and at the first possible moment, recommend a draft resolution to the General Assembly for adoption. The General Assembly then pronounces itself on such requests, and if the General Assembly is also satisfied that the failure is beyond the member state's control, the member state can be permitted to vote for the remainder of the session.

Twice yearly, at the beginning of the session and at the beginning of the new year, the General Assembly is notified by the Secretary-General of those member states that are in arrears and subject to Article 19. The General Assembly takes note of the letter by the Secretary-General. Immediately upon receipt of funds by the Secretariat, the voting rights of the member state are restored. This means that if and when a member state pays the necessary amount a few minutes prior to a meeting during which voting is expected, the Office of the Controller would have to notify the General Assembly and Secretariat immediately so that the voting console at the respective seat can be activated, as was the case during the seventy-eighth plenary meeting of the General Assembly on June 11, 2021.[60] The Legal Counsel has long held that the loss of voting rights also applied in the Main Committees of the General Assembly.[61]

Over the years, the procedure has not changed; however, the number of countries subject to Article 19 has declined considerably. Especially in the 1990s, a significantly larger number of countries were in arrears, including as many as twenty-four member states in 1999.[62]

Contributions and the Liquidity Crisis

If all member states paid their dues and on time, the story would end here. The financial health of the organization depends on member states paying their dues in full and on time every year. As a recent report stated, "the full and efficient implementation of the programme of work depends on the financial support of member states through the adoption of realistic budget levels and the provision of timely contributions to ensure a stable and predictable financial situation throughout the year."[63] However, member states do not all pay their contributions on time. In fact, the pattern of collection is an inverted parabola with a large number of funds being collected in the second half of the year.

For a number of years, the Secretary-General has been signaling that liquidity and structural issues in budget management have to be addressed. A number of measures were proposed in a report on improving the financial situation of the United Nations, but no action was taken by the General Assembly to implement such measures.[64] In recent years, this has led to serious deficits (a negative balance of inflow and outflow), in the amounts of US$520 million at the lowest point in 2019 and US$334 million in 2020.

As a result, the Secretariat has had to put spending controls on program delivery, threatening the ability of the United Nations to implement the mandates that have been entrusted to it, even if budgets are approved and expenditures apportioned. This has resulted in hiring freezes, recruitment stops, and stringent cash management, all costing considerable staff time and impacting mandate implementation. In fact, in view of a severe cash shortage, mandate implementation is no longer exclusively a function of program plans and budgets, but of available cash.

In that report, it was noted that the Secretary-General has repeatedly drawn the attention of member states to the deepening crises and appealed to them to put the United Nations on a sound and stable financial footing. Absent solutions, another report notes, program delivery will continue to be constrained by the lack of an adequate liquidity-bridging mechanism.[65]

Other Sources of Funding

So far I have focused on what is known as the regular budget of the United Nations Secretariat. It is the main budget and also the most complex, even if it is not the largest or most flexible. Traditionally, as far as the funding of the Secretariat is concerned, budget documents distinguish between three streams of funding: the regular budget, "other assessed" sources of funding (including peacekeeping), and extrabudgetary resources. The first two types are assessed—as in, subject to apportionment by the General Assembly using a scale of assessments—and come with the obligation to pay by member states that is set forth in Article 17 of the United Nations Charter.

Even within the regular budget itself, there are different funding modalities: certain entities are funded using a grant or a partial grant to another entity, so that the General Assembly ends up authorizing the transfer of a sum of money. Other entities are funded using a grant to a multiyear account, on which there would be subsequent financial reporting to the General Assembly. In certain cases, the General Assembly has authorized other modalities, such as a subvention grant, which is essentially a reserve that would supplement extrabudgetary contributions in case of funding shortfalls.

Although it is beyond the scope of this chapter to comprehensively catalog these modalities, the type of funding should be recognized as significantly impacting the sustainability of programs and activities, the overall program governance, and the perceived impartiality. Extrabudgetary contributions are oftentimes volatile and earmarked, whereas assessed contributions give continuity; this is a consequence of the former being driven by the priorities of individual donors. While the Secretary-General is required to report on extra-budgetarily-funded programmatic activities in the context of the regular budget, the overall program governance is driven by the priorities and reporting requirements of individual donors. And therefore there is a perceived lack of impartiality. Indeed, the following was pointed out in the Independent Expert Panel Report:

> Whereas there is established under the United Nations Charter a single approval procedure for the United Nations budget—i.e., the General Assembly approves the United Nations budget—no such single procedure exists for establishing and approving all the programmes and activities funded through the Regular Budget, peacekeeping, or extrabudgetary budgets. Decisions on programmes and activities funded by these three sources of funds are made by numerous bodies of the United Nations machinery.[66]

Peacekeeping

The first domain of activities not funded by the regular budget that is usually looked at when analyzing other sources of funding are peacekeeping operations. They constitute by far the largest budgets of the organization in the amount of US$6.379 billion for the period July 2021–June 2022.[67] We will look at this domain through the lenses of mandates, program planning, budgeting, and assessment.

Mandates of Peacekeeping Operations

Unlike the General Assembly and ECOSOC, the Security Council does not have a specific rule in its provisional Rules of Procedure that would provide for the submission of draft resolutions to review program budget implications. However, the Security Council has requested that where a new peacekeeping mission is proposed or where significant change to a mandate is envisaged, an estimate of the resource implications for the mission be provided to it.[68]

Program Planning of Peacekeeping Operations

The program planning of peacekeeping operations follows the overall results-based budgeting methodology. Other than variations in terms of format, the formulation of the budgets is done in keeping with resolution 55/231 in which the General Assembly requests that the Secretary-General ensure that the expected accomplishments and indicators of achievement are directly and clearly linked to the objectives of the programs and in accordance with the different nature of the activities of the programs.[69] This resolution was reaffirmed in one of the crosscutting resolutions on the administrative and budgetary aspects of the financing of UN peacekeeping operations, resolution 61/276.[70]

Budgeting of Peacekeeping Operations

The budget cycle of peacekeeping operations is annual and runs from July to June, in keeping with resolution 49/233 A.[71] In May, the Fifth Committee meets at its second resumed session to discuss the budget proposals for the peacekeeping operations, so that agreement can be reached at the end of the financial period.

In recognition of the volatile nature of certain peace operations, the General Assembly decided in resolution 64/269 that if a decision of the Security Council relating to the start-up phase or expansion phase of peacekeeping operations results in the need for expenditure, the Secretary-General is authorized, with the prior concurrence of the Advisory Committee on Administrative and Budgetary Questions, to enter into commitments up to US$100 million.[72] Once a mandate is entrusted to the Secretariat by the Security Council, this provision gives flexibility in the start-up phase to kick-start operations without having to obtain immediate intergovernmental approval for financing related aspects.

Assessment of Peacekeeping Operations

In addition to the regular budget, which has assessed contributions, there are three other budgets that come with assessed contributions: the international tribunals, the capital master plan, and peacekeeping operations. The assessments for peacekeeping operations are by far the largest.

From the inception of the United Nations, peacekeeping activities have been funded using assessed contributions. The first two peace-keeping operations, the United Nations Truce Supervision Organization (UNTSO, established in 1948) and the United Nations Military Observer Group in India and Pakistan (UNMOGIP, 1949) have histori-cally been funded through the regular budget, as part of section 5, "Peacekeeping Operations," which also provides funding for part of the Department of Peace Operations at Headquarters.[73] Both UNTSO and UNMOGIP have been relatively small missions.

As larger missions were established in 1956 (UN Emergency Force) and 1960 (UN Operation in Congo [ONUC]), an increasing number of member states openly refused to pay their dues for such operations. In fact, at its sixteenth session, the General Assembly, on the basis of a draft resolution recommended by the Fifth Committee following the sub-mission of a draft resolution submitted by Brazil, Cameroon, Canada, Denmark, Japan, the United Kingdom, and the United States, went as far as requesting an advisory opinion from the International Court of Justice if in fact expenditures relating to the UN Emergency Force and consti-tuted "expenses of the Organization" within the meaning of Article 17 of the Charter. The Court, in its Advisory Opinion of July 20, 1962, replied in the affirmative that these expenditures were expenses of the United Nations.[74] The Court also pointed out that under Article 17, paragraph 2, of the Charter, the "expenses of the Organization" are the amounts paid out to defray the costs of carrying out the purposes of the organization.

However, as the number of peace operations and their budgets con-tinued to grow in the second half of the last century, so did the number of discussions in the General Assembly on an alternative scale for peacekeeping, which would provide discounts to specific groups of countries and recognize what was viewed as the special responsibility of the permanent members of the Security Council. For decades, the scale was tinkered with to recognize specific categories of countries and to adjust the scale accordingly. This finally led to resolution 55/235 and the adoption of a new peacekeeping scale in 2000, which remains in place today.[75] The scale continues to be based on a system of discounts, similar to the ones mentioned for the regular budget above.

Extrabudgetary Contributions

A second area not funded by the regular budget relates to extrabudgetary, voluntary contributions that are made by individual member states or other entities. Such contributions are usually made to trust funds. Historically, this category of contributions came about as early as the 1940s through economic and social activities that underlined the importance of technical assistance and, later, capacity-building programs.

In 1949, the General Assembly by resolution 304 (IV) authorized the Secretary-General to set up a special account for technical assistance for economic development and invited all governments to make voluntary contributions as large as possible to the special account, which helped establish the Expanded Program of Technical Assistance (EPTA) as a first program that was authorized to operate outside the governance structures of the assessed contributions.[76] While governance structures were in place with regard to the selection of projects, for example, it was clear that the General Assembly would not determine the size of the EPTA budget, which would be driven by contributions of individual member states.

Mandate for Extrabudgetary Contributions

Trust funds can be established by the General Assembly (such as for EPTA) or by the Secretary-General and used to receive voluntary contributions, whether or not in cash, as set out in Financial Regulation 3.12, as approved by the General Assembly. A dated bulletin and three administrative instructions from 1982 refer to the establishment and management of such funds and related procedures.[77] The bottom line is that funds may only be accepted provided that the purposes for which the contributions are made are consistent with the policies, aims, and activities of the organization. This is more specifically spelled out in Financial Rule 107.6, which provides that no voluntary contribution may be accepted if the purpose is inconsistent with the policies and aims of the United Nations.[78] The purpose of a trust fund and its relationship to the policies, aims, and activities of the organization are usually outlined in a trust fund's "birth certificate," which is kept by the Office of Program Planning, Finance, and Budget of the Department for Management Strategy, Policy, and Compliance.

Program Planning for Extrabudgetary Contributions

In theory, the program planning for extrabudgetary contributions is no different from regular budget programming. PPBME Regulation 1.1 provides that the program planning rules apply to all activities undertaken by the United Nations, irrespective of their source of financing.[79]

While planning for activities to be partially or fully financed by extrabudgetary funds is provisional, and such activities are implemented only if adequate funds are made available, the programmatic frameworks must also cover extrabudgetary contributions. Depending on the nature of the extrabudgetary contribution, donors would likely also have their own reporting requirements, both before and after the funded activity. Although efforts are made to integrate such reporting requirements within the overall program planning cycle to allow for economies of scale, separate frameworks have to be maintained in certain cases.

Budgeting and Assessment of Extrabudgetary Resources

Although estimates of extrabudgetary resources are included in the proposed program budget, the budgeting for extrabudgetary contributions is almost exclusively driven by a donor's budgeting cycle and requirements, and any data presented to the General Assembly is provided for informational purposes only. As stated above, there is no scale of assessment for extrabudgetary resources.

Hybrid Constructs

As mentioned before, there are more funding mechanisms than can be outlined in this chapter. For example, certain funds and programs are funded through a hybrid modality of regular budget, "core budget," and extrabudgetary resources. The regular budget would cover a small share of the overall "assessed" budget, to be supplemented by a "core budget" to which member states commit in an entity's own governing body without being subject to the obligation to pay that would apply if approved by the General Assembly. For example, in the case of the UN Environment Programme (UNEP), approximately 5 percent of its budget is provided through the regular budget approved by the General Assembly. Some 15 percent is provided through the Environment Fund, UNEP's core fund, which is approved by member states but entirely made up of voluntary contributions. The remaining 80 percent is provided through earmarked contributions by individual donors.

Such arrangements create a number of challenges, especially from a program planning perspective. What does it mean if UNEP's governing body, the Environment Assembly, approves an overall program plan and then, while the plan is being implemented, changes are requested to its programmatic framework by the General Assembly? How can such discrepancies be resolved? In an attempt to update the Committee for Program and Coordination on intergovernmental developments in sectoral, functional, and regional bodies, the Program Planning and Budget Division prepares a note with any such action taken.[80]

This was also a subject of review in the *Because Process Matters* report, in which the experts underscored the following:

> The review by relevant intergovernmental bodies is important, not just because this is part of the envisioned process, but because of the expertise available in the programme review bodies. Technically, these are the bodies that may be responsible for originating many of the programmes and activities under review and, therefore, they are the most qualified to pass judgment on the issues referred to them.[81]

Notes

1. Wildavsky, *Politics of the Budgetary Process*.
2. J. Laurenti, "Financing the United Nations," in Krasno, *The United Nations*, p. 271.
3. "The Process of Informals in the Fifth Committee," *UN Chronicle*, no. 1 (2002).
4. UN General Assembly, Resolution 72/266 A., "Shifting the Management Paradigm in the United Nations, 2017, https://undocs.org/a/res/72/266A.
5. Independent Expert Panel, *Because Process Matters: Groundwork for a Reform of Planning and Budgeting at the United Nations*, Permanent Mission of Switzerland to the United Nations, New York, August 2014, p. 60.
6. Wildavsky, *Politics of the Budgetary Process*, p. 7.
7. Rubin, *Politics of Public Budgeting*, p. 2.
8. United Nations, "Shifting the Management Paradigm in the United Nations: Improving and Streamlining the Programme Planning and Budgeting Process," 2017, http://undocs.org/a/72/492/add.1.
9. Lindblom, "The Science of Muddling Through"; Lindblom and Woodhouse, *The Policy-Making Process*; and Dahl and Lindblom, *Politics, Economics, and Welfare*.
10. United Nations, "Rules of Procedure of the General Assembly," 2019 http://undocs.org/a/520/rev.19.
11. For detail on the interpretation of Rule 153 and other rules cited in this chapter, please see the Office of Legal Affairs, United Nations, "Comments on Precedent and Past Practice," 1996, https://legal.un.org/ola/media/GA_RoP_EN. Rule 31 of the ECOSOC rules of procedure has similar implications.
12. For example, at the second plenary meeting of its seventy-sixth session, on September 17, 2021, the General Assembly adopted a number of provisions concerning the organization of the seventy-sixth session (decision 76/505). United Nations, "Book of Resolutions and Decisions (76th Session)," Volume 2, https://undocs.org/a/76/505.

13. United Nations, Official Records, 38th Plenary Meeting at the 75th Session, 2020, https://undocs.org/A/75/PV.38.

14. United Nations, "Regulations and Rules Governing Programme Planning, the Programme Aspects of the Budget, the Monitoring of Implementation and the Methods of Evaluation," 2018, https://undocs.org/st/sgb/2018/3.

15. United Nations, "Book of Resolutions and Decisions (34th session)," p. 264, 1979, https://undocs.org/en/a/34/46(supp).

16. For an example of such an oral statement, please see a recent meeting of the UN General Assembly, Official Records, 71st Plenary Meeting at the 75th Session, 2020, https://undocs.org/A/75/PV.71.

17. For an example of such a deferral, please see a recent meeting of the UN General Assembly, Official Records, 38th Plenary Meeting at the 75th Session, 2020, https://undocs.org/A/75/PV.38.

18. United Nations, "Regulations and Rules Governing Programme Planning, the Programme Aspects of the Budget, the Monitoring of Implementation and the Methods of Evaluation," 2018, https://undocs.org/st/sgb/2018/3.

19. United Nations, "Proposed Programme Budget for 2022: Forward and Introduction," 2021, https://undocs.org/a/76/6 (Introduction).

20. United Nations, "Regulations and Rules Governing Programme Planning, the Programme Aspects of the Budget, the Monitoring of Implementation and the Methods of Evaluation," 2018, https://undocs.org/st/sgb/2018/3.

21. Maurice Bertrand and Joint Inspection Unit, "Report on the Elaboration of Regulations for the Planning, Programming and Evaluation Cycle of the United Nations," 1982, https://undocs.org/jiu/rep/82/3.

22. Ibid.

23. United Nations, ECOSOC Resolution 920 (XXXIV), 2014, http://undocs.org/a/res/2150.

24. United Nations, Proposed Program Budget for 2022: Section 2, p. 13–14, April 30, 2021, https://undocs.org/a/76/6(Sect.2).

25. United Nations, "Report of the Committee for Programme and Coordination on its 54th Session," paragraph 31, February 23, 2015, https://undocs.org/a/69/16.

26. UN General Assembly, Resolution 72/266 A, January 15, 2018, https://undocs.org/a/res/72/266A.

27. United Nations, "Biennial Programme Plan and Priorities for the Period 2018–2019," https://undocs.org/a/71/6/rev.1.

28. UN General Assembly, Resolution 55/231, https://undocs.org/a/res/55/231.

29. United Nations, "Proposed Programme Budget for 2022: Section 16," April 12, 2021, https://undocs.org/a/76/6(Sect.16).

30. Ibid.

31. United Nations, "Report of the Committee for Programme and Coordination on its 48th session," paragraph 28, https://undocs.org/a/63/16(supp).

32. United Nations, "Report of the Committee for Programme and Coordination on its 54th session," paragraph 50, https://undocs.org/a/69/16; UN General Assembly, Resolution 71/6, paragraph 12, https://undocs.org/a/res/71/6; United Nations, "Report of the Committee for Programme and Coordination on its 53rd session," paragraph 33, https://undocs.org/a/68/16.

33. United Nations, "Biennial Programme Plan and Priorities for the Period 2018–2019."

34. United Nations, "Regulations and Rules Governing Programme Planning, the Programme Aspects of the Budget, the Monitoring of Implementation and the Methods of Evaluation," June 1, 2018, https://undocs.org/st/sgb/2018/3.

35. Independent Export Panel, *Because Process Matters,* p. 60.

36. United Nations, "Rules of Procedure of the General Assembly."

37. UN General Assembly, Resolution 75/254 A, 2020, https://undocs.org/a/res/75/254A.

38. New York Police Department, *Report to the Committees on Finance and Public Safety on the Fiscal 2022 Executive Budget for the New York Police Department,* May 2021, p. 12.

39. OECD, *Global Outlook on Financing for Sustainable Development 2021: A New Way to Invest for People and Planet,* 2020, doi: 10.1787/e3c30a9a-en.

40. New York City, *United Nations Impact Report,* 2016, https://www1.nyc.gov/assets/international/dowloads/pdf/UN_Impact_Report.pdf.

41. Government Accountability Office, *Cost Comparison of Actual UN and Hypothetical U.S. Operations in Haiti,* 2016, https://www.gao.gov/assets/gao-06-331.pdf.

42. UN General Assembly, Resolution 68/246, January 17, 2014, https://undocs.org/a/res/68/246.

43. United Nations, "Study on Recosting and Options for the Organization in Dealing with Fluctuations in Exchange Rates and Inflation," September 12, 2014, https://undocs.org/a/69/381.

44. United Nations, "Revised Estimates: Effect of Changes in Rates of Exchange and Inflation," December 11, 2019, https://undocs.org/a/74/585.

45. United Nations, "Proposed Programme Budget for 2022."

46. Ibid.

47. Ibid.

48. UN General Assembly, Resolution 74/267, January 17, 2020, https://undocs.org/a/res/74/267.

49. United Nations, "Rules of Procedure of the General Assembly."

50. UN General Assembly, Resolution 41/213, 1986, https://undocs.org/a/res/41/213.

51. "The Process of Informals in the Fifth Committee," *UN Chronicle,* no. 1, 2002.

52. Ibid.

53. Ibid.

54. Ibid.

55. Ibid.

56. United Nations, "Rules of Procedure of the General Assembly."

57. See the most recent report of the Committee on Contributions on its work at its eighty-first session for the detail of ongoing discussions: United Nations, "Report of the Committee on Contributions on its 81st session," 2021, https://undocs.org/a/76/11.

58. United Nations, "Rules of Procedure of the General Assembly."

59. UN General Assembly, Resolution 54/237 C, 1999, https://undocs.org/a/res/54/237C.

60. United Nations, "Official Records: 78th Plenary Meeting at the 75th Session," 2020, https:undocs.org/A/75/PV.78.

61. United Nations, "Note Verbale Dated 26 July 1968 from Secretary-General Addressed to the Permanent Representative of the USSR," 1968, p. 2 (annex), https://undocs.org/a/7146.

62. United Nations, "Report of the Committee on Contributions on its 59th session," 2004, https://undocs.org/a/59/11.

63. United Nations, "Proposed Programme Budget for 2022," paragraph 26.

64. United Nations, "Improving the Financial Situation of the United Nations," March 26, 2019, https://undocs.org/a/73/809.

65. United Nations, "Financial Situation of the United Nations," October 13, 2020, https://undocs.org/a/75/387.

66. Independent Export Panel, *Because Process Matters*, p. 60.

67. United Nations, "Approved Resources for Peacekeeping Operations for the Period from 1 July 2021 to 30 June 2022," June 29, 2021, https://undocs.org/a/c.5/75/25.

68. United Nations, "Statement by the President of the Security Council," August 2009, https://undocs.org/s/prst/2009/24.

69. UN General Assembly, Resolution 55/231, 2005, https://undocs.org/a/res/55/231.

70. UN General Assembly, Resolution 61/276, 2011, https://undocs.org/a/res/61/276.

71. UN General Assembly, Resolution 49/233 A, 1994, https://undocs.org/a/res/49/233A.

72. UN General Assembly, Resolution 64/269, 2009, https://undocs.org/a/res/64/269.

73. United Nations, "Proposed Programme Budget for 2022: section 5," 2021, https://undocs.org/a/76/6(Sect.5).

74. International Court of Justice, *Certain Expenses of the United Nations (Article 17, paragraph 2, of the UN Charter)*, https://www.icj-cij.org/en/case/49.

75. UN General Assembly, Resolution 55/231, 2000, https://undocs.org/a/res/55/231.

76. UN General Assembly, Resolution 304 (IV), 1949, https://undocs/org/a/res/305(IV).

77. United Nations, "Establishment and Management of Trust Funds," 1982, https://undocs.org/st/sgb/188; United Nations, "General Trust Funds," 1982, https://undocs.org/st/ai/284; United Nations, "Technical Co-operation Trust Funds," 1982, https://undocs.org/st/ai/285; and United Nations, "Programme Support Accounts," 1982, https://undocs.org/st/ai/286.

78. United Nations, "Financial Regulations and Rules," 1982, https://undocs.org/st/sgb/2018/3.

79. United Nations, "Regulations and Rules Governing Programme Planning, the Programme Aspects of the Budget, the Monitoring of Implementation and the Methods of Evaluation," 2018, https://undocs.org/st/sgb/2018/3.

80. United Nations, "Review of the Proposed Programme Plan for 2022 by Sectoral, Functional and Regional Bodies," 2021, https://undocs.org/e/ac.51/2021/9.

81. Independent Export Panel, *Because Process Matters*, p. 60.

11

Confronting the Authority of the Security Council

Jean E. Krasno

Security Council resolutions have the authority to bind all United Nations member states into compliance. Authority is legitimized power based on rules but also contains a threat of coercion if certain parties do not comply. The Council has the right under Chapter VII of the UN Charter to impose sanctions and to authorize the use of force, thus enhancing its authority. However, for situations in which the Security Council is unable to act, in order to maintain a global system based in the rule of law, UN member states had to create a legal means to address crises and transfer that authority temporarily to another body. Following this line of thought, the UN General Assembly passed the Uniting for Peace resolution, 377 (V), in 1950 as just such an instrument to address this vacuum when action was deemed critical. This chapter tells the story of how the Uniting for Peace resolution came into being, why it was necessary, and how it has been used over time.

The Big Question

The big question is how to embolden the United Nations to take action when the Council is deadlocked by the veto. With the increased activity of the Security Council and the expansion of its authority into spheres well beyond the visions of the founders—from peace and security to human rights, humanitarian assistance, and climate change, to name a few—there emerged a need to find a legitimate way to circumvent the

231

Council when it fails to act. Member states first addressed this dilemma in 1950 to pass authority from the normally privileged Security Council to the General Assembly where there is no veto. The purpose originally was to wrestle the use of the veto away from the Soviet Union at a time when the United States and the West wanted the United Nations to legitimize action taken to defend South Korea from encroachment from the Communist North. It was actually not the first time that the Western powers had maneuvered an issue into the General Assembly to avoid Soviet blockage, and it happened several times again after 1950. The question today is: When the Security Council is unable to act for reasons of the veto or any other obstacle, can Uniting for Peace action be utilized as an effective and legitimate strategy? Here I examine the history of this strategic tool, and other similarly inspired maneuvers, and attempt to analyze the potential for its future use.

A Look at the Language

Disgruntlement over inaction and lack of cooperation among Security Council members emerged soon after the United Nations met for the first time in London in January 1946. If the Council continued to be blocked by the veto and unable to take any action, its authority and that of the UN as a whole would wither away. General Assembly resolution 290 (IV), which passed on December 1, 1949, clearly demonstrated that frustration:

> GA resolution 290 (IV) Essentials of Peace
> *The General Assembly*
> *Calls upon the five permanent members of the Security Council,*
> 10. *To broaden* progressively their cooperation and to exercise restraint in the use of the veto in order to make the Security Council a more effective instrument for maintaining peace.[1]

Less than a year later in November 1950, the General Assembly was ready to take up the responsibilities of peace and security and make use of its veto-free advantage. The passage of the Uniting for Peace resolution was initially orchestrated to enable the Assembly to address the conflict in Korea in the face of Soviet objections. In addition, the resolution was intended to establish for the record a mechanism for taking action if and when the Security Council was unable to agree. If legitimate authority is based on rules, then rules had to be put in place to shift authority when needed. The resolution reads:

377 (V) Uniting for Peace
The General Assembly
Recalling its resolution 290 (IV) entitled "Essentials of Peace," which states that disregard of the Principles of the Charter of the United Nations is primarily responsible for the continuance of international tensions, and desiring to contribute further to the objectives of that resolution,

A1. *Resolves* that if the Security Council, because of lack of unanimity of the permanent members, fails to exercise its primary responsibility for the maintenance of international peace and security in any case where there appears to be a threat to the peace, breach of the peace, or act of aggression, the General Assembly shall consider the matter immediately with a view to making appropriate recommendations to Members for collective measures, including in the case of a breach of the peace or act of aggression the use of armed force when necessary, to maintain or restore international peace and security. If not in session at the time, the General Assembly may meet in emergency special session within twenty-four hours of the request thereof. Such emergency special session shall be called if requested by the Security Council on the vote of any of its seven Members, or by a majority of the Members of the United Nations.[2]

The resolution clearly states that if the Security Council is unable to act when there is an imminent threat to international peace and security, the General Assembly may take up the issue under two conditions: (1) that the Security Council votes to do so, today with nine votes in favor among the current fifteen-member Council, or (2) that a majority of UN member states votes to do so. The vote count in the Security Council would not be subject to the veto as it would be considered a procedural matter, as stated in the resolution, voted on by "any of its seven members." Maneuvering around the veto was a clever and useful strategy for a period of time, but could this be repeated effectively today when the West no longer controls the General Assembly? One might also ask the following: Why was the veto created in the first place if it seems to only throw roadblocks in the way of progress and action?

How the Veto Emerged: The Debate at San Francisco

The principle that there should be a veto was settled among the major powers prior to the 1945 San Francisco Conference that finalized the UN Charter, but the issue was again raised during the conference. The word *veto* does not appear in the Charter, and the San Francisco participants often referred to it as the "unanimity clause." The Charter states the following in Article 27:

> Voting: UN Charter, Article 27:
> Each member of the Security Council shall have one vote.
> Decisions of the Security Council on procedural matters shall be made by an affirmative vote of nine members [in 1950, seven members of the then eleven-member Council].
> Decisions of the Security Council on all other matters shall be by an affirmative vote of nine members including the concurring votes of the permanent members.

This explains the careful wording in the Uniting for Peace resolution, using the phrase *lack of unanimity* instead of the word *veto* in reference to the "concurring votes of the permanent members." The establishment of the veto, or unanimity of the five permanent members, was meant to protect the interests of the great powers.[3] It was believed that the major powers—China, France, the Soviet Union (now Russia), the UK, and the United States—that fought together as the Allies to defeat the Axis powers in World War II would need to remain united in a common cause to deter any aggression that might spark a third world war. Any serious disagreement among the powers could in essence initiate a clash and perhaps war. That was to be avoided, and in fact the United States would not have become a member of the UN without the veto. At San Francisco, "smaller countries were generally opposed to the veto, the Latin Americans in particular, but eventually they along with the Philippines and Australia had to retreat, because there would have been no charter without it and they couldn't afford not to have a charter. The final vote in San Francisco on the "unanimity clause" was 33 in favor, 2 against, and 15 abstentions. The smaller powers had agreed to accept the veto on the condition that the General Assembly should be granted under Charter Article 11, paragraph 2, the right to discuss any question and to make recommendations unless the Security Council is seized of the matter.[4]

> UN Charter, Article 11, paragraph 2:
> The General Assembly may discuss any question relating to the maintenance of international peace and security brought before it by any Member of the United Nations, or by the Security Council, or by a state which is not a Member of the United Nations . . . and . . . may make recommendations with regard to any such questions to the state or states concerned or to the Security Council or both.

At San Francisco, the Soviet Union had objected to the General Assembly's right to take up any issue including security, even if its resolutions were only recommendations and not binding. However, under pressure by the United States and the smaller states, particularly from Latin America, the Soviets eventually had to back down. To protect the prerogatives of the Council, the Charter declares that as long as the Security Council is seized of a matter, the General Assembly is not allowed to intervene. Article 12 of the Charter states the following:

> UN Charter, Article 12:
>   While the Security Council is exercising in respect of any dispute or situation the functions assigned to it in the present Charter, the General Assembly shall not make any recommendation with regard to that dispute or situation unless the Security Council so requests.
>   The Secretary-General, with the consent of the Security Council, shall notify the General Assembly at each session of any matters relative to the maintenance of international peace and security which are being dealt with by the Security Council and shall similarly notify the General Assembly, or Members of the United Nations if the General Assembly is not in session, immediately [when] the Security Council ceases to deal with such matters.

The Soviets must have felt a sense of security with that interpretation, not anticipating what would occur only a few years later.

The United Nations Special Commission on the Balkans

It is generally perceived that there was no precedent to the 1950 Uniting for Peace resolution, which allows the General Assembly to make recommendations in lieu of the Security Council on a matter of peace and security. However, the UN Special Commission on the Balkans (UNSCOB) was deployed in 1947 under the authority of the General Assembly, not the Security Council. This observer mission was sent to monitor complaints that outside support for the Communist movement in northern Greece by Communist guerrillas from Albania, Bulgaria, and Yugoslavia was destabilizing the Western-backed Greek government. When the Soviets used their veto to block the mission, the United States maneuvered the issue onto the agenda of the General Assembly. UNSCOB was the first UN-sponsored fact-finding mission deployed in the midst of armed conflict.[5] The creation of UNSCOB by the General Assembly instead of the Security Council demonstrated the first attempt to consider a procedural vote by the Council as a means to circumvent Soviet objections and have a veto-free Assembly address the issue.

The history leading up to UNSCOB illustrates the frustration members had with the Security Council and its inability to act. The failures of the League of Nations were still fresh in the minds of diplomats who did not want the newly created UN to be paralyzed in the same manner the League had been. The issue of violent incidents along the border between Greece and Albania was initially raised by the Ukrainian representative on August 24, 1946. The United States suggested the establishment of an investigative commission to look into the matter. However, the proposal was vetoed by the Soviet Union. On December 3, 1946, the Greek government brought complaints before the Security Council against Albania, Bulgaria, and Yugoslavia for supporting Communist guerrillas in northern Greece. This time the Soviet Union went along with the proposal made by the United States. However, the support was short-lived because UNSCOB found evidence of support for the insurgency, affirming the Greek claim. The Soviet Union disagreed with the results and repeatedly used the veto against Security Council resolutions that were based on the recommendations of the report with regard to the insurgency. The Council then removed the item from its agenda to allow the General Assembly to deal with the matter.[6]

The General Assembly called on all parties for restraint and established UNSCOB on October 21, 1947, to be composed of the then eleven members of the Security Council. However, the Soviet Union and Poland refused to serve on the commission, bringing the number down to nine. A unique trait of the mission was that its members represented and received instructions from their respective states and not the UN. In addition, the military observers reported their findings to their national governments. The commission reports were issued to the General Assembly and not to the Security Council. UNSCOB remained in existence until 1951, submitting regular reports on the growing refugee problems, arms trafficking, and the abduction of children across international frontiers. On December 7, 1951, the General Assembly decided to discontinue the special commission, but due to the situation in the Balkans, it chose to request the Peace Observer Commission to establish a Balkan sub-commission (contemplated in resolution 377 (V), section B).[7]

The Korean Question

In 1950, the Soviet Union had boycotted the Security Council on grounds that the UN had failed to grant the People's Republic of China (Communist China), which had achieved control of the mainland by

1949, the seat of China in the UN and on the Council. Instead the UN continued to recognize the Chiang Kai-shek regime in Taiwan as the legitimate member of the UN. When war broke out between North and South Korea, with the Soviets absent from the Council, the West was free to authorize the use of force under UN auspices without the threat of a Soviet veto.

During this period, the Council passed three resolutions on Korea: the first on June 25, 1950; the second on June 27, 1950; and the third on July 7, 1950. The three gave authority to the member states led by the United States to take action against the North Korean attack. In August 1950, realizing its blunder, the Soviet Union returned, and Soviet Ambassador Jacob A. Malik took up the Council presidency for the month of August. With the Soviets back on the Security Council, it was no longer possible to take action with regard to Korea because of Soviet opposition. They were supporting North Korea. Previous discussions about the role of the General Assembly in the area of peace and security and the experience of UNSCOB encouraged Washington to seek a way to involve the Assembly in finding a solution to the Korean conflict. A careful study of the Charter by legal analysts revealed the right of the General Assembly to discuss questions of peace and security and make recommendations as long as the Security Council was not considering the matter. The United States sought support from other nations and drafted what was referred to as the "multi-power" resolution. The proposal was cleverly named the "Uniting for Peace" resolution to cast a more positive light and obfuscate the fact that it was actually a political and legal maneuver to sideline the Soviets. Leonard Meeker, who was working in the US State Department at the time on UN affairs, recounts:

> During the summer when August first came around and Malik went back to the Security Council to take up the role of President (since it was his turn to be President in August) it was recognized that the Security Council, with the Soviet Union present, would no longer be able to function in regard to Korea. The Soviet veto would prevent any action. There had been earlier discussion about the role of the General Assembly in the field of peace and security and, in fact, a sub-organ called the Interim Committee had been set up a couple of years earlier. As I recall it now, during August of 1950 there were meetings in Washington which included Dean Rusk, Harding Bancroft, John Foster Dulles (who came down from his retreat in northern New York State) and myself to discuss what might be done to put the General Assembly in a position to act in some way in the Korean War. It was recognized that the Security Council at the most had made recommendations. And it was believed by all of us that if you looked carefully at

the different articles of the Charter dealing with the powers of the General Assembly, it could discuss questions affecting peace and security and also could make recommendations. So with that set of ideas we began in the month to draft a resolution for the General Assembly to pass which would set up a framework for General Assembly consideration of a peace and security problem in a situation where the Security Council was unable to act because of the veto. The drafts were pretty well finished and approved along in early September, and I remember going to New York at that time with Mr. Dulles who handled this question in the First Committee of the General Assembly. We had a series of meetings over a few weeks with other delegations to solicit their sponsorship (or at least their support) of the resolution in the General Assembly which eventually became the Uniting for Peace plan.[8]

Debates in the General Assembly in 1950

Complaints about the veto were gathering steam, and several ambassadors referred to the crippling effects of the veto during the General Debate in September 1950. The Brazilian permanent representative at the time, Ambassador Cyro de Freitas Valle, stated: "the right of the veto has been abused."[9] Ambassador Victor Andres Belaunde of Peru complained of the "difficulty resulting from the paralyzing effect of the veto" where "the veto has gone far beyond the purpose for which it was devised . . . the veto is not a right but an obligation . . . to seek unanimity."[10] Moreover, he mentioned the apprehension of the Latin American countries toward the veto at the conference in San Francisco. Emphasizing the power of the General Assembly, Ambassador Belaunde referred to Article 10 of the Charter, asserting that "the Assembly's jurisdiction . . . constitutes . . . the legal foundation for any proposal for convening the Assembly in case of emergency to deal with the exigencies of peace when the Council is paralyzed."[11]

In his speech on September 20, 1950, Dean Acheson, US Secretary of State, openly accused the Soviet Union, stating that, "we have been confronted with many and complex problems, but the main obstacle to peace . . . has been by the policies of the Soviet Union."[12] The United States put forth a set of recommendations before the General Assembly that included the provision of an emergency session within twenty-four hours' notice.[13]

In response to the accusations put forth by the United States, Ambassador Andrei Y. Vyshinsky of the Soviet Union, in his speech at the UN, targeted the United States and earlier resolutions passed on

Korea through the initiative of the United States, stating that, "the United States delegation . . . adopted a number of illegal and unjust decisions on the Korea question . . . to camouflage the armed intervention in Korea."[14] A similar attitude was adopted by the Soviet Union toward the Uniting for Peace resolution as well. The Soviet argument was that the UN could not be strengthened by weakening the Security Council, which would be the result if the proposals were adopted. The responsibility of the Security Council for maintaining international peace and security was an "exclusive" right, and not respecting that right meant ending the unanimity clause in the Charter. Changing the veto would mean amending the Charter, but of course that would require the unanimity of the permanent five members; thus the Soviets were putting forth a specious argument. Yet, the Charter does not actually give the Security Council the exclusive right to maintaining peace and security. UN Charter Article 24, paragraph 1, gives the Council the primary responsibility. Other members claimed that the use of the word *primary* implied that other bodies could play secondary roles.

In a 1991 interview with Canadian diplomat Geoffrey Murray, he stated that Canada was not "too keen on the whole Uniting for Peace procedure—mainly because . . . it irritated the Russians and possibly because we had our own hesitations about its constitutionality in terms of the United Nations Charter."[15]

Discussions in the First Committee of the General Assembly

Once the General Assembly had agreed to include the United States proposal on the agenda, it was referred to the First Committee. A joint effort called the "Seven Power" draft resolution was submitted by Canada, France, the Philippines, Turkey, the UK, the United States, and Uruguay.[16]

Section A of draft resolution A/C.1/576 proposed that the General Assembly could promptly make a recommendation if Security Council action was blocked.[17] Though recommendations of the General Assembly are not binding, past experience on the Korean situation demonstrated that responses to recommendations could be very effective. Fifty-three members out of the total of sixty member states at the time had carried out the recommendations. With regard to the question of whether the provisions of section A in the draft Uniting for Peace resolution calling for special sessions of the Assembly were consistent with Article 20 of the Charter,[18] Younger, the UK representative, stated that the General Assembly had the right to determine the time of its sessions and the circumstances in which they should be called. Action by the Security Council was a procedural matter for which an affirmative vote by seven members would suffice (now nine after the Charter was amended in 1965).[19]

Section B of the joint draft resolution called for the establishment of a peace observation mission with the members to be chosen by the General Assembly from among member states other than the so-called great powers, and examples of Greece and Korea were stated to support the recommendation. Section C of the draft resolution proposed that member countries designate troops drawn from their national militaries to serve under the UN when needed and that a panel of military experts would serve under the authority of the Secretary-General. Under section D of the Seven-Power draft resolution, the Security Council and the General Assembly were to receive reports from a Collective Measures Committee on the whole problem of collective security.[20] Meeker, who worked on the plan, explains how *collective measures* was defined at the time in relation to collective security:

> Well, it's very much related to collective security. The Charter and the UN organization as a whole were created to support and assure collective security. It was originally supposed that the Security Council would be the organ that would arrange all this, and when it turned out that the Council (because of the veto) would not be able to function in some important cases, then a transfer to the forum was decided upon. The General Assembly (which has in it all the Members of the UN) would be designed to assure collective security by using the powers which it had—powers of recommendation—and of course, it could take certain preparatory measures in advance through the Collective Measures Committee by setting up a system of contributions of forces by Member States and providing for their suitable military organization.[21]

In the end, the First Committee approved the draft resolution, as amended, by fifty votes to five (the Soviet Bloc) with three abstentions (Argentina; India, which voted in favor of sections A, B, and E only; and Syria). The General Assembly adopted resolution 377 (V) on November 3, 1950, by fifty votes to five, with two abstentions. Under the resolution, a Peace Observation Commission of fourteen members was established to be dispatched to troubled areas in order to advise the Assembly of any necessary action. A Collective Measures Committee of fourteen members was also established in order to coordinate the actions by the members on the recommendations of the Assembly.

Additional Legal Arguments

In the "Certain Expenses of the United Nations" case of 1962, the International Court of Justice (ICJ) advised in a majority opinion that the Security Council had "primary" but not "exclusive" authority, and that although the taking of enforcement action was the exclusive prerogative of the Security Council under Chapter VII, this did not prevent the Assembly from making recommendations under Article 10 and 14.[22]

The Charter provides for a certain interaction between the Council and the Assembly. It is the General Assembly that elects the Council's ten nonpermanent members as stated in Articles 23(1) and 18(2). Under Article 10, the General Assembly is given the right to discuss any issues falling within the realm of the Charter, which is essentially a very wide range of issues. Moreover, Articles 5 and 6 of the Charter show that the General Assembly and the Security Council work in tandem with regard to suspension and expulsion of defaulting members. Under Articles 15(1) and 24(3), "the Security Council shall submit annual and, when necessary, special reports to the General Assembly for its consideration," thus emphasizing the substantial role of the General Assembly.

Though Article 11(1) limits the General Assembly's involvement to general principles, Article 11(2) along with Article 14 together provide a positive mandate for the General Assembly to assume a secondary role through discussions on issues of international peace and security. Furthermore, Articles 10, 11(2), 14, and 18(2) allow the General Assembly (and even nonmembers) to make recommendations to the Security Council. Therefore, the Uniting for Peace resolution did not confer competence to the General Assembly that it did not already have in the Charter, thus challenging arguments by the Soviet Union that termed the resolution a violation of the UN Charter. Yet, the Charter did not define the concept of consent to take up an issue. The Uniting for Peace resolution simply clarifies that consent process.

Using the Resolution on Korea

The reason for adopting the Uniting for Peace resolution and shifting authority to the Assembly was that the Security Council had failed to exercise its primary responsibility for the maintenance of international peace and security. In addition, in order to follow strictly the legal provisions in the Charter, for the General Assembly to take up an issue, the Council must not be seized of the matter. The Assembly is forbidden to take up an issue for recommendation if the Council is already engaged in the issue. While the Uniting for Peace plan was not technically used by name on Korea, the procedure was used in January and February 1951, soon after the Uniting for Peace resolution was passed in November 1950. The resolution 377 (V) was not written into the documents directly, but the strategy was exercised according to plan. At this time Communist China had entered the war in Korea, and the West was eager to condemn the action. However, the Soviets would not go along. Therefore, on January 31, 1951, the Security Council passed resolution 90 (1951), which states: "The Security Council resolves to remove the item 'Complaint of aggression upon the Republic of Korea' from the list of matters of which the Council is seized."[23]

With that legal obstacle out of the way, the General Assembly could move to take up the issue on February 1, 1951, and the Assembly adopted General Assembly resolution 498 (1951).[24] The resolution called upon the People's Republic of China to withdraw from Korea. It affirmed that the United Nations was determined to continue its action in Korea and called on all countries to assist the UN. The resolution asked for the creation of a Committee of the Collective Measures designated under 377 (V) to, as a matter of urgency, regard additional measures to meet the aggression and report to the General Assembly. In this manner, the General Assembly took up the authority on peace and security.

The 1956 Suez Crisis

Though the Uniting for Peace strategy was executed during the Korean War, the first time the resolution was invoked by name was in response to the 1956 Suez crisis, when under resolution 377 (V) the General Assembly called for an Emergency Special Session. Following the nationalization of the Suez Canal Company by Egyptian leader Gamal Abdel Nasser, Israel—in collusion with France and the UK—invaded Egypt. Nasser had forbidden Israel from using the canal once it was nationalized, a move that Israel considered an act of war. France and Britain in an effort to regain the canal had convinced Israel to make the first move, promising to "come to the rescue" of Egypt by positioning their forces between the warring parties and recapturing the canal. When the Security Council attempted to take action under the UN Charter to end the aggression, the British and French as permanent members exercised their veto. In response, nonpermanent Council member Yugoslavia, with full support of the US president Dwight D. Eisenhower, invoked the Uniting for Peace resolution transferring the Suez question to the General Assembly on October 31.[25] The first emergency special session of the General Assembly was convened November 7–10, 1956. The General Assembly demanded the immediate withdrawal of Israel from the Sinai and the French and British troops from the north and authorized the first-ever deployment of *armed* UN peacekeepers. These first UN peacekeeping troops were sent to Egypt to monitor a buffer zone between Egyptian and Israeli forces as the French and British withdrew. This was the first application of the Uniting for Peace resolution, and it resulted in a UN-led armed military deployment. This time the Soviets were pleased to see the British and French at the other end of the stick.

Other Instances of the Use of the Uniting for Peace Resolution

At the same time as Suez in 1956, Uniting for Peace was utilized by the United States to pressure the Soviet Union to cease its intervention into Hungary. The Soviets had used their veto to prevent the passage of a resolution in the Security Council calling on the Soviet Union not to intervene in the Hungarian uprising. On November 4, 1956, the Hungarian question was referred to the General Assembly, and the Soviet Union was called upon to cease its intervention, with the withdrawal of all "foreign forces."[26] Additionally, the General Assembly requested the UN High Commissioner for Refugees provide assistance. As history shows, the Soviets simply ignored the Assembly's demands.

Two years later, August 8–12, 1958, the General Assembly was once again called into emergency session by the Security Council under Uniting for Peace to deal with the crisis in Lebanon, citing the Council's lack of unanimity among the permanent members. The UN Observation Group in Lebanon was deployed with 600 peacekeeping observers to the Syrian-Lebanese border to report on the alleged infiltration of arms and personnel into Lebanon from Syria.[27]

In another instance, following a Soviet veto in the Security Council over the extent and nature of the UN Operation in the Congo, the case of the Congo was referred to the General Assembly in an emergency session on September 17–19, 1960.[28] Seven years later in a letter dated June 13, 1967, the Soviet Union itself requested the UN Secretary-General to convene an emergency special session of the General Assembly in order to debate the 1967 war in the Middle East. Because the Soviets had never recognized the Uniting for Peace resolution, they requested the special session under Article 11 of the UN Charter, which states that the General Assembly may discuss any questions related to international peace and security. Council calls for a cease-fire had been ignored, and the situation was in crisis. Ninety-eight member states, more than the required majority under Uniting for Peace, agreed to take up the issue, even though the United States voted against it, claiming the Security Council was still considering the matter. The General Assembly session debate continued from June 17 through July 5, 1967, but outside the explicit framework of the Uniting for Peace resolution.[29] Ultimately, a cease-fire was reached, and Security Council resolution 242 (1967) was passed.

Further General Assembly special sessions followed. Regarding the India-Pakistan conflict on December 6, 1971, the East Pakistan (now Bangladesh) question was referred to the General Assembly under the Uniting for Peace resolution. Several years later, the General Assembly held an emergency special session on January 10–14, 1980, on the Soviet invasion of Afghanistan. On July 22–29, 1980, a special session was held on the Israeli invasion of Lebanon, and this session was continued again on other dates in 1982. The General Assembly passed a resolution in a session on September 3–14, 1981, under Uniting for Peace calling for sanctions to be imposed on South Africa because of its continued occupation of South West Africa, now Namibia. Again in January and February 1982, under Uniting for Peace, a session was convened on the Middle East to address the issue of the Occupied Territories captured by Israel during the 1967 war.

Two other events happened in the 1980s that resulted in the General Assembly taking up a matter on international peace and security when the Council was blocked by a permanent member veto. In October 1983, the United States joined by some Caribbean nations militarily intervened in Grenada, following a period of internal unrest. Hundreds of Cuban advisors were in the country, and the tense political nature of events in the eyes of the US policymakers conveyed a sense of Cuban ideological expansionism.[30] At the request of Nicaragua, the Security Council considered the situation in a meeting October 25–28. A draft resolution called for the withdrawal of foreign troops but was vetoed by the United States in a vote that took place on October 28.[31] On October 31, Nicaragua requested that the General Assembly take up the matter under rule 15 of the rules of procedure on the General Assembly. Attached to the ambassador's letter to the Secretary-General making the request was an explanatory memorandum with several items:

[item 4] The examination of this question by the Security Council on 25, 26, 27, and 28 October 1983 unequivocally showed that the majority of the Members of the Organization rejected the military invasion of Grenada and demanded the immediate and unconditional withdrawal of all foreign troops from its territory.

[item 5] The General Assembly should, therefore, adopt the draft resolution submitted by Guyana, Nicaragua, and Zimbabwe to the Security Council which the Council failed to adopt because of the negative vote of one of its permanent members and which is now introduced in a revised form.[32]

On November 2, 1983, the General Assembly adopted resolution A/38/7, condemning the Grenada invasion and calling for the removal of foreign troops. Nicaragua, a friend of the Soviet Union that never recognized the Uniting for Peace resolution, did not invoke 377 (V), but used General Assembly rules of procedure. Nevertheless, the purpose was the same: to circumvent the veto.

Again drawing on rules of procedure of the General Assembly and not Uniting for Peace, on December 21, 1989, the permanent representatives of Cuba and Nicaragua requested an item titled "Grave Situation in Panama" be added immediately to the agenda of the General Assembly.[33] On December 15, 1989, General Manuel Noriega had declared war on the United States. The United States had asked him to step down as president when he did not win reelection. As a result, on December 20, the United States sent in military troops, and in a few days had captured Noriega, removing him from the country. Nicaragua asked for a meeting of the Security Council on the issue of Panama, accusing the United States of an act of aggression by invading Panama. On December 23, the Security Council put to a vote a draft resolution strongly deploring the US intervention and demanding immediate withdrawal. However, the measure was vetoed by three permanent members: France, the UK, and the United States. The United States claimed its purpose was to defend democracy in Panama. On December 29, 1989, the General Assembly adopted resolution 240, deploring the intervention in Panama and calling for an immediate withdrawal and respect for Panama's sovereignty.[34]

In 1997, the Uniting for Peace resolution was once again revived and the Tenth Emergency Special Session was convened to handle the ongoing conflict in the Middle East. Rather than open a new session on the Middle East conflict every time there was a new event, the Tenth Emergency Special Session under resolution 377 (V) is simply reopened when a majority of the General Assembly asks the president of the General

Assembly to resume the session. The Assembly's first Tenth Emergency Special Session was held in 1997 after the Security Council in two separate meetings failed to adopt a draft resolution on a new Israeli settlement south of East Jerusalem. Using the Uniting for Peace formula, a special emergency session of the General Assembly was convened in April and again in July and November of 1997. The same Tenth session resumed in 1998, 1999, 2000, 2001, 2003, 2004, 2006, 2009, 2017, and the latest one in 2018 on the protection of the Palestinian civilian population.[35] The discussions, often ending in long statements with no action, demonstrated the frustration of the Assembly on the inability to find a peaceful solution to the Israeli-Palestinian conflict. But they were equally unable to produce any results. Unfortunately, by using the Tenth Special Emergency Sessions for yet another forum of rhetorical debate, the once useful strategy was threatening to become essentially useless.

Instances When Uniting for Peace Could Have Been Used, but Was Not

The Uniting for Peace resolution was designed, ironically, by the United States for conditions where the use of the veto by one or more of the permanent five had paralyzed the Council. However in 1999, when a humanitarian crisis, including acts of genocide, erupted in Kosovo, and Yugoslavia was accused of carrying out mass killings, neither the Security Council nor the General Assembly was consulted. Without UN authorization, North Atlantic Treaty Organization (NATO) forces engaged in a series of bombing attacks in an attempt to force Yugoslavia to remove its troops and Serb-supported militias from Kosovo. The United States and Europe had anticipated a Russian veto and never brought it to a vote in the Security Council. A de facto, rather backhanded approval of the NATO action became apparent when the Council refused to pass a condemnation of the NATO initiative, with twelve countries voting against the condemnation. Nevertheless, a lack of *disapproval* does not offer legal authorization for the use of force. Council members could have invoked the Uniting for Peace resolution, but that was not done. Why not? Perhaps it was determined that in the face of ongoing genocide, there was not enough time to engage in debate, or perhaps members did not trust that the Assembly would authorize NATO action. It is also possible that the West at the time was in the same position that the Soviet Union was in during the early years—in essence, not having control over the Assembly and what it might do.

Therefore, perhaps protecting the right of the veto in the long run had become more precious. The United States, who had been the early insti-gator of the resolution, has lost much of its influence in the Assembly and could not guarantee an outcome to its liking. Paul Heinbecker, who was the Canadian ambassador to the UN and on the Council at the time of Kosovo, explains what happened:

> As it happened, Canada had the chair of the Security Council in Feb-ruary 1999. . . . And we raised the issue of the "Uniting for Peace res-olution" informally three times. We were warned off each time that we raised it; we should not bring it to the Assembly. In the first instance, we came to the conclusion that there were no doubts the Russians would veto in the Council. And if the Russians did then the Chinese would likely follow suit. . . . But in the circumstances, then we might go for a Uniting for Peace resolution. But we didn't do that. There were two reasons: one was we thought that the Yugoslavs, who were founding members of the Non-Aligned Movement, probably had enough chits out there or enough sympathy that it could have taken time and we might have gotten a watered-down resolution. Meanwhile people were dying. There was another angle that people have lost sight of and that is the P-5 didn't want it. . . . Because none of them wants to deprecate the value of a veto.[36]

Conditions for invoking the Uniting for Peace resolution emerged again in 2003 with regard to Iraq. Iraq had refused to allow UN inspec-tors to return to finish their work of removing weapons of mass destruc-tion. No inspections had been carried out from the end of 1998 through 2002. Despite the fact that the UN had destroyed most or possibly all the weapons, there were still unanswered questions, and the Council had been unable to obtain a full and complete report when the inspec-tors were aborted. By 2002, the United States was ready to take more forceful action, but others on the Council disagreed. The stalemate in the Council pitted the United States, the UK, and Spain on one side calling for the use of force against France and Germany on the other, with France threatening to use the veto against a US resolution. Russia proposed various different solutions, with still no agreement. There was clearly a lack of unanimity in the Council, and it could be interpreted that the Council was unable to act.

Others might say that the Council was fulfilling its role exactly as the founders had anticipated by not approving an action that was con-sidered flawed. The United States once again could have taken the issue to the General Assembly, but most likely there would not have been nine needed votes in the Council to do so nor a majority in the Assem-bly to approve it. Finally, the decision by the United States and the UK with the support of Spain to proceed with the use of force without a further resolution directly meant that the Security Council had achieved neither unanimity among the major powers nor a general consensus.

Nongovernmental organizations (NGOs) and others throughout the world called for a resolution to prevent a US-led attack on Iraq. The Arab Group at the United Nations with twenty-two members and the Organization of Islamic Conference with fifty-seven members had resolved to introduce a resolution to convene an emergency session of the General Assembly demanding an immediate end to the US invasion of Iraq. They appeared intent on demonstrating an overwhelming international opposition to the US-led action and discussing ways to bring about a withdrawal of all foreign troops from Iraq. The Non-Aligned Movement with 115 members and several other governments, including Russia, China, Indonesia, and Jamaica, had also expressed their support for an emergency General Assembly session under the Uniting for Peace resolution. However, neither UN Secretary-General Kofi Annan nor the president of the General Assembly ever received a request from any nation to convene such an emergency session, as would be required.[37]

Had the resolution been invoked, the General Assembly could have called upon Iraq to adhere to the resolutions of the Security Council and allow for complete access to its weapons facilities by the UN inspectors. The condemnation of the use of force against Iraq by a large majority in the General Assembly might have offered such a demanding moral authority that it could have prevented the US-led attack; however, in hindsight this was unlikely.

Other Examples Invoking Uniting for Peace

An interesting use of the Uniting for Peace resolution took place in the fall–winter of 2003. Israel had undertaken to construct a wall dividing Israel proper from the West Bank to protect itself from suicide bombing attacks, which had been increasing at an alarming rate. Parts of the wall had encroached into the Occupied Territories, cutting Palestinians off from sections of their land and from access to towns, water, hospitals, and other necessities. The Security Council had introduced a resolution on October 14, 2003, to condemn the wall, but the United States vetoed the draft, saying that such a statement should also include language condemning the killing of innocent Israeli citizens. Several other drafts on the issue of the wall were also vetoed. Under a provision in the Uniting for Peace resolution that allows members of the General Assembly to take a decision when the Security Council is unable to act—in this case, the use of the veto—the Assembly took up the issue. The Tenth Emergency Special Session established under Uniting for Peace 377 (V) was resumed by the president of the General Assembly, Julian Robert Hunte (of Saint Lucia) at the request of a majority of members. The session was resumed on October 20–21 and again on December 3, 2003.

The resulting General Assembly resolution that passed on December 18, 2003, requested an Advisory Opinion of the ICJ on the legal status of the Wall on the Occupied Territories. The request is described as "Advisory Opinion of the International Court of Justice on the legal consequences of the construction of a wall in the occupied Palestinian territory, including in and around East Jerusalem."[38] The Court accepted the request and by July 2004 issued a majority decision (fourteen to one) declaring the "Wall on the Occupied Territory" to be illegal.[39] The decision, however, failed to say anything about the parts of the wall built within the State of Israel, those sections presumably considered legal. Nevertheless, while Israel refused to acknowledge the jurisdiction of the ICJ over the matter, the process of the Court taking the request and hearing arguments resulted in simultaneous action by the Israeli Supreme Court itself taking up the issue and declaring parts of the wall illegal. As a result, some parts of the wall were moved. While Israel rejected the decision of the ICJ, the process did have some positive results on the ground.

A civil war in Syria broke out in 2011–2012. This followed a year of unrest and turmoil across the Middle East and North Africa—sometimes referred to as the Arab Awakening—during which governments fell in Tunisia, Libya, and Egypt. Growing protests against the Syrian government, emboldened by events, were met with harsh punishment. Efforts by the Security Council to address the fighting even in October 2011 were squashed by vetoes from Russia and China.[40] On February 4, 2012, the Security Council tried again to reach agreement on calling for an end to the violence in Syria only to have Russia and China veto that effort.[41] On February 16, 2012, the General Assembly took up the issue, calling on the Syrian government to immediately end human rights violations and attacks on civilians and to protect its people. The General Assembly plan included the cessation of all violence, the release of political prisoners, the withdrawal of all military forces from cities and towns, and the guarantee of peaceful demonstrations. The resolution also requested that the Secretary-General Ban Ki-moon appoint a special envoy to seek a mediated solution.[42]

The Assembly's resolution mirrored the Security Council's draft resolution vetoed by Russia and China just a few days before. Moving the question to the Assembly in the face of Security Council inaction was taken up through a request by members of the General Assembly, who went to the president of the Assembly, Nassir Abdulaziz Nasser (Qatar), calling for a meeting to address the issue. At first, members wanted to use the Uniting for Peace resolution 377 (V), but due to some objections by certain members, that wording was removed.[43] Implementing the General Assembly resolution, Ban named Annan, his predecessor, as the special envoy. Then on March 21, 2012, the president of the Security Council issued a statement expressing the concern of the Council for the deteriorating situation in Syria and welcoming the joint appointment among the UN, the League of Arab States, and the African Union of Annan as special envoy. Having been embarrassed by the General Assembly taking action when the Council had failed to do so in such a violent crisis, the Council members asked the Security Council president for that month to at least make a statement in lieu of an actual Security Council resolution. Annan began his work as the special envoy and met with leaders in the region, putting together a peace plan. But after several months, he found that the Security Council permanent members were still locked in disagreement. Annan stated: "I lost my team on the Road to Damascus. I turned around and they [the Council members] were fighting each other."[44] He later stepped down as the special envoy, realizing without major power support for any peaceful solution, there was no point in continuing his efforts.

On February 27, 2014, Russian armed forces took over the Ukrainian territory of Crimea. These unidentified and masked alleged "defense forces" entered the parliament building in the capital city of Simferopol. They blocked the Ukrainian air base, captured Ukrainian soldiers, and took over administrative buildings. The existing Ukrainian local government was dismissed, and Sergey Aksyonov was appointed prime minister. He led the Crimean council in declaring the independence of Crimea on March 11.[45] A few days later, a "referendum" was held that offered the voters the option to "reunify Crimea with Russia" or "restore the Constitution of the Republic of Crimea and status as a part of Ukraine."[46] The results of this very quickly held referendum were announced the next day, and Vladimir Putin signed an executive order announcing Crimea's admission as a federal entity of Russia.

> The conduct of the referendum proved chaotic and took place absent any credible international observers. Local authorities reported a turnout

of 83 percent, with 96.7 percent voting to join Russia. The numbers seemed implausible, given that ethnic Ukrainians and Crimean Tatars accounted for almost 40 percent of the peninsula's population. (Two months later, a leaked report from the Russian president's Human Rights Council put turnout at only 30 percent, with about half of those voting to join Russia.)[47]

This recognition of Crimea as a new part of Russia was approved by the Russian parliament and signed by Putin on March 21, 2014—all this occurring in a matter of a few weeks.

The Security Council was unable to take any action or even condemn the Russian aggression because of Russia's veto on the Council. The Council convened seven sessions to address the Crimean crisis; ultimately, its draft resolution S/2014/189 was vetoed by Russia. With the Security Council unable to act, the General Assembly took up the matter and issued General Assembly resolution 68/262 (March 27, 2014), which declared a commitment to the territorial integrity of Ukraine within its internationally recognized borders and called upon member states to announce the nonrecognition of the Crimean referendum and invalidate this act of aggression.[48] In response to the Russian use of force and the annexation of Crimea, the Group of Eight (G-8) ultimately removed Russia from its membership (becoming the G-7), and the United States and the EU imposed a series of sanctions on Russia. While the General Assembly resolution did not compel the UN to do anything, it expressed a *sense* of the Assembly and put on record the reaction of member states to Russia's breach of international law, offering legitimacy to actions taken by the Members. However, this lack of action by the UN emboldened Russia to attack Ukraine again in 2022, as will be discussed later.

Circumventing the Security Council on the Nuclear Issue

The non-nuclear-weapon nations have become increasingly frustrated with the lack of movement on nuclear disarmament and fed up with the veto privileges of the five nuclear powers on the Security Council. A number of treaties and conventions limit nuclear testing, and even the Nuclear Non-Proliferation Treaty (NPT), as one of its three pillars, in Article VI, calls on the five nuclear powers to undertake the disarmament of their nuclear arsenals. NPT review conferences that happen every five years often erupt into accusations by the nonnuclear states that the

P-5 have not lived up to their promises in the Treaty. Having endured this intransigency for decades, these states along with efforts by civil society determined a strategy to completely circumvent the Security Council altogether. Claiming that the threat or use of nuclear weapons along with testing was a violation of humanitarian law, the abolition movement gained a normative, magnetic pull that hit a nerve among those who see nuclear weapons as an existential threat.

The winning strategy was to go directly to the General Assembly, where the voting is by majority rule and there is no veto. The negotiating mandate to begin discussions on the prohibition of nuclear weapons was officially given by the UN General Assembly in December 2016 through its resolution 71/258, adopting the decision to convene a conference in 2017 "to negotiate a legally binding instrument to prohibit nuclear weapons."[49] The UN conference opened its first substantive session in New York at UN headquarters March 27–31, 2017. States and NGOs worked together to form the concepts and wording that would enter the treaty drafts. During the March conference, governments were able to clarify several complex legal and technical issues and begin to formulate their national positions.[50]

The second negotiating conference, under General Assembly auspices, was held again in New York, June 15 to July 7, 2017. The draft text of the treaty, now to be called the Treaty on the Prohibition of Nuclear Weapons (TPNW), was ready to be examined, discussed, and debated, and representatives of civil society were invited to speak. The following consultations by member states were closed, however, and NGOs did not participate in discussing the core provisions. The language was perfected, and a final review of the text was held on July 5. On July 7, 2017, the conference body adopted the TPNW with a vote of 122 in favor, 1 against, and 1 abstention.[51] In addition to prohibiting nuclear weapons, the Treaty obliges the parties to assist victims suffering from the use or testing of nuclear weapons and to take measures to remediate environmental damage done by such use or testing.[52] The nuclear powers refused to participate. The Treaty acquired the needed fifty ratifications in the fall of 2020, went into force on January 22, 2021, and there are a growing number of signatories and ratifications. As of this writing, there are sixty-eight ratifications with ninety-one signatures to the TPNW. The first meeting of the States Parties took place in Vienna, Austria, in June 2022, hosted by the Austrian foreign ministry. While the P-5 have said that the TPNW undermines the NPT, others argue that they are quite compatible by both calling for the disarmament of nuclear weapons.

Russia Attacks Ukraine Again in 2022

After months building up troops along the Ukrainian border, denying any intention to attack Ukraine, and claiming the buildup was only a military exercise, Russia began a major military invasion of the independent nation. The UN had avoided any significant condemnation of Russian actions in Syria during the war that began in 2011–2012 and again in 2014 when Russia occupied Crimea and intervened in Ukraine's eastern region. The international community had not been ready to confront Russia's military. However, the invasion of Ukraine—a democratic European nation—on February 24, 2022, broke that hesitation. Immediately, attempts to confront Russia in the Security Council were obstructed by the Russian veto. However, a few days after the invasion, on February 27, the Security Council, by a procedural vote that does not allow a veto, passed resolution 2623 (2022) calling for "an emergency special session of the General Assembly to examine the question"[53] of Russia's aggression against Ukraine. Under its eleventh emergency special session, the General Assembly issued a resolution on March 1 (with 141 in favor, 5 against, and 35 abstentions) titled "Aggression against Ukraine,"[54] which reaffirmed the importance of promoting the rule of law among nations. The General Assembly resolution "deplores in the strongest terms the aggression by the Russian Federation against Ukraine in violation of Article 2 (4) of the Charter."[55] The resolution also expresses "grave concern" regarding attacks on civilian facilities such as schools and hospitals. It condemns "the decision of the Russian Federation to increase the readiness of its nuclear forces."[56] The resolution also recognizes "that the military operations of the Russian Federation inside the sovereign territory of Ukraine are on a scale that the international community has not seen in Europe in decades and that urgent action is needed to save this generation from the scourge of war."[57] A few months later on October 12, 2022, the General Assembly once again reconvened the Eleventh Emergency Special Session and passed a resolution with 143 votes in favor and 5 against, which condemned Russia's illegal annexation of certain regions of eastern Ukraine. The resolution states that these illegal annexations are violations of Ukraine's sovereignty.[58]

While the General Assembly resolution calls on Russia to cease its use of force, it does not ask member states to impose sanctions against Russia (as the UN has done against North Korea), and it does not call for a UN force to address Russian aggression (as the UN had done during the Korea War). Nevertheless, the importance of the resolution was to confirm on the record that the UN did not accept Russia's aggression and also to establish a legitimate foundation for member states to join stronger efforts such as imposing sanctions or providing military assistance on a country-by-country basis.

Conclusion

While most people outside the UN are completely unaware of it, the Uniting for Peace resolution, particularly as seen in 2022, still provides a means to act when the Security Council is deadlocked and can offer a useful strategy for member states to circumvent the authority of a P-5 member. However, without the backing of at least a few of the major powers, and most particularly the United States, it is unlikely that member states would be capable of implementing General Assembly resolutions other than condemning violence, requesting an advisory opinion, or appointing a mediator, which in themselves do not require troops or economic resources. Nevertheless, the legitimacy offered by such General Assembly resolutions provides normative support to actions by member states.

The Uniting for Peace resolution established a landmark piece of legislation in terms of drawing attention to a latent potential in the Charter itself, supporting what was already there and establishing procedural rules for how to pass authority to the General Assembly. It only borrows that authority under stress when the Security Council is unable to act. The dilemma today is that the nature of conflict has primarily changed from wars between states (with the war in Ukraine as an anomaly) to internal conflicts, and intervention in civil wars means the erosion of the sovereign integrity of the state. Other member states may feel threatened by that concept and might shrink away from setting that kind of precedent. Yet, the expectations placed on the UN to become the protector of human rights and the human condition is becoming a kind of litmus test for the legitimacy of the organization. If the UN cannot do that or is unwilling to take the risks of playing that role, then other organizations may step in to fill that void. From a legal perspective, while General Assembly resolutions are nonbinding, they can covey a moral consensus and perhaps a kind of customary law where members abide by the recommendation because they believe in it. This tool is waiting there ready to be utilized when there is a need. Just open the cupboard door and pull it out.

Table 11.1 lists the instances where the General Assembly has taken up an issue when the Security Council has been unable to act. The list is in chronological order and includes the issue topic involved, the date, which body initiated the move to the General Assembly, and what resolutions emerged from the process.

Table 11.1 Instances of Transfer of Authority

Topic	Document(s)	Date of Session	Who Convened Session	Resolution, Date, and Votes
Northern Greece	Creation of UNSCOB by GA-A/109	October 21, 1947	Security Council	Security Council moved the issue to the GA-S/555, September 15, 1947
Korea	Calling for China to remove its forces, A/498 (V)	February 1, 1951	General Assembly	S/RES/90 (1951) No longer seized of the matter Voting was unanimous
Suez	A/3354 (GAOR, 1st ESS, Suppl. No. 1)	November 1–10, 1956	Security Council	S/RES/119, October 31, 1956 Adopted by 7 votes to 2 (France, UK) with 2 abstentions (Australia and Belgium)
Hungary	A/3355 (GAOR, 2nd ESS, Suppl. No. 1)	November 4–10, 1956	Security Council	S/RES/120, November 4, 1956 Adopted by 10 votes to 1 (USSR) at the 754th meeting
Lebanon	A/3905 (GAOR, 3rd ESS, Suppl. No. 1)	August 8–21, 1958	Security Council	S/RES/129, August 7, 1958 Adopted unanimous at the 838th meeting
Congo question	A/4510 (GAOR, 4th ESS, Suppl. No. 1)	September 17–19, 1960	Security Council	S/RES/157, September 17, 1960 Adopted by 8 votes to 2 (Poland and USSR) with 1 abstention (France)
Middle East 1967 War	A/6798 (GAOR, 5th ESS, Suppl. No. 1)	June 17, September 18, 1967	USSR	Letter from USSR (A/6717): under Article 11 of the Charter
India/Pakistan	A/2832 (26th GA Session)	December 16, 1971	Security Council	S/RES/303, December 6, 1971 Adopted by 11 votes to 0 with 4 abstentions
Afghanistan (Soviet invasion)	A/ES-6/7 (GAOR, 6th ESS, Suppl. No. 1), Press Release GA/6172	January 10–14, 1980	Security Council	S/RES/462, January 9, 1980 Adopted by 12 votes to 2 (Germany, USSR) with 1 abstention (Zambia)
Palestine (Israeli withdrawal)	A/ES-7/14 + Add.1 + Add.1/Corr.1(GAOR, 7th ESS, Suppl. No.1),Press Release GA/6245 + Add.1–4	July 22–29, 1980 April 20–28, 1982 June 25–26, 1982 August 16–19, 1982 September 24, 1982	Senegal (Chairman, Palestinian Rights Committee)	Letter from Senegal (A/ES-7/1), A/37/205-S/14990 Convened pursuant to the Uniting for Peace Resolution

continues

Table 11.1 Continued

Topic	Document(s)	Date of Session	Who Convened Session	Resolution, Date, and Votes
South West Africa/ Namibia (sanctions on South Africa)	A/ES-8/13 (GAOR, 8th ESS, Suppl.No. 1), Press Release GA/6414	September 3–14, 1981	Zimbabwe	Letter from Zimbabwe (A/ES-8/1) Convened pursuant to the Uniting for Peace Resolution
Occupied Arab territories	A/ES-9/7 (GAOR, 9th ESS, Suppl. No. 1), Press Release GA/6560	January 29–February 5, 1982	Security Council	S/RES/500, January 28, 1982 Adopted by 13 votes to none, with 2 abstentions (United Kingdom and United States) at the 2330th meeting
Grenada	On the issue of US intervention: GA res. A/38/7	November 2, 1983	General Assembly	Draft resolution vetoed by United States, S/16077/Rev.1 Nicaragua request GA meet under rule 15
Panama	Intervention of United States to remove Manuel Noriega; GA res. A/44/240	December 29, 1989	General Assembly	Draft resolution on December 23, vetoed by France, United Kingdom, and United States; letter by Cuba and Nicaragua request GA meeting under rule 15
Occupied East Jerusalem and the rest of the Occupied Palestinian territory (10th Emergency Session)	A/ES-10/5 1/ES-10/L.1 + Add.1 1/ES-10/L.2/ Rev.1 1/ES-10/L.3 + Add.1 1/ES-10/L.4/ Rev.1 + Rev.1/Add.1 1/ES-10/L.5/ Rev.1 A/ES-10/L.6 A/58/ES-10/L.13 A/58/ES-10/L.16 [Add.1] A/58/ES-10/L.17 [Add.1] A/RES/ES-10/2-11	April 24–25, 1997 July 15, 1997 November 13, 1997 March 17, 1998 February 5, 8, 9, 1999 October 18 and 20, 2000 December 20, 2001 May 7, 2002 August 5, 2002 September 19, 2003 October 20–21, 2003 December 3, 2003	Qatar	Letter from Qatar Convened pursuant to the Uniting for Peace Resolution
Israeli security wall (resumption of 10th ES)	Resolution passed on the wall A/RES/58/3 Request to the ICJ for an advisory opinion A/RES/ES-10/14	October 21, 2003; December 3 and 8, 2003	General Assembly	Vetoed Security Council draft resolution S/2003/980, October 14, 2003

continues

Table 11.1 Continued

Topic	Document(s)	Date of Session	Who Convened Session	Resolution, Date, and Votes
Situation in the Arab Republic	A/RES/66/253 A	February 16, 2012	General Assembly	A/66/PV.97, February 16, 2012 GA/11207 137 in favor, 12 against, 17 abstentions
Territorial integrity of Ukraine	A/RES/68/262	March 27, 2014	General Assembly	A/68/PV.80, March 27, 2014 GA/11493 100 in favor, 11 against, 58 abstentions
Taking Forward Nuclear Disarmament Negotiations	A/RES/71/258	December 23, 2016	General Assembly	A/71/PV.68, December 23, 2016 GA/11882 113 in favor, 35 against, 13 abstentions
Illegal Israeli actions in Occupied East Jerusalem and the rest of the Occupied Palestinian Territory	A/RES/ES-10/19 Status of Jerusalem	December 21, 2017	Turkey and Yemen	Letter from Turkey and Yemen (A/ES-10/769) A/ES-10/PV.37, December 21, 2017 128 in favor, 9 against, 35 abstentions
Illegal Israeli actions in Occupied East Jerusalem and the rest of the Occupied Palestinian Territory	A/RES/ES-10/20 Protection of the Palestinian civilian population	June 13, 2018	Turkey and Yemen	Letter from Turkey and Yemen (A/ES-10/786) A/ES-10/PV.38, June 13, 2018 120 in favor, 8 against, 45 abstentions
Russian aggression against Ukraine	A/ES-11L.1, Eleventh ESS; 141 in favor, 5 against, 35 abstentions	March 1, 2022	Security Council	S/RES/2623 (2022), February 27, 2022 11 in favor, 1 against (Russia), 3 abstentions (China, India, and United Arab Emirates) ES/GA/12458
Russian annexation of Ukraine territory	GA/12458; 143 in favor, 5 against	October 12, 2022	General Assembly	

Source: Adapted from a United Nations Department of Public Information table with additions by the authors.
Notes: ES = Emergency Special Session; GA = General Assembly; GAOR = General Assembly Official Records.

Notes

1. GA resolution 290 (IV) Essentials of Peace, A/RES/290 (IV), 1949.
2. GA resolution 377 (V) Uniting for Peace, A/RES/377 (V), 1950.
3. Krasno, "Founding the United Nations: An Evolutionary Process," in Krasno, *The United Nations,* forthcoming.
4. Ibid.
5. Birgisson, "United Nations Special Committee on the Balkans," in Durch, *Evolution of UN Peacekeeping,* 1993.
6. Ibid.
7. Ibid.
8. Leonard Meeker, Yale-UN Oral History Interview, July 24, 1990.
9. UN General Assembly records 1950, Document A/PV.279, September 20, 1950.
10. Ibid.
11. Ibid.
12. Ibid.
13. UN General Assembly, Document A/1373 (1950), paragraphs 43–49.
14. UN General Assembly, Document A/1456 and A/1481.
15. Geoffrey Murray, Yale-UN Oral History interview, January 10, 1991.
16. Sohn, *Cases on United Nations Law,* 1956, pp. 4–8.
17. UN General Assembly, Document A/C.1.576, 1950.
18. UN Charter Article 20: "The General Assembly shall meet in regular annual sessions and in such special sessions as occasion may require. Special sessions shall be convoked by the Secretary-General at the request of the Security Council or of a majority of the Members of the United Nations."
19. Amendment to Charter Article 23 that enlarges the membership of the Security Council from eleven to fifteen was adopted by the General Assembly on December 17, 1963, and went into force on August 31, 1965.
20. Sohn, pp. 4–8.
21. Meeker, interview.
22. International Court of Justice, "Certain Expenses of the United Nations (Article 17, Paragraph 2, of the Charter) Advisory Opinion of 20 July 1962," https://www.icj-cij.org/public/files/case-related/49/5261.pdf.
23. UN Security Council, Resolution 90, 1951.
24. UN General Assembly, Resolution A/498 (V), "Intervention of the Central People's Government of the People's Republic of China in Korea," February 1, 1951.
25. "Question Considered by the Security Council at Its 749th and 750th Meetings, Held on 30 October 1956," A/RES/1003 (ES-I); and "1st Emergency Special Session Suez," convened by A/RES/377 (V) ("Uniting for Peace"), and S/RES/119 (1956) of October 31, 1956.
26. "2nd Emergency Special Session Hungary," convened by A/RES/377 (V) ("Uniting for Peace") of 1950; and S/RES/120 (1956) of November 4, 1956.
27. "3rd Emergency Special Session Lebanon," convened by A/RES/377 (V) ("Uniting for Peace") of 1950; and S/RES/129 (1958) of August 7, 1958.
28. "4th Emergency Special Session Democratic Republic of the Congo," convened by A/RES/377 (V) ("Uniting for Peace") of 1950; and S/RES/157 (1960) of September 17, 1960.
29. *United Nations Yearbook* 1967, p. 191.
30. *United Nations Yearbook* 1983, pp. 211–217.
31. UN Security Council, Draft Resolution S/16077/Rec.1.

32. UN General Assembly, Resolution A/38/245, 1983.

33. UN General Assembly, Resolution A/44/906, 1989.

34. *United Nations Yearbook* 1989, pp. 172–176.

35. UN General Assembly, Resolution A/RES/ES-10/20; a full list of the Special Emergency Sessions can be found at the UN Dag Hammarskjöld Library under UN General Assembly Special Emergency Sessions.

36. Paul Heinbecker, Yale-UN Oral History interview, November 8, 2004.

37. Jeremy Brecher, "Uniting for Peace: The UN General Assembly Provides a Crucial Opportunity for Global Peace Movement," *Outlook India,* April 2, 2003, https://www.outlookindia.com/website/story/uniting-for-peace.

38. UN General Assembly, Resolution A/RES/ES-10/14, December 18, 2003.

39. International Court of Justice, "Legal Consequences of the Construction of a Wall on the Occupied Palestinian Territory (Advisory Opinion)," ICJ Reports, www.icj-cij.org/icjwww/idocket/imwp/imwp/iframe.html.

40. UN Security Council, Draft Resolution S/2011/612, and Meeting Record S/PV.6627, from October 4, 2011.

41. UN Security Council, Draft Resolution S/2012/77, and Meeting Record S/PV.6711, from February 4, 2012.

42. UN General Assembly, Resolution A/RES/66/253, February 16, 2012.

43. Interview with a staff member of the UN Office of Legal Affairs at the UN on February 24, 2012.

44. Smith, "Kofi Annan on War and Peace."

45. Antonello Tancredi, "The Russian Annexation of the Crimea: Questions Relation to the Use of Force," *Question of International Law (Questions de Droit International/Questioni di Diritto Internazionale*), May 2014, http://www.qil-qdi.org/wp-content/uploads/2014/05/CRIMEA_Tancredi_FINAL-1.pdf.

46. Bowring, "Who Are the 'Crimea People' or 'People of Crimea'?"

47. Steven Pifer, "Crimea: Six Years After Illegal Annexation," Brookings blog, March 17, 2020, https://www.brookings.edu/blog/order-from-chaos/2020/03/17/crimea-six-years-after-illegal-annexation/.

48. Grant, "Annexation of Crimea."

49. UN General Assembly, Resolution 71/258, "Taking Forward Nuclear Disarmament Negotiations," January 11, 2017, Document A/Res/71/258, paragraph 8.

50. Krasno and Szeli, *Banning the Bomb,* p. 99.

51. Ibid., p. 102.

52. Treaty on the Prohibition of Nuclear Weapons, Part I, paragraph two, Document A/CONF.229/2017/8, July 7, 2017.

53. UN Security Council, Resolution 2623 (2022), adopted by the Security Council at its 8980th meeting, on February 27, 2022.

54. UN General Assembly, Resolution A/ES-11/L.1.

55. UN General Assembly, Resolution A/ES-11/L.1, Item 5.

56. Ibid.

57. Ibid.

58. UN General Assembly, Resolution GA/12458, October 12, 2022.

12

Achievements and Challenges

Jean E. Krasno

The United Nations has survived more than seven decades and witnessed dramatic global changes: the intransigency of the Cold War, the exuberance of the anticipated rapprochement as the Cold War drew to a close, and now a return to obstructionism as the major powers collide on many, particularly security, issues—the war in Ukraine being a case in point. In 2020, the UN celebrated its seventy-fifth anniversary; unfortunately, this celebration was in a nearly empty General Assembly Hall due to the global Covid-19 pandemic, which also dampened the hopes for achieving the aspirations of the Sustainable Development Goals (SDGs) by 2030. An understanding and perspective of where the UN has been and where it is going is aptly described by Yale professor Paul Kennedy in his book *The Parliament of Man:*

> There is an old analogy about perspective and history that suggests we are all members of a vast caravan that winds its way through the desert, with a range of mountains to one side. Those peaks appear to have a certain shape when advancing from the south. Yet they look different when the observers draw level to the mountains, and different again when casting a backward glance upon them. Perhaps we should approach our understanding of the UN in rather the same manner.[1]

Countries from the Global South may view the UN quite differently than do those in the more industrialized world. Experiencing the inequality within nations and between nations may exacerbate frustrations that the UN should do more to level the playing field. In confronting the global crisis of climate change where the nations of the world have to work in unison to reduce greenhouse gas emissions, members of the developing world rightfully blame the industrialized countries for polluting the atmosphere and cry for justice as they seek energy for their own deserved development. Yet all must work together to keep the growth in global temperatures to below 2 degrees Celsius or even less. These differing perspectives will determine how one might perceive the UN's achievements, failures, and the challenges ahead. In this closing segment, I highlight some of the key factors presented in the previous chapters and add some new thoughts not covered.

Achievements

Promotion of Human Rights and Accountability

The United Nations has done more to promote human rights than any efforts prior to its creation. While the League of Nations adopted the Declaration on the Rights of Man and included some protections for indigenous peoples in its mandate system, it was not until the wording in the 1945 UN Charter "to reaffirm faith in fundamental human rights,"[2] and the Universal Declaration of Human Rights (UDHR) accepted by the UN General Assembly in 1948, that the world had the normative language that clearly supported human rights standards.[3] Shortly following the General Assembly's approval of the UDHR, the Convention on the Prevention and Punishment of the Crime of Genocide went into force in 1951, adding to the work of the international community to address human rights violations and heinous crimes such as genocide. The international Bill of Rights includes the UN Charter, the UDHR, the Covenant on Civil and Political Rights, and the Covenant on Economic, Social, and Cultural Rights. The latter two treaty-based obligations split the spirit of the UDHR into two concepts: what a government cannot take away from its citizens (civil and political rights such as freedom of press, expression, assembly, etc.) and what the state must provide for its people (a standard of living, housing, healthcare, education, etc.).

Included within this UN treaty-based system are the Convention on the Elimination of All Forms of Racial Discrimination; the Convention on the Elimination of All Forms of Discrimination Against Women; the Convention on the Rights of the Child; the Convention Against Torture and Other Cruel, Inhuman, or Degrading Treatment or Punishment; the 1951 Refugee Convention and its 1967 Protocol; and the Convention on the Rights of Persons with Disabilities. There are other agreements in this comprehensive system that all add to the sense of obligation and precision of language to promote and protect human rights. The problem, of course, is enforcement. There is no UN police force to hold states accountable for human rights violations. However, many of these agreements have oversight committees that investigate violations and make full reports with an effort to shame countries into compliance.

The organization also promotes human rights within its own UN bodies—for example, the UN High Commissioner for Refugees, the UN High Commissioner for Human Rights and its rapporteurs, the Human Rights Council, UN Women, and the UN agencies and funds such as the UN Children's Fund (UNICEF). The UN Secretariat also has offices on the prevention of sexual abuse and exploitation and a focus on children and armed conflict. UN peace operations now incorporate human rights components, and Security Council mandates also include language on the protection of civilians in peace operations. This represents a long list of achievements by the UN in promoting, defining, and laying out human rights obligations, but as stated above, the problem lies in enforcement and compliance with these delineated norms.

Inside the UN, Secretary-General António Guterres has been committed to improving gender equality within the UN ranks. Taking office in 2017, by the following year he had accomplished his goal of appointing women to 50 percent of the top positions. Among them was Deputy Secretary-General Amina Mohammed, who oversees the SDGs, under-secretaries-general, and assistant secretaries-general. In addition, the UN "has increased the number of women heads and deputy heads of peace operations, peacekeepers and mediators."[4] During the pandemic, the UN placed women at the center of attention with many types of assistance, some of which prevented "nearly 40,000 maternal deaths."[5] It assisted two million "women per month in overcoming pregnancy and childbirth complications," and supported forty-five member states in increasing women's participation in electoral processes."[6]

Human Development

The World Bank measures world development in terms of production as gross domestic product, which as it suggests is a gross economic formulation. However, in the early 1990s, the UN turned that measurement on its head, stating that development must focus on human development, not a factor of gross production. Per capita income calculated by dividing gross domestic product by population was not an accurate measure of the *quality* of development. The UN, reflecting the interests of all its member states, began to examine how economies affected human beings: life expectancy, infant mortality rates, levels of education, health, and gender equity. The UN Development Programme thus created the *Human Development Report* to complement the World Bank reports. Publication of the *Human Development Report* meant gathering data along all these indicators in nations across every continent to offer a truer picture of the human condition. This information was used to build a database, evaluating each country on a scale of more developed and less developed to formulate the Human Development Index. While some countries showed a life expectancy of well into the seventies, others suffered very low life expectancy, even in terms of thirty-eight to forty years. This annual report revealed to the world a new way of looking at development and how it affected the quality of human life.

In 2000, the fifty-fifth anniversary of the UN, the then Secretary-General, Kofi Annan, wanted to use this landmark year to focus the attention of the international community on the "peoples" of the world, reflecting the opening words of the Charter's preamble: "We the peoples of the United Nations." His purpose was to capture the attention of member states to work toward the alleviation of poverty, improve maternal health, reduce infant mortality, and tackle global warming. Annan utilized the expertise in the Secretariat to draft a Millennium Report launched in March 2000,[7] which was then given to the General Assembly for discussion and amendments. The General Assembly approved the Millennium Declaration during its Millennium Summit held in September 2000. The Declaration led to the creation of the eight Millennium Development Goals (MDGs) to be achieved by the target year of 2015. At the sixtieth anniversary of the UN in 2005, the member states approved the Outcome Document, which states the following:

II. Development
    17. We strongly reiterate our determination to ensure the timely and full realization of the development goals and objectives agreed at the major United Nations conferences and summits, including those agreed at the Millennium Summit that are described as the Millennium Development Goals, which have helped to galvanize efforts towards poverty eradication.[8]

The MDGs achieved relative success in 2015, having survived a global recession, mainly by building partnerships and focusing the international community on the issue of addressing global poverty. A few years before the 2015 deadline, the new UN Secretary-General Ban

Ki-moon reinforced the importance of continuing this effort to eradicate poverty and in 2012 organized the UN to begin thinking about the post-2015 steps that would need to be taken.[9] The global 2012 conference in Rio on sustainable development took up the issue, and member states began to formulate a continuation of the process. Having seen the successes of the MDGs, the whole membership began working together to devise a more expanded list of goals, now the seventeen SDGs, Agenda 2030. The process evolved from being the creation of the UN Secretariat in devising the MDGs to a broader and more inclusive dialogue among member states and civil society. The end date for the SDGs is 2030, but the goals and targets have been greatly expanded, and even collecting the data is a challenge. Nevertheless, countries, nongovernmental organizations (NGOs), and much of the global community are working in tandem to accomplish these goals, despite the Covid-19 pandemic and the resulting economic downturn.

Responding to Humanitarian Crises

A number of UN agencies constitute the response teams when crises occur. The UN refugee agency, the High Commissioner for Refugees (UNHCR), provides both emergency and long-term assistance by establishing camps with shelter, food, water, and security for people fleeing conflict, earthquakes, floods, and more. They work with UNICEF to provide temporary schools for children. The World Health Organization (WHO) also coordinates with other UN bodies to attend to health needs within the camps. The World Food Programme (WFP) brings in emergency food aid, medicine, and water. The UN also cooperates with organizations such as the International Committee of the Red Cross, Doctors Without Borders, and other NGO partners. In past years, with climate change, extreme weather condition, and the pandemic, the UN has had to scramble to meet these global needs. By July 2022, some 280 million people were forcibly displaced by conflict, violence, extreme weather, or to seek a better life and found themselves in serious need of humanitarian assistance.[10]

Recently, disasters have become more frequent and more devastating. "In 2020, the United Nations worked with partners to mobilize a record US$19.1 billion to assist 264 million people in 64 countries."[11] At times, UN efforts to provide humanitarian assistance in terms of food, water, and healthcare are caught in the middle of a conflict where parties to the conflict have blocked the delivery of aid, such as in Ethiopia in 2021. Then UN negotiators have had to step in to find a solution. During these emergencies, contributions by member states are often too slow in coming, and people may be left to suffer. Yet, there is no other global organization that can replace the UN in responding to humanitarian crises.

Security, Peace, and Peacebuilding

Chapter 6 lays out the history and evolution of UN peacekeeping, so I will not repeat that here. However, in addition to sending troops to the twelve UN peace operations deployed to date, the UN conducts some twenty-eight special political missions to protect civilians and advance peace efforts.[12] Through envoys and special representatives, the Secretary-General utilizes their "good offices" for mediation and quiet diplomacy to meet with parties to a conflict to de-escalate disputes, seek peaceful solutions, and call for cease-fires, as was done to attempt to bring a halt to fighting during efforts to alleviate the health crisis brought on by the Covid-19 pandemic in 2020 and 2021. In addition, the UN contributed to the creation of the Covid-19 Vaccine Global Access (COVAX) Facility to establish a global response to the distribution of vaccines.[13]

Peacebuilding has been given a greater seat at the table, and the former Department of Political Affairs was renamed the Department of Political and Peacebuilding Affairs to enhance the UN's activities at building a nation's capacity to maintain peace and stability. In 2020, the Peacebuilding Commission engaged in fifteen countries and regions that included multi-partner support for peacebuilding. "The Peacebuilding Fund provided nearly $174 million in investments across 39 countries in 2020, 97 per cent of which contributed to targets of the Sustainable Development Goals."[14]

The UN's role in disarmament has been mixed as member states continue to protect their own interests in retaining and selling weapons. However, in addressing the curb on weapons of mass destruction (WMDs), the UN has played a major role. The UN Special Commission (UNSCOM) was created as a part of UN resolution 687 of April 1991 to eliminate and monitor Iraq's weapons of mass destruction following the end of the 1991 Gulf War. Inspectors began their work shortly afterward in May 1991 and by fall 1998 had eliminated nearly all of Iraq's WMDs, except for a small percentage of items that were considered "unaccounted for." The Compendium, which was a final report prepared by the UN, noted that their records on the destruction or removal of all WMDs did not completely match the paperwork they had amassed.[15] Nevertheless, the UN inspectors had disarmed and eliminated the threat of WMDs by Iraq, something that had never been done before by an international organization.

It was said at the time that the UN would never be able to do such a task again. However, never say never, because when there is a need, the UN will be asked once more. This happened in 2013 when it was discovered that chemical weapons were being used in Syria. The Organization for the Prohibition of Chemical Weapons (OPCW) reported to the UN Secretary-General that there was evidence of the use of chemical weapons in the war in Syria in 2013. Secretary-General Ban dispatched a team of inspectors to Syria led by the High Commissioner for Disarmament and head of the UN Office of Disarmament Affairs, Angela Kane. Their report confirmed that chemical weapons were being used. This led to the UN and OPCW being tasked with removing all chemical weapons and their ingredients, which was completed in the spring of 2014.[16] Following the removal and destruction of Syria's chemical weapons, evidence reappeared of their use, and the UN Security Council formed the UN-OPCW Joint Inspection Mechanism (JIM) headed by Virginia Gamba to look into these allegations and report back to the Security Council. The team confirmed that there had indeed been some continued use of chemical weapons by various parties to the conflict. However, the JIM's mandate expired in 2017. Disagreement among the P-5 members of the Security Council, mainly Russia, brought an end to the reporting.

Informal Ad Hoc Groups of Friends

Another contribution to the work of the UN is the formation of "groups of friends," an ad hoc mechanism to assist in peace processes. This phenomenon first appeared in December 1989 at a meeting of UN advisor Alvaro de Soto with the rebel group FMLN in the conflict in El Salvador. As de Soto explained in an interview, "one of the ideas that came up at this meeting that I had was whether it would ever be possible for the Secretary-General to create a group of countries that would act as a kind of support for the Secretary-General and counter-balance the political weight of the Security Council."[17] This concept led to the creation of the Friends of the Secretary-General on El Salvador and included four countries: Mexico, Colombia, Venezuela, and Spain. The ad hoc mechanism in this case worked very well because the Group of Friends was small, they all were dedicated to finding a peaceful solution, they were well respected by the parties to the conflict, and they were effective in pressuring the parties to work together. Their contribution to the peace process successfully resulted in the peace agreement of January 1992.

Since its inception, groups have proliferated. They are primarily attached to issues of peacekeeping, but others have formed around global movements, such as the Group of Friends of Water, the Group of Friends on Climate and Security, and the Group of Friends of R2P (Responsibility to Protect). Some have since dissolved, and others simply faded away. More recent ones include Group of Friends of Women in Afghanistan, launched in November 2019; Group of Friends for Victims of Terrorism, June 2019; and Group of Friends United Against Human Trafficking, February 2019. To date, there are over forty such groups of friends.[18]

Interestingly, because Venezuela was a member of the original Group of Friends, one of the four countries that came forward to help the peace process in El Salvador, it is now the subject of concern for a new group called the Group of Friends of the Quito Process established in 2018. The Group has thirteen member states, all from Latin America and the Caribbean, and was created to promote cooperation among countries receiving Venezuelan migrants and refugees. It aims "to specifically address this humanitarian situation separate and apart from political questions about Venezuela's future."[19] Venezuela, however, is not supportive of any intervention into its sovereignty and has become a member of another group of friends: the Group of Friends in Defense of the UN Charter.[20] Venezuela's membership in this group of friends is in reference to the UN Charter's Chapter I, Article 2, paragraph 7, which states: "Nothing contained in this present Charter shall authorize the United Nations to intervene in matters which are essentially within the domestic jurisdiction of any state or shall require the Members to submit such matters to settlement under the present Charter." By joining this group, Venezuela is firmly declaring its opposition to any form of interference into its sovereignty.

Challenges

The Veto

While the United Nations has continued to change and adapt to the evolving global environment, it also serves as a mirrored reflection of the world around it. Challenges facing the world also challenge the UN. The pendulum appears to be swinging back to the Cold War era when the major powers were tangled in a web of mistrust and intransigence within the Security Council body. At first, it was the Soviets that deployed the veto when the West had greater control through its members in the UN. Then as those dynamics morphed, the United States began to resort to the veto to defend its interests. To date, there have been 246 resolutions vetoed in the Security Council (of course, often by more than one country).[21] Nevertheless, it is interesting to note how many vetoes each P-5 member has cast: 145 by Russia/Soviet Union, 86 by the United States, 30 by the United Kingdom, 19 by the People's Republic of China, and 18 by France.[22] Recent vetoes have been cast by Russia and China working in tandem—fourteen of China's recent vetoes have been done hand-in-hand with Russia.[23]

The perception of the UN is that the Security Council is consistently deadlocked. In fact, that is not really true. The Security Council has reached cooperative decisions more than 2,600 times. Security Council resolutions are numbered consecutively, and the numbering continues over from year-to-year. Therefore, a recent Council resolution of July 12, 2022, number S/RES/2642 (2022), on the situation in the Middle East demonstrates that 2,642 resolutions have passed since 1946 when the Council met for the first time. Thus, the vetoed resolutions constitute less than 10 percent of resolutions considered; over 90 percent have reached agreement. Nevertheless, the most recent use of the veto, primarily by Russia (China abstained) was to block any condemnation of its aggression in Ukraine. The vetoes by Russia and China together have been to block access of humanitarian aid to Syria, and by Russia, to impede investigations into the continued use of chemical weapons in Syria. So, this obstructionism has serious consequences. If this pattern continues, member states may look to other organizations for leadership.

Security Threats

Security failures are a result of a lack of cooperation and resolve among the major powers, who have the capacity to act. As discussed in previous chapters, Ukraine is an excellent example. The international community, the UN, the EU, and other entities have struggled to address Russia's violent attacks on Ukraine and its perpetration of multiple human rights violations. Some have likened the conflagration to the onset of World War II. In addition, Syria, Yemen, Ethiopia, Libya, Ukraine, Afghanistan, Mali, and terrorist groups in the Sahel account for some of the security challenges today. The sheer number of threats is overwhelming and beyond the capabilities of the UN alone. UN political envoys, working with the backing of member states, can try to cajole leaders in a civil conflict to find a peaceful solution, but if even one party to the conflict is determined to win, there can be no cease-fire or room for the UN to seek a peaceful solution, no matter how many times the Security Council may take up the issue.

Terrorism

Pervasive acts of terrorism persist in all parts of every continent. They involve different actors and different targets, but the methods are recognizable: attacks on innocent civilians to exact a political, ideological, or religious goal. Terrorists have also exploited the socioeconomic crisis brought about by the Covid-19 pandemic in conflict-affected regions, and acts by such groups as the Islamic State of Iraq and Syria (ISIS), Daesh, al-Qaeda, and their affiliates have been compounded by growing concerns over neo-Nazi and other ethnically motivated nationalist groups who have resorted to terrorist violence.[24] The UN has addressed this issue in a number of ways. Security Council resolution 1373 (2001) under Chapter VII, following the attacks on 9/11, "obliged states to prevent and suppress the financing of terrorists acts; criminalize the provision or collection of funds; freeze bank accounts of terrorists and their supporters; deny safe haven; prevent their movements; and cooperate in international investigations of terrorist acts."[25]

In addition, Security Council resolution 1540 (2004) requires states to prevent nonstate actors from acquiring weapons of mass destruction. Both Security Council resolutions have established committees to oversee the implementation of these obligations, and states have been cooperating: "within two years every state had submitted reports in compliance with Security Council resolution 1373."[26] Working in cooperation, the UN Office on Counter-Terrorism coordinates information gathering by holding meetings of member states to share strategies in addressing the threat. The Office has involved 175 countries in counterterrorism capacity building.[27] While these are valiant efforts to prevent terrorist acts, heinous attacks, supported by criminal enterprises and dark money, continue to kill and harm innocent people, challenging the international community in every part of the globe.

Democracy

One of the UN's major activities since the end of the Cold War has been to assist and support democratic capacity building. This is a component of every peace operation, the goal of peacebuilding, and the key UN strategy for settling internal disputes arising from civil conflict, authoritarian rule, and the resulting inequity when one dominant group suppresses others. This involves such things as assisting in free and fair elections; building democratic institutions like rule-of-law, rights-based justice systems; and helping to rewrite constitutions to include equal human rights, freedom of speech, and freedom of assembly. But power struggles have thrown obstacles in the path of these UN endeavors, and hopes for democracy appear to be eroding; some examples are Russia, Sudan, Myanmar, Turkey, Hungary, Poland, and the Philippines, to name a few. Even the United States and its Western allies have witnessed some backsliding in areas like judicial independence and fair elections. These findings appear in the data collected by a Sweden-based nonprofit called V-Dem that records "countries' level of democracy across a host of indicators."[28] This trend can threaten, or challenge, the work of the UN and its claim on the legitimacy of democratization when the beacons of democratic role models are dimming.

Global Warming and Climate Change

The biggest challenge threatening the entire planet today is global warming, brought about by greenhouse gas emissions that have already caused oceans to warm, water levels to rise, and extreme weather conditions to proliferate, leading to floods, droughts, and massive wildfires. The UN has been the focus of efforts to address climate change by forming the UN Framework Convention on Climate Change (UNFCCC) and conducting regular scientific assessments on global warming by the Independent Panel on Climate Change (IPCC). In December 2015, the Paris Agreement on climate change was signed, in which countries made some very significant steps forward: (1) they all agreed that climate change was happening; (2) they agreed that it was in part man-made; and (3) they agreed that all countries must work together to limit global warming to 2 degrees Celsius or even 1.5 degrees from the pre-industrialized era.

The Conference of Parties 26 (COP26) that met in Glasgow, Scotland, in November 2021 demonstrated only modest results as a follow-up to Paris. COP27, held in Egypt in November 2022, promised more support for countries suffering from the results of global warming. On a positive note, countries expressed a greater sense of urgency, and agreements were reached on curbing methane gas emissions, limiting deforestation, and changing the ultimate goal of reducing global warming from 2 degrees Celsius to the lower rate of 1.5 degrees. Nevertheless, many criticized the conference for not providing any means of enforcement as all of these agreements and commitments are voluntary. Yet, if countries believe the dangers have already arrived and that there must be a global response with every country playing its part, there may be relative success going forward.

Other Challenges

This list covers only some of the major threats facing the planet and the United Nations. Threats include the stresses of migration as people flee conflict, poverty, and disasters caused by climate change and war. All these factors are compounded by the deadly Covid-19 pandemic that has hit every continent. While some countries have reached significant levels of vaccination, others see less than 5 percent of their citizens vaccinated. The WHO estimates that 15 million people have died worldwide—over 1 million in the United States alone. The UN has instituted the COVAX dissemination of vaccines, but it is nowhere near enough. Mutations develop among those who are not vaccinated, which means that this is a global problem that must be solved. The UN is doing much to address these challenges but often has a problem getting its message out; the news media generally covers what is not working and focuses on the failures of the Security Council to take action. As stated in the beginning of this chapter, your perspective of the work of the United Nations will depend on where you sit as you view the winding path between the desert and the mountains that loom above. The challenge for the UN is to remain engaged and relevant.

Notes

1. Kennedy, *The Parliament of Man,* p. 243.
2. UN Charter, Preamble, second paragraph.
3. Buergenthal, "The Evolving International Human Rights System."
4. Guterres, *Report of the Secretary-General on the Work of the Organization 2021,* p. 13.
5. Ibid.
6. Ibid., p. 21.
7. Krasno, *Collected Papers of Kofi Annan,* p. 1015.
8. United Nations, "Resolution Adopted by the General Assembly on 16 September 2005," Document A/RES/60/1.
9. Krasno, *Collected Papers of Secretary-General Ban Ki-moon.*
10. *World Migration Report 2022,* published by the International Organization for Migration, p. 1. Guterres, *Report of the Secretary-General,* p. 96.
11. Ibid., p. 91.

12. Ibid., p. 13.

13. Ibid., p. 9.

14. Ibid., p. 58.

15. Krasno and Sutterlin, "Destroyed and Rendered Harmless." See also the UN Oral History interviews on UNSCOM. The Yale-UN Oral History interviews are housed in the UN Dag Hammarskjöld Library, New York, and the Yale University Archives and Manuscripts Library, New Haven, CT.

16. Organization for the Prohibition of Chemical Weapons, "Syria and the OPCW," www.opcw.org/media-centre/featured-topics/Syria-and-opcw. Also see Krasno, *Collected Papers of Secretary-General Ban Ki-moon.*

17. Alvaro de Soto, Yale-UN Oral History interview, April 9, 1996.

18. David Joseph Deutch, "What Are Friends For?: 'Groups of Friends' and the UN System," Universal Rights Group NYC, Beyond the Council blog, March 31, 2020, https://www.universal-rights.org/blog/what-are-friends-for-groups-of-friends-and-the-un-system/.

19. "International Technical Meeting on Human Mobility of Venezuelan Citizens in the Region (Quito Process)," UN International Organization on Migration (IOM), accessed November 20, 2021, https://iom.int/node/103049.

20. Simon Garcia, "Venezuela Reaffirms the Formation of the Group of Friends in Defense of the UN Charter," January 10, 2020, Group of Friends in Defense of the Charter of the United Nations, https://en.wikipedia.org/wiki/Group-of-Friends-in-defence-of-the-UN-Charter-of-the-United-Nations.

21. Loraine Sievers and Sam Daws, *The Procedure of the UN Security Council,* Table 4, "Vetoes of Draft Resolutions and Proposed Amendments Cast in Formal Security Council Meetings, 1946 to Present," July 8, 2022, SCProcedure.com.

22. Ibid.

23. Ibid.

24. Guterres, *Report of the Secretary-General,* p. 117.

25. Doyle, "The UN Charter: A Global Constitution?" p. 75.

26. Ibid., p. 76.

27. Guterres, *Report of the Secretary-General,* p. 121.

28. Max Fisher, "U.S. and Allies Spur Much of World's Democratic Decline, Data Shows," *New York Times,* November 17, 2021, p. A11.

Acronyms

ACABQ	Advisory Committee on Administrative and Budgetary Questions
AIDS	acquired immunodeficiency syndrome
AMISOM	African Union Mission in Somalia
AU	African Union
CAR	Central African Republic
CD	Conference on Disarmament
COP	Conference of Parties
CPC	Committee for Program and Coordination
CTBT	Comprehensive Nuclear Test Ban Treaty
DDR	demobilization, disarmament, and reintegration
DESA	Department of Economic and Social Affairs
DGC	Department of Global Communications
DMSPC	Department of Management Strategy, Policy, and Compliance
DOS	Department of Operational Support
DPKO	Department of Peacekeeping Operations
DPPA	Department of Political and Peacebuilding Affairs
DPO	Department of Peace Operations
DRC	Democratic Republic of Congo
EAD	Electoral Assistance Division
ECOSOC	Economic and Social Council
ECOWAS	Economic Community of West African States
EPTA	Expanded Program of Technical Assistance
EU	European Union

FAO	Food and Agriculture Organization
FMLN	Farabundo Martí National Liberation Front
G-8	Group of Eight
G-7	Group of Seven
G-77	Group of 77
GA	General Assembly
GATT	General Agreement on Tariffs and Trade
GCD	general and complete disarmament
GHG	greenhouse gas
GNI	gross national income
HIV	human immunodeficiency virus
IAEA	International Atomic Energy Agency
IBRD	International Bank for Reconstruction and Development
ICAO	International Civil Aviation Organization
ICC	International Criminal Court
ICJ	International Court of Justice
ICMPD	International Centre for Migration Policy Development
ICNRD	International Conference for New and Restored Democracies
IDA	International Development Assistance
IDP	Internally displaced person
IFAD	International Fund for Agricultural Development
IFC	International Finance Corporation
ILC	International Law Commission
ILO	International Labour Organization
IMF	International Monetary Fund
IMO	International Maritime Organization
IOM	International Organization for Migration
IPCC	Intergovernmental Panel on Climate Change
ITU	International Telecommunications Union
JIM	Joint Inspection Mechanism
MDGs	Millennium Development Goals
MERS	Middle East respiratory syndrome
MIGA	Multilateral Investment Guarantee Agency
MINURSO	United Nations Mission for the Referendum in Western Sahara
MINUSCA	United Nations Multidimensional Integrated Stabilization Mission in the Central African Republic
MINUSMA	United Nations Multidimensional Integrated Stabilization Mission in Mali

MONUC	United Nations Organization Mission in the Democratic Republic of Congo
MONUSCO	United Nations Organization Stabilization Mission in the Democratic Republic of the Congo
MOU	memorandum of understanding
NATO	North Atlantic Treaty Organization
NGO	nongovernmental organization
NPT	Nuclear Non-Proliferation Treaty
OAS	Organization of American States
OCHA	Office for the Coordination of Humanitarian Affairs
OECD	Organisation for Economic Co-operation and Development
OHCHR	Office of the High Commissioner for Human Rights
OLA	Office of Legal Affairs
ONUC	UN Operation in the Congo
OPCW	Organization for the Prohibition of Chemical Weapons
OSCE	Organization for Security and Cooperation in Europe
P-5	permanent five members of the Security Council
PICUM	Platform for International Cooperation on Undocumented Migrants
PLO	Palestine Liberation Organization
PPBME	program planning, budget, monitoring, and evaluation
RC	Resident Coordinator
RUF	Revolutionary United Front
SARS	severe acute respiratory syndrome
SDGs	Sustainable Development Goals
SSOD	Special Session on Disarmament
TPNW	Treaty on the Prohibition of Nuclear Weapons
UDHR	Universal Declaration of Human Rights
UK	United Kingdom
UN	United Nations
UNAIDS	Joint United Nations Programme on HIV/AIDS
UNAMSIL	United Nations Mission in Sierra Leone
UNCTAD	United Nations Conference on Trade and Development
UNDC	United Nations Disarmament Commission
UNDOF	United Nations Disengagement Observer Force
UNDP	United Nations Development Programme
UNEF	United Nations Emergency Force
UNEP	United Nations Environment Programme
UNESCO	United Nations Educational, Scientific and Cultural Organization

UNFCCC	United Nations Framework Convention on Climate Change
UNFICYP	United Nations Peacekeeping Force in Cyprus
UNFPA	United Nations Population Fund
UNHCHR	United Nations High Commission for Human Rights
UNHCR	United Nations High Commissioner for Refugees
UNICEF	United Nations Children's Fund
UNIDIR	United Nations Institute for Disarmament Research
UNIDO	United Nations Industrial Development Organization
UNIFIL	United Nations Interim Force in Lebanon
UNIMIR	United Nations Assistance Mission for Rwanda
UNISFA	United Nations Interim Security Force for Abyei
UNITAR	United Nations Institute for Training and Research
UNMIK	UN Mission in Kosovo
UNMIL	United Nations Mission in Liberia
UNMISS	United Nations Mission in South Sudan
UNMOGIP	United Nations Military Observer Group in India and Pakistan
UNODA	United Nations Office on Disarmament Affairs
UNODC	United Nations Office on Drugs and Crime
UNOMOZ	United Nations Operation in Mozambique
UNSCOB	United Nations Special Committee on the Balkans
UNSCOM	United Nations Special Commission
UNSDG	United Nations Sustainable Development Group
UNTAC	United Nations Transitional Authority in Cambodia
UNTAG	United Nations Transition Assistance Group for Namibia
UNTSO	United Nations Truce Supervision Organization
UNU	United Nations University
UPR	Universal Periodic Review
USAID	US Agency for International Development
WFP	World Food Programme
WHO	World Health Organization
WIPO	World Intellectual Property Organization
WMD	weapons of mass destruction
WMO	World Meteorological Organization
WTO	World Trade Organization

Bibliography

Alhashimi, Hana, Andres Fiallo, Toni-Shae Freckleton, Mona Ali Khalil, Vahd Mulachela, and Jonathan Viera (eds.). *The Future of Diplomacy After COVID-19: Multilateralism and the Global Pandemic.* New York: Routledge, 2021.

Alston, P., and F. Mégret (eds.). *The UN and Human Rights*, 2nd ed. (London: Oxford University Press, 2020).

Annan, Kofi. *Interventions: A Life in War and Peace.* New York: Penguin, 2012.

Arghiros, Daniel, Horacio Boneo, Simon Henderson, Sonia Palmieri, and Therese Pearce Laanela. *Making It Count: Lessons from Australian Electoral Assistance 2006–2016.* Canberra: Australian Government Department of Foreign Affairs and Trade, 2017.

Aris, Stephen, and Andreas Wenger (eds.). *Regional Organisations and Security: Conceptions and Practices.* New York: Routledge, 2014.

Autessere, Severine. *The Frontlines of Peace: An Insider's Guide to Changing the World.* New York: Oxford University Press, 2021.

Ban Ki-moon. *Resolved: United Nations in a Divided World.* New York: Columbia University Press, 2021.

Barros, James (ed.). *The United Nations. Past, Present and Future.* New York: The Free Press, 1972.

Berdal, Mats. "The United Nations in Bosnia, 1992–1995: Faithful Scapegoat to the World?" In Jean E. Krasno, Don Daniel, and Bradd Hayes, (eds.), *Leveraging for Success in United Nations Peace Operations.* Westport, CT: Praeger, 2003.

Betts, Alexander, and Paul Collier. *Refuge: Rethinking Refugee Policy in a Changing World.* Oxford: Oxford University Press, 2017.

Birgisson, Karl Th. "United Nations Peacekeeping Force in Cyprus." In Durch, *The Evolution of UN Peacekeeping,* 1993, 219–236.

———. "United Nations Special Committee on the Balkans." In William Durch (ed.), *The Evolution of UN Peacekeeping: Case Studies and Comparative Analysis,* 77–83. New York: St. Martin's Press, 1993.

The Blue Helmets: A Review of United Nations Peace-Keeping, 3rd ed. New York: United Nations, 1996.

Boneo, Horacio. "Elections and the United Nations." In Banerjee and Sharma, *Reinventing the United Nations,* 95–110.

279

Boulden, Jane, Ramesh Thakur, and Thomas G. Weiss (eds.). *The United Nations and Nuclear Orders* (Tokyo: UN University Press, 2009).

Boulden, Jane, and Thomas G. Weiss (eds.). *Terrorism and the UN.* Bloomington: Indiana University Press, 2004.

Bowring, Bill. "Who Are the 'Crimea People' or 'People of Crimea'? The Fate of the Crimean Tatars, Russia's Legal Justification for Annexation, and Pandora's Box." In Sergey Sayapin and Evhen Tsybulenko (eds.), *The Use of Force Against Ukraine and International Law,* 21–40. The Hague: T.M.C. Asser Press, 2018.

Brown, Stephen. "Foreign Aid and Democracy Promotion: Lessons from Africa." *European Journal of Development Research* 17, no. 2 (2005): 179–198.

Browne, Stephen. *Sustainable Development Goals and UN Goal-Setting.* New York: Routledge, 2017.

———. *UN Reform: 75 Years of Challenge and Change.* Cheltenham, UK: Edward Elgar, 2019.

Browne, Stephen, and Thomas G. Weiss (eds.). *Routledge Handbook on the UN and Development.* New York: Routledge, 2021.

Buergenthal, Thomas. "The Evolving International Human Rights System." In Charlotte Ku and Paul Diehl (eds.), *International Law: Classic and Contemporary Readings.* Boulder: Lynne Rienner Publishers, 2009.

Burri, Thomas. "Two Points for the International Court of Justice in *Chagos*: Take the Case, All of It—It Is a Human Rights Case." *Questions of International Law (QIL), Zoom Out* 55 (2018) (online version posted January 2, 2019).

Caballero, Paula, and Patti Londoño. *Redefining Development: The Extraordinary Genesis of the Sustainable Development Goals.* Boulder: Lynne Rienner Publishers, 2022.

Carroll, David J., and Avery Davis-Roberts. "The Carter Center and Election Observation: An Obligations-Based Approach for Assessing Elections," *Election Law Journal: Rules, Politics, and Policy* 12, no. 1 (2013): 87–93.

Chasek, Pamela S., David L. Downing, and Janet Welsh Brown. *Global Environmental Politics,* 7th ed. Boulder: Westview Press, 2017.

Chesterman, Simon. *You, The People: The United Nations, Transitional Administration, and State Building.* Oxford: Oxford University Press, 2004.

Clapham, Andrew. "The General Assembly (August 4, 2012)." In Alston and Mégret, *The UN and Human Rights.*

Claude, Inis, Jr. *The Changing United Nations.* New York: Random House, 1968.

———. *Swords Into Plowshares: The Problems and Progress of International Organization,* 4th ed. New York: Random House, 1984.

Conte, Alex, and Richard Burchill. *Defining Civil and Political Rights: The Jurisprudence of the United Nations Human Rights Committee.* London: Routledge, 2016.

Cornia, Giovanni A., Richard Jolly, and Frances Stewart (eds.). *Adjustment with a Human Face.* Oxford: Clarendon, 1987.

Cronin, Bruce, and Ian Hurd (eds.). *The Security Council and the Politics of International Authority.* New York: Routledge, 2008.

Dahl, R. A., and C. E. Lindblom. *Politics, Economics, and Welfare.* New York: Transaction Publishers, 1976.

Dallaire, Romeo. *Shake Hands with the Devil: The Failure of Humanity in Rwanda.* New York: Carroll & Graf, 2004).

Dayal, Anjali K. *Incredible Commitments. How UN Peacekeeping Failures Shape Peace Processes.* New York: Cambridge University Press, 2021.

Doyle, Michael. "The UN Charter: A Global Constitution?" In Ian Shapiro and Joseph Lampert (eds.), *Charter of the United Nations*. New Haven: Yale University Press, 2014.

Dulles, John Foster. "The General Assembly." *Foreign Affairs* 24, no.1 (October 1945).

Durch, William (ed.). *The Evolution of UN Peacekeeping*. New York: St. Martin's Press, 1993.

———. "The UN Operation in the Congo: 1960–1964." In Durch, *The Evolution of UN Peacekeeping*, 323–324.

——— (ed.). *UN Peacekeeping, American Policy, and the Uncivil Wars of the 1990s*. New York: St. Martin's Press, 1996.

Ebersole, Jon. "The United Nations' Response to Requests for Assistance in Electoral Matters." *Virginia Journal of International Law* 33, no. 1 (October 1992): 91–121.

Fikentscher, Wolfgang. "United Nations Codes of Conduct: New Paths in International Law." *American Journal of Comparative Law* 30, no. 4 (Autumn 1982): 577–604.

Fomerand, Jacques. "North-South Issues at the 2002 Monterrey Conference on Finance and Development." *Development and Finance* (Quarterly Hungarian Economic Review Published by the Strategic Advisory Board of the Hungarian Development Bank), August 2003.

Foresti, Marta, and Daniel Harris. *Democracy Support Through the United Nations*. Oslo: Norad, 2010).

Freedman, Rosa. "The Council and Commission on Human Rights." In Alston and Mégret, *The UN and Human Rights*.

Frulli, M. "The Contribution of International Criminal Tribunals to the Development of International Law: The Prominence of *opinion juris* and the Moralization of Customary Law." *The Law and Practice of International Courts and Tribunals (LAPE)* 14 (2015): 80–93.

Fukuda-Parr, Sakiko. *Millennium Development Goals: Ideas, Interests and Influence*. New York: Routledge, 2017.

Fukuda-Parr, Sakiko, Carlos Lopes, and Khalil Mlik (eds.). *Capacity for Development: New Solutions to Old Problems*. London: Earthscan, 2002.

Fukuyama, Francis. *The End of History and the Last Man*. New York: Free Press, 1992.

Gowlland-Debbas, Vera. "The ICJ and the Challenges of Human Rights Law." In Mads Andenas and Eirik Bjorge (eds.), *A Farewell to Fragmentation (Reassertion and Convergence in International Law* (Cambridge: Cambridge University Press, 2015)), pp. 109–145.

Grant, Thomas D. "Annexation of Crimea." *The American Journal of International Law,* 109.1 (2015): 68–95.

Guterres, António. *Report of the Secretary-General on the Work of the Organization 2021* (New York: United Nations, 2021).

Haack, Kirsten. *The United Nations Democracy Agenda: A Conceptual History*. Manchester, UK: Manchester University Press, 2011.

Hennebel, Ludovic. "The Human Rights Committee." In Alston and Mégret, *The UN and Human Rights*.

Hess, Martin, Therese Pearce Laanela, and William Maley. *Preparing for Elections in Afghanistan: Prospects and Challenges: Summary Report*. Canberra: Australia National University–Asia-Pacific College of Diplomacy, 2012.

Higgins, Rosalyn. *Problems and Process: International Law and How We Use It*. Oxford: Clarendon Press, 1996.

————. *United Nations Peacekeeping, 1946–67: Documents and Commentary*, vol. 3, *Africa*. Oxford: Oxford University Press, 1980.

Hill, William Martin. *The Economic and Financial Organisation of the League of Nations: A Survey of Twenty-Five Years' Experience*. Washington, DC: Carnegie Endowment for International Peace, 1946.

Hopgood, Stephen. *The End Times of Human Rights*. Ithaca, NY: Cornell University Press, 2013.

Hosli, Madeleine O., Taylor Garrett, Sonja Niedecken, and Nicolas Verbeck (eds.). *The Future of Multilateralism: Global Cooperation and International Organizations*. Lanham, MD: Rowman & Littlefield, 2021.

Howard, Lise Morjé. *Power in Peacekeeping*. Cambridge: Cambridge University Press, 2019.

————. *UN Peacekeeping in Civil Wars*. Cambridge: Cambridge University Press, 2008.

Human Development Report, 1990. New York: Oxford University Press, 1990.

Hurd, Ian. *International Organizations: Politics, Law, Practice*. Cambridge: Cambridge University Press, 2011.

————. *International Organizations: Politics, Law, Practice*, 2nd ed. Cambridge: Cambridge University Press, 2014.

James, Alan. *The Politics of Peacekeeping*. New York: Praeger, 1969.

Johnstone, Ian. *Rights and Reconciliation: UN Strategies in El Salvador*. Boulder: Lynne Rienner Publishers, 2007.

Joyner, Christopher. "The United Nations and Democracy." *Global Governance* 5, no. 3 (1999): 333–357.

Kane, Angela. *The New Zealand Lectures on Disarmament*, UNODA Occasional Papers 26. New York: UNODA, June 2014.

Kateb, George. *Human Dignity*. Cambridge, MA: Harvard University Press, 2011.

Kennedy, Paul. *The Parliament of Man: The Past, Present, and Future of the United Nations*. New York: Random House, 2006.

Kirdar, Uner. *The Structure of United Nations Economic Aid to Underdeveloped Countries*. The Hague: Nijhoff, 1966.

Knobler, Stacey, Adel Mahmoud, Stanley Lemon, and Leslie Pray (eds.). *The Impact of Globalization on Infectious Disease Emergence and Control: Exploring the Consequences and Opportunities: Workshop Summary*. Institute of Medicine Forum on Microbial Threats (Washington, DC: National Academies Press, 2006).

Korey, William. *NGOs and the Universal Declaration of Human Rights*. New York: Palgrave/Macmillan, 2001.

Krasno, Jean E. (ed.). *The Collected Papers of Kofi Annan: UN Secretary-General 1997–2006*. Boulder: Lynne Rienner Publishers, 2012.

———— (ed.). *The Collected Papers of Secretary-General Ban Ki-moon*. JSTOR, 2022.

————. "Founding the United Nations: An Evolutionary Process." In Krasno, *The United Nations: Confronting the Challenges of a Global Society*, 19–46.

————. "Namibian Independence: A UN Success Story." In Shapiro and Lampert, *Charter of the United Nations*, 174–192.

———— (ed.), *The United Nations: Confronting the Challenges of a Global Society*. Boulder: Lynne Rienner Publishers, 2004.

Krasno, Jean E., and James Sutterlin. "Destroyed and Rendered Harmless: UNSCOM's and IAEA's Achievements." In Jean E. Krasno and James Sutterlin, (eds.), *The United Nations and Iraq: Defanging the Viper*, 159–175. Westport, CT, and London: Praeger, 2003.

Krasno, Jean E., and Elisabeth Szeli. *Banning the Bomb: The Treaty on the Prohibition of Nuclear Weapons.* Boulder: Lynne Rienner Publishers, 2021.

Lampert, Joseph. "Science and Politics on a Warming Planet: The IPCC and the Representation of Future Generations." In Shapiro and Lampert, *Charter of the United Nations.*

Lauwaars, R. H., et al. *International Organisation and Integration,* 2nd ed. The Hague: Martinus Nijhoff Publishers, 1981.

Leterme, Yves. "Elections in International Democracy Assistance." In *Brown Journal of World Affairs* 24, no. 2 (2018): 81–95.

Lindblom, C. E. "The Science of Muddling Through." *Public Administration Review* 19 (Spring 1959).

Lindblom, C. E., and E. J. Woodhouse. *The Policy-Making Process.* New York: Prentice Hall, 1993.

Lowi, Theodore J. "Four Systems of Policy, Politics, and Choice." *Public Administration Review* 32, no. 4 (July–August 1972): 298–310.

Lübermann, Anna. *UN Electoral Assistance: Does It Matter for the Quality of Elections?* V-Dem Working Paper No. 27. Gothenburg, Sweden: Department of Political Science, University of Gothenburg, 2016.

Ludwig, Robin. "Democratization and the UN: New Mandate for a New Millenium." In Roy Oshiba et al. (eds.), *Democratization and the United Nations,* 209–239. Nishinomiya, Japan: Japan Association for United Nations Studies, Kwansei Gakuin University, 2004.

———. "Free and Fair Elections: Letting the People Decide." In Krasno, *United Nations,* 115–162.

Lyons, Terrence. "Post-conflict Elections and the Process of Demilitarizing Politics." *Democratization* 11, no. 3 (2004): 36–62.

Martini, Alice. *The UN and Counter-Terrorism. Global Hegemonies, Power and Identities.* New York: Routledge, 2021.

McGaughey, Fiona. *Non-governmental Organisations and the United Nations Human Rights System.* London: Routledge, 2021.

McInnes, Colin, and Kelley Lee. *Global Health and International Relations.* New York: Wiley, 2012.

Mégret, Frédéric. "The Security Council." In Alston and Mégret, *The UN and Human Rights.*

Meron, T. *The Humanization of International Law.* Leiden: Martinus Nijhoff, 2006.

Mertus, Julie. *The UN and Human Rights.* London: Routledge, 2009.

Micinski, Nicholas R. *UN Global Compacts: Governing Migrants and Refugees.* New York: Routledge, 2021.

Moller, J. Th., and A. de Zayas. *United Nations Human Rights Committee Case Law 1977–2008.* New York: N. P. Engel, 2009.

Narasimhan, P. S. "Technical Assistance for Economic Development of Underdeveloped Countries." *India Quarterly* 8 (April–June 1952): 142–155.

Nayyar, Deepak. *Catch Up: Developing Countries in the World Economy.* Oxford: Oxford University Press, 2013.

Newman, Edward, and Roland Rich (eds.). *The UN Role in Promoting Democracy: Between Ideals and Reality.* New York: United Nations University Press, 2004.

Nolan, Aoife, Rosa Freedman, and Thérèse Murphy. *The United Nations Special Procedures System.* London: Brill, 2017.

Oudraat, Chantal de Jonge, and Michael Brown (eds.). *The Gender and Security Agenda: Strategies for the 21st Century.* New York: Routledge, 2020.

Packard, Randall M. *A History of Global Health: Interventions into the Lives of Other Peoples.* Washington, DC: Johns Hopkins University Press, 2016.

Patz, Ronny, and Klaus H. Goetz. *Managing Money and Discord in the UN: Budgeting and Bureaucracy.* Oxford: Oxford University Press, 2019.

Pearce Laanela, Therese, Sead Alihodžić, Antonio Spinelli, and Peter Wolf, *Supporting Elections Effectively.* Stockholm: Elanders Sverige, 2021.

Ponzio, Richard. *Democratic Peacebuilding: Aiding Afghanistan and Other Fragile States.* Oxford: Oxford University Press, 2011.

Răduleţu, S. "The Role of International Criminal Tribunals in Promoting Human Rights." *International Journal of Law and Jurisprudence* 11, no. 1 (2021).

Ramcharan, Bertrand (ed.), *The Right to Life in International Law.* The Hague: Martinus Nijhoff, 1985.

———. *UN Protection of Humanity and Its Habitat.* The Hague: Martinus Nijhoff, 1983.

Ratner, Steven R. *The New UN Peacekeeping: Building Peace in Lands of Conflict After the Cold War.* New York: St. Martin's Press, 1996.

Reuveny, Rafael, and William R. Thompson. *North and South in the World Political Economy.* Oxford: Backwell, 2008.

Rittberger, Volker, Bernhard Zangl, and Matthias Staisch. *International Organization. Polity, Politics and Policies.* New York: Palgrave MacMillan, 2006.

Romaniuk, Peter. *Multilateral Counter-terrorism.* New York: Routledge, 2010.

Rubin, Irene S. *The Politics of Public Budgeting: Getting and Spending, Borrowing and Balancing.* New York: CQ Press, 2019.

Russell, Ruth B. *A History of the United Nations Charter: The Role of the United States, 1940–45.* Washington, DC: Brookings Institution, 1958.

Rydell, Randy. *Explaining Hammarskjöld's "Hardy Perennial": The Role of the United Nations in Nuclear Disarmament.* London: UK/United Nations Association, 2013.

———. "The Guterres Disarmament Agenda and the Challenge of Constructing a Global Regime for Weapons." *Journal for Peace and Nuclear Disarmament* 3, no. 1 (May 2020): 21–40.

Sachs, Jeffrey D. *The Age of Sustainable Development.* New York: Columbia University Press, 2015.

Samarsinghe, Natalie. "Human Rights: Norms and Machinery." In Thomas G. Weiss and Sam Daws (eds.), *The Oxford Handbook on the United Nations,* 2nd ed. Oxford: Oxford University Press, 2018.

Scheinin, Martin, ed. *Terrorism and Human Rights.* Herndon, VA: Edward Elgar, 2013.

Sénit, Carole-Anne. "Leaving No One Behind? The Influence of Civil Society Participation on the Sustainable Development Goals." *Environment and Planning C: Politics and Space* 38, no. 4 (2020)): 693–712.

Seygin, Zeynep, and Dennis Dijkzeul. *The New Humanitarians in International Practice: Emerging Actors and Contested Principles.* New York: Routledge, 2016.

Shapiro, Ian, and Joseph Lampert (eds.). *Charter of the United Nations.* New Haven and London: Yale University Press, 2014.

Shelton, Dinah (ed.). *The United Nations System for Protecting Human Rights,* Vol. 4 of *The Library of Essays on International Human Rights,* edited by Stephanie Farrior. London: Routledge, 2016.

Simangan, Dahlia. *International Peacebuilding and Local Involvement: A Liberal Renaissance?* New York: Routledge, 2019.

Simma, Bruno. "The International Court of Justice." In Alston and Mégret, *The UN and Human Rights.*

Smith, Karen, and Katie V. Laatikaiden (eds.). *Group Politics in UN Multilateralism.* London: Brill, 2020.

Smith, Patrick. "Kofi Annan on War and Peace and the Art of Interventions." *Africa Report*, February 8, 2013.

Sohn, Louis B. *Cases on United Nations Law.* Brooklyn, NY: Foundation Press, 1956.

Sohn, Louis B., and Thomas Buergenthal (eds.). *The International Protection of Human Rights.* Indianapolis: Bobbs-Merrill, 1972.

Tesner, Sandrine, and Georg Kell. *The United Nations and Business: A Partnership Recovered.* New York: St. Martin's Press, 2000.

Thakur, Ramesh. *Reviewing the Responsibility to Protect: Origins, Implementation and Controversies.* New York: Routledge, 2018.

Tistounet, Eric. *The UN Human Rights Council: A Practical Anatomy.* New York: Edward Elgar Publishing, 2020.

Turan, Tuba. *Positive Peace in Theory and Practice: Strengthening the United Nations' Pre-conflict Prevention Role.* Danvers, MA: Brill, 2016.

United Nations. *The Millennium Development Goals Report 2015.* New York: United Nations, 2015.

———. *The Sustainable Development Goals Report 2019.* New York: United Nations, 2019.

United Nations Group of Experts on the Structure of the United Nations System. *A New United Nations Structure for Global Economic Co-operation.* New York: United Nations, 1975.

van Boven, Theo C. "Partners in the Promotion and Protection of Human Rights." *Netherlands International Law Review* 24 (1977): 55–71.

Wallensteen, Peter, and Anders Biurner. *Regional Organizations and Peacemaking: Challenges to the UN?* New York: Routledge, 2015.

Weeramantry, C. G. *The Slumbering Sentinels—Law and Human Rights in the Wake of Technology.* New York: Penguin, 1983.

Weiss, Thomas G., Tatiana Carayannis, and Richard Jolly. "The 'Third' United Nations." *Global Governance* 15, no. 1 (January–March 2009).

Weiss, Thomas G., and Ramesh Thakur. *Global Governance and the UN: An Unfinished Journey.* Bloomington: Indiana University Press, 2010.

Weiss, Thomas G., and Rorden Wilkinson (eds.). *International Organization and Global Governance.* New York: Routledge, 2014.

Wildavsky, A. B. *The Politics of the Budgetary Process.* New York: Little Brown, 1964.

Willetts, Peter. "The Cardoso Report on the UN and Civil Society: Functionalism, Global Corporatism, or Global Democracy." *Global Governance* 12, no. 3 (July–September 2006): 305–324.

———. *Non-governmental Organizations in World Politics: The Construction of Global Governance.* Abingdon: Routledge, 2011.

Zacker, Mark W. *The United Nations and Global Commerce.* New York: United Nations, 1999).

Contributors

Jacques Fomerand joined the UN Secretariat in 1977, serving in the office of the under-secretary-general of the former Department for International Economic and Social Affairs. From 1992 to June 2003, when he retired from UN service, he was director of the United Nations University Office in North America. Since 2002, Fomerand has taught in the UN program of Occidental College and is now assistant director of the program. He also teaches at the Colin Powell School for Civic and Global Leadership at the City College of New York.

Kimberly Gamble-Payne is lecturer in the Department of Global Health at George Washington University and in the MA program in international relations at the City College of New York. Previously, she worked at the United Nations for some twenty years.

Jean E. Krasno is on the faculty of the Department of Political Science at the City College of New York (CCNY) and also a lecturer at Columbia University. She is also editor of the collected papers of Secretaries-General Kofi Annan and Ban Ki-moon. She served for five years as executive director of the Academic Council on the United Nations System.

Wannes Lint has worked for the United Nations since 2013, focusing on intergovernmental affairs and governance and strategic planning. He recently supported intergovernmental consultations on the "Our Common Agenda" report. In previous assignments, he helped implement elements of the Secretary-General's reform agenda while working in the Executive Office of the Secretary-General, drafted an integrated strategic framework for the United Nations in Iraq, and supported budget negotiations in the Fifth Committee of the General Assembly.

Therese Pearce Laanela is head of the electoral processes team at the International Institute for Democracy and Electoral Assistance, and she has thirty years of experience in elections and electoral assistance at the field, headquarters, and policy levels. Previous affiliations include the Carter Center and the United Nations, and she has served on numerous international election observer and assistance missions in Africa, Europe, and Asia for organizations such as the Organization for Security and Co-operation in Europe and the European Union.

Bertrand Ramcharan spent three decades with the United Nations, including as chief speechwriter in the Office of the Secretary-General, director of the Department of Political Affairs, director of the International Conference on the Former Yugoslavia, and acting UN High Commissioner for Human Rights. Ramcharan has also lectured on international law at the Geneva Graduate Institute and Columbia University.

Randy Rydell is an executive advisor of Mayors for Peace, an international nongovernmental organization headquartered in Hiroshima, Japan. Previously, he served as a senior political affairs officer in the UN Office for Disarmament Affairs, a nonproliferation advisor to US Senator John Glenn, and an international political analyst at the Lawrence Livermore National Laboratory.

Massimo Tommasoli is director of Global Programmes, as well as the institute's permanent observer to the United Nations at the International Institute for Democracy and Electoral Assistance. He has worked at the Organisation for Economic Co-operation and Development, the Italian Ministry of Foreign Affairs, and the UN Educational, Scientific, and Cultural Organization. He also has been a lecturer at the Colin Powell School for Civic and Global Leadership, City College of New York.

Index

ACABQ (Advisory Committee on Administrative and Budgetary Questions), 215, 217
Acheson, Dean, 238
Administrative and Budgetary Committee (Fifth Committee), 202–203, 210, 215, 217–218
Advisory Board on Disarmament Matters, 186
Advisory Committee on Administrative and Budgetary Questions (ACABQ), 215, 217
Advisory Opinion on Reservations to the Genocide Convention, ICJ, 95
Afghan Joint Electoral Management Body (JEMB), 158n36
Afghanistan, 149, 158n36, 244
African Union (AU), 128
African Union Mission in Somalia (AMISOM), 128
Aideed, Mohamed Farah, 127
Albania, 235–236
Alexandretta, League of Nations and, 107
AMISOM (African Union Mission in Somalia), 128
Angola, electoral assistance in, 141, 148
Annan, Kofi, 6, 11–13, 117–118; on disarmament machinery, 182–183; election of, 21; on global health, 160–161; MDGs creation and, 264;

Rwanda peacekeeping and, 129; as special envoy for Syria, 250
Argentina, 38, 41
Arms control. *See* Disarmament
Arrhenius, Svante, 166
Arusha Agreement, 128–129
Assessed contributions, for peacekeeping, 223–224
ATMIS (AU Transition Mission in Somalia), 128
Atomic bomb, 51
AU (African Union), 128
AU Transition Mission in Somalia (ATMIS), 128

Ban Ki-moon, 12, 13, 20, 117, 120, 167, 249; disarmament agenda of, 189–190; election of, 21
Barcelona Traction case, 95
Baril, Maurice, 129
Barre, Said, 127
Because Process Matters report, 198, 210, 227
Belaunde, Victor Andres, 239
Belgium, Congo crisis and, 112–116
Berdal, Mats, 130
Bertrand, Maurice, 204
Bilateral diplomacy, 30
Biological Weapons Convention, 184
Bioterrorism, global health and, 165
Boneo, Horacio, 140, 142–143, 146–147

Bosnia, 130, 149
Boutros-Ghali, Boutros, 12–13, 21, 119, 129
Boven, Theo van, 100–101
Brazil, 7
Bretton Woods Institutions, 22, 61, 75–76; flagship reports, 80*tab*
Brown, Stephen, 142
Bruce Committee, League of Nations, 59
Budget, 55*n*30; ACABQ and, 215, 217; acting without specific mandates, 203–204; assessment of, 211; *Because Process Matters* report on, 198, 210, 227; breaking down, 212, 213*tab,* 215; contributions to, 218–221; expectations of, 27–28; extrabudgetary contributions and, 224–226; Fifth Committee on, 202–203, 210, 215, 217–218; funding modalities for, 221–222; hybrid constructs in, 226–227; importance of, 197; incrementalism theory and, 199; legal framework for, 210–211; mandates and, 200–201; mandates for 2022, 216*tab*; for peacekeeping, 106, 222–224; politics and, 199; preparation of, 211–212; program, 201–203; stages of, 198; theory and, 199–200; 2021, 211. *See also* Mandates; Program planning
Budgetary incrementalism theory, 199
Bulgaria, 235–236
Bunche, Ralph, 36, 111–115
Burri, Thomas, 95–96
Bush, George H. W., 127, 167
Byelorussia, 38–39

Cadogan, Alexander, 37
Cambodia, electoral assistance in, 141, 144
Canada, 23–24, 110–111
Capacity building, electoral assistance and, 148–149
CAR (Central African Republic), 133–134
Carter, Jimmy, 118
CD (Conference on Disarmament), 184–185
Central African Republic (CAR), 133–134
Central Emergency Response Fund, 73, 84*n*46
"Certain Expenses of the United Nations" case, 241
Chagos Island case, 95–96

Chain of events theory, 49, 56*n*41
Chapultepec Conference, 41
Chemical Weapons Convention, 184
China: Belt and Road Initiative of, 163; Dumbarton Oaks meeting and, 36–37; on P-5, 7–8; WHO's memorandum of understanding with, 163
Churchill, Winston, 38–41
Claude, Inis, 31, 52, 77–78
Climate change, 3; challenges of, 271–272; Germany and, 169; human security and, 166–170; impact of, 169–170; IPCC and, 166, 271; Kyoto Protocol and, 167; Paris Agreement on, 167–169; UNFCCC and, 166–168, 271
Clinton, Bill, 127–128, 130
Cold War, 51, 53, 261; democratization following, 143; peacekeeping and thaw of, 118–120
Collective Measures Committee, 240
Colombia, 107–108
Commission on Human Rights, 76
Committee for Program and Coordination, 205–206
Comprehensive Nuclear Test Ban Treaty (CTBT), 184
Concert of Europe, 30–31
Conditionality of aid, for democratization, 142
Conference of Parties 15 (COP15), 167
Conference of Parties 26 (COP26), 168–169, 271
Conference on Disarmament (CD), 184–185
Congo crisis, Belgium and, 112–116
Congress of Vienna, 30
Connally, Tom, 35, 56*n*47
Consensus, 18
Contributions: assessed, for peacekeeping, 223–224; Committee on, 219; consequences of not paying, 219–220; debt burden adjustment and, 218; determining, 218–219; extrabudgetary, 224–226; liquidity crisis and, 220–221
COP15 (Conference of Parties 15), 167
COP26 (Conference of Parties 26), 168–169, 271
Côte d'Ivoire (Ivory Coast), 125–126
COVAX (Covid-19 Vaccine Global Access) Facility, 266, 272

Covid-19 pandemic, 3, 24; challenges of, 272; development system and, 65, 78; global health and, 161–162, 165; human security and, 159–160, 175
Covid-19 Vaccine Global Access (COVAX) Facility, 266, 272
CTBT (Comprehensive Nuclear Test Ban Treaty), 184
Cuba, 244–245
Cyprus, UNFICYP and, 116–117

Dahl, R. A., 199
Dallaire, Roméo, 128–129
Danzig, League of Nations and, 107
"Days," UN designation of special, 69–70
Dayton Accords, 1995, 126, 130
DDR (demobilization, disarmament, and reintegration) program, 123, 187
Debt burden adjustment, contributions and, 218
"Decades," UN designation of special, 69–70
Declaration of Principles for International Election Observation, 155
Decolonization, General Assembly overseeing, 10, 54, 143
Demobilization, disarmament, and reintegration (DDR) program, 123, 187
Democratic Republic of Congo (DRC): Belgium and crisis in, 112–116; peacekeeping in, 132
Democratization, 3; challenges facing, 270–271; after Cold War, 143; conditionality of aid for, 142; in Guyana, 141–142; ICNRD and, 152–153; International Democracy Day and, 153; knowledge networking and, 156; leadership and agenda setting for, 155; member states and, 152–154; norm setting for, 154–155; in Portugal, 141; in Somalia, 140; in Togoland, 151; trajectory of UN involvement in, 139–143; UNDP and, 143, 150, 153–154, 156. *See also* Electoral assistance
Department for Management Strategy, Policy and Compliance (DMSPC), 211–212
Department of Global Communications (DGC), 14

Department of Peace Operations (DPO), 150
Department of Peacekeeping Operations (DPKO), 119–120
Department of Political and Peacebuilding Affairs (DPPA), 120, 150
Deputy Secretary-General, 11
Developing countries, terminology of, 58–59
Development Decades, UN, 69
Development system: achievements of, 263–265; Bruce Committee and, 59; contributions of, 58; Covid-19 pandemic and, 65, 78; "days," "weeks," "years," "decades" commemorated in, 69–70; ECOSOC and, 60–61; Fabianism and, 66–67; flagship reports and, 79*tab*; General Assembly and, 60; Global Compact and, 63; global conferences of, 67, 68*tab*, 69; humanitarian assistance and, 71–73; influence of, 58; institutions and structures in, 59–62; leadership challenges for, 77–78; neoliberalism and, 65–66; NGO partnerships in, 62–63; North and, 63–64; objectives of, 57; RCs and, 76–77; redistributive policies of, 70–73; reform of, 71, 75–77; regulatory policies and, 73–75; resources and capacity of, 70–71; South and, 64; staffing and finances of, 61–62; tasks of, 59–60; terminology of, 58–59; uncertain mandate of, 63–65; UNDP and, 67; World Bank, IMF and, 61. *See also* Sustainable Development Goals; UN Development Programme
DGC (Department of Global Communications), 14
Dhlakama, Afonso, 148
Dignity: in human rights system, 91–92; international orders conducive to human, 92–94
Disarmament, 3; achievements in, 266–267; Advisory Board on, 186; Annan on machinery of, 182–183; Ban Ki-moon's agenda for, 189–190; Conference on, 184–185; evolving structures of, 182–188; future of, 193; goals of, 181; Guterres' agenda for, 190–191, 196*n*45; history of, 179–180; importance of, 179; League of

Nations and, 180; multilateral treaties on, 188, 188*tab*; NGOs and, 192; norms on, 182, 187; obstacles to, 192–193; OPCW and, 267; primary functions of centers on, 181–182; SSOD-I and, 183; "taboo," 192; TPNW and, 191–192, 252; UN Atomic Energy Commission and, 180–181; UNDC and, 183–184; UNIDIR and, 186; UNODA and, 185–186, 190

DMSPC (Department for Management Strategy, Policy and Compliance), 211–212

DPKO (Department of Peacekeeping Operations), 119–120

DPO (Department of Peace Operations), 150

DPPA (Department of Political and Peacebuilding Affairs), 120, 150

DRC. *See* Democratic Republic of Congo

Duarte, Sergio, 193

Dumbarton Oaks meeting, 35–38

EAD (Electoral Assistance Division), 150

East Timor (Timor Leste), 10; electoral assistance in, 148–149; peacekeeping in, 126–127

Ebersole, Jon, 147–148, 150

Economic and Social Council (ECOSOC): Bruce Committee and, 59; Committee for Program and Coordination and, 205–206; criticism against, 14; development system and, 60–61; elections to, 14; establishment of, 13; evolution of, 54; NGOs and, 13–14, 60, 62; proposal to abolish, 75; Yalta Conference on, 40

Economic Community of West African States (ECOWAS), 133

ECOSOC. *See* Economic and Social Council

ECOWAS (Economic Community of West African States), 133

Eden, Anthony, 38–39

Egalitarian voting, 18

Egypt, 20, 109–112, 242–243

Eisenhower, Dwight D., 243

El Salvador: Friends of the Secretary-General on, 267–268; peacekeeping in, 122–123

Electoral assistance, 3; acceptance of results and, 144–145; in Afghanistan, 149, 158*n*36; in Angola, 141, 148; in Bosnia, 149; in Cambodia, 141, 144; capacity building and, 148–149; conditionality of, 142; costs of, 145–146, 153; DPO and, 150; in East Timor, 148–149; expanding engagement in, 150–152; fieldwork choices shaping, 146–150; in Haiti, 147–148, 151; in Iraq, 149; Jammu-Kashmir crisis and, 140; knowledge networking and, 156; leadership and agenda setting for, 155; in Mozambique, 144–145, 148; in Namibia, 141, 146–147; in Nicaragua, 147, 151; norm setting for, 154–155; special characteristics of, 144–146; trajectory of UN involvement in, 139–143; UNDP and, 143, 150, 153–154, 156; UNTCOK and, 140. *See also* Democratization

Electoral Assistance Division (EAD), 150

Elite privilege voting, 18–19

EPTA (Expanded Program of Technical Assistance), 225

Equality, in human rights system, 91–92

Esquipulas II Agreement of 1987, 147

EU Pact on Migration and Asylum, 174

European Commission, 149

Evatt, Herbert, 49

Expanded Program of Technical Assistance (EPTA), 225

Extrabudgetary contributions, 224–226

Fabianism, development system and, 66–67

FAO (Food and Agricultural Organization), 61

Farabundo Martí National Liberation Front (FMLN), 122–123

Fawzi, Mohammed, 112

Fifth Committee (Administrative and Budgetary Committee), 202–203, 210, 215, 217–218

Finkelstein, Lawrence, 46, 48–50, 56*n*47

Flag, UN, 29

Flagship reports, UN, 79*tab*

FMLN (Farabundo Martí National Liberation Front), 122–123

Food and Agricultural Organization (FAO), 61

Food insecurity, 170
Force, San Francisco Conference on use of, 51
Foreign Assistance Act of 1961, 142
France: Alexandretta, League of Nations and, 107; CAR and, 134; on P-5, 7–8; Saar Basin, League of Nations and, 106–107; on Secretary-General's election, 50; Suez Canal crisis of 1956 and, 20, 109–110, 243; Syria and, 45
Freedom House, 93
Freitas Valle, Cyro de, 239
Friends of the Quito Process, 174–175
Friends of the Secretary-General on El Salvador, 267–268

Gamba, Virginia, 267
Garcia Robles, Alfonso, 41, 44–45
GATT (General Agreement on Tariffs and Trade), 25
Gbagbo, Laurent, 125–126
Gender: equality, 263; human rights system and, 88; of Secretary-General, 13
General Agreement on Tariffs and Trade (GATT), 25
General Assembly: authority of, 9; committees of, 9–10; decolonization role of, 10, 54, 143; development system and, 60; Fifth Committee and, 202, 210, 215; function of, 8; on Grenada invasion of 1983, 244–245; observer status in, 10; on Panama invasion of 1989, 245; resolution 290 (IV), 232; resolutions of, 8–9; Russia's war of aggression in Ukraine and, 89; on Russia's war of aggression on Ukraine, 253–254; San Francisco Conference on competency of, 44–45; Security Council circumvented by, 255*tab*; Social and Humanitarian Committee of, 99; TPNW and, 252; UDHR and, 87–88; Uniting for Peace resolution debates in, 239–240; veto debates in 1950 in, 238–239; voting in, 20–21; Yalta Conference on competency of, 40. *See also* Uniting for Peace resolution
Germany, 8; climate change action of, 169; Danzig, League of Nations and, 107; Saar Basin, League of Nations

and, 106–107; Upper Silesia, League of Nations and, 107
GHG (greenhouse gas) emissions, 166–170. *See also* Climate change
Global Action Plan for Healthy Lives and Well-Being for All, 165
Global Compact, UN, 63
Global Compact for Safe, Orderly and Regular Migration, 171–174
Global conferences, UN, 67, 68*tab*, 69
Global Environment Outlook, 79*tab*
Global health, 3; bioterrorism and, 165; Covid-19 pandemic and, 161–162, 165; emergence of, 162–163; food insecurity and, 170; HIV/AIDS and, 161; human security and, 160–166; international relations agenda and, 164–166; International Sanitary Conferences for, 162; MDGs and, 161. *See also* World Health Organization
Global Report on Adult Learning and Education, 81*tab*
Global South, terminology of, 58–59
Global warming. *See* Climate change
"Good offices," of Secretary-General, 11
Gorbachev, Mikhail, 118
Gore, Al, 166
Gowlland-Debbas, Vera, 95
Greece, 235–236
Greenhouse gas (GHG) emissions, 166–170. *See also* Climate change
Grenada invasion of 1983, 244–245
Gromyko, Andrei, 37, 44
Gross violations of human rights, 96
"Group of Friends," 267–268
Guterres, António, 12–13, 71, 77, 165; disarmament agenda of, 190–191, 196*n*45; gender equality agenda of, 263
Guyana, democratization in, 141–142

Habibie, B. J., 126
Habyarimana, Juvénal, 129
Hague Peace Conventions of 1899 and 1907, 180
Haiti, electoral assistance in, 147–148, 151
Halff, Maarten, 140, 150
Halsey, William Frederick, Jr., 35
Hammarskjöld, Dag, 12, 13, 109–115, 181, 185
Harriman, Averell, 49

Heinbecker, Paul, 247
Hezbollah, 118
Higgins, Roselyn, 16–17
Hiss, Alger, 32, 36–39, 51–53
HIV/AIDS, 24, 161
Holocaust, 52
Hopkins, Harry, 49
Hull, Cordell, 33, 35, 38
Human development. *See* Development system, UN
Human Development Index, UNDP, 23
Human Development Report, 2, 23–24, 67, 79*tab,* 264
Human Rights Committee, 94–95
Human Rights Council, 76, 88, 97–99
Human rights system: achievements of, 262–263; components of national, 93; core circles of, 101; dignity and equality in, 91–92; gender equality and, 263; gross violations of, 96; ICC tribunals and, 96–97; ICJ and, 86, 95–96; international law and, 94–96; international orders conducive to human survival, dignity, and rights promoted by, 92–94; NGOs and, 97–101; normative and jurisprudential architecture of, 86–89; overview of, 85–86; right to life and, 89–91; Russia's war of aggression in Ukraine and, 89–90; San Francisco Conference and, 52; treaty supervisory bodies in, 99–100; UDHR and, 52, 87–88, 90–93; UPR and, 97; women and, 88
Human security, 3; achievements in, 266–267; climate change and, 166–170; concept of, 159; Covid-19 pandemic and, 159–160, 175; food insecurity and, 170; global health and, 160–166; migration and, 170–175; national security and, 159
Human survival, dignity, and rights, international orders conducive to, 92–94
Humanitarian assistance: achievements of, 265–266; critiques of, 73; development system and, 71–73; North-South tensions overshadowing, 72
Hungary, 243
Hunte, Julian Robert, 249
Hybrid budget constructs, 226–227

IAEA (International Atomic Energy Agency), 22, 61
IBRD (International Bank for Reconstruction and Development), 22
ICAO (International Civil Aviation Organization), 115
ICC (International Criminal Court), 18, 96–97
ICJ. *See* International Court of Justice
ICMPD (International Centre for Migration Policy Development), 172–173
ICNRD (International Conference for New and Restored Democracies), 152–153
IDA (International Development Assistance), 22
IDPs (internally displaced persons), 25
IFAD (International Fund for Agricultural Development), 61
ILO (International Labour Organization), 61
IMF. *See* International Monetary Fund
Independence, San Francisco Conference on, 47
India, 38, 140, 244
Industrial Development Report, 81*tab*
Inter-American Conference on the Problems of Peace and War, 41
Intergovernmental Panel on Climate Change (IPCC), 166, 271
Internally displaced persons (IDPs), 25
International Atomic Energy Agency (IAEA), 22, 61
International Bank for Reconstruction and Development (IBRD), 22
International Centre for Migration Policy Development (ICMPD), 172–173
International Civil Aviation Organization (ICAO), 115
International Conference for New and Restored Democracies (ICNRD), 152–153
International Court of Justice (ICJ): Advisory Opinion on Reservations to the Genocide Convention of, 95; advisory opinions of, 17; annual dues of, 17; authority of, 15–16; *Barcelona Traction* case, 95; cases heard by, 16–17; on "Certain Expenses of the United Nations" case, 241; *Chagos Island* case, 95–96; elections to, 16,

21; human rights system and, 86, 95–96; membership of, 15; on Russia's war of aggression in Ukraine, 89–90

International Criminal Court (ICC), 18, 96–97

International Democracy Day, 153

International Development Assistance (IDA), 22

International Foundation for Electoral Systems, 149

International Fund for Agricultural Development (IFAD), 61

International Health Regulations, 165

International human rights law, 94–96

International Labour Organization (ILO), 61

International Law Commission, 88

International Monetary Fund (IMF): criticism against, 23; development system and, 61; function of, 22

International orders conducive to human survival, dignity, and rights, 92–94

International Organization for Migration (IOM), 61, 149

International Sanitary Conferences, 162

International Telegraph Union, 31

IOM (International Organization for Migration), 61, 149

IPCC (Intergovernmental Panel on Climate Change), 166, 271

Iraq, 107; electoral assistance in, 149; Uniting for Peace resolution not used for US invasion of, 247–248; WMDs and, 266–267

Israel, 244; ICJ advisory opinions on, 17; Lebanon and PLO attacks on, 117–118; Six-Day War of 1967 and, 112; Suez Canal crisis of 1956 and, 20, 109–112, 242–243; Uniting for Peace resolution on Palestinian conflict with, 245–246, 248–249; UNTSO and, 109; Yom Kippur War and, 112

Ivory Coast (Côte d'Ivoire), 125–126

Jammu-Kashmir crisis, 140

Japan, 7, 8

Jebb, Gladwyn, 40

JEMB (Afghan Joint Electoral Management Body), 158n36

John D. and Catherine T. MacArthur Foundation, 196n46

Jordan, 109

Kane, Angela, 192–193, 267

Kant, Immanuel, 91

Kasavubu, Joseph, 113

Kashmir, 140

Keeling, Charles, 166

Kelapile, Collen Vixen, 197

Kennedy, Paul, 261

KFOR (Kosovo Force), 126

Khadduri, Majid, 45–46, 49

Kirk, Grayson, 36

Kissinger, Henry, 190

de Klerk, F. W., 121

Knowledge networking, democratization, electoral assistance and, 156

Korea, Uniting for Peace resolution and, 19–20, 237–238, 241–242

Korean War, 4

Kosovo, 10; ICJ advisory opinions on, 17; peacekeeping in, 126; Uniting for Peace resolution not used for crisis in, 246–247

Kosovo Force (KFOR), 126

Kyoto Protocol, 167

Laurenti, Jeffrey, 197

Law, international human rights, 94–96

League Assembly, 32

League Council, 31–32

League of Nations: authority of, 33; Bruce Committee of, 59; consensus rules of, 32; Covenant of, 32–33; creation of, 31–33; disarmament and, 180; formation of, 106; peacekeeping operations during, 106–108

Lebanon, 109, 244; peacekeeping in, 117–118; Uniting for Peace resolution and, 243

Lee, Kelley, 164–165

Legwaila, Joseph, 122

Leticia, League of Nations and, 107–108

Liberia, peacekeeping in, 124–125

Lie, Trygve, 13

Lindblom, C. E., 199

Liquidity crisis, 220–221

Lithuania, 38, 107

Lobbying, voting and, 17–18

logo design, UN, 42–43

Lumumba, Patrice, 113–115

Lundquist, Oliver, 42–43

Majoritarianism voting, 18, 19

Mali, peacekeeping in, 133

Mandates: acting without specific, 203–204; concept of, 200–201; for extrabudgetary contributions, 225; incremental, 204; for peacekeeping, 222–223; for 2022, 216*tab*. *See also* Budget

Mandela, Nelson, 144

Mauritania, 131

McInnes, Colin, 164–165

MDGs. *See* Millennium Development Goals

Measuring the Information Society Report, 81*tab*

Meeker, Leonard, 237–238, 240

Memel, League of Nations and, 107

Migration, 3; challenges of, 272; EU Pact on, 174; Friends of the Quito Process and, 174–175; Global Compact for, 171–174; history of human, 170–171; human security and, 170–175; influx of, 172–173; objectives for, 173–174; PICUM and, 174; refugee rights and, 171–172; UDHR on, 171

Millennium Declaration, 6

Millennium Development Goals (MDGs), 2, 67, 69; achievements of, 264–265; creation of, 264; expanding, 74; global health and, 161; influence of, 73; RCs and, 76–77

MINURSO (UN Mission for the Referendum in Western Sahara), 131

MINUSCA (UN Multidimensional Integrated Stabilization Mission in the CAR), 133

MINUSMA (UN Multidimensional Integrated Stabilization Mission in Mali), 133

Mohammed, Amina, 11, 76, 263

Molotov, Vyacheslav, 38, 44, 49

MONUC (UN Organization Mission in DRC), 132

MONUSCO (UN Organization Stabilization Mission in the DRC), 132

Morocco, 131

Moscow Declaration, 33–34

Mosul, League of Nations and, 107

Mozambique, electoral assistance in, 144–145, 148

Murray, Geoffrey, 239

Namibia, 244; electoral assistance in, 141, 146–147; peacekeeping in, 121–122

Nasser, Gamal Abdel, 20, 109, 112, 242

Nasser, Nassir Abdulaziz, 250

National security, human security and, 159

NATO (North Atlantic Treaty Organization), 246

Neoliberalism, development system and, 65–66

Nervo, Padilla, 41

NGOs. *See* Nongovernmental organizations

Nicaragua: electoral assistance in, 147, 151; on Grenada invasion of 1983, 244–245; on Panama invasion of 1989, 245

Nongovernmental organizations (NGOs): development system partnerships with, 62–63; disarmament and, 192; ECOSOC and, 13–14, 60, 62; Global Compact and, 63; human rights system and, 97–101; importance of, 100

North: Covid-19 pandemic and, 65; development system and, 63–64; humanitarian assistance and South tensions with, 72; terminology of, 58–59

North Atlantic Treaty Organization (NATO), 246

Norway, 23–24

Nuclear Non-Proliferation Treaty (NPT), 184, 251–252

Obama, Barack, 167–168

Objectives, in program planning, 206–207

Observer status, in General Assembly, 10

Office for the Coordination of Humanitarian Affairs (OCHA), 73

Office of the High Commissioner for Human Rights (OHCHR), 93–94, 150

ONUC (UN Operation in the Congo), 112–116, 224

OPCW (Organization for the Prohibition of Chemical Weapons), 267

Optional Protocol to the Covenant on Civil and Political Rights, 98

Organization for Security and Cooperation in Europe (OSCE), 149

Organization for the Prohibition of Chemical Weapons (OPCW), 267

OSCE (Organization for Security and Cooperation in Europe), 149

Ouattara, Alassane, 125–126

P-5 (permanent five members), 7–8
Pakistan, 140, 244
Palau, 15
Palestine Liberation Organization (PLO),
    117–118
Palestine/Palestinians: as "Non-Member
    Observer State," 10; Uniting for
    Peace resolution on Israel conflict
    with, 245–246, 248–249
Panama invasion of 1989, 245
Paris Agreement on climate change, 167–
    169
Paris Peace Accords, 148
The Parliament of Man (Kennedy), 261
Parra Perez, C., 41
Pasvolsky, Leo, 36, 55*n*10, 56*n*41
Peacebuilding Commission and Fund, 1,
    76, 134, 152, 266
Peacekeeping, 1, 3; achievements in, 266–
    267; assessed contributions for,
    223–224; in Bosnia, 130; budget for,
    106, 222–224; in CAR, 133–134; Cold
    War's thaw and, 118–120; in Côte
    d'Ivoire (Ivory Coast), 125–126;
    current and ongoing operations in,
    130–134; in Cyprus, 116–117;
    defining, 105; DPKO and, 119–120;
    DPPA and, 120; in DRC, 132; in East
    Timor, 126–127; failures in, 127–130;
    first UN missions for, 108–109;
    "Group of Friends" for, 268; in
    Kosovo, 126; League of Nations and,
    106–108; in Lebanon, 117–118; in
    Liberia, 124–125; in Mali, 133;
    mandates for, 222–223; in Namibia,
    121–122; ONUC, Belgian Congo
    crisis and, 112–116; program planning
    of operations in, 223; in Rwanda, 128–
    129; in Sierra Leone, 124; in Somalia,
    127–128; successes in, 120–127; Suez
    Canal crisis of 1956 and, 109–112;
    UNEF for, 111–112; UNSCOB and,
    108; in Western Sahara, 131
"Peace-loving nations," definition of, 38
Pearson, Lester Bowles, 110, 112
Pérez de Cuéllar, Javier, 12, 13, 21, 122
Pérez Guerrero, Manuel, 41, 42
Performance information, program
    planning and, 206
Permanent Court of International Justice,
    31
Permanent five members (P-5), 7–8

Peru, 107–108
PICUM (Platform for International
    Cooperation on Undocumented
    Migrants), 174
Plan outline, 209
Platform for International Cooperation
    on Undocumented Migrants
    (PICUM), 174
PLO (Palestine Liberation Organization),
    117–118
Poland, 39, 52, 56*n*54; UNSCOB and,
    236; Upper Silesia, League of Nations
    and, 107; Vilna, League of Nations
    and, 107
Politics, Economics, and Welfare (Dahl
    and Lindblom), 199
Politics of the Budgetary Process
    (Wildavsky), 197, 199
Portugal, democratization in, 141
PPBME (Program Planning, Budget,
    Monitoring, and Evaluation), 202,
    204, 209, 225
Program budget, 201–203
Program planning: activities and outputs
    in, 207–208; Committee for Program
    and Coordination and, 205–206; for
    extrabudgetary contributions, 225–
    226; local intergovernmental bodies'
    relationship to, 209–210; objectives
    in, 206–207; origins of, 204; of
    peacekeeping operations, 223;
    performance information and, 206;
    plan outline in, 209; results in, 208–
    209; system of, 204–205
Program Planning, Budget, Monitoring,
    and Evaluation (PPBME), 202, 204,
    209, 225
Progress of the World's Women, 80*tab*

Ramayana, 179
RCs (Resident Coordinators), 76–77
Red Cross, 62
Redistributive policies, of development
    system, 70–73
Refugee rights, 171–172. *See also*
    Migration
refugees, definition of, 24–25
Resident Coordinators (RCs), 76–77
Results, in program planning, 208–209
Revolutionary United Front (RUF), 124
Right to life, human rights system and,
    89–91

Rio 2012 UN Conference on Sustainable Development, 73–74
Rockefeller, Nelson, 43–44
Romulo, Carlos, 47, 49, 54
Roosevelt, Eleanor, 52, 98
Roosevelt, Franklin D., 33–35; death of, 42; Dumbarton Oaks meeting and, 35–38; Yalta Conference and, 38–41
Roschin, Alexei, 33–34, 37, 51
Rubin, Irene, 199
RUF (Revolutionary United Front), 124
Rural Development Report, 80*tab*
Russell, Ruth, 33, 50, 55*n*30
Russia: CAR and, 134; Crimea seized from Ukraine by, 250–251; Hungarian uprising and, 243; on P-5, 7–8; Ukraine war of aggression by, 20, 89–90, 193, 252–254. *See also* Soviet Union
Rwanda, 97, 119, 128–129

Saar Basin, League of Nations and, 106–107
San Francisco Conference: on colonialism, 46–47; on General Assembly competency, 44–45; on human rights, 52; on independence and self-determination, 47; logo design at, 42–43; on membership, 43–44; on Secretary-General's role, 50; on self-defense, 47–48; on Trustee Council, 45–47; on use of force, 51; veto debate at, 48–50, 233–235
Saudi Arabia, 42
Sayadi and Vinck v. Belgium, 94
Schlesinger, Thomas, 217
SDGs. *See* Sustainable Development Goals
Secretariat: departments and offices of, 11; evolution of, 53; functions of, 10–11; program planning and, 204–205; Security Council compared to, 11
Secretary-General: Advisory Board on Disarmament Matters and, 186; authority of, 12; budget mandates and, 200–201; election of, 11–12, 21, 50; evolution of, 53; gender of, 13; "good offices" of, 11; importance of, 5; list of, 13; role and impartiality of, 12; San Francisco Conference on role of, 50; UNODA and, 185–186
Securing Our Common Future (UNODA), 190

Security. *See* Human security
Security Council, 2, 4, 89; circumventing, 231–232; evolution of, 53–54; General Assembly circumventing, 255*tab*; General Assembly resolution 290 (IV) on, 232; Korea resolutions of, 237–238; membership of, 7; reform attempts of, 8; resolution passage procedures of, 8; responsibilities of, 5, 7; on Russia's war of aggression on Ukraine, 253; Secretariat compared to, 11; Soviet Union boycott of, 236–237; UNTSO and, 109; veto challenges of, 268–269; veto debate at San Francisco Conference, 49–50, 233–235; voting system of, 18–19. *See also* Uniting for Peace resolution
Security threat challenges, 269–270
Self-defense, 47–48
Self-determination, 47, 143
Sierra Leone, 24, 124
Sirleaf, Ellen Johnson, 125
Six-Day War, 1967, 112
Social and Humanitarian Committee, of General Assembly, 99
Somalia, 127–128, 140
de Soto, Alvaro, 122, 267
South: Covid-19 pandemic and, 65; development system and, 64; humanitarian assistance and North tensions with, 72; terminology of, 58–59
South Africa, 121–122, 244
South Sudan, 10
Soviet Union, 56*n*54; Dumbarton Oaks meeting and, 36–37; on Secretary-General's election, 50; Security Council boycotted by, 236–237; Uniting for Peace resolution and, 19–20, 243–244; UNSCOB and, 235–236; veto debate at San Francisco Conference and, 48–49; Yalta Conference and, 38–41. *See also* Russia
Spain, 153
Special Session on Disarmament (SSOD), 183
Stalin, Joseph, 38–41, 49
Stassen, Harold, 35, 47–48
State of Food and Agriculture, 80*tab*
State of the Global Climate Report, 81*tab*

State of the World Population, 79*tab*
State of the World's Children, 79*tab*
State sovereignty, 5–6
Stettinius, Edward, 36–37, 38, 41, 43
Stunting, food insecurity and, 170
Suez Canal crisis of 1956, 20, 109–112,
    242–243
Survival, international orders conducive
    to human, 92–94
Sustainable Development Goals (SDGs),
    2, 6, 67, 69, 71, 83*n*29; cost to
    implement, 84*n*48; formation of, 74–
    75, 265; influence of, 73; Mohammed
    overseeing, 76; RCs and, 76–77; Rio
    2012 Conference on, 73–74; World
    Bank and, 76
Sweden, 153
Syria, 20, 45, 107; chemical weapons in,
    267; Uniting for Peace resolution and,
    249–250

Taiwan, 10
Terrorism challenges, 270
Thant, U, 13, 92, 112, 115
Thirty Years' War, 30
Timor Leste. *See* East Timor
Togoland, democratization in, 151
TPNW (Treaty on the Prohibition of
    Nuclear Weapons), 191–192, 252
Treaty of Versailles, 106, 107
Treaty of Westphalia, 30
Treaty on the Prohibition of Nuclear
    Weapons (TPNW), 191–192, 252
Treaty supervisory bodies, in human
    rights system, 99–100
Truman, Harry, 42, 44, 49
Trump, Donald, 168
Trustee Council: function of, 14; future
    of, 15; membership of, 15; San
    Francisco Conference on, 45–47;
    Togoland democratization and, 151;
    Yalta Conference on, 39–40
Tshombe, Moise, 115–116
Tueni, Ghassan, 117, 118
Turkey, 107, 117

UDHR (Universal Declaration of Human
    Rights), 52, 87–88, 90–93, 171, 262
UK. *See* United Kingdom
Ukraine, 38–39; Russia's seizure of Crimea
    in, 250–251; Russia's war of aggression
    on, 20, 89–90, 193, 252–254

UN. *See* United Nations
UN Assistance Mission for Rwanda
    (UNAMIR), 119, 128–129
UN Assistance Mission in Afghanistan
    (UNAMA), 158*n*36
UN Atomic Energy Commission, 180–
    181
UN Chronicle, 197, 217
UN Conference on Trade and
    Development (UNCTAD), 64
UN Development Programme (UNDP),
    2, 22, 67; capacity of, 70; creation of,
    70–71; democratization, electoral
    assistance and, 143, 150, 153–154,
    156; function of, 23; Human
    Development Index, 23; *Human
    Development Report* and, 2, 23–24,
    67, 79*tab,* 264; RCs and, 76–77;
    USAID contributions to, 149–150
UN Disarmament Commission (UNDC),
    183–184
UN Education, Scientific, and Cultural
    Organization (UNESCO), 61
UN Emergency Force (UNEF), 111–112,
    224
UN Environment Programme (UNEP),
    226–227
UN Framework Convention on Climate
    Change (UNFCCC), 75, 166–168,
    271
UN High Commission for Human Rights
    (UNHCHR), 93–94, 265
UN High Commissioner for Refugees
    (UNHCR), 24–25
UN Institute for Disarmament Research
    (UNIDIR), 186
UN Institute for Training and Research
    (UNITAR), 60
UN Interim Force in Lebanon (UNIFIL),
    117–118
UN International Children's Emergency
    Fund (UNICEF), 2, 22; function and
    governance of, 23; ONUC and, 115
UN Military Observer Group in India
    and Pakistan (UNMOGIP), 224
UN Mission for the Referendum in
    Western Sahara (MINURSO), 131
UN Mission in Kosovo (UNMIK), 126
UN Mission in Liberia (UNMIL), 124–
    125
UN Mission in Sierra Leone
    (UNAMSIL), 124

UN Multidimensional Integrated Stabilization Mission in Mali (MINUSMA), 133

UN Multidimensional Integrated Stabilization Mission in the CAR (MINUSCA), 133

UN Observer Group in Lebanon, 117

UN Office for Disarmament Affairs (UNODA), 185–186, 190

UN Office of Drugs and Crime (UNODC), 207, 208

UN Office on Counter-Terrorism, 270

UN Operation in Mozambique (UNOMOZ), 148

UN Operation in Somalia (UNOSOM), 128

UN Operation in the Congo (ONUC), 112–116, 224

UN Organization Mission in DRC (MONUC), 132

UN Organization Stabilization Mission in the DRC (MONUSCO), 132

UN Peacekeeping Force in Cyprus (UNFICYP), 116–117

UN Special Commission (UNSCOM), 266

UN Special Committee on the Balkans (UNSCOB), 108, 235–236

UN Sustainable Development Group (UNSDG), 71, 77, 83*n*29

UN Temporary Commission on Korea (UNTCOK), 140

UN Transition Assistance Group for Namibia (UNTAG), 121–122, 141, 146–147

UN Truce Supervision Organization (UNTSO), 109, 224

UN University (UNU), 60

UN Verification Mission in Angola II (UNAVEM II), 141

UN Women, 151–153, 156

UN World Water Development Report, 81*tab*

UNAMA (UN Assistance Mission in Afghanistan), 158*n*36

UNAMIR (UN Assistance Mission for Rwanda), 119, 128–129

UNAMSIL (UN Mission in Sierra Leone), 124

Unanimity, 18, 19

Unanimity clause, 48

UNAVEM II (UN Verification Mission in Angola II), 141

UNCTAD (UN Conference on Trade and Development), 64

UNDC (UN Disarmament Commission), 183–184

UNDP. *See* UN Development Programme

UNEF (UN Emergency Force), 111–112, 224

UNEP (UN Environment Programme), 226–227

UNESCO (UN Education, Scientific, and Cultural Organization), 61

UNFCCC (UN Framework Convention on Climate Change), 75, 166–168, 271

UNFICYP (UN Peacekeeping Force in Cyprus), 116–117

UNHCHR (UN High Commission for Human Rights), 93–94, 265

UNHCR (UN High Commissioner for Refugees), 24–25

UNICEF. *See* UN International Children's Emergency Fund

UNIDIR (UN Institute for Disarmament Research), 186

UNIFIL (UN Interim Force in Lebanon), 117–118

UNITAR (UN Institute for Training and Research), 60

United Kingdom (UK): Dumbarton Oaks meeting and, 36–37; on P-5, 7–8; on Secretary-General's election, 50; Suez Canal crisis of 1956 and, 20, 109–112, 243; Yalta Conference and, 38–41

United Nations (UN): achievements of, 262–268; challenges facing, 4, 261–262, 268–272; Chapultepec Conference and, 41; conflict prevention mission of, 6–7; "days," "weeks," "years," "decades" designated by, 69–70; democracy challenges facing, 270–271; democratization and electoral assistance trajectory of involvement, 139–143; Dumbarton Oaks meeting and, 35–38; evolution of, 1–2, 5, 28, 53–54; first peacekeeping missions of, 108–109; flag of, 29; flagship reports, 79*tab*; Global Compact, 63; global conferences of, 67, 68*tab*, 69; historical basis for, 30–31; logo design for, 42–43; membership to, 43–44; organizations supported by, 2;

principle bodies of, 5, 7–17; programs, funds, and special agencies of, 22–27; rationale for, 29–30; reforming, 75–77; resources of, 27–28, 55*n*30; Roosevelt, F. D., US and formation of, 33–35; San Francisco Conference and, 42–52, 233–235; security threat challenges facing, 269–270; signing and ratifying Charter of, 52–53; terrorism challenges facing, 270; voting procedures within, 17–21; Yalta Conference and, 38–41. *See also specific committees; specific topics*
United Nations Transitional Authority in Cambodia (UNTAC), 141
United States (US): on colonialism at San Francisco Conference, 46–47; Dumbarton Oaks meeting and, 35–38; Grenada invasion of 1983 and, 244–245; Iraq invasion and, 247–248; on P-5, 7–8; Panama invasion of 1989 and, 245; on Secretary-General's election, 50; UN creation and, 33–35; veto debate at San Francisco Conference and, 48–49; Yalta Conference and, 38–41
Uniting for Peace resolution, 4, 231; Collective Measures Committee and, 240; General Assembly debates on, 239–240; Hungary and, 243; Iraq invasion and no use of, 247–248; Israeli-Palestinian conflict and, 245–246, 248–249; Korea and, 19–20, 237–238, 241–242; Kosovo crisis and no use of, 246–247; language of, 232–233; Lebanon and, 243; legacy of, 254; legal arguments on, 241; passage of, 232; purpose of, 19–20, 241; Russian aggression in Ukraine and, 20; Soviet Union and, 19–20, 243–244; Suez Canal crisis of 1956 and, 20, 242–243; Syria and, 249–250; UNSCOB and, 235–236; veto debate at San Francisco Conference and, 233–235
Universal Declaration of Human Rights (UDHR), 52, 87–88, 90–93, 171, 262
Universal Periodic Review (UPR), 97
Universal Postal Union, 31
UNMIK (UN Mission in Kosovo), 126
UNMIL (UN Mission in Liberia), 124–125

UNMOGIP (UN Military Observer Group in India and Pakistan), 224
UNODA (UN Office for Disarmament Affairs), 185–186, 190
UNODC (UN Office of Drugs and Crime), 207, 208
UNOMOZ (UN Operation in Mozambique), 148
UNOSOM (UN Operation in Somalia), 128
UNSCOB (UN Special Committee on the Balkans), 108, 235–236
UNSCOM (UN Special Commission), 266
UNSDG (UN Sustainable Development Group), 71, 77, 83*n*29
UNTAC (UN Transitional Authority in Cambodia), 141
UNTAG (UN Transition Assistance Group for Namibia), 121–122, 141, 146–147
UNTCOK (UN Temporary Commission on Korea), 140
UNTSO (UN Truce Supervision Organization), 109, 224
UNU (UN University), 60
Upper Silesia, League of Nations and, 107
UPR (Universal Periodic Review), 97
Urquhart, Brian, 109–112, 114–115
US. *See* United States
US Agency for International Development (USAID), 149–150
US Rangers Delta Force, 127
USAID (US Agency for International Development), 149–150
Use of force, San Francisco Conference on, 51

Vandenberg, Arthur, 35, 44
V-Dem, 271
Venezuela, 174–175, 268
Veto debates: challenges of, 268–269; in General Assembly in 1950, 238–239; at San Francisco Conference, 48–50, 233–235. *See also* Uniting for Peace resolution
Vigier, Henri, 108
Vilna, League of Nations and, 107
Voting: consensus and, 18; egalitarian, 18; elite privilege and, 18–19; in General Assembly, 20–21; in ICJ elections, 21; lobbying and, 17–18;

majoritarianism and, 18, 19; in Secretary-General election, 21; Security Council's system of, 18–19; unanimity and, 18, 19; Uniting for Peace resolution and, 19–20. *See also* Uniting for Peace resolution
Vyshinsky, Andrei Y., 238–239

Waldheim, Kurt, 13
Wasting, food insecurity and, 170
Weapons adaptable to mass destruction (WMDs), 180–181, 189, 266–267. *See also* Disarmament
"Weeks," UN designation of special, 69–70
WESA (World Employment and Social Outlook), 80*tab*
Western Sahara, peacekeeping in, 131
WFP (World Food Programme), 2, 265
WHO. *See* World Health Organization
Wildavsky, Aaron, 197, 199–200
Wilson, Woodrow, 32
WMDs (weapons adaptable to mass destruction), 180–181, 189, 266–267. *See also* Disarmament
Women, human rights system and, 88. *See also* Gender; UN Women
World Bank, 263–264; criticism against, 23; development system and, 61; function of, 22; origins of, 22; SDGs and, 76
World Cities Report, 79*tab*
World Court. *See* International Court of Justice
World Development Report, 80*tab*
World Drug Report, 79*tab*
World Economic and Social Survey, 79*tab*

World Economic Outlook, 80*tab*
World Economic Situation and Prospects, 79*tab*
World Economic Survey, 67
World Employment and Social Outlook (WESA), 80*tab*
World Food Programme (WFP), 2, 265
World Health Assembly, 163
World Health Organization (WHO), 2; China's memorandum of understanding with, 163; critiques on, 163; establishment of, 162–163; function of, 24; ONUC and, 115
World Health Report, 80*tab*
World Intellectual Property Report, 81*tab*
World Investment Report, 79*tab*
World Migration Report, 81*tab*
World Survey on the Role of Women in Development, 80*tab*
World Trade Organization (WTO), 61; Dispute Settlement Body of, 26; Dispute Settlement Mechanism of, 26; function of, 25
World War I, 106
World War II, 29–30, 107
WTO. *See* World Trade Organization

Xi Jinping, 168

Yalta Conference, 38–41
"Years," UN designation of special, 69–70
Yom Kippur War, 112
Yugoslavia, 235–236

Zimbabwe, 24

About the Book

The United Nations has a vast outreach through its many agencies, funds, and programs—but that very fact can make it difficult for "outsiders" to understand.

Among the questions that arise: How can the UN promote human rights when its charter prohibits its intervention in the domestic affairs of sovereign states? Why do the five permanent members of the Security Council have veto power? Can a dysfunctional Security Council be circumvented? How is consensus on policy ever reached? Where does the money to run this enormous system come from? The list goes on. In response, this new text clearly explains the UN's history, functions, and day-to-day operations.

Ranging from development to disarmament, from electoral assistance to finance, the authors unveil the processes involved as diplomats and practitioners navigate the challenges of serving the common good while balancing opposing interests.

Jean E. Krasno is on the faculty of the Department of Political Science at the City College of New York (CCNY) and also a lecturer at Columbia University.